VALUING ENVIRONMENTAL
USING STATED CHOICE STUDIES

MW01222021

THE ECONOMICS OF NON-MARKET GOODS AND RESOURCES

VOLUME 8

Series Editor: Dr. Ian J. Bateman

Dr. Ian J. Bateman is Professor of Environmental Economics at the School of Environmental Sciences, University of East Anglia (UEA) and directs the research theme Innovation in Decision Support (Tools and Methods) within the Programme on Environmental Decision Making (PEDM) at the Centre for Social and Economic Research on the Global Environment (CSERGE), UEA. The PEDM is funded by the UK Economic and Social Research Council. Professor Bateman is also a member of the Centre for the Economic and Behavioural Analysis of Risk and Decision (CEBARD) at UEA and Executive Editor of Environmental and Resource Economics, an international journal published in cooperation with the European Association of Environmental and Resource Economists. (EAERE).

Aims and Scope

The volumes which comprise *The Economics of Non-Market Goods and Resources* series have been specially commissioned to bring a new perspective to the greatest economic challenge facing society in the 21st Century; the successful incorporation of non-market goods within economic decision making. Only by addressing the complexity of the underlying issues raised by such a task can society hope to redirect global economies onto paths of sustainable development. To this end the series combines and contrasts perspectives from environmental, ecological and resource economics and contains a variety of volumes which will appeal to students, researchers, and decision makers at a range of expertise levels. The series will initially address two themes, the first examining the ways in which economists assess the value of non-market goods, the second looking at approaches to the sustainable use and management of such goods. These will be supplemented with further texts examining the fundamental theoretical and applied problems raised by public good decision making.

For further information about the series and how to order, please visit our Website
www.springer.com

Valuing Environmental Amenities Using Stated Choice Studies

A Common Sense Approach to Theory and Practice

Edited by

Barbara J. Kanninen

Arlington, Virginia, USA

 Springer

A C.I.P. Catalogue record for this book is available from the Library of Congress.

ISBN-10 1-4020-5313-4 (e-book)
ISBN-13 978-1-4020-5313-9 (e-book)

Published by Springer,
P.O. Box 17, 3300 AA Dordrecht, The Netherlands.

www.springer.com

Printed on acid-free paper

TABLE OF CONTENTS

CONTRIBUTING AUTHORS

W.L. (Vic) Adamowicz, Canada Research Chair and Professor, Department of Rural Economy, University of Alberta, Edmonton, Alberta, Canada T6G 2H1, email: Vic.Adamowicz@Ualberta.ca.

Anna Alberini, Associate Professor, Department of Agricultural and Resource Economics, University of Maryland, College Park, MD, U.S.A. and Fondazione ENI Enrico Mattei, e-mail: aalberini@arec.umd.edu.

Matthew Bingham, Principal Economist, Veritas Economic Consulting, LLC, 1851 Evans Road, Cary, NC 27513, USA., e-mail: matthewbingham@nc.rr.com.

Patricia Champ, Economist, U.S. Forest Service, Rocky Mountain Research Station, 2150 Centre Ave., Bldg A, Fort Collins, CO 80526, U.S.A., e-mail: pchamp@fs.fed.us.

William H. Desvousges, President, W.H. Desvousges & Associates, Inc., 7824 Harps Mill Road, Raleigh, NC 27615, U.S.A., e-mail: wdesvousges@aol.com.

Miranda L. Freeman, Triangle Economic Research, 11000 Regency Parkway, West Tower, Suite 205, Cary, NC 27511-8518, U.S.A., e-mail: mfreeman@ter.com.

Glenn W. Harrison, Professor of Economics, Department of Economics, College of Business Administration, University of Central Florida, Orlando, FL, 32816-1400, U.S.A., e-mail: gharrison@research.bus.ucf.edu.

Daniel Hellerstein, e-mail: danielh@crosslink.net.

David A. Hensher, Institute of Transport and Logistics Studies, School of Business, Faculty of Economics and Business, The University of Sydney, Australia, e-mail: davidh@itls.usyd.edu.au.

F. Reed Johnson, Principal Economist and RTI Fellow, RTI International, 3040 Cornwallis Road, P.O. Box 12194, Research Triangle Park, NC, 27709-2194, U.S.A., e-mail: frjohnson@rti.org.

Barbara Kanninen, e-mail: barbkann@aol.com, URL: www.barbarakanninen.com.

Alan Krupnick, Senior Fellow and Director, Quality of the Environment Division, Resources for the Future, 1616 P Street N., Washington, D.C. 20036, U.S.A., e-mail: krupnick@rff.org.

Alberto Longo, University of Bath, Bath, UK, e-mail: alongo@arec.umd.edu.

Carol Mansfield, RTI International, 3040 Cornwallis Road, P.O. Box 12194, Research Triangle Park, NC, 27709-2194, U.S.A., e-mail: carolm@rti.org.

Kristy E. Mathews, Principal Economist, Veritas Economic Consulting, LLC, 1851 Evans Road, Cary, NC 27513, USA., e-mail: kmathews1@nc.rr.com.

Semra Özdemir, Research Health Economist, RTI International, 3040 Cornwallis Road, P.O. Box 12194, Research Triangle Park, NC, 27709-2194, U.S.A., e-mail: sozdemir@rti.org.

Subhrendu Pattanayak, RTI Fellow and Senior Economist, RTI International, 3040 Cornwallis Road, P.O. Box 12194, Research Triangle Park, NC, 27709-2194, U.S.A., e-mail: subrendu@rti.org.

V. Kerry Smith, W.P. Carey Professor of Economics, Arizona State University, Tempe, Arizona, U.S.A.

Joffre Swait, Partner, Advanis Inc., Suite 1600, Sun Life Place, 10123 99th Street, Edmonton, Alberta   T5J 3H1, Canada, email: Joffre_Swait@Advanis.ca, URL: http://www.swaitworld.org/

Marcella Veronesi, Department of Agricultural and Resource Economics, University of Maryland, College Park, MD, U.S.A., e-mail: mveronesi@arec.umd.edu.

Michael P. Welsh, Senior Economist, Christensen Associates, 4610 University Avenue, Suite 700, Madison, WI 53705, U.S.A., e-mail: mpwelsh@lrca.com.

PREFACE

When I was a graduate student, I fell in love with choice models. After years studying the econometrics of the standard linear model, discrete choice offered so many new, cool twists. With contingent valuation (CV) studies abounding, data was plentiful and varied. Every CV dataset had its own kinks and quirks that begged to be addressed through innovative modeling techniques. Dissertation topics were not scarce.

We economists like to assume. There are jokes written about this. My assumption, as I slaved over the statistical properties of the double-bounded CV model, was that CV data was good data, representing valid economic choices made by survey respondents. Before I received my Ph.D., this assumption was called into question big time.

In 1989, the Exxon-Valdez oil tanker spilled 11 million gallons of oil into Prince William Sound, Alaska. The accident killed a lot of birds, devastated fisheries, harmed area economies and ruined a reputation or two. It also changed the field of environmental valuation. What was once a research field dominated by environmental economists interested in obtaining nonmarket values for environmental amenities was now a legal battleground pitting environmental economists against "traditional" economists who were skeptical of the techniques and procedures used with CV. If Nobel prizes are indicators of quality – and I'm fairly certain they are – the Exxon-Valdez oil spill drew the best and the brightest to scrutinize our field.

I mention the Exxon-Valdez not because it sets the agenda for this book, but because without that event, this book might not be. As suggested above, the scrutiny inspired by the Exxon-Valdez shook down the field of environmental valuation and forced economists like me to ask ourselves about the quality of our data. In a sense, all the questions boil down to this one: are the data meaningful? By now, I think we have concluded that the answer is yes, at least when a study is well-designed and well-executed.

This book is not about natural resource damage assessment. Though large legal cases do go on with millions of dollars invested, most environmental economists today find themselves working on relatively smaller questions: is it worth the effort to reduce the smog that obscures scenic vistas of the Grand Canyon? Should we allow snowmobilers to ride through Yellowstone National Park? Should a small village in Central America invest in a clean water system? Of course, many of these questions are not small at all. What are often small are the budgets for the studies, and that is what this book is about: doing high quality studies on (possibly) low budgets, principally for benefit-cost analysis.

High quality valuation studies require high quality effort and care on a wide array of topics from survey design and methodology to econometric modeling to policy interpretation. It is, truly, impossible for someone to become expert in all of these areas. My hope is that this book will provide researchers with a solid summary of state-of-the-art techniques, covering all the basic issues necessary for developing and implementing a good valuation study.

The issue is this. We, humans, care about a lot of things that are not bought or sold in the marketplace. We care about our families, our neighbors, our world; and the interconnectedness of our world means that we even care about things we no nothing or very little about. Yet things go on every day that may be affecting our interests: over-fishing, over-hunting, over-grazing, over-developing, over-polluting, to name a few. Many of these activities occur on scales so large that they can only be dealt with by corporate decision-making or government policy-making, and that means that if we want good decisions and good policies to be made, we need solid information about the benefits and costs of these activities. Nonmarket valuation studies are our attempt to obtain that solid information.

We conduct nonmarket valuation studies when we have no means of obtaining standard, market information. Much of our natural world fits into this category. We do not buy or sell the ivory-billed woodpecker or the beauty of Acadia National Park. We do not buy or sell clean air. But these are "goods" that people care about and hold values for. In the absence of markets (such as real estate or travel, for example), the only way we economists have found to learn about these values is to ask people about them. This approach has come to be known as stated choice or stated preference.

This book focuses on the practice of conducting stated choice studies, looking at the entire process from start to finish. Within the discussion, a lot of theory is covered, but the book is meant to be, first and foremost, a practical guide. It begins at the beginning: when researchers start to think about a problem and plan their study.

In chapter 1, Carol Mansfield and Subhrendu Pattanayak provide a thorough and rather handy explanation of how they have gone about planning their own stated-choice studies. This is the kind of information that usually gets left out of journal articles and theory books. Good planning is a fundamental part of a good study.

In Chapter 2, Patty Champ and Michael Welsh provide a summary of survey methodology issues and approaches. Survey techniques seem to be changing before our eyes as computer assisted technologies and internet-based approaches proliferate. Champ and Welsh summarize pretty much everything that is out there right now and what the trade-offs are in terms of cost, sample size and sample selection. This is a field to keep close watch on, though, as it may be changing even as this book goes to press.

Beginning in Chapter 3, the book moves into issues with writing the survey. One of the general concerns I have when it comes to surveys is respect for our respondents' time. It is terrific that so many people continue to be willing to respond to surveys, but we should not take our subjects' generosity for granted. We should do all we can to minimize the amount of time it takes for people to respond. We can do this by careful planning: cutting questions we do not need to use for later analysis and framing questions in the most appropriate manner to obtain the most useful information possible. To this end, Alan Krupnick and Vic Adamowicz have provided an innovative chapter that discusses what they call "supporting questions," that is, all the questions that are not directly focused on obtaining choice or willingness to pay information. In many studies, supporting questions take up most of the survey, yet the literature has focused so little attention on this topic. Krupnick and Adamowicz have taken a first stab at filling this gap in the literature.

Chapters 4 through 6 address different aspects of the actual choice question(s). There is a lot for the researcher to think about here. First is the question of whether we can get respondents to provide truthful responses to our questions. In chapter 4, Glenn Harrison addresses this crucial issue, providing a critical look at the difficult question of whether or not hypothetical bias can be reduced, eliminated, or at least, better understood. Harrison's conclusion, based on his work in experimental economics, is that there may be ways to do this, using techniques that can be applied either before or after the survey. We certainly need more research in this area, especially from researchers who have the goal of making responses more informative (as opposed to simply finding examples where they are not informative).

In Chapter 5, Kristy Mathews, Miranda Freeman and Bill Desvousges address another crucial issue: how do we supply respondents with new, complex information about the goods they are being asked to value? A good survey will help respondents make informed, rational choices by providing them with clear, unbiased information. Fortunately, the authors practice what they preach. Their chapter is clear and straightforward and provides tons of useful information.

In Chapter 6, David Hensher addresses a topic that he elegantly refers to as "attribute processing." I like to call it "what are respondents thinking?" because that is the real question. We have long understood that economic decision-making is very much of a psychological issue. We also have understood that some of our stated-choice questions can be rather complex and hard to answer. We call this problem "cognitive burden." Hensher looks at the psychological literature and presents some of his own, new research based on a dataset that is truly to die for.

The next chapters move into the statistics of choice models, starting with the issue of experimental design and moving into the econometrics. I like to think, by this format, that I am following the teaching of Frank Yates, a prominent statistician, who once argued that statistics books and courses should first address the topic of experimental design and then turn to the more traditional topic of statistical inference. This is rarely done in practice, but I find his argument compelling. The study of experimental design gives a nice grounding to what statistics is all about. And, after all, you do need to collect your data before you begin to model it.

As many of you know, I have been actively involved in the study of optimal designs for stated choice studies. This is a smaller field within the general field of experimental design. My early work focused on CV models; later work addressed multinomial logit. As I, and my co-authors Reed Johnson and Matt Bingham, try to show in Chapter 7, the problem of generating choice tasks takes us out of the world of standard experimental design and introduces some unique features that sometimes turn the standard theory on its head. Some of these issues are only now being realized and many questions remain unanswered. I would love to see more researchers get involved in this area of study.

Though I like to think there are many reasons to buy this book, Chapters 8 and 9 are, in my opinion, the most obvious ones. I do not think you will find two better chapters on the econometrics of choice models anywhere. I could go on raving about Anna Alberini and Joffre Swait, their command of their topics, and their friendly styles of presentation, but I'd rather you just turn to those chapters and get started. I have a feeling there will be a lot of copies of these chapters floating around graduate departments all over the world.

If you blink while you're flipping through the pages of this book, you might miss chapter 10 by Dan Hellerstein. In true computer guru fashion (that would be, succinctly), Dan invites the readers of this book to check out his software package, GRBL, which is capable of estimating many of the models presented in Anna's and and Joffre's chapters. It is available free via the internet. Dan is working to update GRBL, so if the model you want isn't there, contact him via e-mail. He's a nice guy and will probably do his best to help you.

Ever since the Exxon-Valdez case, our field has talked a lot about judging quality. We have conducted experiments, set standards, and generated new tests, but at the end of the day, it seems to me that meaningful results come from well-conducted, high-quality studies. In Chapter 11, entitled "Judging Quality," Kerry Smith brings this whole topic full circle. Quality, he shows, happens at every stage of the game and, frankly, Smith's chapter could have been placed at the beginning of the book just as well as at the end. Quality is not an after-the-fact question. It has to be integrated into the study plan. Read Kerry's chapter before you begin your study. Better yet, read this whole book before you begin your study!

I still love choice models. I am awed to see how far this field has come in terms of econometric sophistication. I am also awed to see how many other directions our field has taken, delving into psychology, experimentation and new, applied branches of economics. My hope is that this book will provide a sense of what we have learned along the way and give researchers in all sorts of fields, including health, transportation, marketing and others, the tools they need to conduct meaningful stated choice studies for valuation purposes.

Barbara Kanninen

ACKNOWLEDGEMENTS

People say I'm lucky. They're right. I'm lucky to have a fine set of colleagues who know their stuff, are passionate about it, and were willing to commit to the long, sometimes tedious, process of putting together this book. All the authors in this book are top-notch and I am lucky that I get to call them friends. I thank them from the bottom of my heart for their contributions. This book simply would not exist without them.

I thank Julie Hewitt, who over lunch one day suggested I think about working on a book. I have to admit, it had never occurred to me that I might be at "that stage" in my career. But Julie's gentle nudging convinced me that, perhaps, it was time to give such a project a try.

When Ian Bateman, Springer's series editor, responded to my initial, tentative e-mail with complete enthusiasm, there was no turning back. I had a project. I thank Ian for his wise advice, support and patience throughout the process. He is a pro. Similarly, I thank Esther Verdries at Springer, whose patience knows no bounds.

I have benefited greatly over the years from working with a number of high-quality people including, but not limited to Michael Hanemann, Anna Alberini, Richard Carson, John Loomis, John Stoll, John Bergstrom, David Chapman, Carol Jones, Bengt Kriström, Karl-Göran Mäler, Dan Hellerstein, Mary Ahearn, Craig Mohn, Jackie Geoghegan, Ed Schuh and Reed Johnson.

And then there is my family. What can I say except that my boys are a constant reminder that life is a balancing act -- fortunately a forgiving one. I know they will be very proud of me, at least for a moment, when they see this book. They, by the way, are responsible for all remaining errors in it.

My husband Kevin Wolf is my biggest fan. He seems to think I can manage just about anything and I suppose his support often makes it so. I thank him for that, but more importantly, I thank him for his extraordinary word processing skills. If you can read this book, you have Kevin to thank.

CHAPTER 1

GETTING STARTED

CAROL MANSFIELD

RTI International, Research Triangle Park, North Carolina, U.S.A.

SUBHRENDU PATTANAYAK

RTI International, Research Triangle Park, North Carolina, U.S.A.

1. INTRODUCTION

Valuing environmental goods covers a wide range of topics from animals and habitats, to reduced risk of disease, to improvements in air or water quality. You may be interested in values that are specific to a particular context or group of people or in values that can be easily transferred to a variety of situations. Studies can be designed to provide data for a policy or regulatory analysis, or studies may explore a research hypothesis unrelated to the good or service valued in the choice experiment. Within this almost unlimited list of potential projects, a carefully designed stated-choice (SC) study follows the same basic path from idea to completion.

SC studies describe goods or services as a collection of attributes (see Figure 1 for an example). By varying the attribute levels, the researcher creates different "goods." For this reason, SC studies resemble experiments in which the researcher can manipulate attributes and levels to see how people react. SC studies represent an important form of experimentation that lies somewhere along the spectrum between laboratory experiments and observational studies (Harrison and List 2004). Survey-based "field experiments" represent a practical mix of control and realism. Control comes from the design of the survey sample and the structure of the survey instrument. Contrasted to the laboratory settings of experimental economics, realism comes from interviewing people, often in their homes, about goods and services that are important to their daily lives. As you plan your survey, take advantage of the chance to experiment. Plan a survey that uses the combination of experimental control and realism embodied in a SC study to your advantage.

1

B.J. Kanninen (ed.), Valuing Environmental Amenities Using Stated Choice Studies, 1–20.
© 2006 *Springer*.

The key to a successful SC study is the extent to which you can capture the important attributes of the good, service, or policy you wish to describe without confusing or overburdening the respondents. You are asking the respondents to tell you what they would do if they were faced with the choice you describe. There is always the danger that they will reject the whole exercise or particular attribute combinations. While our collective experience suggests that most respondents carefully consider their answers, this does not happen by accident—it is the result of careful planning and pretesting.

CHOICE 3: Which do you prefer—Trip A, Trip B, or "Not Visit"?
Please check ONE box at the bottom of the table to indicate whether you prefer Trip A, Trip B, or Not Visit. If you choose Trip A or Trip B, write the number of days you would spend on a trip doing only that activity. Note that we shaded the boxes that are the same for both trips. The conditions and prices described in this question may be different than what the parks are like today.

		Trip A	Trip B	Not Visit
Activity		Take an unguided snowmobile trip in Yellowstone starting at the North entrance (near Gardiner)	Take a guided tour into Yellowstone on a snowcoach shuttle to cross-country ski or hike starting at the West entrance (near West Yellowstone)	I would not enter Yellowstone or Grand Teton National Park if these were my only choices
Conditions during day trip	**Daily snowmobile traffic at the entrance where you started**	Low (200 or fewer snowmobiles)	Moderate (300 to 600 snowmobiles)	
	Snowmobile traffic at most crowded part of the trip	Low (200 or fewer snowmobiles)	Low (200 or fewer snowmobiles)	
	Condition of snow on the road or trail surface for all or most of the trip	Bumpy and rough	Smooth	
	Highest noise level experienced on trip	Moderate (Like a busy city street)	Low noise, occasional	
	Exhaust emission levels	Noticeable	Noticeable	
	Total Cost for DAY per person	$150	$100	
I would choose... (check only one)		☐	☐	☐

FIGURE 1. Sample Stated Choice Question

2. OVERVIEW

The chapters in this book provide step-by-step advice on each element of a SC study. The chapters correspond roughly to the following stages of survey development and analysis:

1.   planning the survey (which includes selecting the mode of administration, selecting sampling frame, and determining the methodology for drawing the sample),
2.   writing the survey,
3.   analyzing the data, and
4.   evaluating the success of the survey.

In this chapter, we focus on Stage 1, planning the survey. To illustrate the process, we use examples from three of our own SC studies. The first example is a survey of winter visitors to Yellowstone National Park (the Yellowstone study). Funded by the National Park Service (NPS), the survey was designed to provide willingness to pay (WTP) values for a benefit-cost analysis of proposed winter regulations regarding snowmobile use in the park. The second study, funded by a grant from the Environmental Protection Agency, collected data on WTP by parents to prevent restrictions on outdoor time for their children (the outdoor time study). The SC study was one component of a larger study in which we collected data from activity diaries on the actual amount of time children spent outdoors on high and low air pollution days. The final example comes from Sri Lanka, where the World Bank was interested in evaluating household demand for improved water infrastructure (the Sri Lanka study). Table 1 contains information about the main features of each survey.

2.1. The Planning Process

Figure 2 presents the process we recommend to start planning a survey. The survey planning stage takes you through most of the major decisions you need to make to move forward with the survey. By the end of the survey planning stage, you should have:

*   a detailed understanding of the issues related to conducting a survey about your selected topic,
*   a rough draft of the survey instrument, and
*   concrete ideas about the sampling frame and how the survey will be administered.

Following Figure 2, the process starts with an examination of the question you wish to answer. As you start the survey planning process, you may have only a general idea of what you want to learn from the survey. It may be a hypothesis you want to evaluate or you may need data from the survey to conduct an analysis. The goal of

TABLE 1. Survey Examples

	Yellowstone study	Outdoor time study	Sri Lanka study
Time frame for data collection	December 2002 to March 2003	June 2003	August and September 2003
Sample population	Winter visitors to Yellowstone National Park	Members of an online panel who had children aged 2 to 12 and a parent at home over the summer in the 35 U.S. cities with the worst air pollution	Households in the Greater Negombo and the coastal strip from Kalutara to Galle in Southwest Sri Lanka
Mode of administration	Intercepted on site to get address, survey conducted by mail	Administered over the Web through an existing online panel	Administered in person
Commodity being valued	Winter day trips to Yellowstone National Park	Preventative medication that required restrictions on time outdoors while the child took the medication	Alternative infrastructure designs to supply the household with water
Number of attributes	Nine attributes	Three attributes	Five attributes
Labeled or unlabeled design	Unlabeled	Unlabeled	Labeled

the planning process is to learn more about your topic and to determine the data you need from your survey. With a topic in mind, you then develop the theoretical framework and empirical model you will use to analyze the survey data and provide evidence to answer your question or inputs for your analysis. Whether you are conducting the survey to support a benefit-cost analysis or to address an academic research question, the more specific you can be in the planning stage about the evidence you need, the empirical models you plan to estimate, the variables that need to be included, and the values that need to be calculated, the more successful your survey will be. From here, the process proceeds on three parallel tracks: instrument design, sample selection, and determination of the budget and schedule. The first track involves developing the draft survey instrument. Developing draft questions and survey layouts to evaluate and refine during the survey writing phase is part of the planning stage, and these topics are covered in more detail in Chapters 3 through 5. Second, you need to make decisions about your sample (Chapter 2).

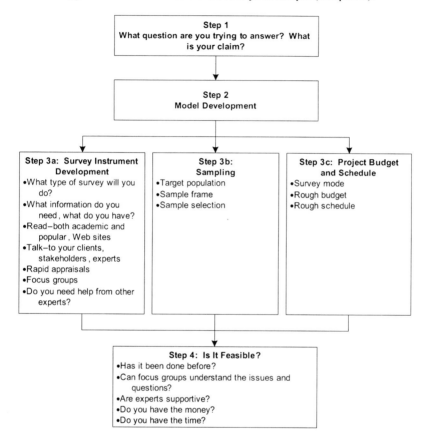

FIGURE 2. *Getting Started*

Finally, you need to think about the project budget and timeline. You need to design a survey that is capable of eliciting the information you need from a particular group of people within a given budget and schedule. Data collection will most likely represent the single largest element of your budget, and Chapter 2 presents a discussion of alternative survey administration modes that affect the budget.

Of course, survey planning is not a linear process. New decisions you make have an impact on issues you thought you had already decided. Inevitably, you will need to return to earlier decisions about question wording, sample selection, and survey administration as the process moves forward. If you plan your survey carefully, you will minimize the need to make last minute changes later in the process, which can be costly and disruptive. If changes are necessary, careful planning can help you minimize the impact of the changes on your budget and schedule. For example, suppose you decided to recruit a new set of respondents. The survey instrument text depends in part on the education and experience of the sample population you select. Early focus groups or discussions with stakeholders will help you understand how you can tailor the survey to different populations. As another example, the hourly rates for field staff living in different areas can vary greatly and in remote areas it may be difficult to find staff. Past experience in one setting may not apply in another setting. The realities of staffing cost and logistics are an important variable in your decisions about sample size, survey administration mode, and the length of time you expect the survey to be in the field.

2.2. Stated Choice Studies

Figure 2 presents a fairly generic planning process. However, SC studies raise some unique issues. SC studies define a hypothetical good or service using a limited number of attributes. For example, the Yellowstone survey described winter trips using nine attributes that included three attributes describing the activity, five attributes describing conditions in the park (noise, crowding, and fumes), and the cost attribute. In contrast, the outdoor time study included three attributes, and the Sri Lanka questions included five attributes. Each attribute can take on several levels, ideally no more than four or five. By varying the levels using an experimental design, the researcher creates a series of goods or services from which the respondent will select. Chapters 6 and 7 present detailed discussions of experimental design.

SC studies have some advantages over other types of stated preference studies, such as contingent valuation surveys, including the ability to manipulate attributes and attribute levels to create a variety of new goods and services. However, this ability also creates challenges for survey design and administration. During the planning stage, you will want to assess:

- the need to provide visual information, either on paper or a computer, which limits the use of telephone administration (Chapters 2 and 5);
- the need for a precise description of a hypothetical good or service, including the mechanism through which it will be provided, the form the payment will take, and other features of the hypothetical market (Chapters 4 through 6);
- the need for a statistically sound design to construct choices from the set of attributes and the levels of these attributes (Chapter 7);
- the cognitive burden imposed by the number of attributes and levels used to describe the good and the unfamiliar nature of many of the goods and services being valued (Chapter 6); and
- the sample size, in particular the trade-off between the number of choice questions per respondent and the number of respondents (Chapters 2, 6 and 7).

3. THE SURVEY PLANNING PROCESS IN DETAIL

3.1. Step 1: What is your claim and how will data from a SC study support it?

In *The Craft of Research*, Booth, Colomb and Williams (1995) describe research as stating a claim and then providing evidence to support it. The claim might be a hypothesis or the claim that you have calculated the benefits and costs of a regulation. The purpose of the survey is to provide evidence to support your claim. Earlier we presented SC studies as falling somewhere between pure laboratory experiments and fieldwork. The design of the survey scenarios (the attributes and levels selected to describe the good or service) create the experiment that you run in the survey to produce the evidence you need. Choice experiments provide flexibility to collect a variety of data. For example, you do not have to value changes solely in monetary units. You could leave out cost entirely and value the maximum risk the respondent would accept in exchange for improved therapeutic benefit from a drug. SC studies can provide data on the amount individuals would pay for improvements in attribute levels or the compensation they would require if attribute levels worsened (willingness to accept or WTA). In addition, attribute levels can be used to create entirely new goods. Responses from SC studies can be used to calculate market demand for a new or improved product or market share for one brand relative to another. It is also possible to combine the data from a SC study with revealed preference (RP) data collected through a survey or from secondary sources.

The ability to gather evidence for a specific claim through a SC study will depend in part on the unique features of the situation. This is one reason that the planning process needs to begin with research on the topic and feedback from stakeholders or other knowledgeable people. In the Yellowstone study, the very first draft was written to value management alternatives. We quickly realized that describing management plans, which set limits on decibel levels and other technical criteria, required too much detailed information about the changes occurring all over 3the park. Asking respondents to value management plans also invited protest responses. Early on, we switched to valuing trips to the park with characteristics (such as crowding or noise) that could be affected by the management alternatives under consideration by the park. Respondents found it easier to think about trips, but creating the trip descriptions required information on the attributes of trips that are important to visitors and how the management alternatives affected these attributes—information we got from NPS staff and other stakeholders.

The survey planning process can be initiated through a series of steps that focuses on conducting initial meetings, reviewing the literature, collecting existing survey instruments, building the survey team, and visiting the field (if necessary and permitted by the budget). Some of the techniques introduced below, for example, focus groups, will be useful at other stages of the survey design process. At the end of this section, we discuss "rapid appraisals (RAs)," a somewhat more formalized approach to survey planning that incorporates initial conversations with different stakeholders, field visits, and more structured data collection.

3.1.1. Conduct Initial Meetings

As with any project, the planning phase of a survey includes a kickoff meeting of the survey team and the client, if you have a client. The meeting should include a discussion of the project goals, project team, budget, and suggested schedule. The Yellowstone survey started with meetings involving NPS staff to help us understand the regulatory options they were considering, their reasons for selecting these options, and how different details of the management plans might change the experience of winter visitors in the park. Using the right words and details in the scenarios created for a SC study makes the survey more relevant and realistic to the respondents. In addition to meeting with the client or funding agency, meetings with other stakeholders can be useful. These meetings might come at the beginning of the project or later in the design phase.

In the case of the Yellowstone study, the Office of Management and Budget (OMB), which had to approve the survey instrument and sampling plan, was a critical stakeholder; so we brought them into the process early in the design phase to explain our plans.

The World Bank funded the Sri Lanka study, but the Sri Lankan government department of urban infrastructure was an important stakeholder because its policies would be affected by study findings. Initial meetings were conducted with government staff to review all aspects of the study design—goals, methods, sample, surveys, and planned analysis; to seek comments and set a timetable for feedback on sampling and the survey; and to plan a dissemination strategy.

Most people have a general idea about the uses of surveys, but few people have experience with SC studies. In the initial meetings, you may want to provide your client and the rest of your team with either a hypothetical or an actual example of a SC study on a similar topic. Survey development will move more smoothly if everyone has a basic understanding of the design process (Chapter 7), in particular, how to select attributes and attribute levels. For example, people often want to include a level for each possible outcome of the attribute. However, each additional level adds complexity to the design and increases the sample size requirements. In addition, discussing the types of questions that can be answered with different SC survey designs is helpful. If you want to assess a particular policy, then the attributes should reflect the factors affected by the policy. In the case of the Yellowstone study, we needed to assess WTP for a range of policies including limiting or banning snowmobiles in the park, technology requirements for snowmobiles, and a requirement that all snowmobiles be on commercially guided tours. To evaluate the impact of these different policies separately and in combination, we had to be able to map the attribute levels in the SC survey to conditions in the park under each policy.

3.1.2. Review the Literature

The first and often most substantive step in the survey planning process is to review the existing literature on the topic. The literature review should take stock of knowns and unknowns regarding the topic; provide an understanding of the past, current, and future situation as it is relevant to the survey; and assess the availability of related or secondary data that could help in designing and analyzing the survey.

The literature review should not be confined to the academic literature. The media, position papers written by nonprofit organizations, and Web sites created by stakeholder groups can provide not only information, but also context and a sense of any controversy that exists about the topic. The proposed winter management plans for Yellowstone were highly controversial, and we gathered a variety of useful information from the media and advocacy group Web sites. The media reports and Web sites also served as a reminder to the survey team about the political environment in which we would be operating.

A variety of databases exists that may be useful for your literature search: Environmental Valuation Reference Inventory (EVRI), the Beneficial Use Values Database, ingenta, AGRICOLA (Agricultural Online Access), and ECONLIT. E-mail listservs devoted to environmental economics provide another avenue for collecting information about relevant literature, especially unpublished studies.

3.1.3. Collect Other Survey Instruments

As part of the literature review, you may identify other relevant surveys. You can often ask the lead investigators of other studies for copies of their surveys. The databases mentioned above provide a good starting place for identifying other surveys. Furthermore, the questions or the layout of other surveys can provide useful models in the early stages of the survey planning process. To develop the activity diary component of the outdoor time study, we found a variety of activity diaries used in other studies through an Internet search.

You may want to incorporate questions from existing surveys. For example, using questions from nationally representative surveys can provide a way to compare your sample with a national sample. Alternatively, you might be interested in asking a different sample a question from another study, for example, in a different country or a different age group. Often the questions in these surveys have already been tested and validated.

Depending on your topic, you may also be interested in specialized questionnaires designed for specific purposes, such as medical surveys. A number of questionnaires have been developed to measure the severity of specific diseases such as asthma or multiple sclerosis. The authors of the questionnaire have often developed a scoring method to produce one or several indices of disease severity or quality of life. In the outdoor time study, we used existing survey instruments designed to measure the severity of an individual's asthma as a basis for our asthma severity questions. Remember that you may need permission from the survey designer to use their survey instrument. In addition, the disease-specific survey instruments may be too long to include in your survey instrument—talk to the researchers who developed the instrument; sometimes a shorter version exists.

Beyond the survey design itself, other studies provide useful information on the population that was sampled, how the survey was administered, what response rate was achieved, how the data analysis was conducted, and what conclusions the authors were able to reach.

3.1.4. Build Study Teams

Finally, team members should be assembled to complement your own knowledge and expertise. SC studies usually require sophisticated experimental design and data analysis techniques, so the team should include people with expertise in these areas. In addition, the team needs to include experts on the topic of the survey—economists, natural scientists, health care professionals, or others. As discussed above, members of the survey team need to understand the basics of designing a SC study to understand their role in the survey process. The outdoor time survey team included scientists who specialized in air quality exposure assessment. In Sri Lanka, it was critical to include researchers who had studied the water sector and understood the policy issues and options for delivering potable water. Furthermore, interest in the spatial dimension of service delivery led to the inclusion of geographic information systems (GIS) specialists.

3.1.5. Visit the Field

In the introduction, we contend that survey-based SC studies are good examples of "field experiments" by representing a practical mix of control and realism. This realism starts with the analysts and investigators visiting the field and learning the lay of the land. We learn about the types of questions to ask and the way to ask them by observing respondents in their natural setting making choices over a range of goods and services of interest (to the analyst) while facing income, time, and information constraints. In addition, field visits provide a wealth of data on logistical issues related to travel, coordination, costs, and management. In Sri Lanka, for example, we conducted a 10-day scoping visit in May 2003 prior to returning with the full team in July 2003 to finalize the study and launch the survey. The rapid appraisal methods described below present a special type of preparatory field visit.

3.1.6. Rapid Appraisals Methods

Moving beyond these basic steps, a more formalized method of preparing for surveys is a rapid appraisal. RA methods are "quick and dirty," low-cost methods for gathering information. They lie somewhere along the continuum of data collection options ranging from informal short field visits and casual conversations to fully developed census, surveys, or experiments. While most of us have been exposed to procedurally precise, highly structured, systematic surveys or experiments at some point in our lives, as respondents, enumerators, or designers, many of the activities you use to prepare for a survey would fall into the category of RA methods.

These methods emerged in the 1970s in the field of social anthropology so that urban professionals and outsiders could learn about agricultural systems. The methods emphasize the importance and relevance of situational local knowledge and of getting the big things broadly right rather than achieving spurious statistical accuracy. The methods use a style of listening research and a creative combination of iterative methods and verification. The most well known verification strategy relies on "triangulation" of data from different sources (i.e., using two different methods to view and confirm the same information). As you can imagine, RA methods can quickly and cheaply generate a comprehensive picture of the situation at hand only if they are administered by highly trained and skilled professionals who compensate for the speed and cost savings through a wealth of experience and knowledge. Some of the most common examples of RAs include key informant interviews, focus groups, direct observations, community surveys or workshops, and mini-surveys.

1. *Key informant* interviews typically constitute talking to 15 to 25 knowledgeable and diverse experts from the study area. These interviews are semi-structured, qualitative in nature, and essentially in-depth discussions.

2. *Focus groups* are discussions among 8 to 12 individuals, who constitute a homogeneous group, regarding issues and experiences of interest to the researcher. A moderator introduces the topic, facilitates and stimulates discussion, and avoids domination by a few.

3. *Direct observations* essentially involve teams of observers recording what they see, hear, and experience into a pre-specified detailed observation form. The observations could relate to objects, structures, processes, activities, or even discussions.

4. *Community surveys or workshops* are similar to focus groups in purpose, except that they are typically conducted at a public meeting and involve an extensive amount of interaction between the participants and the interviewers (often through question-and-answer sessions). This type of group-wide data collection is sometimes better accomplished in a workshop setting.

5. *Mini-surveys* are structured but short (1 to 2 page) questionnaires (usually including close-ended questions) that are administered to 25 to 75 individuals using a nonprobability sampling strategy.

These methods are often complemented (or even substituted) by one or more of the following: review of secondary sources; foot transects;[1] familiarization and participation in activities; mapping and diagramming; biographies, local histories, and times; ranking and scoring; and rapid report writing in the field.

The strengths of RA methodologies include the fact that they are cheap, quick, flexible, and contextually and evidentially rich. Their primary weaknesses are that their results are unreliable or potentially invalid, not generalizable to the large population, and not sufficiently rigorous and credible for key decision makers. Thus, they are best used to help understand your topic; the population you will be surveying; and the types of information you will need by providing:

- qualitative, descriptive information;
- assessments of attitudes and motivations;
- interpretations of quantitative data from surveys and experiments;
- suggestions and recommendations; and
- questions, hypotheses, and approaches to be tested by surveys and experiments.

3.2. Step 2: Model Development

The initial assessment process is designed to gather information about the topic and to generate more specific testable hypotheses or research claims that provide direction for the survey instrument and sample design. The next stage is to develop an analysis plan. The theoretical and empirical models you select define the framework in which to analyze and interpret your data. If you are testing a hypothesis about how people behave, then the theoretical model from which the hypothesis is derived will be a prominent focus of the project. Other projects may involve applying a well-developed theory, for example, a benefit-cost analysis. The theoretical model is always important, even for a straightforward application. For example, the primary impact of the Yellowstone National Park winter management plans on local businesses was indirect (by changing the number of customers they served), rather than direct (mandating the use of certain technology). As part of the project design, we consulted benefit-cost analysis textbooks to determine the circumstances under which these indirect impacts should be included in a benefit-cost analysis. Without thinking carefully about your theoretical model, you may misinterpret the meaning of your regression coefficients or fail to collect the specific data needed to calculate WTP or other desired output measures. You may also miss the opportunity to explore additional questions. For example, in the outdoor time survey, we did not ask about the child's height and weight. Given the current focus on childhood obesity, more thought about our theoretical model would have revealed interesting trade-offs between risks from lack of exercise and risks from exposure to air pollution. The theoretical and empirical models should be specified early in the study to avoid collecting survey responses and then trying to force them into a model that does not fit or discovering you forgot to ask a crucial question.

The job of the empirical model is to develop quantitative and statistically testable versions of the research and/or policy question that is the reason for the survey. In SC studies, a couple of basic decisions have an impact on the approach you will use to analyze the data.

- The number of alternatives the respondents select among: If respondents select between two alternatives, you will use a binary choice model. If respondents select from more than two alternatives, you will need a multinomial model.
- A labeled or unlabeled design:[2] Labeled designs require an alternative-specific constant as part of the estimating equation.
- The attribute levels: It is harder to generate a good experimental design as the number of attributes grows. Likewise, creating the experimental design and analyzing the data are more difficult when there are restrictions on the attribute levels.[3]
- Forced choice or not: In a forced choice, respondents who do not like either alternative must still select the one they dislike least. In contrast, one of the alternatives can be an "opt-out" that allows the respondent

to indicate he would not select either alternative. The empirical strategy differs for each case.

- Using RP data: SC studies provide a logical framework for combining RP and SP data. Jointly estimating RP and SP data requires that the two data sets contain information on similar attributes.

Chapters 9 and 10 in this book discuss common empirical approaches to estimating SC models, including calculating WTP.

The model will help guide both the selection of dependent and independent variables and the format in which the data need to be collected. The theoretical model may contain variables like the prices of substitute goods that need to be collected or highlight the possibility of confounding variables. Confounding variables, often referred to as confounders, are variables that may not be the focus of the study but need to be controlled for in the empirical specification to produce efficient, unbiased estimates of the coefficients. The outdoor time study was part of an effort to evaluate the impact of high levels of ozone pollution on time spent outdoors. Ozone and temperature are highly correlated; thus, one issue in designing the outdoor time study was controlling for temperature.

In addition, there are often a variety of empirical measures for a single variable, such as measuring attitudes, awareness, or risk perceptions. The theoretical and empirical models may help determine the appropriate measure of a particular variable (of course, pretesting the variable on actual respondents is also important). For example, one common problem in designing SC studies is how to link physical measures of environmental goods with services or experiences people care about. For example, it can be difficult to link chemical measures of water or air quality or decibel measures of noise with services people care about such as fishing, a spectacular view, or natural quiet. Chapter 3 contains advice on determining the questions you need to ask to capture the variables of interest.

3.3. Step 3: Planning the Instrument Design, Sample Selection, Budget and Schedule

With the topic of the survey well defined and the model specified, the next steps in the planning process are to make preliminary decisions about the survey instrument, sample, budget and schedule. These topics are interdependent and should be considered together.

3.3.1. Step 3a: Survey Instrument

The planning process we describe here includes creating a draft of the survey instrument. It will not be the final draft, but a working draft so you can assess the feasibility of the project by getting a basic idea of what might work and how long respondents will take to complete the survey.

If at all possible, it is useful to conduct some focus groups on the survey topic during the planning stage. After the planning stage, when you are actually writing your survey instrument, you may use focus groups to evaluate different versions of the survey instrument, information provided in the survey, and visual aids used in the survey to convey information (as discussed in chapter 5). Focus groups can also be useful as a way to gauge awareness of the issues and knowledge of the topic and to identify potential problems for the survey design phase.

In our opinion, focus groups should be used sparingly with a clear understanding of their strengths and weaknesses as information-gathering tools. Focus groups are typically small (8 to 12 people), nonrandom groups of people. The discussion in a focus group can be dominated by an individual or two, even with the most skillful moderator, and group dynamics will affect the direction of the discussion. While focus groups provide useful information, you need to be careful not to overreact to comments from one or two people.

Focus groups explore topics related to the survey. At the planning stage, you may want to assess the public's familiarity with the subject, the language people use to talk about the subject, and any cultural or political sensitivities related to the topic. In addition, it is never too early to start assessing possible attributes and attribute levels that you will use to design the survey (i.e., understanding characteristics of the good, service, or policy being evaluated that are important to people). It is important to have an experienced moderator who understands the research question you are asking and the type of information you need to start designing your SC study, so that she can follow-up on unexpected revelations and steer the group away from unimportant issues.

We recommend giving the focus group a writing task at the beginning of the discussion to get the group thinking about the topic and to gain a sense of people's opinions before the group discussion starts. Using questions from other surveys on the same or similar topic can be a useful method for gathering information that can then be compared to the results of other studies for differences and similarities.

In addition to focus groups, drafts of the survey can be tested using one-on-one interviews, sometimes called cognitive interviews. Respondents talk aloud as they answer questions, and the interviewer can probe for unclear directions, poorly worded questions, or missing information.

In all of our surveys, we have used techniques such as focus groups and cognitive interviews both formally and informally and have found them to be immensely helpful in understanding the topic. In the Yellowstone study, testing early drafts of the instrument led us to change the focus of the SC study from evaluating management options to evaluating trips whose characteristics were influenced by changes in management. Questions centered around management options appeared to invite protest responses and were difficult for the respondents to understand. Instead we created stated choice questions that described day trips the visitor could choose between. The survey did contain a question about management alternatives, but in the form of a stated behavior question (it asked how visitors would change their current vacation plans in response to different management alternatives).

Using the information you collected previously, ideas from other survey instruments, and feedback from the focus groups, you can create an outline of the survey and fill in the outline with possible questions. To help with the planning process, you need an idea of:

- the approximate length of the survey instrument;
- the possible need for visual aids such as photographs, charts or diagrams;
- the amount of background information that might be needed; and
- possible formats for the SC choice questions.

The earlier you make decisions on these issues, the more accurate your budget forecast will be. Professional survey research firms base their cost estimates on assumptions about the length of the survey and details such as the need for skip patterns, the number of open-ended questions, and the use of visual aids.

It is also important to consider how you will assess the success of your survey and the reliability of the estimates derived from the survey. The success of a SC survey is judged by the degree to which the values produced by the survey conform to intuition and economic theory. Several measures have been discussed as methods for evaluating SC studies, including scope tests and convergent validity. Ideally the results will be responsive to variables such as price, income, and the size or scope of the good being valued. In addition, tests of respondent rationality and consistency, such as repeating a question, asking questions where one choice is clearly dominant, and more subtle tests for transitivity, can be incorporated in the survey design. Split samples can test for the impact of information, visual aids, or other characteristics of the survey design or sample on the responses. Finally, you can include questions that ask the respondent factual questions to test their knowledge of the topic. Furthermore, survey quality measures such as the overall response rate to the survey and item nonresponse will be important. Many of these tests need to be purposefully included as part of the survey design. In the survey planning stage, you need to decide how you will evaluate the results of your survey and build these elements into the survey design.

3.3.2. Step 3b: The Sample

At the start of the survey design process, you must determine the population whose values your survey is designed to capture or the population to which you want to be able to extrapolate the results. Sometimes, the population is well defined, either by your client or the needs of a report. Other times, you have more flexibility. If you are having a difficult time figuring out whose values you want to measure, then you may want to return to the first step and think harder about the goals of your survey and your research questions.

The sample you choose to study has implications for survey instrument design, the budget, and the method used to recruit people into your sample. The survey instrument design will be affected by the level of knowledge the people in the sample have about the topic, the level of education within the sample (often self-administered surveys are designed for an eighth grade reading level), and the use of computer-administered surveys. The budget will obviously be affected by the size of the sample. However, the criteria you use to select the sample (limiting the age, gender, or race of the sample, for example) will also affect the cost and how you recruit individuals into your sample. Again, professional survey administration firms will want to know what criteria you plan to use to select your sample and the incidence of people who meet the criteria in the population. For example, in the outdoor time study we needed parents who were staying at home with their children over the summer. To develop preliminary budget estimates, we worked with the online marketing firm that administered the survey to estimate the probability that the families they contacted would meet this criterion based on national survey data on the percentage of parents who stay home with their children.

The sample frame is the population from which respondents for the survey will be drawn. Because you should only generalize the results within your sampling frame, ideally, the sampling frame would include everyone in the population of interest and each person would have a known probability of selection for the sample. Often, this is not possible, and the degree to which your sample frame captures the population of interest will depend on the method of sampling.

In the Yellowstone study, our sampling frame included all winter visitors during the winter of 2002 to 2003. We selected a random sample of this population by intercepting visitors at the four entrances to the park using a statistical sampling plan. Thus, the results of the survey could be generalized to all visitors during the winter of 2002 to 2003. But the population of interest was actually wider than current visitors, because under some of the management plans the park expected new people to visit the park. Because the benefit-cost analysis was being prepared for a regulatory analysis, we were not permitted to use a convenience sample of these potential visitors (for example, membership lists from cross-country ski clubs). Most surveys funded by the U.S. government must be approved by the Office of Management and Budget (OMB) under the Paperwork Reduction Act (44 U.S.C. chapter 35). OMB issues guidelines that describe their expectations for the design, administration, and analysis of surveys conducted by the federal government. We considered random-digit dialing to locate individuals who might be interested in visiting Yellowstone in the future; however, the incidence of such people was believed to be low in the general population, and our budget could not support a sample of the likely size needed. Unfortunately, these potential visitors had to be excluded from the sample. Note that excluding these people resulted in an underestimate, which has the advantage of being considered a conservative estimate (and therefore more acceptable to skeptics) but the disadvantage of ultimately being inaccurate.

After selecting the sampling frame, you must choose the method of sampling from that frame. Selecting a random sample of individuals from your sampling frame allows you to generalize your results to the rest of the sampling frame. A wide range of strategies exists for drawing random samples and for over-sampling certain subpopulations within a random design. Chapter 2 reviews sampling methods.

In between fully random and convenience samples, there is a large literature on experimental design that offers strategies for selecting the sample that allows you to test your hypothesis or gather the data you need to answer your central question. The purpose of the study will often determine the importance of your sampling frame and whether you draw a random sample or a convenience sample or follow another experimental design strategy. Often, surveys that test methodological issues, for example, how the number of attributes in a SC question affects the results, use convenience samples. The outdoor time survey was conducted using an online market research panel. The panel is recruited through various Web portals, and respondents agree to participate in surveys in exchange for points they can use to purchase merchandise. The firm that operates the panel provides weights that can be used to calibrate your sample to national averages based on both demographics and likelihood of taking online surveys. As part of the outdoor time survey, we were interested in testing the use of online activity diaries to collect our data. The online marketing panel provided a cost-effective method of testing the methodology and for locating stay-at-home parents of young children with asthma in 35 major metropolitan areas.

Finally, planning for the survey involves some decisions about sample size or at least a range of sample sizes. Sample size balances the cost of alternative data collection methods with the desired level of precision in your estimates. Power calculations provide estimates of expected precision based on the best information you have about your population. Power calculations for SC studies need to account for the panel nature of the data (multiple, but correlated, observations per respondent). If you want to compare two or more groups, then you also need information about the fraction of the population in each group and whether your sample will have enough people in each group to generate estimates at the level of precision you want. For example, suppose you need to compare people with a certain health condition to those without the condition. If you plan to draw a representative sample of the population, you need information on the prevalence of the health condition in the population to determine whether your sample is likely to include enough people with the condition to make inferences. For rare health conditions, the cost of finding these people through random-digit dialing, for example, is often so large that using disease registries or other lists of patients is more practical.

3.3.3. Step 3c: Budget and Timeline
The third track of the survey planning process involves estimating the budget and schedule for the survey.

Budget

Survey research is more complicated and expensive than most people anticipate. Data collection often devours most of the budget for a survey, leaving inadequate resources for a careful analysis of the data. There is a temptation to think that if you can just get the data collected, you will be able to find additional time and money to analyze it.

Conducting surveys on a limited budget presents challenges. The size of your budget will affect all of the decisions you make about the target population, sample size, mode of survey administration, amount of pretesting, complexity of the survey, and the level of analysis. As part of the planning process, you need to determine whether you can achieve the study's goals with the available budget. Below we summarize some of the main cost drivers in survey research.

1. **Survey Mode**: The survey mode and the target population will probably have the greatest influence on the cost of your choice experiment. Chapter 2 discusses the different survey modes. In general, in-person interviewing is most expensive, while mail surveys are the least expensive in the United States. However, the actual cost of using a particular mode will depend, among other things, on your sample size. For example, conducting the survey over the Web or with a computer could involve upfront fixed costs for programming that may seem high if you are interested in a small sample size. However, because collecting data over the Web or on a computer reduces the cost of data entry associated with mail surveys, it may be more cost-effective to use a computer-administered survey for larger samples or for on-site interviews.

2. **Target Population**: Your target population and the type of sample you intend to draw also have a large impact on your survey costs. If you need a random sample of your target population, then your survey costs will generally be higher. In addition, the more specific the population of interest, the more expensive it will be to survey them, unless you are targeting a group of people who are part of an association or other organization that will provide (or sell) a list of members.

3. **Topic**: If the topic is unfamiliar or complicated, then you will want to conduct careful pretesting to determine the attributes, attribute levels, and additional information to be included in the survey.

4. **Design**: Because SC surveys must be created according to a statistical design process, you will need to include someone on your team who is familiar with SC experimental design.

5. **Data Analysis**: SC studies require sophisticated data analysis techniques, so you will need a team member familiar with these techniques. In addition, analyzing SP choice data often takes more time than surveys for which results can simply be tabulated or expressed as a percentage.

Schedule

The schedule for your survey will depend not only on the deadlines faced by you or your client, but also on your budget, the survey mode, the level of analysis anticipated, and the report format. Just as budgets are often underestimated, it is also common to vastly underestimate the amount of time needed to design, implement, and analyze a choice experiment. Determining the time frame includes not just how much time you have to develop, administer, and analyze the survey data, but also whether you need to collect data during a particular season, before or after a particular event, and the number of times you intend to contact people. For example, the Yellowstone survey had to be ready to field in late December when snowmobile season starts. Because we wanted a sample that was representative of all winter visitors, we intercepted visitors from late December through early March. After mailing the surveys and follow-up reminders, the majority of the surveys were returned by May, but we were still receiving surveys in late June. The data collection phase of the Sri Lanka survey took approximately 40 days, from mid-August to the end of September 2003. The primary influence on the schedule was the need to conduct a public forum during the process.

The other element of the schedule involves securing approval for the survey from institutional review boards and, if necessary, from OMB for surveys conducted by federal agencies. Approval from review boards, while sometimes quick, can often add weeks or months to your schedule.

3.4. Step 4: Is It Feasible?

Returning to Figure 2, you have now completed Steps 1, 2, and 3, and it is time to assess the feasibility of the plan you have developed. Of course, you have probably been asking yourself "Will this work? Can we really do this?" since the first day you started planning. Although there are no hard and fast rules for assessing feasibility, feasibility encompasses two issues that we refer to as theoretical feasibility and practical feasibility. Theoretical feasibility can be thought of as whether a survey can be designed to assess the research question of interest. Can the good or service be described using a SC study in a way that is both easy to understand and scientifically accurate? Do nonmonetary trade-offs work better than using cost as an attribute? Can the goods or services described in the survey be linked to the policy or hypothesis you want to evaluate? Instrument design work, including focus groups and pretests, will help determine if it is theoretically possible to conduct the survey. Discussions with experts in the field or researchers who have attempted surveys on the same topic can also help you determine whether your project is feasible. SC studies have many advantages compared to other methods of collecting nonmarket valuation data, but they are not the right format for every topic.

Practical feasibility relates more to questions of budget and schedule. What is theoretically feasible may not be doable within a constrained budget or schedule. If you cannot accomplish what you need to, you will need to revisit the design of the survey instrument, the size and composition of the sample, the method of recruiting the sample, and the survey administration mode to create your final plan.

4. SUMMARY

The choices you make in designing a SC study should always be motivated by your research question. Nothing is more important than starting with a clear statement of the question you want to answer and what data you will need to answer it. Taking the time in the beginning of the project to plan carefully, to explore the survey topic and to understand the implications of different SC designs will help you make good decisions about your survey.

All good quality surveys share a similar planning process. SC surveys require additional effort to select the attributes and attribute levels, and the survey team needs to include someone with expertise in choice experiment design and data analysis. But the reward for investing additional effort in the survey design process is the flexibility of the SC approach – an approach that can be used to explore the impact of key attributes on individual choice for a wide variety of topics.

---

5. ENDNOTES

[1] A foot transect refers to the act of surveying an area by walking in a systematic way and recording what you see.

[2] In a labeled design, the alternatives have labels such as the names of actual companies or products. You might, for example, ask respondents to select between a Gateway and a Dell laptop with different features. An unlabeled design would present laptops A and B.

[3] Attribute levels may be restricted if certain combinations of attributes create alternatives that do not make sense.

6. REFERENCES

Booth, W.C., G.G. Colomb and J.M. Williams, 1995, *The Craft of Research,* Chicago: University of Chicago Press.

Harrison, G. and J. List, 2004, "Field Experiments," *Journal of Economic Literature,* XLII: 1009-1055.

CHAPTER 2

SURVEY METHODOLOGIES FOR STATED CHOICE STUDIES

PATRICIA A. CHAMP

U.S. Forest Service, Rocky Mountain Research Station, Fort Collins, Colorado, U.S.A.

MICHAEL P. WELSH

Christensen Associates, Madison, Wisconsin, U.S.A.

1. INTRODUCTION

In this chapter, we focus on administration of stated choice (SC) surveys. Many decisions you make regarding methodology will directly impact the quantity and quality of the data. Should you administer the survey through the mail, or in-person, or on the web? How many people should you contact? What do you do when individuals do not complete and return the survey? How do you know if you have a good response rate? Although there are not hard and fast rules, there are generally-agreed upon best practices.

In this chapter, we synthesize the survey literature relevant to conducting SC surveys and offer some of our practical knowledge about best practice. In the next section, we discuss sample design and the process of selecting the individuals who will receive the survey. In Section 3, we describe potential sources of error that can impact data quality. Section 4 covers survey administration and Section 5 provides important guidelines for managing your SC survey.

2. SAMPLE DESIGN

The sample design specifies the population of interest, the sampling frame, and the technique for drawing a sample from the sampling frame. Researchers usually choose the survey mode (see Section 4) and develop the sample design at the same

B.J. Kanninen (ed.), Valuing Environmental Amenities Using Stated Choice Studies, 21–42.

time, as the two issues are closely related. How the survey is administered – the survey mode -- will impact how a sample is drawn. For example, if the choice survey is going to be administered on-site at participants' homes and the desired study participants do not need to be contacted in advance, the sample might be drawn based on a geographical designation such as a census block or a city block. However if the survey is going to be administered via mail, a sample frame that includes addresses would be needed. Conversely, the sample design impacts which modes of administration are feasible. If it is not possible to develop a sample frame of addresses for the study population then a mail survey may not be an option.

2.1. Study Population

SC surveys are used in many contexts including benefit-cost analyses, natural resource damage assessments, and policy analyses. Each of these situations may call for a different standard for defining the relevant study population. An important consideration is to ask whose values matter. In some cases, defining the study population will be straightforward. For example, if you are administering a study to investigate preferences of anglers over a range of fishery management options, the relevant population may be current fishing license holders. However, if you are interested in *potential* anglers, you would want to consider a population broader than current fishing license holders to try to capture individuals who, statistically speaking, might choose to become anglers in the future.

It is also important to think about the types of values to be measured. For example, there is much discussion in the broader valuation literature about measuring use and passive use values. Policy relevant studies often require measurement of both types of values. Identification of the relevant study population for measurement of passive use values can be challenging as the benefits may extend beyond the population who has direct contact with the good. Loomis (2000, p. 312) argues,

> If the public good provides benefits well beyond the immediate jurisdiction where the good is located, then either federal grants-in-aid or even federal provision may be needed to improve the allocation of resources involving the public good. Comparing only the local public benefits to marginal cost of supply will result in under provision if substantial spillover benefits to other nonpayers are ignored.

Likewise, this issue of whose benefits should be measured has been described by Smith (1993, p. 21) as, ". . . probably more important to the value attributed to environmental amenities as assets than any changes that might arise from refining our estimates of per unit values." Empirical studies of goods with a large passive use value component (Loomis, 2000; Sutherland and Walsh, 1985) verify that only small percentage of the aggregate economic benefit is accounted for by the immediate jurisdiction where the good is located. Unfortunately, no simple rule of thumb exists for defining the study population. We recommend thoughtful consideration of who will pay for the good as well as who will benefit from its provision.

2.2. Sample Frame

The sample frame is the list from which sample units – people or households, for example -- are selected to be surveyed. If we are conducting a study to investigate preferences for library services at Colorado State University (CSU), the relevant study population could be all students enrolled at CSU plus CSU faculty and staff. One sample frame that could be considered would be the CSU directory. Ideally, the sample frame perfectly matches the study population. This is an important issue and warrants careful thought. The researcher should ask what types, if any, of individuals are being systematically excluded from the study population by using any particular sample frame. For example, if the intent of a study is to provide information about all households in a specified geographic area, telephone listings would under-represent the study population because they omit households that do not have telephones as well as those that do not list their telephone number. A better sample frame in this case might be developed from multiple sources such as telephone listings and voter and automobile registration lists. Such lists can be purchased from survey research firms. Although coverage of the study population using such lists may not be perfect, it is often very good.

Sometimes a good sample frame does not exist for the relevant sample population. One option is to conduct in-person surveys using sampling techniques that do not require an initial sample frame. This approach is discussed in Section 4.1.1. Another option when a good sample frame does not exist is to use random digit dialing, a method where potential study participants are contacted via randomly generated phone numbers (See Section 4.1.2). The National Survey on Recreation and the Environment, an ongoing national recreation survey that began in 1960, is an example of a national survey that currently employs random digit dialing to identify potential survey participants. If a sample frame can be identified, budget constraints usually require the selection of only a portion of the units in the sample frame to receive the survey. The sample selection process involves two decisions: *How* will sample units be selected and *How many* sample units will be selected?

2.3. Probability Sampling

When we use probability sampling, every unit in the sample frame has a known, nonzero probability of being chosen for the sample. If statistical inference is the goal of a SC survey, probability sampling is most appropriate. Several probability sampling techniques exist, the most straightforward of which is simple random sampling (see Kish, 1967, Cochran, 1977, or Särndal, Swensson and Wretman, 1992, for more extensive discussions of survey sampling). Simple random sampling requires a list of the entire sample frame. Since sampling lists are not usually arranged in random order, sample units must be pulled from the list in a random manner. If the list is very long – a phone book, for example, -- simple random sampling could be cumbersome. In this case, it might be better to use a systematic sampling technique in which the first sample unit is randomly drawn and after that, every n^{th} unit is selected. Random sampling is best suited for telephone, mail, or e-mail surveys. If the sample frame is geographically dispersed, in-person survey costs with random sampling can be exorbitant, due to travel costs between geographically scattered interviews.

Another commonly used probability sampling technique is stratified sampling. With stratified sampling, the entire study population is divided into nonoverlapping subpopulations called strata based on some measure that is available for the initial sample frame. Within each stratum, a variety of methods can be used to select the sample units. For example, if sample units are randomly selected from each stratum, the procedure is called stratified random sampling.

Stratified sampling is primarily used in three situations. First, stratified sampling can be used to ensure adequate sample size within a stratum for separate analysis. This is important when the strata are of particular interest. For example, consider a SC survey with the primary objective of estimating mean willingness to pay (WTP) for improved access to a recreational area and a secondary goal of comparing the mean WTP between urban and rural populations. In this situation, a simple random sample may not provide an adequate number of rural respondents to allow for detection of a statistical difference. The sample could be stratified into rural and urban strata with the rural stratum more heavily sampled to ensure an adequate number of respondents for analysis. Another situation in which stratified sampling is used is when the variance on a measure of interest is expected to not be equal across the strata. In this case, more of the sample can be drawn from the stratum with the larger variance to increase overall sample efficiency. In the rural-urban example above, there could be higher variance of WTP for the urban population relative to the rural population, perhaps due to varied levels of environmental avidity among urban residents. The third situation in which a stratified sample might be used is when the cost of obtaining a survey response differs by strata. An example of this would be an Internet survey combined with a mail survey for individuals who do not have an Internet account. Survey responses from the mail survey stratum will be more costly than those from the Internet survey stratum. For a fixed budget, drawing a disproportionate amount of the sample from the lower cost stratum would most improve the sample variance. Sudman (1983) provides the details of how to stratify a sample for strata with differing costs.

A third type of probability sampling, cluster sampling, can be used with in-person surveys to minimize the travel costs between interviews. The general idea is that respondents are chosen in groups or clusters. For example, a simple cluster sample may define blocks in a city as clusters. First, blocks are selected, then survey participants within each of the blocks are chosen. Cluster sampling can be quite complicated, and consulting a survey statistician to design the sampling procedures is a good idea. Frankel (1983) provides a detailed explanation of cluster sampling.

Multistage area sampling is a similar technique for in-person surveys that does not require a complete sample frame. A multistage area sample involves first sampling geographic regions, then sampling areas within each region. Carson et al. (1992) implemented a multistage area sample with their contingent valuation study of the lost passive use values resulting from the Exxon Valdez oil spill. In the first stage, they sampled 61 counties or county groups from a list of all counties in the U.S. In the second stage, 330 blocks were chosen from within the 61 counties. Finally, 1,600 dwelling units were chosen from within the 330 blocks. This sample design with appropriate sample weighting allowed Carson et al. to generalize the results of their study to the population of the United States.

2.4. Nonprobability Sampling

In nonprobability sampling each individual in the population does *not* have a known nonzero probability of being chosen for the sample. Examples of nonprobability sampling could include using students in a class or recruiting subjects in a shopping mall. Nonprobability sampling is best suited for studies that do not require generalization from the survey sample to a broader population. Such samples are frequently used to investigate methodological questions such as how behaviors or responses vary under different treatments. The field of experimental economics largely relies on observations of behaviors using nonprobability samples.

Harrison and Lesley (1996) recommend the use of nonprobability convenience samples to estimate a behavioral model for estimating contingent values. This model uses sample averages of population characteristics to predict behavior for the population. Their approach, however, remains controversial. We recommend the use of probability sampling if generalizations from the survey sample to a broader population are to be made.

2.5. Sample Size

Closely related to the "how" to choose the sample is deciding *how many sample units to choose*. Sampling error and the power of statistical tests are two important considerations in determining sample size. First, sampling error is a function of sample size. Sampling error arises because a sample does not provide complete information about the population of interest (see Section 3.2 for a more complete description). For small study populations, a relatively large proportion of the population is needed in the sample to maintain an acceptable level of sampling error. For example, for a study population of size 1,000, approximately 200-300 observations are required for ±5% sampling error. The sensitivity of the sampling error to sample size decreases as the population increases in size. Whether the size of the study population is 10,000 or 100,000,000, a sample size of approximately 380 is needed to provide a ±5% sampling error. Interestingly, this sample size is not much more than the sample size of 200-300 for the study population of 1,000 mentioned above (see Salant and Dillman, 1994, p. 55, for a table of final sample sizes for various population sizes and characteristics).

A second consideration is that the power of statistical testing is related to the sample size. The power function, which measures the probability of rejecting the null hypothesis when it is false, increases as the sample size increases. To give full consideration to this issue, one should think about all the statistical tests that might be conducted with the data. If statistical testing will use sub-samples of the data, the number of observations in each of the sub-samples must be adequate. Mitchell and Carson (1989) provide a nice exposition of the power of contingent valuation hypothesis tests. Of course, the final sample size (i.e. the number of completed observations) is usually smaller than the initial sample, so the initial sample should also be selected with consideration of the expected response rate.

Ignoring project costs, bigger is better when it comes to sample size. Choosing a sample size under a budget constraint involves deciding how much error is acceptable and determining whether the budget allows for a large enough sample to keep error within this range. The sample size is also related to the mode of administration. With a fixed budget, choosing a more expensive mode of administration, such as in-person, implies a smaller sample size than choosing a less expensive mode. This highlights the point made at the beginning of this section about the interconnectedness of decisions related to sampling and mode of administration.

3. SOURCES OF ERROR

Throughout the survey process, the researcher should be aware of issues that could give rise to errors in the survey data. Such errors can influence study results and possibly reduce the validity of the results as well. As complete avoidance of errors is impossible, the realistic goal of good survey design is to *minimize errors*. Four types of potential error are described in this section.

3.1. Coverage Error

One source of error introduced in the sample design stage is coverage error, which arises when the population of interest does not correspond with the sample frame. If, for example, the population of interest is all residents of the U.S., a sample frame of registered voters will not fully represent that population, as many residents of the U.S. do not register to vote. As SC studies often focus on public goods, the study population may be the general public for which no comprehensive list exists. In such cases, one option is to administer the survey via a mode that does not require an initial list, such as a random digit dialing telephone survey. Another option is to create a list of individuals that combines lists from multiple sources such as telephone listings or vehicle registration.

3.2. Sampling Error

Sampling error results from collecting data from only a subset, rather than all, of the members of the sample frame (Dillman, 2000, p. 196). As discussed in the earlier section on sample size, sampling error is a function of the sample size and the size of the population. Sampling error is often summarized as the "margin of error." Survey results, such as opinion polls, are often reported with a margin of error. For example, the results of a political poll might report 80 percent of Americans favor a particular presidential candidate with a margin of error of 3 percentage points. To keep sampling error within an acceptable range, the researcher must make sure the sample size is sufficient. As mentioned in Section 2.5, the necessary sample size for a specific level of sampling error depends on the size of the study population, though as the study population gets larger, the needed sample size does not increase proportionately.

3.3. Measurement Error

Measurement error is the result of poor question wording or the questions being presented in such a way that inaccurate or uninterpretable answers are obtained (Dillman, 2000, p.11). While measurement error can be an issue with all surveys, it can be a serious issue with SC surveys when goods or programs are not familiar to respondents. For example, consider a choice study on wolf reintroduction programs where one of the attributes is the number of wolves being reintroduced (either 20 or 100 wolves). If the study participants are not able to differentiate between the impacts of 20 wolves versus 100 wolves, they may not know if 100 wolves are better or worse than 20 wolves and as a result their responses to the choice sets may be inconsistent. Desvousges et al. (this volume) provide guidance on how to develop SC questions that allow for measurement of the intended construct.

3.4. Nonresponse Error

Even well designed surveys with substantial budgets will not get responses from all the individuals in the chosen sample. Salant and Dillman (1994, p. 20) define nonresponse error as occurring when "... a significant number of people in the survey sample do not respond to the questionnaire *and* are different from those who do in a way that is important to the study." The second part of this definition is often overlooked. While a higher response rate would likely reduce nonresponse error, a low response rate does not necessarily mean that nonresponse error is a problem. The best way to investigate whether nonresponse error is significant is to conduct surveys of nonrespondents. However, as these nonrespondents did not respond to the attempts to convince them to participate in the initial survey, they may also be reluctant to participate in a follow-up survey of nonrespondents. General population data, such as U.S. Census data, can often be used to assess whether the population of survey respondents is similar to the sample population in terms of standard demographics. However, this approach assumes that demographic variables are related to responses. That may not always be the case as some public goods may be viewed positively by some and negatively by others. For example, open space is a positive good for some individuals but considered a negative by individuals who would rather see the land used for development. In such a case, we do not know how results might be affected if we have more high income individuals in the response population than in the actual population.

As we mentioned, the higher the response rate, the less likely it is that nonresponse error will be substantial. There are many factors that can influence response rates. One of the major influences is the salience of the survey topic to the sample. Surveys on interesting topics that resonate with respondents, such as recreation, are likely to be more salient than surveys on electricity usage. Attempts should be made to link the individual's participation in the survey with some personal benefits (for example, "your participation will help inform decision makers about this very important issue"). The mode of administration can also impact response rates but it is not clear if the differences in response rate impact nonresponse error.

Advance letters are sometimes sent out to potential respondents to let them know they will be receiving a survey. These letters have been found to improve response rates in some situations (Goldstein and Jennings, 2002). Incentives such as including a few dollar bills or a pen with the survey can also improve response rates. Another approach is to send an incentive to respondents who return the survey by a specified date.

There has been some research on the impact of time of year on response rates to surveys. The summer and the month of December are generally considered poor times to administer surveys, but there are not many published studies to document seasonal effects. The technique that clearly has a positive impact on the number of surveys returned is the use of follow-up contacts. Dillman (2000) details survey implementation procedures, including number of and timing of follow-up mailings for mail and Internet surveys. Survey researchers have been experimenting with using different modes for follow-ups to improve response rates.

4. ADMINISTERING THE SURVEY

A SC survey can be conducted in one of two ways: an interviewer can ask the survey questions and record the respondents' answers (interviewer-administered) or survey respondents can record their own answers (self-administered). Interview-administered surveys can be conducted face-to-face with the survey respondent or over the telephone. Self-administered surveys can be conducted through the mail, phone, Internet, or on-site. In this section, we describe the different ways to administer SC surveys and the tradeoffs associated with each of the modes. We also describe emerging techniques, as survey administration is continually adapting to accommodate trends in communication. Two important adaptations in recent years include mixing different modes of administration within a survey and administering surveys with new technologies. The most obvious example of using new technology is the proliferation of web-based surveys.

4.1. Interviewer-Administered Surveys

Interviewers are used to administer SC surveys when the researcher wants to retain substantial control over how the information is presented and the order in which questions are asked. The interviewer can also clarify issues for the respondent if needed. While this control is positive, there is an associated tradeoff: the presence of the interviewer can affect responses to the survey. In this section, we describe how an interviewer can administer a SC survey and the tradeoffs associated with doing so. We describe two common ways for interviewers to administer surveys: in-person and over the telephone.

4.1.1. In-Person Surveys

One of the more common ways for an interviewer to administer a SC survey is face-to-face with an interviewer asking questions and recording respondents' answers. Such surveys can be administered in a variety of locations such as respondents' homes, shopping malls, on the street, or in places where the participants of targeted activities tend to congregate. For example, surveys about recreational preferences are often administered at the site of the recreational activity, such as a hiking trailhead, boat landing, or campsite.

As mentioned earlier, the primary advantage of in-person surveys comes from the control the interviewer has while administering the survey. The interviewer controls the question order and can use visual aids. The interviewer can also verify that the individual chosen to respond to the survey is the one to complete the survey. Likewise, complex surveys that may need some interviewer clarification are administered more easily in-person. Another potential advantage of in-person surveys is that one does not necessarily need a pre-existing list of names of the individuals in the survey population, as individuals can be intercepted on-site or interviewers can approach individual homes. These approaches might allow interviewers to reach people who would not respond to a telephone, mail, or Internet survey.

In-person interviews, however, tend to be much more expensive than other modes of administration due to training, salary, and travel costs for interviewers. Additionally, in-person surveys are subject to potential interviewer influences (Singer and Presser, 1989). One type of interviewer influence is "social desirability bias," which occurs when respondents respond to questions in ways they think the interviewer wants to hear. Respondents may overstate their contributions to charitable organizations if they perceive charitable giving as a socially desirable activity (Bradburn, 1983). Social desirability bias is more likely to occur with an in-person interview than with other modes of administration that allow for more anonymity.

Leggett et al. (2003) investigated social desirability bias in a contingent valuation survey. They implemented a split sample experiment in which one sample was administered a contingent valuation survey in-person and the other sample self-administered the survey. The topic of the survey was WTP to visit Fort Sumter National Monument in South Carolina. A "ballot box" into which respondents placed their response to the contingent valuation question was used to reduce the chances of respondents providing socially desirable responses. Despite this effort to minimize social desirability bias, Leggett et al. (2003) found responses to the contingent valuation question in the in-person survey to be more positive than responses in the self-administered survey. The mean WTP for the in-person surveys was $7.51, which was significantly higher than $5.71 for the self-administered surveys. Likewise, Bateman and Mawby (2004) found that the attire of the interviewer affected stated WTP in an in-person survey. Specifically, they found that when the interviewer (a male) wore a formal suit, statements of WTP were significantly higher than those from interviews where the same interviewer wore casual attire (t-shirt, denim shorts and tennis shoes).

One issue that has not been well researched is the impact of having others present during the survey interview. In general, interviewers try to discourage the presence of others during the interview for reasons of privacy. However, interviewers may not want to enforce this rule if they are concerned about refusals. In particular, spouses and children are often present during in home interviews and are often invited to participate in or observe the interview by the interviewee. Zipp and Toth (2002) looked at the impact of having a spouse present during in-person interviews for the British Household Panel Study. While previous research reported little evidence of social desirability bias associated with the presence of a spouse during the interview, Zipp and Toth (2002) investigated a somewhat different hypothesis. They hypothesized and found evidence that having a spouse present during the interview process resulted in greater agreement between the husband and wife on attitudinal and behavioral questions. This result highlights the need to be aware of the many factors that can influence survey responses. While not all influences can be controlled for, they should at least be acknowledged. In the case of third parties being present, the interviewer may want to record if a third party is present and who it is (child, spouse/partner, for example). Zipp and Toth (2002) do not suggest that the third party influences result in responses that are less valid, rather they make the point that the presence of a third party and the interviewer define the social context of the interview and that there is not a "true" or "optimal" social context.

In-person surveys had previously been thought to produce higher quality data than surveys administered by other modes. However, research over the last two decades has challenged this belief (Lyberg and Kasprzyk, 1991). The circumstances specific to a study will dictate which mode of administration is most appropriate. If the survey involves a well defined study population and is on a topic with which the study population is already familiar, the benefits of using an interviewer may not justify the additional costs. Likewise the particular design of a SC survey might better lend itself to being self-administered. The researcher must carefully consider the tradeoffs in terms of cost, sampling needs, how much information can reasonably be provided, and interviewer effects among the various modes of administration. In the end, the circumstances of a specific SC study will dictate which mode of administration is most appropriate.

To summarize, the advantages of in-person-administered surveys are the control the interviewer has over the question order, ease of providing additional information, such as visual aids to the respondent, and the ability to work from a sample frame that is not complete with names, addresses and/or telephone numbers. The drawbacks of in-person surveys are that interviewers and the presence of third parties can influence responses to the surveys and in-person surveys are expensive.

4.1.2. Interviewer-Administered Telephone Surveys

The proliferation of telemarketing and difficulties experienced by potential respondents in distinguishing between legitimate research surveys and telemarketing calls has made interviewer administered telephone surveys more problematic in recent years. Administering a SC survey over the telephone is even more challenging because the need for the respondent to understand the differing levels of the identified attributes in each of the choices may not lend itself well to verbal description over the phone. One option is to mail a survey describing the attributes, levels, and choice sets prior to the phone call so the survey respondent has the opportunity to look over the choices he or she will be asked to make. The mailing of the survey prior to the telephone interview may also make the initial phone call seem less abrupt, as the respondent would be expecting it. The initial mailing also provides an opportunity to communicate the legitimacy of the choice survey as a research method rather than a marketing ploy. The advantage of having an interviewer elicit responses over the phone rather than simply having the respondent fill out the survey and mail it back, is that the interviewer can clarify any sources of confusion, maintain control over the order in which questions are asked and potentially get responses from individuals who would not return a mail or other type of survey.

Another option is to use the telephone interview to obtain agreement from the respondent to complete a survey that can be administered via mail or Internet. One advantage of a telephone survey is that it can be conducted without a pre-existing list of names or telephone numbers by use of random digit dialing. With random digit dialing, the researcher identifies the three-digit prefix within a particular area code, then the following four digits are randomly generated. Of course, when the interviewer reaches a potential survey respondent, he does not know the respondent's name, so the introduction of the survey may seem impersonal to the respondent. If an individual agrees to complete a mail survey, the telephone interviewer obtains the mailing information and a survey is sent out soon after the call.

Telephone interviews with residential samples are usually scheduled for evenings and weekends, times when individuals are most likely to be home. The proliferation of cellular telephones also affects the practicality of conducting telephone interviews. While legitimate surveys are currently exempt from do-not-call lists, the current Federal Communications Commission regulations prohibit calls to cell phone numbers using an automated dialing system if the receiver of the call is charged for the call. As cellular phone plans vary with respect to charges for individual calls, it is nearly impossible to know if the receiver of the call is being charged. Differentiating between cell phone numbers and land lines can be difficult if individuals list their cellular phone number in the phone book or switch their residential number to their cell phone number. The FCC regulations will continue to change as the use of cellular phones rises. If you plan to implement a telephone survey, our advice is to understand the current regulations and do what you can to adhere to them.

In summary, the advantages of administering a SC survey via the telephone include the control maintained by the interviewer and the ability of the interviewer to clarify information. Telephone surveys tend to be less expensive relative to in-person surveys. However, we do not recommend use of a strict telephone survey to implement a SC study. The telephone might be best used in conjunction with some other mode of administration.

4.2. Self-Administered Surveys

Surveys are self-administered when the respondent reads the questions and records his own responses. Self-administered surveys can be distributed in a number of ways such as sending the survey by mail, handing surveys out at a public location, such as a shopping mall or recreation site, or having respondents go to a website. Most SC surveys are self-administered.

Removing interviewers from the survey process has some advantages and a few drawbacks. One advantage of self-administered surveys is that they are generally less costly as there is no expense associated with training and employing interviewers. There are also no interviewer effects and the respondent can control the pace at which he or she completes the survey.

On the other hand, when the respondent administers the survey him or herself, the investigator has much less control over the survey process. The respondent may not answer the questions in the desired order, or at all. Likewise, there is no interviewer available to clarify survey information. In some situations, the investigator cannot be sure the survey respondent is the person who was selected to be in the survey sample.

4.2.1. Paper Surveys

The most common mode for administering paper surveys is through the mail. However, paper surveys can also be administered on-site. As mentioned earlier, many recreation surveys are handed out at boat launch sites, trailheads, or other such locations. If paper surveys are handed out on-site, respondents can be asked to complete the survey later and return it, or the respondents may be asked to complete the survey immediately. Paper surveys can also be administered at a "central site facility" or a "laboratory" where individuals are paid to show up at a designated location and complete a paper survey. These types of surveys often involve convenience samples rather than samples that can be generalized to a population.

The advantages of paper surveys include the ability of respondents to complete the survey at their convenience and at their own pace. Respondents may also feel more comfortable offering honest responses to sensitive questions if they record their responses themselves rather than having to tell an interviewer. Paper surveys tend to be less expensive than in-person or telephone surveys. Inclusion of additional information, such as photographs and maps, is easily facilitated. Paper surveys can also be used in combination with other technologies. For example some researchers have conducted SC surveys (Loomis et al., 2006) by including a videotape that the respondent can watch while, or before, filling out the paper survey.

As mentioned earlier, the downside of paper surveys is the lack of control over the order in which the respondent answers the questions. Respondents may go back and change responses to earlier questions in the survey based on their responses to later questions. The order of the choice questions cannot be randomized as easily as they can be if the survey were administered on a computer. Likewise, inconsistent response patterns cannot be checked by asking respondents to review the question(s) and perhaps revise their answer(s). Another concern is that the pool of respondents may be biased if individuals look over the survey before they decide whether to respond. For example, a mail survey on rock climbing in National Forests may result in a disproportionate number of rock climbers responding. Also, there can be a substantial lag between the respondent receiving the survey and the survey being returned. Despite some of the shortcomings of mail surveys, mail remains a popular mode. Breffle et al. (1999), for example, chose mail to conduct a SC survey to assess the natural resource damages resulting from releases of polychlorinated biphenyls (PCBs) in the lower Fox River/Green Bay ecosystem in northeast Wisconsin.

4.2.2. Computer-Administered Surveys

Use of computer-administered surveys has increased substantially in recent years due to the wide range of advantages they offer to survey researchers. Visual materials such as maps, charts, graphics, streaming video and auditory stimulus can be integrated into the survey. Choice sets can be randomly or systematically generated as part of the study design. Inconsistent responses can also be checked by having respondents answer the question(s) again. A high degree of control is maintained over the presentation of questions and the order in which questions are answered. Computer-administered surveys may also dramatically reduce implementation expenses by avoiding interviewer time, postage, printing, data entry and/or mail handling expenses

There are, however, potential drawbacks associated with computer-administered surveys. Perhaps the largest drawback of computer-administered surveys is that the population of interest may not have access or the ability to complete a computer-based survey. In addition, while the marginal costs per respondent may be low for a computer-administered survey, the fixed costs of survey preparation may be high. These factors must be weighed carefully when deciding if a computer-administered survey is appropriate in the context of a specific research project.

Computer-administered surveys can take a variety of forms. In the next three sections we discuss some of these forms and associated implementation issues.

4.2.3. Computer-Administered without Internet

When a SC survey is computer-administered without use of the Internet, the researcher prepares a computer program to collect responses and write them to an electronic database. This approach can be implemented through the mail or by recruiting respondents to a central location.

Implementing this approach through the mail involves mailing the program on a computer disk to potential survey respondents and asking the respondents to complete the survey and return the disk containing the survey data. In this case, samples based on mailing addresses, which may be easier to obtain than samples of e-mail addresses, can be used. However, a sample based on physical addresses is subject to the concern that all members of the sample may not have access to computers and therefore may not be able to complete the survey. In addition, concerns about computer viruses can make potential respondents wary of running the survey program. A further issue is that the computer program must be able to run on a variety of operating systems found on the potential respondents' computers. While administering a SC survey via a computer through the mail provides some of the benefits of computer-administered surveys, it still requires the expenses associated with preparing and tracking mailings. This mode of implementation is likely not the best option for most SC surveys.

One approach to dealing with concerns about computer access and compatibility is to recruit potential respondents to a central location (for example a market research facility or meeting room) where computers containing the survey program are made available. Laptop computers have also made it easier for individuals to complete computer-administered surveys in less conventional locations, such as the public library.

4.2.4. E-mail-Administered Surveys

When SC surveys are administered via e-mail, the first order of business is to identify a sample of e-mail addresses. The survey can then be embedded in the e-mail message or sent as an attachment. If the survey is embedded in the e-mail message, it may be difficult to control the appearance of the survey instrument as viewed through the respondents' e-mail programs. Likewise it can be difficult to set up the response form so that it is easy and straightforward for the respondent to provide answers.

Providing the survey to a respondent in a form that can be easily manipulated by the respondent can pose difficulties. For example, respondents can modify questions by crossing out and/or inserting words and then answer the modified question. These types of modifications are easily detected during the data coding/entry process associated with a paper survey but could go undetected in an e-mail survey since the survey responses are already in an electronic format. Some of these problems can be mitigated by including the survey as an attachment. This allows the researcher more control over the appearance of the survey and may allow respondents to select responses using mouse clicks. However, the use of attachments means that the respondent must have access to appropriate software to view the survey, indicate responses, and save the completed survey form.

The use of e-mail to distribute the survey poses additional logistical issues for the survey researcher. First, the researcher must be able to create and send large numbers of e-mails. Ideally, these e-mails will be sent to individual e-mail addresses and may be customized. Individualized e-mail messages are likely to be perceived as more important than e-mail messages distributed using a large number of addresses in the "cc" field. Likewise, if respondent confidentiality is important, the presence of other survey respondents e-mail addresses in the "cc" field may be problematic. There are ways around these problems. For example, the researcher may consider including the recipients in a "blind cc" field. Doing so prevents each recipient from seeing the list of other recipients but raises the problem of what gets inserted in the "To" field. Another approach is to use standard mail merge techniques and direct the output to an e-mail message. This approach allows customization of each e-mail message, but may not be feasible because of security settings on the sender's computer system. For example, since some viruses spread by attempting to send e-mail messages to all the addresses in a contact list, some operating systems require the user to manually verify each e-mail message generated as the result of a mail merge process. This can be a time consuming process. Likewise, the respondent might not recognize the sender and delete the message without reading it due to concerns about computer viruses. Regardless of how these issues are addressed, the survey researcher must be sure that the appropriate hardware, software, and procedures are in place and functioning properly before initiating the survey.

4.2.5. Web-Based Surveys

The most promising approach for administering computer-based SC studies may be to have the survey reside at a website and have the respondent go to that website to complete the survey. The use of these web-based forms is relatively new and appears to be growing in popularity. In this mode, a survey form is posted on a computer connected to the Internet. Respondents answer questions using either a mouse and/or keyboard. Sometimes access to the survey can be open, allowing anyone with the appropriate URL or even anyone that just happens to arrive at the URL to access and complete the survey. Other times, respondents must enter a unique "key" to access the survey that prohibits any one individual from answering the survey more than once. The unique key can be provided to respondents by a variety of methods such as mail, e-mail, or a telephone call. When implementing a web-based survey, it is important to make sure that it functions correctly with a variety of browsers. Of all the computer-administered survey approaches, web-based surveys offer the greatest control over presentation and format of the survey instrument.

4.2.6. Self-Administered Telephone Surveys

Self-administered telephone surveys are a relatively new mode for administering surveys. We do not know of any published SC studies that have been self-administered over the telephone, however, we think readers will be interested in this new technology. The technology is referred to by various names such as interactive voice response, touchtone data entry, and telephone audio computer-assisted self-interviewing (Tourangeau, Steiger, and Wilson, 2002). All three of these labels refer to the technology where individuals respond to recorded questions by pressing keys on the telephone. While few people may have experience with taking a survey this way, many people have had a similar experience when calling an airline, bank, or other business. Interviewers can call potential respondents to initiate the interview and then switch the respondents to the interactive voice response system. Another option is for respondents to dial directly into the interactive voice response system. The advantages of this approach over interviewer-administered telephone surveys include less concern over social desirability bias and reduced costs. However, the technology may not work well for long or complex surveys. Only the simplest SC survey could conceivably be administered in this manner. One concern is that respondents have been found to hang up before the interview is done or hang up when they are switched from an interviewer to the interactive voice response system.

4.2.7. Mixed Modes

As mentioned in several places in this chapter, there are many situations where using more than one mode to administer a SC survey is likely to improve the response rate. However, research has shown that administering surveys with different modes can affect the results.

Modes can be mixed within the sample. For example, having part of the sample complete a web-based survey and the other part a paper mail survey. This might be done if part of the sample does not have access to the Internet. If funds are limited, it will be less expensive to have the part of the sample with Internet access complete the web-based survey rather than sending paper surveys to everyone. Modes can also be mixed within a survey. For example, if individuals do not respond to a mail survey, a telephone follow-up might work.

5. SURVEY MANAGEMENT

Once the decision has been reached regarding the survey mode, sampling plan, and final instrument design, the survey is ready to go into the field. Regardless of the attention paid to survey design and sample selection, quality results are still dependent upon careful implementation of the survey. In this section, we discuss some of the issues related to implementation of surveys.

5.1. Day- to-Day Management

Many researchers fielding a SC survey for the first time are surprised by the number of details that must be attended to, and the level of effort required, to get a survey in the field. For all types of surveys it is critical to establish a mechanism for tracking the contacts with each member of the sample and recording the final disposition or status of each member of the sample. A unique identification number is assigned to each sample unit. Then in an electronic database of some sort, all information about that sample unit is input. A careful tracking of survey contacts is critical for managing survey implementation tasks. For instance, in a mail survey, tracking the surveys that are not deliverable from an advance mailing and/or initial survey mailing allows the survey manager to reduce postage and handling costs in follow-up mailings. For mail surveys, the contact history would include the dates of all efforts to contact the potential survey respondent. The researcher should document the dates for mailing the advance letter, initial survey, thank you/reminder postcard, follow-up survey mailings, and dates on which a final disposition was reached. For telephone interviews, these details would include the time and date of each attempted call and the interviewer for all calls in which an interviewer actually spoke with a potential respondent.

For personal interviews, details frequently tracked include the time and date of each attempt made to contact the potential survey respondent and the interviewer attempting the interview. For computer-administered surveys administered to a known sample, contact details include dates of any contacts with potential survey respondents.

A tally of final dispositions is essential for calculating survey response rates. A discussion of response rates and final dispositions will also help inform the user of your survey results of possible strengths and weaknesses of your survey data. For mail surveys final dispositions usually fall into one of the following categories: various types of undeliverable surveys (for example, invalid address, forwarding order expired, intended respondent is deceased), returned but unusable surveys (for example, a blank survey, a note indicating a refusal to complete the survey, surveys that are substantially incomplete), and returned usable surveys. For telephone interviews, final dispositions typically fall into one of the following categories: invalid number (for example, disconnected/no longer in service, fax number, wrong number) refusal (and point of the interview at which the refusal occurred), and completed interview. Final dispositions for web-based surveys often include the following categories: no response, partial response and complete.

It is very important to have designed and tested a system to accommodate the survey tracking effort before the survey is fielded. If a survey tracking system is not in place, the survey researcher may find him or herself unable to cope with time sensitive data. For example, in a mail survey the researcher must record returns on a daily basis. This can be a time consuming effort – particularly in the early stages of the survey when the bulk of completed surveys, undeliverable surveys and refusals arrive. Likewise, imagine a mixed mode survey employing a telephone screening survey used to recruit respondents to complete a web-based survey. During the telephone screening process, the respondent is asked to provide an e-mail address to which the survey researcher will send a message explaining the survey, how to contact the survey researcher if problems are encountered accessing the web-based form and a unique "key" (as discussed earlier) to access the web-based form. In this case it is very important to minimize the time interval between the telephone screening call and the e-mail contact. This goal is hard to meet unless the survey researcher has designed and tested procedures that will be used to coordinate the telephone screening with the e-mail contact before the telephone screening begins.

5.2. Creation of Datasets

If the data are entered directly into a computer as the survey is administered (such as a web-based survey) the data do not need to be transferred from the original format to an electronic format. Some surveys, for example, a self-administered paper survey or a response form completed by an interviewer during a personal interview, require that the data be entered into an electronic format. Prior to data entry, the data must be "coded." Coding the data refers to the process of translating each survey response into a numeric value. For example, a "yes" response may be coded as a 1 and a "no" response coded as a 2. A separate code is designated for each potential response, including lack of a response. Often times, surveys are set up with numerical responses that can be entered directly with no need for coding. However, rules should be established to cover situations, such as individuals skipping questions that they were supposed to answer, or individuals answering questions they were supposed to skip.

After the surveys have been coded, they are ready for data entry. This task is frequently accomplished using software that automatically checks the data as it is entered. For example, the software might check for keystroke errors taking the form of out-of-range values and/or values indicating inconsistent skip patterns. If the survey forms contain any questions with open-ended responses, these responses must be reviewed and assigned a numeric code. In some cases, open-ended responses may be entered verbatim into an electronic database.

Once the data have been entered into an electronic format, data summaries such as frequencies and cross tabulations should be examined to identify any remaining data entry or coding errors. Errors identified at this stage can be resolved by reference to the physical copy of the completed survey materials.

The data entry and verification process is simpler for telephone surveys that are administered using either computer-assisted telephone interviewing (CATI) systems or web-based surveys. In these two modes, software creates an electronic copy of the data as the survey is completed. Even so, it is critical to pay close attention to actual functioning of the software controlling the survey and producing the data. For example, if a web-based survey is designed to write a value of "1" to the electronic data base when the respondent chooses the response category "Yes", it is worthwhile to answer the question on-line and observe that a value of "1" is written to the data base when the "yes" response is selected. Having complete confidence that the software is producing correct values in the database is essential for CATI surveys and web-based surveys. The resulting electronic database is the only record that will exist once the survey is completed.

5.3. Documentation of the Survey Process

After the data collection is completed, it is desirable to document the survey collection effort. The documentation typically includes all survey materials, samples used, a narrative description of the survey timeline, including dates on which key events occurred, a record of any transformations that were used in translating the raw data set to a final data set, the final data set, and a codebook completely describing the final data set. With the possible exception of the sample and the final data set, it is generally desirable to include both electronic and "hard copy" forms of the documentation. Documentation is made easier if during the survey process, the researcher systematically collects the information and materials to be documented.

Creating a careful documentation of the survey process takes a substantial effort and is best undertaken as soon as the data set is finalized. Human nature being what it is, there is sometimes a temptation to minimize the documentation or skip it altogether. For researchers conducting their own data analysis, it is usually more exciting to work with their data than to document the dataset. Likewise, having just developed an intimate knowledge of the data and the process by which it was created, many researchers find it hard to believe that they would ever forget these details. Experienced survey researchers know that the existence of extensive documentation can save many hours of effort if any questions ever arise about the data, or if other researchers ask for copies of the data to verify published results. This last concern is particularly important if you intend to publish your results in a peer-reviewed journal as providing a data set upon request is frequently a condition for publication.

5.4. Other Survey Management Issues

In addition to the general survey management topics just discussed there are additional issues that arise in the context of specific types of surveys and research approaches. As mentioned earlier, in nearly all survey efforts it is important to assign a unique identifier to each member of the sample. In choosing this identifier it is sometimes useful to choose a number that will convey information about the sample point. For example, in a study with four treatments, with each treatment being administered to 1,500 potential respondents, the first treatment might be given numbers from 10001 through 11500, the second treatment might be assigned numbers from 20001 through 21500, etc. This scheme allows quick identification of the survey treatment by simply looking at the first digit of the identifier. Furthermore, once the final data set has been created it is easy to select observations from a particular treatment by reference to the identifying number.

For web-based studies, identifiers may be chosen to meet other objectives. Frequently each member of a web-based survey is assigned a unique identifier that is used as a key to gain access to the web-based survey. For security reasons, this identifier should be nonguessable to prevent unauthorized users from accessing the web-based survey. On the other hand, the key should be short enough that the potential respondent does not have difficulty correctly typing it. One possible approach is to assign each potential respondent a random combination of three letters and three digits. The random letters should specifically avoid the use of the letters "I" and "l" to avoid confusion with the numeral 1. Likewise, the letters "O" and "o" should not be used to avoid the possibility of confusion with the numeral 0. All randomly created identifiers should be subjected to a "social acceptability test". It is remarkable how many potentially offensive three letter combinations may be generated by a random process.

If the survey is to be administered on paper, all printed materials should be reviewed and proofread prior to being sent to the printer or copy shop. If the review is primarily intended to make sure that the prepared materials "make sense" and do not contain typos or grammatical errors this review is best done by someone with only a peripheral knowledge of the project. In other cases, it is essential that the final review is conducted by someone with complete knowledge of the survey effort. For example, some survey treatments may be designed to investigate the effects on responses of minor wording changes. Verification that the two survey versions contain the correct words requires the review of someone with an in-depth knowledge of the research effort. The best approach would be to have two individuals carefully review the survey, one for typos and grammatical errors and the other for content. For paper mail surveys and interviewer administered surveys, it essential to perform a spot check once the materials come back from the printer or copy shop to verify that the printed copies are consistent with the originals. It is much easier to deal with a printing problem before the materials are mailed out than when it is discovered during the data entry process.

Some surveys employ multiple versions of survey instruments and/or supporting materials. In these applications, it is important to ensure that the correct materials are being mailed to the correct survey respondent. To help achieve this goal, survey materials can be prepared with a treatment code discretely placed somewhere on the survey materials. For example, include a survey version designation in the fold of the center facing pages of a survey booklet. Likewise, different color covers can be used to designate different survey versions. Mailing staff need to understand these codes and the implications of the codes in assembling a mailing. In addition to the use of codes, it may be useful to allow the mailing preparation staff to have access to only one set of survey materials at a time. Once the mailing for one treatment or experimental design point has been prepared, the materials for this treatment are sealed and removed. Prior to sealing of the mailing packets it may be desirable to conduct a final random check of prepared packets.

6. SUMMARY

In this chapter, we have provided an overview of the decisions that need to be made when implementing a SC survey. The resources available to implement the survey will affect many of the decisions. If a SC survey is well funded, it may be best to hire a professional survey research firm to administer the survey. The researcher would still need to be closely involved with development of the survey but could leave the details of administering the survey to professionals. However, many SC surveys are conducted through universities or organizations that might not have much experience with administering surveys. In such cases, it is essential that the researcher understand the survey administration process and take extra care to make sure the individuals helping with the survey are well trained and knowledgeable about the process. While it can be a challenge to implement a SC survey for the first time, careful attention to details will allow collection of high-quality data.

7. REFERENCES

Bateman, I. J. and J. Mawby, 2004, "First Impressions Count: Interviewer Appearance and Information Effects in Stated Preference Studies," *Ecological Economics,* 49: 47-55.

Biemer, P. P., R. M. Groves, L.E. Lyberg, N.A. Mathiowetz and S. Sudman, Eds., 1991, *Measurement Errors in Surveys,* New York, John Wiley & Sons, Inc.

Bradburn, N.M., 1983, "Response Effects," in *Handbook of Survey Research*, P.H. Rossi, J.D. Wright and A.B. Anderson, Eds., San Diego, Academic Press, Inc.

Breffle, W.S., E.R. Morey, R.D. Rowe, D.M. Waldman and S.M. Wytinck, 1999, "Recreational Fishing Damages from Fish Consumption Advisories in the Waters of Green Bay," Report prepared for U.S. Fish and Wildlife Service, U.S. Department of Interior, U.S. Department of Justice, Stratus Consulting Inc., Boulder, CO.

Carson, R. T., R. C. Mitchell, W.M. Hanemann, R.J. Kopp, S. Presser, and P.A. Ruud, 1992, "A Contingent Valuation Study of Lost Passive Use Values Resulting from the Exxon Valdez Oil Spill," Report to the Attorney General of the State of Alaska.

Cochran, W. G., 1977, *Sampling Techniques*, New York, John Wiley & Sons.

Dillman, D. A., 2000, *Mail and Internet Surveys: The Tailored Design Method*, New York, John Wiley & Sons, Inc.

Frankel, M., 1983, "Sampling Theory," in *Handbook of Survey Research*, P. H. Rossi, J. D. Wright and A. B. Anderson, Eds., San Diego, Academic Press, Inc.

Harrison, G. W. and J. C. Lesley, 1996, "Must Contingent Valuation Surveys Cost So Much?" *Journal of Environmental Economics and Management*, 31(1): 79-95.

Goldstein, K.M. and M.K. Jennings, 2002, "The Effect of Advance Letters on Cooperation in a List Sample Telephone Survey," *The Pubic Opinion Quarterly*, 66(4): 608-617.

Kish, L., 1967, *Survey Sampling*, New York, John Wiley & Sons, Inc.

Leggett, C. G., N.S. Kleckner, K.J. Boyle, J.W. Duffield, and R.C. Mitchell, 2003, "Social Desirability Bias in Contingent Valuation Surveys Administered Through In-Person Interviews," *Land Economics*, 79(4): 561-575.

Loomis, J. B., 2000, "Vertically Summing Public Good Demand Curves: An Empirical Comparison of Economic Versus Political Jurisdictions," *Land Economics*, 76(2): 312-321.

Loomis, J., J. Miller, A. Gonzalez-Caban, and J. Champ, 2006, "Testing Convergent Validity of Videotape Survey Administration and Phone Interviews in Contingent Valuation," *Society and Natural Resources*, 19: 1-9.

Lyberg, L. and D. Kasprzyk, 1991, "Data Collection Methods and Measurement Error: An Overview," *Measurement Errors in Surveys*, P. P. Biemer, R. M. Groves, L. Lyberg, N. A. Mathiowetz and S. Sudman, New York, John Wiley & Sons, Inc.

Mitchell, R. C. and R. T. Carson, 1989, *Using Surveys to Value Public Goods: The Contingent Valuation Method*, Washington D.C., Resources for the Future.

Salant, P. and D. A. Dillman, 1994, *How to Conduct Your Own Survey*, New York, John Wiley & Sons, Inc.

Särndal, C., B. Swensson, and J. Wretman, 1992, *Model Assisted Survey Sampling*, New York, Springer.

Singer, E. and S. Presser, eds., 1989, *Survey Research Methods*, Chicago, The University of Chicago Press.

Smith, V. K., 1993, "Nonmarket Valuation of Environmental Resources: An Interpretive Appraisal," *Land Economics*, 69(1): 1-26.

Sudman, S., 1983, "Applied Sampling," in *Handbook of Survey Research*, P. H. Rossi, J. D. Wright and A. B. Anderson, San Diego, Academic Press, Inc.

Sutherland, R. J. and R. G. Walsh, 1985, "Effect of Distance on the Preservation Value of Water Quality," *Land Economics*, 61(3): 281-291.

Tourangeau, R., D. Steiger, and D. Wilson, 2002. "Self-Administered Questions by Telephone: Evaluating Interactive Voice Responses," *Public Opinion Quarterly*, 66(2): 265-78.

Zipp, J. F. and J. Toth, 2002, "She Said, He Said, They Said: The Impact of Spousal Presence in Survey Research," *Public Opinion Quarterly,* 66(2): 177-208.

CHAPTER 3

SUPPORTING QUESTIONS IN STATED CHOICE STUDIES

ALAN KRUPNICK

Resources for the Future, Washington, D.C., U.S.A.

W.L. (VIC) ADAMOWICZ

Department of Rural Economy, University of Alberta, Alberta, Canada

1. INTRODUCTION

The purpose of this chapter is to provide a modest beginning to a more systematic treatment of the "supporting questions" in stated choice (SC) surveys – those questions that support the key questions eliciting willingness to pay (WTP). Below, we consider the various roles played by these supporting questions, e.g., to serve as covariates versus to eliminate respondents who do not understand key concepts; issues that have surrounded some of these questions; and challenges for using these questions in a WTP analysis. We close with a section that begins drawing lessons about using supporting questions, including implicit trade-off decisions such as between comprehensiveness and fatigue, in deciding on survey length.

We are not covering aspects of question design, e.g. specific question wording, question ordering, etc. These are very important issues. For instance, Schwarz et al. (1991) find that a scale including negative numbers (from –5 to +5) leads to different responses than a scale in the positive domain (0-10) with equal intervals. An example of the importance of question wording is provided by Holbrook et al. (2000) in which the authors show that violating conversational conventions results in poorer quality data and more noise around attitudinal questions. Additional examples are given in Mitchell and Carson (1989) chapter 5. However, the reader is directed to the survey design literature to examine these issues, as they are broader than the

B.J. Kanninen (ed.), Valuing Environmental Amenities Using Stated Choice Studies, 43–65.
© 2006 *Springer.*

issues we examine here, which are focused specifically on SC studies. Good references in the survey design and implementation literature include Tourangeau et al. (2000) and Dillman (2000). The newest of the how-to books on SC techniques is Bateman et al. (2002).

Furthermore, we do not discuss concepts that are part of the valuation question itself. That is, we do not discuss the wording of uncertainty questions (e.g. Li and Mattsson, 1995) or "cheap talk" scripts (Cummings and Taylor, 1999) that are usually included immediately after and before, respectively, valuation response questions. These questions are discussed by Harrison (this volume).

To begin, here is a list of types of "supporting questions" we will be considering:

i)   basic demographic and economic information at the personal or household level (e.g., age, income);

ii)   special personal or household characteristics associated with the specific purpose of the survey (e.g., detailed health status questions, membership in environmental organizations);

iii)   questions about relevant behavior (e.g., how much water do you drink and from what sources);

iv)   questions about prior knowledge (e.g., have you ever heard that acid rain causes damage to trees? knowledge about factors affecting water quality);

v)   questions to test or fix understanding of a key aspect of a survey (e.g., tests of understanding of the concept of probability or life expectancy, tests of understanding the effects of the water quality program being described.);

vi)   debriefing questions to test whether various aspects of the survey were understood and accepted (e.g., did you believe the baseline we gave you? Did you believe the approach to cleanup we discussed would work?) and whether extraneous concepts to the survey were being considered (e.g., did you think of the health improvements to your community when you answered the WTP question about a measure that would help only you?);

vii)   attitudinal questions (e.g., do you think your taxes are too high?, do you believe that economic development is more important than environmental protection?).

2. THE ROLE FOR SUPPORTING SURVEY QUESTIONS

Our fundamental rule for survey questions is that every question should have a specific purpose defined *ex ante*. A second rule is that there is a trade-off between collecting more information and adding burden to the respondent. This second consideration will differ by survey context, type of respondent and cultural factors. In this section we provide a general outline of the role for supporting questions.

We define the focus of valuation surveys as the valuation task or the questions that directly elicit trade-offs between money and the environmental / public good. To formalize this, consider the following stylized model of choice. In this stylized model, based on Swait et al. (2002), D is the strategy used to make a decision, C is the choice set, j indexes alternatives, n indexes individuals and t indexes time. V is the (indirect) utility function expressed here as a function of income (M) and environmental quality (Q) and prices (P). ε is an error process that arises because elements of the process are not observed by the researcher. This decision structure generates a chosen alternative i_{nt}^{*} :

$$i_{nt}^{*} \longleftarrow D_{n} \underset{j \in C_{nt}}{\{V_{jnt}(M,Q,P), \varepsilon_{jnt}\}} \tag{1}$$

In developing estimates of compensating variation we are most interested in V_{jnt}. Information in V_{jnt} is also of importance in development of a measure of the *expected value* of compensating or equivalent variation. Supporting questions will provide useful information about all elements of this process and will aid in the understanding of the responses. The role of supporting questions can be classified as follows:

A. Providing covariates that allow for the understanding of observed heterogeneity of preferences (heterogeneity in V_{jnt}). This includes demographic factors like income and age. In some cases these covariates will enter in a fashion identified by theory (income,[1] demographic scaling[2]), while in other cases the specification will be somewhat *ad hoc*. When covariates and their expected role in V_{jnt} are described by theory, these covariates provide a measure of construct validity.

B. Providing information about the error component (ε) and the variance of the error. It is possible that the error component is systematically affected by demographic factors or individual characteristics. Variance may be a function of characteristics, like experience with a certain health condition. Error variance may be smaller for subsets of individuals who have experienced a given illness. These experiences may also affect preferences directly and would then enter into (A) above.

C. Providing information that helps identify the decision strategy (D_n) being used by the respondent and whether that decision strategy changes over valuation questions (for instance, in a sequence of stated-choice tasks). For example, if an individual states that they would never say yes to an environmental program that reduced the number of wetland acres in the state, even if other environmental attributes improved, he or she may be exhibiting a form of elimination by aspects strategy (Tversky, 1972) or a type of lexicographic preference (Fishburn, 1975). If these decision strategies are being used then respondents are not making trade-offs between public goods and money or between attributes of publics goods and money; rather, they are making choices based on individual components of the programs achieving a particular level. Commonly used econometric models rely on fully compensatory decision strategies and thus accounting for noncompensatory strategies (e.g. Yang and Allenby, 2000) or at least identifying those respondents who may be using noncompensatory strategies will be important.

D.   Identifying strategies that individuals use to simplify choices. A particular choice strategy -- choosing not to choose (Dhar, 1997) or to choose randomly --is of particular interest. Supporting questions may be able to identify these individuals, but it is also the case that "warm up questions" early in the survey may help to motivate thought and consideration about the topic and focus cognitive effort on the valuation question (see Tourangeau et al., 2000) In this sense, for example, information and questions about a respondent's personal consumption of drinking water may motivate them to internalize the information on a drinking water program and put effort into determining their response to a valuation question that they may otherwise think is inapplicable to them.

E   Identifying the degree to which the respondent's understanding of the baseline and changed level of Q (the component being valued) conforms to the researcher's description of the problem. If the researcher presents a scenario where a program will lengthen the respondent's life, but the respondent does not believe that the program will do so, the response to the valuation question will not be relevant to the program the researcher is assessing. Supporting questions, therefore, provide a basis for selecting subsets of individuals for analysis or rejecting some groups of respondents from further analysis.

F.   Showing readers and reviewers that the survey descriptions and questions are understandable, unbiased, and, overall, demonstrate the validity of the survey. For instance, debriefing questions about whether the respondent considered what they would give up if they paid for the commodity in question, or whether they thought the wording of the survey was unbiased are included more for the subsequent review of the research than for the benefit of the respondent.

These six ways that supporting questions can aid in developing valuation estimates and bolstering their credibility provide a categorization, but do not provide much guidance for researchers. Below we reframe these roles of supporting questions in terms of the way they enter surveys.

3. CATEGORIES OF SUPPORTING QUESTIONS

In this section, we discuss i) introductory, warm-up questions and attitudinal questions, ii) debriefing questions and iii) demographic/individual characteristics questions as three sections of surveys that provide supporting information. Within the discussion of warm-up and attitudinal questions we examine the use of these questions as methods of identification of preference heterogeneity and decision strategy. Also, we examine the use of questions that indicate understanding of the issues presented in the survey, specifically probability concepts. Finally, we examine questions that are used to indicate and perhaps alleviate "warm glow" around the survey topic. All of these questions provide information about preference heterogeneity, decision strategy, or the nature of understanding of the issues by the respondent. In the discussion of debriefing questions we illustrate the use of various forms of questions that help categorize respondents and identify understanding and strategies. We conclude with a discussion of the elicitation of demographic information that can also be used in identification of heterogeneity of preferences.

3.1. "Warm-Up" Questions: Focusing Respondent Effort and Identifying Experience and Attitudes

Respondents have varied experience with the goods that they are asked to value and there is significant heterogeneity in attitudes over the respondent groups. Researchers often ask introductory questions about the respondent's experience with goods or services related to the good being valued early in the survey, often following a brief introduction and just before a detailed discussion of the good and the quality change. In a survey of water quality, for example, respondents could be asked about their consumption of bottled water. Surveys of land use options (parks, protected areas) could ask about the respondent's recreation behavior and membership in environmental organizations. In addition, surveys typically include rating scale questions in these early sections of a survey to identify the respondent's interest and focus his /her mind on the good / service being evaluated.

These attitude and experience questions are primarily asked to focus the respondent on the issue at hand. Questions about how safe a person feels their drinking water is generally precede a description of a water quality program change. Questions about a respondent's opinion regarding endangered species management can be found early in a survey valuing land use options or protected area management plans. While these types of questions have commonly been employed, they have seldom been used in analysis of valuation questions. At times they are used as covariates in valuation functions but often responses to these questions are correlated and thus only a small number are used in statistical models. In a sense these questions triangulate the willingness to pay estimates, as it should not be surprising that individuals who rate the importance of endangered species protection as "very high" would also be willing to pay more for such programs. Table 1 provides some examples of attitudinal and motivation questions.

An alternative approach to eliciting information from attitudinal statements is Maximum Difference Scaling (Cohen, 2003). This approach has been proposed as an alternative to typical rating scale information because these common scales often show little sensitivity to the different statements (e.g. a respondent always chooses between 2 and 4 on a 5 point scale). In contrast, Maximum Difference Scaling of a ratings task eliciting the importance of various factors presents sets of these statements to the respondent and the respondent must choose the "most important" or "least important" from the set. This forces the respondent to implicitly place the statements on a scale. While this is an interesting alternative to rating scale tasks it should be recognized that information cannot easily be interpreted directly from the results, rather, the responses need to be analyzed with some form of statistical model (e.g. multinomial logit model) before interpretation can begin.

TABLE 1. Examples of Attitudinal Questions

To identify preference groups in the valuation of wilderness canoe areas, Boxall and Adamowicz (2002) use a series of 20 statements that represent reasons why the individual visited backcountry or wilderness areas. Respondents were asked to rate the level of importance of each statement on a 5 point Likert scale (Tourangeau et al., 2000) ranging from "Not at all important" to "Very important." The statements used for this purpose were derived from research on leisure motivations (Beard and Ragheb, 1983). The scores of the respondents were used to derive a scale to measure motivations for visiting wilderness areas and were used in a latent class model.

	Not at all Important			Very Important	

To challenge my skills and abilities   1   5
To develop my skills
To be in charge of a situation
To feel independent
To feel free from society's restrictions
To challenge nature
To be alone
To feel close to nature
To observe the beauty of nature
To obtain a feeling of harmony with nature
To find quiet places
To enjoy the sights, sounds, and smells of nature
To be with my friends or family
To strengthen relationships with friends or family
To do things with other people
To be with people with similar interests
To escape from the pressures of work
To relieve my tensions
To get away from my everyday routine
To be away from other people

The following is a list of statements attempting to elicit attitudes towards environment/development. These statements were presented to respondents with instructions to respond 1 = strongly disagree to 5 = strongly agree.

Technology can and will solve most of the problems faced by people
Human knowledge should seek to understand and then control most natural processes in the environment
Human population is only a problem because of starving people
Human population is not limited by the environment but rather technological innovations
The economy can and should continue to grow indefinitely
Human happiness is linked to economic success
Environmental issues should be solved by "experts" and the public need only be educated and informed of the decisions

Attitudinal questions are included in econometric analyses as covariates. They may also be used to form classes of respondents as a type of segmentation. Such classification may simply involve partitioning the sample according to specific questions, or using more involved techniques such as factor analysis. More recently, there have been attempts to use these attitude and experience questions in more formal approaches for categorization of respondents or explanations of preference heterogeneity. McFadden (1986) provided a conceptual approach for the incorporation of "psychometric" information into economic models of choice. Swait (1994) employed such information as components of a latent class model[3] of choice within an attribute based choice framework. In the environmental literature, Boxall and Adamowicz (2002) employed factor analysis to identify core aspects of rating scale questions and then incorporated the factor scores into a latent class model to help explain heterogeneity within the sample. While there are some challenging econometric issues regarding endogeneity of the responses to rating questions, historical use questions and valuation questions (see below) these questions can provide useful information about preference categories and heterogeneity. Recent advances in this linkage of "hard" information on choices, demographics and attributes with "soft" information on attitudes and psychometric measures can be found in the discussion of the Hybrid Choice Model (Ben Akiva et al. 1999, Ben-Akiva et al., 2002), which combines these different forms of information into a more robust view of preferences and decision strategy.

Swait (2001) developed a novel approach to using attitude and experience responses to understand noncompensatory decision frameworks. Recall that almost all econometric models used in valuation assume compensatory behavior. He uses simple binary questions about respondent preferences to develop a model of "cut-offs" of the consumer's attribute space. Respondents are asked to identify acceptable attribute ranges. For example, respondents are asked if there are some price levels that are too high for the brand of product being presented, or an attribute level that is too low (and such an option will never be selected). These binary questions provide information about single attributes that a consumer would find "unacceptable." Swait then incorporates these as "soft constraints" into an econometric model. This results in a noncompensatory model of choice in that the consumers are not always willing to make trade-offs but they do have some boundaries that have costs associated with them (shadow prices on the constraints).

3.2. Reducing Warm Glow[4]

Surveys attempting to value public goods, such as an improvement to a park, can face a significant problem of "warm glow." This term refers to the hypothesis that people will say they will pay a few dollars for any type of public good just to appear public spirited. But the good feelings (i.e., warm glow) in giving only apply to the first commodity they are asked to value. After that, the warm glow may disappear. Warm glow may also arise when subjects refuse to play the "trade-off game," i.e., they will not admit that to gain some environmental or health improvement, resources (money) will be needed. As valuation/preferences should not depend on where in an order one asks WTP questions for a particular commodity or whether a respondent buys the notion of trade-offs, researchers attempt to "bleed off" warm glow through a variety of techniques. One is to be vague with subjects about the purpose of the survey (e.g., to gather information on your spending priorities for government tax dollars) and then ask subjects to rate various types of programs governments could spend taxes on, specifically whether more or less should be spent in the various areas (e.g., crime prevention, providing and maintaining natural areas). The commodity in question is listed among these areas. The survey is described as one of many, with the other surveys addressing such diverse topics as infant health care and fire protection. This is an effort to bleed off warm glow by putting the damages to the commodity in question in context, with respondents realizing that their funds can only go so far. Note that answers to these questions are not necessarily used in any econometric analyses – they serve primarily to reduce warm glow.

The example in Table 2 is illustrative. It appears in several existing surveys (Carson et al., 1994). The survey (Banzhaf et al., forthcoming) is about eliciting WTP for an improvement in the Adirondacks ecosystem, but this initial page is meant to begin positioning the survey as one of many surveys, each on different topics. It also serves to help identify people who would tend to vote against any public good funded by increasing taxes (a "cold glow," if you will) and provide preference information about various types of general government programs.

3.3. Testing Understanding of Probability

Many SC studies value commodities as if they were certain. For example, studies valuing reduction in an individual's acute health effects ask for the WTP to reduce a symptom-day sometime in the very near future (Krupnick and Alberini, 2000; Loehman, et al., 1979). In reality, an individual has a *probability or risk* of experiencing a symptom-day and some policy intervention may result in that probability being lowered by a small amount. This departure from reality is made for simplicity. It is easier to describe a deterministic commodity and ask to value its elimination than it is to describe a change in probability; and it is easier for the respondent to understand as well. As many instances of this type of commodity may be experienced over any given time period, we think that such a simplification is acceptable.

However, some commodities must be described in probabilistic or risk terms, for instance, mortality risks and risks of developing chronic disease. Properly communicating risks and changes in risks is the subject of an enormous literature and lies outside our scope here (see Corso, et al., 2001). What is germane, though, is how to test whether such communications have been understood.

TABLE 2. *Example of Questions to Diminish/Identify Warm and Cold Glow*

Government Priorities and the Taxes You Pay:
We first would like to know: Did you pay New York state income taxes last year?

      Yes ___
      No____

What is your opinion about the level of state income taxes that you pay? Do you feel that the amount of state income taxes you pay is (please circle one):

      a) Too high
      b) Too low
      c) About right

We would also like to know your opinions about state spending on public services. For each of the government-provided services listed below, please tell us if you personally think funding for these services should be changed. Please keep in mind the effect such changes would have on the amount of taxes you pay. Improving government services usually requires the government to increase taxes. Similarly, reducing government services would allow the government to lower taxes. *(Across any row, please check the box that best applies to you.)*

Desired Change in Program Area Spending:

Program Area	Reduce Substantially	Reduce Somewhat	No Change	Increase Somewhat	Increase Substantially	Not Sure
Education services in elementary and secondary schools						
Crime prevention programs						
Providing access to medical care						
Providing and maintaining natural areas and wildlife refuges						
Enforcing air and water pollution control programs						
Providing road infrastructure						

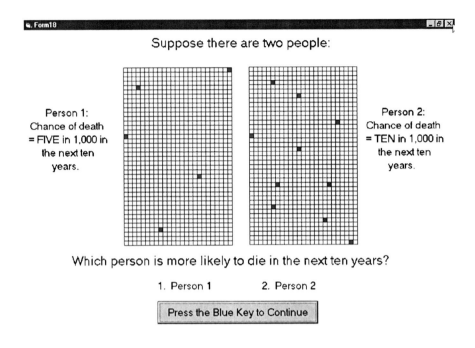

Suppose there are two people:

Person 1:
Chance of death
= FIVE in 1,000 in
the next ten
years.

Person 2:
Chance of death
= TEN in 1,000 in
the next ten
years.

Which person is more likely to die in the next ten years?

1. Person 1   2. Person 2

Press the Blue Key to Continue

FIGURE 1.

The literature on mortality valuation often uses test problems, i.e., the respondent is asked to solve a problem or series of problems involving the risk or probability concept he has been "taught" earlier in the survey. Depending on the respondent's answers to such problems, researchers can then decide *ex post* to the survey, how they want to apply these answers in screening out individuals who did not understand the concept.

For instance, in a Krupnick et al. (2002) mortality risk survey, respondents were shown graphics depicting mortality risks faced by two individuals and asked which individual faced the most risk. A wrong answer led to a follow-up tutorial and another chance at answering a similar problem. Then, the individual was given a question asking which person they would rather *be*. The latter captures continued lack of understanding or some perverse thinking that we occasionally see. Either way, if a person says they want to be the individual with a higher risk of death, their subsequent WTP answers are suspect. In addition, Krupnick et al. use a debriefing question to ask the respondents to evaluate their own understanding of probability on a scale.

Figure 1 provides the probability understanding questions mentioned above. Table 3 shows the results from using this table and the follow-up questions in surveys administered in Canada and the U.S. The table shows that about 10% of the sample got the question in Table 3 wrong, but when educated and re-tested, this amount fell to 1-2 %. About the same percentage chose the individual "they wanted to be" as the one with the higher death risk. Again, these "mistakes" fell to 1% of the sample on re-test. A cross tab of the answers reveals that only around 3% of the sample got both the first probability test question and the first probability choice question wrong, indicating that both questions may be needed to catch people that have problems understanding probability. It's also worth noting that on a separate debriefing question asked at the end of the survey, most of those who had trouble answering the probability test question claimed to understand probability concepts poorly. Finally, note that answers to these questions were turned into "flags," essentially dummy variables. FLAG1 was used as a basic subsetting variable to drop individuals. The use of other flag variables as subsetting or as explanatory variables did not affect the results.

3.4. Debriefing Questions

A surprisingly large number of SC surveys do not use debriefing questions, i.e., questions at the end of a survey that ask respondents what they felt or thought as they read text or answered questions. While such questions lengthen a survey, in our judgment, such questions are an excellent opportunity to find out essential information needed to interpret responses and results, delete observations, and shore up the credibility of the survey.

There are several kinds of debriefing questions. These include questions on the understanding of the text and questions on the acceptance of the factual information in the text (including both rejecting stated information and adding unstated information), opinions about survey bias, questions to elicit biases the respondent may have, and questions to probe further the factors underlying the choice.

Understanding the survey. Stated choice surveys generally provide large amounts of complex written and diagrammatic information to respondents. In spite of the considerable refinement that goes into the specific language and sequencing of information in a SC survey, not all respondents will understand it. This lack of understanding may lead to answers that are different than they would be with better understanding. Thus we use debriefing questions to test this understanding by asking people in some detail whether they understood the most important aspects of the survey, e.g. the baseline (present and, if applicable, future), the program, and the program's effectiveness and costs. Because people can be hesitant about admitting they do not understand something, we provide them with a scale, so they can admit they had a little bit of trouble. With this knowledge, respondents that lacked any degree of understanding can be flagged and either dropped or have their responses corrected for in subsequent analyses.

Acceptance. Probably the most prevalent problem in SC surveys is that people do not "buy" one or more critical elements of the survey. This is very serious and can have unpredictable effects on the results. People can doubt some aspect of the survey, but nevertheless vote as if the information were true – just to be cooperative. Or, respondents may vote differently than they would if they believed the survey. Or, if they outright reject information, they may vote zero, as in protest. Thus, most of our debriefing questions are directed at testing whether respondents accepted survey elements or rejected them, and if rejected, whether their vote was affected, and if affected, in what direction. One can telescope this series of questions if needed for space. Pretests are helpful here to limit the questions. If the pretest reveals that certain aspects of the survey led to rejection, in addition to revising it, one can ask more detailed questions about vote influence. Otherwise, just a basic acceptance/ rejection question could do. Nevertheless, in general, we find it best to avoid yes/no answers to these questions. In terms of acceptance questions (but this principle applies more generally) many people think the environmental baselines are always somewhat worse than given in a survey. By allowing people to say they believed the baseline or thought it was a little bit too optimistic or way too optimistic, many of the mild environmental skeptics can be identified and segregated from people with more serious problems with the baseline.

TABLE 3. Comparison across Canada and U.S. Mortality Risk Studies: Probability Comprehension

	Percent of the sample	
	CANADA	U.S.
Probability test questions answered incorrectly:		
1st probability test question	11.6	12.2
2nd probability test question (FLAG4)	1.1	1.8
Indicates preference for individual with higher risk of death in:		
1st probability choice question	13.0	10.8
Follow-up "confirmation" question (FLAG5)	1.3	1.3
Fails both probability test and choice questions (FLAG1)	2.6	3.7
Claims to understand probability poorly (FLAG6)	7.0	16.2

Once this information is collected, it can be used in validity regressions to check out whether respondents were being consistent. For instance, if some respondents claimed that they thought they would not benefit as much as the survey said from a new medical product, then a dummy variable for this question could be used to see if WTP for such people was lower than for other respondents. Such variables are best left out of the final regression, however, because of endogeneity concerns. If such responses are not too numerous they can be dropped.

Table 4 provides an example of such debriefs from the Adirondacks study. The question asks about whether the future baseline is believable, allowing for gradations of belief.

TABLE 4. *Examples of Debriefing Questions*

The survey described the health of lakes, forests and bird populations. When you voted, did you believe the current condition of the Adirondacks was:

a.   Much better than described in the survey
b.   Somewhat better than described in the survey
c.   About the same as described in the survey
d.   Somewhat worse than described in the survey
e.   Much worse than described in the survey

Survey bias. If respondents feel that the survey is biased, either by its sponsorship or wording, they may not reveal their true preferences. Such perceptions of bias can come from three sources. First is the survey sponsorship. In many surveys, researchers do not have a choice about listing the sponsors of the survey. In this case, sponsorship can be problematic because the names of organizations can carry heavy connotations, even unintended ones, e.g., Resources for the Future may be thought by some to be an environmental NGO (non-governmental organization). If researchers have the freedom to omit sponsorship or manipulate the parties listed, bias can be addressed to a certain extent. Of course, the respondent may have a sponsor in mind even if none is provided. Thus, it could be important to have a question about sponsorship in the debrief section.

Second is the actual wording and facts presented in the survey. Even the most balanced and fastidious survey researcher can inadvertently ring alarm bells for respondents through survey wording. For instance, listing three bullets for why one could vote against a proposal and four for why one might vote for, could lead to a charge of bias. Third, and perhaps the hardest to address is that for many people the very existence of the survey confers a bias towards voting Yes, because in their words, "why would anyone go to the trouble of doing a survey to elicit No votes?"

In our work in the Adirondacks, we have addressed this topic with the following question, which seems to comport with respondents' views of what bias is:

> Thinking about everything you have read in the survey, overall, did it try to push you to vote one way or another, or did it let you make up your own mind about which way to vote:
>
> Pushed me to vote for the program
> Let me make up my own mind
> Pushed me to vote against the program

This question could also be worded to give respondents five options, including strongly and weakly biased for or against the program in question and neutral. We find that few people will answer "neutral," but many people who think the survey is basically neutral but have problems with one or two questions or diagrams will say the survey is biased. By offering people the weakly biased options, a well-designed balanced survey may escape getting falsely branded as biased.

Identifying Problematic Attitudes. One of the most difficult aspects of interpreting survey results is to account for problematic attitudes that respondents bring to the survey. In surveys valuing public environmental goods, there are basically two important types of attitudes: those who vote "For" because the environment must be saved and those who vote "Against" because they think their taxes are already too high – to put it in political terms, the tree huggers and the tax haters. These positions may be forms of "protests" or they may be ways to simplify the task and reduce the costs of examining the trade-offs carefully. Much of our effort at survey design is meant to both mitigate creation of these feelings when taking the survey and to identify people who have such feelings so they can be flagged or dropped from the survey. Debriefs about whether a person is an environmentalist or an active environmentalist are a start, as are open-ended questions asking why people voted the way they did. In addition, we ask questions of those voting For about whether there is any cost of the program that would cause the respondent to vote against it. Of those voting against, we ask whether they think their taxes are already too high and whether they would vote for the program if they could be assessed the fee another way.

Factors affecting choice. SC surveys generally ask respondents to indicate why they made particular choices, using open-ended questions. We feel it is inadvisable to provide respondents with too specific a list of factors explaining their vote because they may pick items from the list that they were not thinking about at the time of the vote. Nevertheless, open-ended responses can be quite incomplete or even incoherent. Thus, many surveys use debriefing questions to probe their thinking further. We either explicitly limit their response to "what you were thinking when you voted" or limit questions to factors that were part of the choice. This latter approach is particularly important for stated choice studies, where there are many attributes that may or may not be considered in a particular choice. It should be noted, however, that identifying the decision strategy used by the respondent using debriefing questions is very difficult, if not impossible. Nesbitt and Wilson (1977) provided the original research in psychology identifying the difficulty in identifying respondent decision strategies after the fact and found that respondents have a great deal of difficulty explaining the strategy they used and may anchor on strategies provided to them by the researcher. Therefore, most debriefing questions ask about fairly concrete items relating to importance of attributes, recollection of facts, and not precise decision strategies employed.

In attribute-based stated choice tasks it is very common to ask respondents to indicate which attributes are important to them and which are not. This is also commonly done using rating scale questions. For example, if a task contains 5 attributes, these attributes will be listed and respondents will be asked to indicate on a 1 to 5 scale how important these are in determining which option is chosen (Table 5 presents such an example). These ratings should correspond to the choices that the individual makes. Of course it will be difficult to link these responses to an econometric model based on aggregate responses, however, some relationships should be found. Casual examination of the data should reveal consistency between the rating questions and the choice questions. (Note: inconsistency here can be a sign of respondent inconsistency in survey response. See Johnson et al., 2001. These inconsistencies can be captured by careful design of the valuation questions. Note that there are other potential uses for the type of question presented in Table 5. This information could be use to help identify "cut-off" information (Swait, 2001) or information indicating that respondents ignore certain attributes when making decisions.

4. DEMOGRAPHIC QUESTIONS / INDIVIDUAL CHARACTERISTICS (HEALTH STATUS, ETC.)

SC surveys carry special burdens to show that their results are valid. One particular concept of validity – termed *construct validity* – gives rise to a number of considerations in the inclusion and design of "supporting questions." Construct validity is the idea that the factors found to influence WTP estimates should generally comport with theory, when the appropriate theory exists and is unambiguous. Thus in the design of a SC survey, the analyst must have a good knowledge of what factors are predicted to have an influence on WTP for the particular case at hand, in what direction, and in what magnitude.

Income and Wealth. One factor that enters all conceptual models underlying WTP is income (often household income) or wealth. Whether or not gross income is the appropriate measure, practical problems of respondent recall have led most researchers to ask for gross income. In the environmental/health area, we are not aware of any studies that ask for wealth. This is not surprising.

Household wealth is a very complicated concept. For instance, when the Federal Reserve Board administers its Survey of Consumer Finances Survey, which is designed to gather the data to compute household wealth, the survey takes an average of 90 minutes (Fries, Starr-McCluer and Sunden, 1998). Obviously, no SC survey can capture the detailed data needed to compute wealth with this precision.

Is including wealth important, or is income good enough? It depends on the commodity being valued and the group doing the valuation. One can argue that income is a reasonable proxy for wealth over some range of family life-cycle and for homogeneous groups, particularly if one can also identify a few factors that correlate well with wealth, such as home ownership vs. renting (Di, 2001),[5] whether the family holds stocks and/or has a retirement account or pension, race, and income.

However, where comparisons of WTP between the elderly and other age groups are concerned, such as in the recent controversies over the use of mortality valuation measures (value of statistical life versus value of a statistical life year), measures of wealth could be important. Some studies have found that the WTP for risk reductions is relatively insensitive to age (Alberini, et al., 2004) and that income effects, while significant, are small. The issue here is whether the elderly's high wealth, relative to their incomes, is contributing to this high WTP, or whether this high WTP is more dependent on other factors, such as a growing preciousness of life as one ages. Furthermore, more detailed analysis of income and wealth is required if an intra-household model is being considered (Browning and Chiappori, 1998).

TABLE 5*. Examples of Questions about Importance of Attributes*

When you were making your choices between alternative programs with cancer and microbial illness and mortality reduced, how much influence did each of the characteristics below have in your decision? Please circle the appropriate number, where 1 = not important at all to your decision and 5 = extremely important to your decision.

	Not Important at All	Not Important	Somewhat Important	Very Important	Extremely Important
Numbers of microbial illnesses	1	2	3	4	5
Numbers of deaths from microbial illness	1	2	3	4	5
Numbers of cancer illnesses	1	2	3	4	5
Deaths from cancer illnesses	1	2	3	4	5
Costs to my household	1	2	3	4	5

Even if income is used, for its own sake or as a proxy for wealth, there is still a question about specification of this variable in the subsequent regression analysis. Our experience with health surveys suggests that income, by itself, irrespective of the specific form of the measure, is not as reliable as income per household member.

Finally, in Banzhaf et al. (2006), we found that the current income variable was less robust as a predictor of WTP than a simple categorical variable for whether the respondent expected their future income (in five years) to increase, stay the same, or decrease relative to their current income. Whether this is a general result cannot be known because the specific payment taking place over a ten-year period may have influenced this result.

Environmental Activism. Factors to include may not necessarily have to comport with fully developed neoclassical theory. For instance, most people would expect that an activist environmentalist would be more inclined to vote for a program to improve the environment (other things equal) than a person who characterizes himself as not an environmentalist. Thus, including a question about whether a person characterizes him or herself as an environmentalist or not, may allow a point to be made for the survey's credibility if the outcome is in line with one's priors (see Schuman and Presser, 1996). This attempt to triangulate results of the valuation with supporting questions is a common and helpful use of these questions.

TABLE 6. Examples of Health Status Questions

Do you have any of the following long-term health conditions?

Please circle all that apply.
a.	Food allergies
b.	Any other allergies
c.	Asthma
d.	Arthritis or rheumatism
e.	Back problems, excluding arthritis
f.	High blood pressure
g.	Migraine headaches
h.	Chronic bronchitis or emphysema
i.	Sinusitis
j.	Diabetes
k.	Epilepsy
l.	Heart disease
m.	Cancer (Please specify type _____)
n.	Stomach or intestinal ulcers
o.	Effects of a stroke
p.	Any other long-term condition that has been diagnosed by a health professional (Please specify _____)

Health Status. Another set of important demographic variables to consider in health surveys is current and future expected health status. There is no clear presumption in theory for the sign of health status on WTP for mortality risk reductions or morbidity reductions. Those in worse health may not think it worthwhile to spend additional resources on prolonging their life, when its quality is not so good. Yet, individuals are very adaptable to their conditions and there are many studies showing that self-rated health status of seriously disabled individuals is no lower than that of healthy people. Further, ill people may find their mortality more real and be willing to pay more to reduce the risk, in spite of their poor baseline health.

How should health status be specified? The choices include presence/absence of specific diseases (see Table 6), the same for functional limitations, aggregate measures such as the presence /absence of any chronic condition, frequency of acute conditions, duration of chronic conditions, and scores from any number of health indices. One we have used is SF-36 (Hays et al., 1993), which asks a series of 36 questions about mental and physical functioning. The advantages of using this or similar indices are that many other groups use it (experiences can be more easily shared and compared by researchers) and respondents do not need to rely on a doctor's diagnosis, but need provide only how well they move around or solve every day problems. Also, such indices produce a host of standardized variables to test for heterogeneity in models. The SF-36 produces eight aggregate measures: limitations in physical activities, limitations in social activities, limitations in usual activities due to physical problems, bodily pain, general mental health, limitations in usual activities due to emotional problems, vitality and general health perceptions. Having listed all these advantages, we must say that these variables have not performed well in regressions. Rather variables for the presence/absence of cancer or lung disease, for example, seem to outperform this variable (Alberini et al., 2004).

Risk Attitudes and Behavior. A final item that is often worth eliciting is the respondent's risk attitudes and their expression in risk taking or avoidance behavior. This can be accomplished in the abstract, for instance, by asking respondents about their preferences for gambles versus fixed amounts or their preferences over gambles. For example, respondents would be asked if they prefer a gamble with a 1/10 chance of winning $2 and a 9/10 chance of winning $1 or a gamble with a 1/10 change of winning $3 and a 9/10 chance of winning $1. Clearly, the second choice is preferred by risk-seekers. A series of these questions will generate bounds on the level of risk aversion of the individual (see Holt and Laury, 2002, for an example). These questions can be incorporated in an incentive compatible fashion by using rewards and incentives. This task can also be accomplished by asking questions about respondent behavior. Do they smoke? Do they hold life insurance? How much? Do they jaywalk? Speed? The resulting risk information can be used as covariates explaining WTP, especially in those cases where risks and probabilities are involved.

5. CHALLENGES IN THE ANALYSIS OF RESPONSES TO SUPPORTING QUESTIONS

5.1. Endogeneity

The main objective of valuation tasks is to identify preferences and trade-offs so that measures of welfare can be derived. Supporting questions are often used in the statistical analysis. However, these supporting questions are very often endogenous as they are also measures of preference, outcomes of choice that arise from preferences, or in some other way linked to the preferences of the respondent. Rating scales on attitudes toward an environmental quality change, for example, are based on the same preferences as those forming the valuation function for a contingent valuation question. Use of these attitudinal questions within the valuation function will likely lead to endogeneity problems. The respondent's history of bottled water consumption is based on the same preferences that will be elicited in a valuation task on water quality improvements. What this issue raises is that analysts must be careful when including supporting questions in statistical analysis and may choose to exclude these factors or use them in other ways. These variables may be used in a form of preliminary classification that then leads to statistical analysis of the groups developed in the classification. A more sophisticated approach is described by Ben Akiva et al. (2002) in which the endogeneity between rating scale responses and choice responses is explicitly recognized in a statistical model (see also Ben Akiva et al., 1999).

5.2. Identification Issues

Information collected in supporting questions can be used in a variety of ways. This information can be used to classify preferences or explain heterogeneity (covariates, latent class models, mixed logit model[6] with systematic explanation of the distribution around preferences[7]). These variables can also be used to explain error variances or forms of heteroskedasticity. Complex surveys, for example, may generate higher error variance in those people with lower incentives to respond (e.g. those not interested in the subject matter). In addition, demographic and attitudinal factors may affect decision strategies (compensatory or noncompensatory). The most challenging element is identifying where in the overall model of choice (equation 1) these supporting variables best fit. They could be placed in multiple categories, but the econometric identification problem would be enormous. Note that this is in some ways an extension of the issue described in A. above to other elements beyond preference. Ben Akiva et al. (2002) provide an interesting overview of the identification issues and some of the techniques recently developed to address these issues.

6. CONCLUSION: DEALING WITH SURVEY DESIGN TRADE-OFFS

There is a complex relationship among incentives to respond to a survey (financial incentives, social incentives, interest in the issue), effort devoted to the survey, and the cognitive burden placed on the respondent. These trade-offs are context specific and population specific and are difficult to judge in advance. They also vary by mode of administration. Nevertheless, the researcher must always keep in mind the trade-offs between fatigue and information collection. Tourangeau et al. (2000) provide a conceptual model of incentives and responses to surveys that is somewhat consistent with an economic model of benefits and costs associated with the activity of completing a survey. They discuss the various ways in which the costs of response can be reduced with careful design and implementation.

In any event, we have not found fatigue to be a factor in pretest and focus groups where in-person, internet or mail surveys addressing all the above issues and of about one-half hour in length on average are administered, and verbal debriefs are used on this point. We do not have experience in phone surveys, which probably cannot be used if all the challenges are to be met.

Unfortunately, there are additional considerations that further constrain surveyor choices. One of the least discussed, but arguably the most important, is taking into account peer review, both at journals and by advisory committees that often are organized to help guide and (hopefully) bless the survey design. There are any number of questions that need to be asked to address expert concerns, but which have no other necessary role. A good example is questions about bias. Respondents who think a survey is biased may ignore the bias in their voting, may be swayed by the bias, or may act in the opposite direction from the bias as a kind of protest. Such a variable is unlikely to be useful in explaining results, although respondents who think a survey is clearly biased may need to be dropped. The primary market for this question is peer reviewers who (rightly) would tend to question the credibility of a survey that participants felt was biased. Leaving such a question out of the survey is no solution, of course, as the bias question cannot be ignored.

Our guidance to researchers is not particularly satisfying – there are no hard and fast rules here. Rather, we suggest that researchers rely on focus groups and pilot tests to identify the best design and implementation choices as well as see where questions or descriptive text can be cut or their readability improved. These focus groups and pilots should be conducted not only on the valuation or choice questions, but also on the supporting questions. Beyond this, the good being valued may offer some clues about trade-offs. Probably the most intensely scrutinized commodities for valuation by SC methods are those with *a priori* significant nonuse values. Peer reviewer concerns should perhaps dominate choices here. And for many commodities some of the types of supporting questions we discuss in this paper are clearly inapplicable. Warm glow-type questions will not be needed when the good is private, e.g., mortality risk reduction to the individual. Probability understanding questions may not be needed when valuing public goods because one may face the easier task of describing effects per total number of people in a community, rather than – what amounts to the same thing -- the probability any one individual would be affected.[8]

In general, we advise that all types of supporting questions we list should be represented in every survey, with the key decisions being their specific wording, placement, and the number of each type. The use of these questions will vary depending on the context of the survey, but should include (a) triangulation or support of the results from the valuation questions, (b) explanation of the variation in responses to valuation questions (covariates on preferences, decision strategy variation), and (c) categorization of individuals that includes exclusion of some sub groups from further analysis. Supporting questions may be used in econometric analysis; however, supporting questions will often simply provide the researcher with the ability to discern certain types of responses and describe the reasons for these responses. They may be most valuable when they uncover responses that do not fit in the economic model of informed, compensatory decisions.

---

7. ENDNOTES

[1] Hanemann and Kanninen (1999) provide an overview of the economic foundations of the statistical discrete choice model that includes discussion of the way that income and other demographics enter the analysis.

[2] For example see Lewbel (1985).

[3] A latent class model is an econometric model that classifies respondents into categories. These categories are not predetermined (e.g. are not based on income levels) and are determined by the data. In valuation applications these methods typically result in a number of preference categories where membership in these categories is probabilistically influenced by characteristics of the individual. See Swait (this volume).

[4] See Andreoni (1989) for one popular definition of this term, which is used in the context of charitable giving. In the case developed here, individuals are asked to commit themselves and others to paying a tax to obtain the public good. We use the term loosely to describe that portion of WTP responses that are not subject to trade-offs.

[5] On average, according to Survey of Consumer Finance data for 1998, the value of primary residences makes up 28% of total household assets. With the stock market down, this value is undoubtedly higher today. In addition, median household net wealth of owners is 33 times that of renters, with this ratio being around 26 for age groups from 35 to 64 and 65 and over and for whites, with blacks and Hispanics in the high 30's. New wealth of owners to renters falls dramatically by income group, from 70 in the under $20,000 group to 4.6 for the $50,000 and over category.

[6] A mixed logit or random parameters logit model relaxes the assumption of common preferences over the sample and explains the degree of (unobserved) heterogeneity in the sample using distributions on the preference parameters.

[7] The distribution of the preference parameters in a mixed logit model can be made a function of underlying respondent characteristics. For example, the distribution of the price coefficient may shift with levels of income or age.

[8] That this task is "easier" is a conjecture on our part and has been criticized (comments by Reed Johnson, AEA Meetings, San Diego, January 3-5, 2004).

8. REFERENCES

Alberini, A., M. Cropper, A. Krupnick and N. Simon, 2004, "Does the Value of Statistical Life Vary with Age and Health Status? Evidence from the U.S. and Canada," *Journal of Environmental Economics and Management* 48(1): 769-792.

Andreoni, J., 1989, "Giving with Impure Altruism: Applications to charity and Ricardian Equivalence," *Journal of Political Economy* 97(6): 1447-1458.

Banzhaf, S., D. Burtraw, D. Evans and A. Krupnick, 2006, "Valuation of Natural Resource improvements in the Adirondacks," Land Economics 82(3): 445-464. Also, see RFF Report with the same title, September, 1994.

Bateman, I., R.T. Carson, B. Day, W.M. Hanemann, N. Hanley, T. Hett, A. Jones, G. Loomes, S. Mourato, E. Ozdemiroglu, D.W. Pearce, R. Sugden and J. Swanson, 2002, *Economic Valuation with Stated Preferences Techniques. A Manual,* Cheltenham: Edward Elgar.

Beard, J.G. and M.G. Ragheb, 1983, "Measuring Leisure Motivation," *Journal of Leisure Research,* 15:219-228.

Ben-Akiva, M., M.J. Walker, A.T. Bernardino, D.A. Gopinath, T. Morikawa, and A. Polydoropoulos, 2002, "Integration of Choice and Latent Variable Models," in *Perpetual Motion: Travel Behavior Research Opportunities and Application Challenges,*" H.S. Mahmassami, Ed., Pergamon.

Ben-Akiva, M., D. McFadden, T. Gärling, D. Gopinath, J. Walker, D. Bolduc, A. Börsch-Supan, P. Delquié, O. Larichev, T. Morikawa, A. Polydoropoulou, and V. Rao, 1999, "Extended Framework for Modeling Choice Behavior," *Marketing Letters* (10):187-203.

Boxall, P.C. and W. Adamowicz, 2002, "Understanding Heterogeneous Preferences in Random Utility Models: the Use of Latent Class Analysis," *Environmental and Resource Economics*. 23:421-446.

Browning, M. and P.-A. Chiappori, 1998, "Efficient Intra-Household Allocations: a General Characterization and Empirical Tests," *Econometrica*, 1241-78.

Carson, R. T., W.M. Hanemann, R.J. Kopp, J.A. Krosnick, R.C. Mitchell, S. Presser, P.A. Ruud, and V.K. Smith, 1994, Prospective Interim Lost Use Value Due to DDT and PCB Contamination in the Southern California Bight (Washington, DC: National Oceanic and Atmospheric Administration, September 1994, two volumes).

Cohen, S.H., 2003, "Maximum Difference Scaling: Improving Measures of Importance and Preference for Segmentation," Sawtooth Software Research Paper Series. www.sawtoothsoftware.com.

Corso, P.S., J.K. Hammitt, and J.D. Graham, 2001, "Valuing Mortality-Risk Reduction: Using Visual Aids to Improve the Validity of Contingent Valuation," *Journal of Risk and Uncertainty*, 23(2): 165-184.

Cummings, R. and L. Taylor, 1999, "Unbiased Value Estimates for Environmental Goods: A Cheap Talk Design for the Contingent Valuation Method," *American Economic Review*, 89(3): pp. 649-65.

Dillman, DA., 2000, *Mail and Internet Surveys: The Tailored Design Method*, New York: Wiley.

Dhar, R., 1997, "Consumer Preference for a No-Choice Option," *Journal of Consumer Research*, 24: 215-231.

Fishburn, P. C., 1975, "Axioms for Lexicographic Preferences," *Review of Economic Studies*, 42: 415-419.

Fries, G. M. Starr-McCluer and A.E. Sundén, 1998, "The Measurement of Household Wealth using Survey Data: An Overview of the Survey of Consumer Finances," Federal Reserve Board of Governors, Paper prepared at the 44th annual conference of the American Council on Consumer Interests, Washington D.C.

Hanemann, W.M. and B.J. Kanninen, 1999, "The Statistical Analysis of Discrete-Response CV Data," in *Valuing Environmental Preferences: Theory and Practice of the Contingent Valuation Method in the US, EU and Developing Countries*, I.J. Bateman and K.G. Willis, eds., Oxford: Oxford University Press.

Hays R.D., C.D. Sherbourne and R.M. Mazel, 1993, "The RAND 36-Item Health Survey 1.0," *Health Economics*. 2:217-227.

Holbrook, A.L., J.A. Krosnick, R.T. Carson and R.C. Mitchell, 2000, "Violating Conversational Conventions Disrupts Cognitive Processing of Attitude Questions," *Journal of Experimental Social Psychology* 36: 465–494.

Holt, C. A. and S.K. Laury, 2002, "Risk Aversion and Incentive Effects," *American Economic Review*, 92(5): 1644-1655.

Johnson F.R. and K.E. Mathews, 2001, "Improving the Connection between Theory and Empirical Analysis of Stated Preference and Conjoint Data: Sources and Effects of Utility-Theoretic Inconsistency in Stated-Preference Surveys," *American Journal of Agricultural Economics*, 83(5): 1328-1333.

Krupnick, A. and A. Alberini., 2000, "Cost of Illness and WTP Estimates of the Benefits of Improved Air Quality in Taiwan," *Land Economics* 76 (1).

Krupnick, A.K., A. Alberini, M. Cropper, N. Simon, B. O'Brien, R. Goeree and M. Heintzelman, 2002, "Age, Health and the Willingness to Pay for Mortality Risk Reductions: A Contingent Valuation Study of Ontario Residents," *Journal of Risk and Uncertainty*, 24: 161-186.

Lewbel, A., 1985, "A Unified Approach to Incorporating Demographic or Other Effects into Demand Systems," *Review of Economic Studies,* 52: 1–18.

Li, Chuan-Zhong and Leif Mattsson, 1995, "Discrete Choice under Preference Uncertainty: An Improved Structural Model for Contingent Valuation," *Journal of Environmental Economics and Management,* 28:256-269.

Loehman, E.T., S.V. Berg, AA. Arroyo, and Others, 1979, "Distributional analysis of Regional benefits and Costs of Air quality control," *Journal OF Environmental Economics and Management* 6: 222-43.

McFadden, D., 1986, "The Choice Theory Approach to Market Research," *Marketing Science* 5: 275–297.

Mitchell, R.C. and R.T. Carson, 1989, *Using Surveys to Value Public Goods: The Contingent Valuation Method,* Washington, DC: Resources for the Future.

Nisbett, R. E. and T. D. Wilson, 1977, "Telling More than we Can Know: Verbal Reports on Mental Processes," *Psychological Review,* 84(3): 231–259.

Schuman, H. and S. Presser, 1996, *Questions and Answers in Attitude Surveys: Experiments on Question Form, Wording, and Context,* San Diego: Sage Publications.

Schwarz, N., B. Knauper, H. Hippler, E. Noelle-Neumann and L. Clark, 1991 "Rating Scales: Numeric Values May Change the Meaning of Scale Labels," *Public Opinion Quarterly* 55: 570-582

Swait, J. R., 1994, "A Structural Equation Model of Latent Segmentation and Product Choice for Cross-Sectional Revealed Preference Choice Data," *Journal of Retailing and Consumer Services,* 1: 77–89.

Swait, J., 2001, "A Non-Compensatory Choice Model Incorporating Attribute Cutoffs," *Transportation Research Part B,* 35: 903-928.

Swait, J., W. Adamowicz, M. Hanemann, A. Diederich, J. Krosnick, D. Layton, W. Provencher, D. Schkade and R. Tourangeau, 2002, "Context Dependence and Aggregation in Disaggregate Choice Analysis," *Marketing Letters,* 13(3):193-203.

Tourangeau R., L.J. Rips and K. Rasinski, 2000, *The Psychology of Survey Response,* New York: Wiley.

Tversky, A., 1972, "Elimination by Aspects: A Theory of Choice," *Psychological Review,* 79: 281-299.

Yang, S. and G. M. Allenby, 2000, "A Model for Observation, Structural, and Household Heterogeneity in Panel Data," *Marketing Letters,* 11(2): 137-149.

Zhu Xiao Di, 2001, "The Role of Housing as a Component of Household Wealth," Working Paper 01-6, Joint Center for Housing Studies, Harvard University.

CHAPTER 4

MAKING CHOICE STUDIES INCENTIVE COMPATIBLE

GLENN W. HARRISON

University of Central Florida, Orlando, Florida, U.S.A.

1. INTRODUCTION

An allocation mechanism or institution is said to be incentive compatible when its rules provide individuals with incentives to truthfully and fully reveal their preferences. When the choice is binary, it is a simple matter to design incentive compatible mechanisms. However, when the domain of the choice task extends beyond two alternatives, things quickly become harder. In this chapter, we examine the conceptual issues involved in testing whether a choice experiment is incentive compatible, whether the evidence supports the claims that they are , and what one can do to enhance the incentive compatibility of choice experiments. We also identify several open issues.

There are many variants of "choice experiments" in use. In the context of this volume, it can refer to any situation in which a decision-maker is asked to rank or choose from two or more alternatives and where there are several choices to be made in which one or more attributes of the alternatives are varied. Thus, a single question in which someone is asked if they would be willing to buy an apple at $1 would not qualify, since there is no variation in any attribute of the apple. But if three questions are asked in which the person has to choose between the apple and parting with $1, $2 or $3, respectively, we have the most rudimentary choice experiment, or stated-choice (SC) study, as the term is used in this volume. In fact, elementary ordered tasks of this kind have become a popular means of eliciting valuations in experiments, and are known as Multiple Price Lists (MPL).[1] In general, there are many more attributes than prices that are varied, and we shall refer to those as Conjoint Choice Experiments.

There appears to be no logical reason to restrict the term "choice experiments" to hypothetical tasks, although that is common in the area of nonmarket valuation and

B.J. Kanninen (ed.), Valuing Environmental Amenities Using Stated Choice Studies, 67–110.

marketing. In fact, the comparison of hypothetical responses and real responses lies at the heart of tests for incentive compatibility, where the expression "real responses" is a short hand for any task for which the choices of the decision-maker are related in a salient manner to real outcomes. In the case of our apple experiments, the individual would have to part with the money before getting a real apple.

In many social policy settings, the connection may be more probabilistic and tenuous than the crisp experiments that have been the focus of the academic literature. The survey may have some ill-defined "advisory" role in terms of influencing policy, in some manner that is often maddeningly vague to experimental economists. But there are sometimes good reasons for such ambiguity, such as when it honestly reflects the true state of scientific knowledge or the political and legal process. We know very little about the effects of these types of ill-defined social consequences for incentive compatibility. We therefore focus here on the crisp, light experiments that involve real and transparent consequences, but we also consider how lessons about incentive compatibility drawn from the harsh contrasts of the laboratory can be transferred to more practical settings in which contingent valuation (CV) studies are applied.

In Section 2, we review the concept of incentive compatibility. The practical lesson is that this concept means more than providing real consequences of the choices that respondents make. The connection between different choices and different consequences has to make it in the best interest of the respondent to respond truthfully. Further, this connection has to be behaviorally transparent and credible, so that the respondent does not start to second-guess the incentive to respond truthfully.

In Sections 3 and 4 we evaluate the importance of making responses incentive compatible.[2] The most directly relevant evidence comes from laboratory experiments, where one can crisply compare environments in which the responses are incentive compatible and those where they are not. This distinction has typically been examined by just looking at choices made when the consequences are hypothetical or imagined, and comparing them to choices made when the consequences are real. There is systematic evidence of differences in responses across a wide range of elicitation procedures. The evidence is not universal, and there are some elicitation procedures and contexts in which the problem of incentive compatibility does not appear to be so serious. But there is no "magic bullet" procedure or question format that reliably produces the same results in hypothetical and real settings.

Section 5 changes gears. The evidence from Sections 3 and 4 establishes that there is a problem to be solved: one cannot just assume the problem of incentive compatibility away, at least if one wants to cite the literature in a systematic way. But there are several constructive ways in which one can mitigate hypothetical bias, or correct for it. One is by "instrument calibration," which is the use of controlled experiments with a particular survey population, scenario, and valuation task to identify the best way to ask the question. In effect, this represents the use of experiments to put operationally meaningful teeth in the "focus group" activities that CV researchers undertake already, at least for large-scale CV studies used for policy or litigation. The other calibration approach is ex post the survey, and uses "statistical calibration" procedures to try to correct for any biases in responses. Again, experiments are used to complement the survey, in this case to identify possible differences in hypothetical and real responses that might be systematically correlated with observable characteristics. These statistical methods can then be used to correct for biases, and also to better identify the appropriate standard errors to attach to estimates derived from CV studies.

Section 6 discusses a number of open issues that have been ignored in previous work. One such issue is the manner in which one should interpret advisory referenda, a popular format for CV studies. Should they be viewed as literal referenda, or as stylized metaphors for the type of voting process that is used in a referenda? In one case the incentives for respondents to respond truthfully are clear, but in the other case they are not at all clear. This ambiguity in interpretation translates into respondent confusion with respect to the incentive compatibility of the procedure, and an inability to draw reliable inferences from observed behavior.

Another open issue is scenario ambiguity. Many of the scenarios presented to respondents are simply incredible or implausible. Of course, one of the reasons we perform CV studies is to evaluate counter-factual policies or scenarios, but incredibility and implausibility are different concepts than hypotheticality. Of immediate concern here is scenario ambiguity with respect to the provision rules relating the choices the respondent can make and any real outcomes. The concern here is separate from the hypothetical-real distinction: even if the consequences were real, the scenario simply does not explain how one or the other response might affect outcomes. Again, the practical result is the inability to claim that a CV study has reliably elicited anything meaningful.

Section 7 draws some conclusions for practical application of the notion of incentive compatibility. These conclusions might seem harsh, but they need to be if stated choice is to achieve its great potential to inform debates over environmental policy. The objective is to force SC researchers to confess to the potential problem they face, and do something constructive about it. The current practice is simply to quote the literature selectively, which allows the low-level policy applications of SC studies to survive casual scrutiny. Higher-level applications are another matter, where the academic, adversarial and policy stakes are substantial enough to force more scrutiny. In those settings the reputation of the SC approach, as currently practiced, is questioned by many and completely dismissed by some. But that could change quickly if the problem of incentive compatibility is addressed.

2. WHAT IS INCENTIVE COMPATIBILITY?

To illustrate the concept of incentive compatibility in relation to choice behavior, we focus initially on voting behavior in referenda. Apart from the popularity of advisory referenda in nonmarket valuation settings, the context of voting matches the history of thought on these matters. It is then easy to see the implications for choice experiments defined in a nonvoting context.

Specifically, consider the design of voting mechanisms for referenda that are incentive compatible and nondictatorial.[3] In the case of voting mechanisms involving the selection of one alternative among k-alternatives, $k \geq 3$, it is well known that, in fact, no such voting procedure exists.[4] It is, however, easier to devise a voting mechanism involving choice among only two alternatives ($k = 2$) that is incentive compatible. One such voting mechanism is simple majority rule. Typically, incentive compatibility for this mechanism requires, in addition to the restriction to two alternatives, the assumption that individuals perceive that their utilities are affected by the outcome of the vote. Thus, if the voter thinks that his behavior will have some impact on the chance that one or the other alternative will be implemented, and that his utility will be affected by the outcome, the voter has a positive incentive to behave truthfully and vote honestly.

Recent work on institution design using the Revelation Principle employs incentive compatibility as a formal constraint. This formulation uses a much stronger assumption, called Epsilon Truthfulness: if the agent is indifferent between lying and telling the truth, assume he tells the truth.[5] It is important that one recognize Epsilon Truthfulness for what it is: an assertion or assumption that is regarded by many as excessively strong and that does not enjoy an empirical foundation. The validity of Epsilon Truthfulness remains an open empirical question.[6]

In the literature concerned with the use of the CV method for valuing environmental goods, the Epsilon Truthfulness assumption is often applied to hypothetical referenda. For example, Mitchell and Carson (1989; p.151) state that:

> We also showed that the discrete-choice referendum model was incentive-compatible in the sense that a person could do no better than vote yes if her WTP for a good being valued by this approach was at least as large as the tax price, and to vote no if this was not the case. This finding offers the possibility of framing contingent valuation questions so that they possess theoretically ideal and truthful demand-revelation properties.

Since one cannot know a priori whether or not subjects in a CV study will feel that their utilities will be affected by the outcome of a hypothetical vote, such assertions of incentive compatibility require that one assume that subjects will behave as they do in real referenda; i.e., one invokes a form of the Epsilon Truthfulness assumption.

The question as to whether or not a hypothetical referendum using majority rule is incentive compatible has become an important policy issue given its prominence in proposed guidelines for applications of CV for estimating environmental damages. In proposed rules for using the CV method, both the Department of the Interior (DOI) (1994; p.23102) and the National Oceanographic and Atmospheric Administration (NOAA) (1994; p.1144) assert that, in applications of CV,

> ... the voting format is incentive compatible. If respondents desire the program at the stated price, they must reveal their preferences and vote for the program.[7]

This proposed prescription for public policy is based on an assumption that presupposes acceptance of the hypothesis: a voter's behavior is independent of the use of a real or hypothetical referendum mechanism. This hypothesis, and therefore the credibility of the incentive compatibility assumption for hypothetical referenda, has been empirically tested by Cummings et al. (1997).

Our focus will be on one reason for the lack of incentive compatibility of SC experiments: hypothetical bias. This bias is said to occur whenever there is a difference between the choices made when the subjects face real consequences from their actions compared to the choices made when they face no real consequences from their actions. However, in many settings of interest to SC researchers who deal with public goods, there may be another source deriving from the propensity to free ride on the provision of others. The propensity to free ride[8] has been shown to be alive and well in the laboratory, as the survey by Ledyard (1995) documents. Harrison and Hirshleifer (1998) also show that it varies theoretically and behaviorally with the nature of the production process used to aggregate private contributions into a public good, such as one finds with threshold effects in many public goods (e.g., health effects of pollutants, species extinction). It is difficult to say a priori if the free riding bias is greater than the hypothetical bias problem. In fact, there is a dearth of studies of the interaction of the two biases.

To answer the question posed at the outset, incentive compatibility will be measured in terms of differences in responses between hypothetical and real environments, and where the real environment has been designed to encourage truthful responses. A "real environment" is one in which the respondent bears some real consequences from making one response or the other. This will normally mean that the scenario is not imaginary, but it is the consequence that is the behavioral trace that we use to identify deviations from incentive compatibility.

Knowledge that the respondent will answer truthfully normally comes from a priori reasoning about rational responses to known incentives. But we will also want to be cognizant of the need to ensure that the respondent sees what is a priori obvious to the (academic) analyst.[9] For example, we prefer mechanisms for which it is a dominant strategy to tell the truth, where this can be explained to the respondent in a nontechnical manner, and where the verification of this fact is a simple matter for the subject. Sometimes we cannot have this ideal behavioral environment. Rational responses may be truthful only in some strategic Nash Equilibrium, so the respondent has to make some guess as to the rationality of other players. Or, the respondent might not understand the simple explanation given, or suspect the surveyor of deception, in which case "all bets are off" when it comes to claims of incentive compatibility.

3. PREVIOUS EVIDENCE

We begin the review of previous evidence by considering the simple cases in which one elicits choices over two alternatives, or where the only attribute that is varied is the cost of the alternative. If we cannot say whether choices are incentive compatible in these settings, we had better give up trying to do so in the more complex settings in which there are more than two alternatives varying in terms of some nonmonetary dimension. We simplify things even further by considering elicitation over a private good, for which it is easy to exclude nonpurchasers.

A dichotomous-choice (DC) elicitation in this setting is just a "take it or leave it" offer, much like the posted-offer institution studied by experimental economists for many years. The difference is that the experimenter presents the subjects with a price, and the subject responds "yes" or "no" to indicate a desire to purchase the good or not at that price. The subject gets the commodity if and only if the response is "yes," and then parts with the money. The consequences of a "yes" response are real, not imagined. Incentive compatibility is apparent, at least in the usual partial-equilibrium settings in which such things are discussed.[10]

Cummings, Harrison and Rutström (1995) (CHR) designed some of the simplest experiments that have probably ever been run, just to expose the emptiness of the claims of those that would simply assert that hypothetical responses are the same as real responses in a DC setting. Subjects were randomly assigned to one of two rooms, the only difference being the use of hypothetical or real language in the instructions. An electric juicer was displayed, and passed around the room with the price tag removed or blacked-out. The display box for the juicer had some informative blurb about the product, as well as pictures of it "in action." Subjects were asked to say whether or not they would be willing to pay some stated amount for the good.

The hypothetical subjects responded much more positively than the real subjects. Since the private sources funding these experiments did not believe that "students were real people," the subjects were nonstudent adults drawn from church groups. The same qualitative results were obtained with students, with the same commodity and with different commodities. Comparable results have been obtained in a willingness to accept setting by Nape et al. (2003).

In response to the experimental results of CHR, some proponents of hypothetical surveys argued that their claims for the incentive compatibility of the DC approach actually pertained to simple majority rule settings in which there was some referendum over just two social choices. It was argued that this setting "somehow" provides the context that subjects need to spot the incentive compatibility. To be blunt but precise: it is apparent that this context is strictly incentive compatible if and only if subjects face real consequences.[11]

Cummings, Elliott, Harrison and Murphy (CEHM) (1997) therefore undertook simple majority rule experiments for an actual public good. After earning some income, in addition to their show-up fee, subjects were asked to vote on a proposition that would have each of them contribute a specified amount toward this public good. If the majority said "yes," all had to pay. The key treatments were again the use of hypothetical or real payments, and again there was significant evidence of hypothetical bias.[12]

4. EVIDENCE FROM CHOICE EXPERIMENTS

We now reconsider more closely the evidence for hypothetical bias from several published studies. In each case we evaluate the raw data using comparable statistical methods. Overall, the evidence is that hypothetical bias exists and needs to be worried about: hypothetical choices are not reliably incentive compatible. But there is a glimmer or two of good news, and certain settings in which the extent of hypothetical bias might be minimal. The task is to try to understand this variation in the behavioral extent of the bias, not just to document it. Only by understanding it can we design SC studies that mitigate it reliably.

4.1. Multiple Price Lists

A direct extension of the DC choice task is to implicitly offer the subject three choices: buy the good at one stated price, buy the good at another stated price, or keep your money. In this case, known in the experimental literature as a MPL auction, the subject is actually asked to make two choices: say "yes" or "no" to whether the good would be purchased at the first price, and make a similar choice at the second price. The subject can effectively make the third choice by saying "no" to both of these two initial choices. The MPL can be made incentive compatible by telling the subject that one of the choices will be picked at random for implementation.

The MPL design has been employed in three general areas in experimental economics: in the elicitation of risk attitudes by Holt and Laury (2002) and Harrison et al. (2005), in the elicitation of valuations for a commodity by Kahneman et al. (1990) and Andersen et al. (2006b), and in the elicitation of individual discount rates by Coller and Williams (1999) and Harrison and Lau (2005).

The MPL has three possible disadvantages. The first is that it only elicits interval responses, rather than "point" valuations. The second is that some subjects can switch back and forth from row to row, implying inconsistent preferences. The third is that it could be susceptible to framing effects, as subjects are drawn to the middle of the ordered table irrespective of their true values. Each of these potential problems can be addressed using appropriate designs and statistical procedures (e.g., Andersen et al., 2006a).

4.1.1. Discount Rates

Coller and Williams (1999) provide a test for hypothetical bias in the MPL format in the context of eliciting discount rates, and find that hypothetical bias does exist. They show (p.121) that elicited discount rates are significantly higher in their hypothetical treatment, and exhibit a higher residual variance after correcting for differences in the demographic characteristics of their samples.

We confirm their finding when we consider the evidence from their experiments that is directly comparable in terms of hypothetical bias. Their experiments with real rewards varied several of the characteristics of the task, such as the use of a "front-end delay" in the two options presented to subjects and the provision of information on implied annual effective rates. Their experiments with hypothetical rewards consisted of one session, and did not include these variations. Therefore one can undertake a tighter statistical test of hypothetical bias by restricting the sample to tasks that were otherwise comparable. In effect, this allows us to draw inferences about hypothetical bias without having to maintain the assumption that hypothetical bias does not interact with these other task characteristics.

Following Coller and Williams (1999) we estimate an interval regression model in which the interval selected by the subject is the dependent variable. Subjects that switched back and forth in a nonmonotonic manner simply have "fatter intervals," reflecting the relatively imprecise information obtained from them. Such behavior could be due to confusion, boredom with the task, or indifference between the options. We control for the same variables that Coller and Williams (1999) employed, using their definitions: age, sex, race, household income, parental income, household size, and a dummy variable to detect the real task. We also control for whether the subject was a junior, a senior, an Accounting major, or an Economics major. After dropping subjects who did not report information on income, there were 30 subjects in the hypothetical treatment and 29 subjects in the real treatment.

Using the basic interval regression specification, we estimate that elicited discount rates are 15.6 percentage points higher in the hypothetical treatment. The average predicted discount rate from this specification is 19.2 percentage points, so this is a large difference.[13] The average effect of hypothetical context has an estimated standard error of 6.4 percentage points, and a p-value of 0.015, so we can conclude that there does appear to be a statistically and substantively significant increase in the elicited discount rate when hypothetical tasks are used.

To anticipate an important theme of some of the work on choice experiments from marketing, we also consider the possibility that the residual varies with the source of the response. This amounts to allowing for some form of structural heteroskedasticity, and has been identified as important in experimental economics by Rutström (1998) in the context of alternative institutions for eliciting an open-ended willingness to pay (WTP). The same approach was employed by Coller and Williams (1999), who also noted that allowing for "scale variability" between elicitation sources could be important in drawing reliable inferences.

We first modify the basic specification discussed above to allow variation in the residual that is correlated with age, sex, race and the use of real rewards. We estimate significant effects on the error from sex, and from the covariates taken jointly. There appears to be a reduction in the residual when discount rates are elicited with real rewards, but it is not statistically significant.[14] There is relatively little change in the average effect of using hypothetical rewards: the elicited discount rate is now 17.4 percentage points higher instead of the 15.6 percentage points estimated from the basic specification.

When we extend the specification to include all of the demographic and treatment controls, however, we find that the average effect from using a hypothetical task drops to only 6.8 percentage points. The estimated standard error on this effect is 1.3 percentage points, so the p-value is less than 0.001 and the effect remains significant. In this case the real treatment is associated with an estimated standard error that is 52% lower than the estimated standard error for responses from the hypothetical treatment, although this estimate only has a p-value of 0.20. The intriguing result here is that the estimated size of hypothetical bias is sensitive to the "care and handling" of the error terms.

4.1.2. Risk Attitudes

Holt and Laury (2002) also provide a test of hypothetical bias in the MPL format, and show that it exists, with hypothetical risk attitudes being significantly lower than comparable real risk attitudes. Unfortunately, their design suffers from a simple confound, noted in Harrison et al. (2005): the comparable hypothetical and real responses are collected in a fixed order from the same subjects, so one cannot say whether it is the hypothetical consequences or the order that is generating differences in results.

In response, Holt and Laury (2005) agreed with the potential and estimated effects of order, and extended their earlier experiments to consider the effects of hypothetical bias without any potential confounds from order. Specifically, they conducted four sessions. One session had 1x payoffs with real rewards, and one session had 1x payoffs with hypothetical rewards. The other two sessions were the same but with 20x payoffs. Each session used different subjects, so the comparisons are all between subjects. Each of the sessions with real rewards used 48 subjects, and each of the sessions with hypothetical rewards used 36 subjects.[15] We use these new data to consider the effect of hypothetical bias.

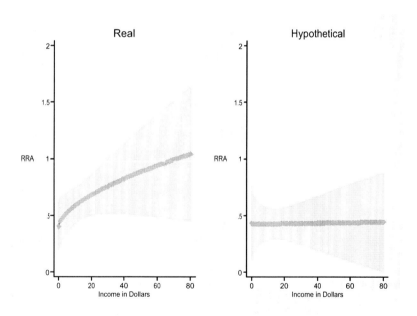

FIGURE 1. *Hypothetical Bias in Elicited Risk Attitudes*
Source: Experiments of Holt and Laury (2005)
Predicted RRA from Maximum Likelihood Expo-Power Model

Holt and Laury were concerned with two issues at once: the constancy of risk aversion over the income domain that they scaled payoffs over, and the effect of hypothetical responses compared to real responses. To allow for the possibility that relative risk aversion is not constant we follow Holt and Laury and estimate a flexible functional form: the Expo-Power (EP) function proposed by Saha (1993). The EP function can be defined as $u(y) = [1-\exp(-\alpha y^{1-r})]/\alpha$, where y is income and α and r are parameters to be estimated using maximum likelihood methods. Relative risk aversion (RRA) is then $r + \alpha(1-r)y^{1-r}$. So RRA varies with income if $\alpha \neq 0$. This function nests the popular Constant Absolute Risk Aversion (CARA) specification of utility, as r tends to 0, but is not defined for α equal to 0. Even if the limit does not exist, as α tends to 0 the popular Constant Relative Risk Aversion (CRRA) specification of utility also emerges, approximately, as a special case.

Maximum likelihood estimates of the EP model can be used to calculate the RRA for different income levels. The likelihood function we use here employs the same function used by Holt and Laury (2002) to evaluate their laboratory data, and indeed we replicate their estimates exactly.[16] Their likelihood function takes the ratio of the expected utility of the safe option to the sum of the expected utility of both options, where each expected utility is evaluated conditional on candidate values of α and r. Their likelihood specification also allows for a noise parameter, μ, to capture stochastic errors associated with the choices of subjects.

One important econometric extension of their approach is to allow each parameter, r and α, to be a separate linear function of the task controls and individual characteristics, where we can estimate the coefficients on each of these linear functions. We also allow for the responses of the same subject to be correlated, due to unobserved individual effects. The data from Holt and Laury (2005) do not include information on individual characteristics, which is unfortunate since the treatments involve between-subject comparisons for which it is particularly important to control for observable differences in samples.

The detailed results from maximum likelihood estimation of the EP model are reported and discussed in Harrison (2006a). Treatment dummies are included for the tasks in which the order of presentation of the lotteries was reversed (variable "reverse"), although this treatment had no statistically significant effects. This model allows for the possibility of correlation between responses by the same subject, since each subject provides 10 binary choices.[17] These results indicate that the real responses differ from the hypothetical responses solely in terms of the α parameter, which controls the nonconstancy of RRA in this EP specification. Since CRRA emerges in the limit as α tends to 0, the hypothetical responses are consistent with CRRA roughly equal to 0.38 (the constant term on the r parameter). That is also the value for RRA with real responses when income levels are sufficiently low, since RRA is equal to r at zero income levels. These inferences are confirmed in Figure 1, which displays the predicted RRA in each treatment, along with a 95% confidence interval. At low levels of income there is virtually no discernible difference between RRA for the hypothetical and real responses, but at higher income levels the real responses exhibit much higher RRA. Thus,hypothetical rewards provide reliable results precisely when they save the least money in terms of subject payments.[18]

4.2. Conjoint Choice Experiments

The other "new kid on the valuation block" involves several choices being posed to subjects, in the spirit of the revealed-preference logic. Each choice involves the subject reporting a preference over two or more bundles, where a bundle is defined by a set of characteristics of one or more commodities. The simplest example would be where the commodity is the same in all bundles, but price is the only characteristic varied. This special case is just the MPL discussed above, in which the subject may be constrained to just pick one of the prices (if any). The most popular variant is where price and nonprice characteristics are allowed to vary across the choices. For example, one bundle might be a lower quality version of the good at some lower price, one bundle might be a higher quality version at a higher price, and one bundle is the status quo in which nothing is purchased. The subject might be asked to pick one of these three bundles in one choice task (or to provide a ranking).

Typically there are several such choices. To continue the example, the qualities might be varied and/or the prices on offer varied. By asking the subject to make a series of such choices, and picking one at random for playing out,[19] the subjects' preferences over the characteristics can be "captured" in the familiar revealed-preference manner. Since each choice reflects the preferences of the subject, if one is selected for implementation independently[20] of the subject's responses, the method is obviously incentive compatible. Furthermore, the incentive to reveal true preferences is relatively transparent.

This set of variants goes by far too many names in the literature. The expression "choice experiments" is popular, but too generic to be accurate. A reference to "conjoint analysis" helps differentiate the method, but at the cost of semantic opacity. In the end, the expression "revealed-preference methods" serves to describe these methods well, and connect them to a long and honorable tradition in economics since Samuelson (1938), Afriat (1967) and Varian (1982, 1983).

Several studies examine hypothetical bias in this revealed preference elicitation method, at least as it is applied to valuation and ranking.

4.2.1. Allocating Money to Environmental Projects

Carlsson and Martinsson (2001) allow subjects to allocate real money to two environmental projects, varying three characteristics: the amount of money the subject personally receives, the amount of money donated to an environmental project by the researchers, and the specific World Wildlife Fund project that the donation should go to. They conclude that the real and hypothetical responses are statistically indistinguishable, using statistical models commonly used in this literature. However, several problems with their experiment make it hard to draw reliable inferences. First, and most seriously, the real treatments were all in-sample: each subject gave a series of hypothetical responses, and then gave real responses. There are obvious ways to test for order effects in such designs, as used by CHR for example, but they are an obvious confound here. Directly comparable experiments by Svedsäter and Johansson-Stenman (2001) suggest that order effects were in fact a significant confound. Second, the subjects were allocating "house money" with respect to the donation, rather than their own. This made it hard to implement a status quo decision, since it would have been dominated by the donation options if the subject had even the slightest value for the environmental project. There is a concern that these are all artificial, forced decisions that might not reflect how subjects allocate monies according to their true preferences (unless one makes strong separability assumptions). Third, all three environmental projects were administered by the same organization, which leads the subject to view them as perfect substitutes. This perception is enhanced by a (rational) belief that the organization was free to re-allocate un-tied funds residually, such that there is no net effect on the specific project. Thus,the subjects may well have rationally been indifferent over this characteristic.[21]

4.2.2. Valuing Beef

Lusk and Schroeder (2004) conduct a careful test of hypothetical bias for the valuation of beef using revealed-preference methods. They consider 5 different types of steak, and vary the relative prices of each steak type over 17 choices. For the subjects facing a real task, one of the 17 choices was to be selected at random for implementation. Subjects also considered a "none of these" option that allowed them not to purchase any steak. Each steak type was a 12-ounce steak, and subjects were told that the baseline steak, a "generic steak" with no label, had a market price of $6.07 at a local supermarket. Each subject received a $40 endowment at the outset of the experiment, making payment feasible for those in the real treatment. Applying the statistical methods commonly used to analyze these data, they find significant differences between hypothetical and real responses. Specifically, they find that the marginal values of the attributes between hypothetical and real are identical but that the propensity to purchase, attributes held constant, is higher in the hypothetical case.

More experimental tests of the revealed-preference approach are likely. I conjecture that the experimental and statistical treatment of the "no buy" option will be critical to the evaluation of this approach. It is plausible that hypothetical bias will manifest itself in the "buy something" versus "buy nothing" stage in decision-making, and not so much in the "buy this" or "buy that" stage that conditionally follows.[22] Indeed, this hypothesis has been one of the implicit attractions of the method. The idea is that one can then focus on the second stage to ascertain the value placed on characteristics. But this promise may be illusory if one of the characteristics varied is price and separability in decisions is not appropriate. In this case the latent-utility specification implies that changes in price spill over from the "buy this or buy that" nest of the utility function and influence the "buy or no-buy" decision.

4.2.3. Ranking Mortality Risks

Harrison and Rutström (2006b) report the results of a conjoint-choice ranking experiment in which there was a marked lack of hypothetical bias. Their task involved subjects ranking the 12 major causes of death in the United States. The task was broken down for each subject according to broad age groups. Thus, a subject aged 25 was asked to state 12 rankings for deaths in the age group 15 to 24, 12 more rankings for deaths in the age group 25 to 44, 12 more rankings for the age group 45 to 64, and finally 12 rankings for those 65 and over. In the real rewards treatment the subject was simply paid $1 for every correct ranking. Thus,the subject could earn up to $48 in the session.

The hypothetical versions of the survey instrument replaced the text in the original versions, which described the salient reward for accuracy. The replacement text was very simple:

> You will be paid $10 for your time. We would like you to try to rank these as accurately as you can, compared to the official tabulations put out by the U.S. Department of Health. When you have finished please check that all cells in the table below are filled in.

The experiment was otherwise administered identically to the others with salient rewards, using a between-subjects design. There were 95 subjects in the hypothetical-rewards experiments[23] and 45 subjects in the salient-rewards experiments. The rank errors for the hypothetical (H) sessions are virtually identical to those in the real (R) sessions. The average rank error in the H sessions is 2.15, compared to 2.00 in the R sessions. Moreover, the standard deviation in the H sessions is 1.95, which is also close to the 1.90 for the R sessions. Although there has been some evidence to suggest that average H responses might be the same as R responses in some settings, it is common to see a significantly higher variance in H responses as noted earlier. A regression analysis confirms the conclusion from the raw descriptive statistics when appropriate controls are added.

This conclusion from the hypothetical survey variant is a surprise, given the extensive literature on the extent of hypothetical bias: the responses obtained in this hypothetical setting are statistically identical to those found in a real setting. The hypothetical setting implemented here should perhaps be better referred to as a nonsalient experiment. Subjects were rewarded for participating, with a fixed show-up fee of $10. The hypothetical surveys popular in the field rarely reward subjects for participating, although it has occurred in some cases. There could be a difference between our nonsalient experiment and "truly hypothetical" experiments.

One feature of the vast literature on hypothetical bias is that it deals almost exclusively with valuation tasks and binary-choice tasks, rather than ranking tasks.[24] The experimental task of Harrison and Rutström (2006b) is a ranking task. It is possible that the evidence on hypothetical bias in valuation settings simply does not apply so readily to ranking tasks.

This conjecture is worth expanding on, since it suggests some important directions for further research. One account of hypothetical bias that is consistent with these data runs as follows. Assume that subjects come into an experiment task and initially form some beliefs as to the "range of feasible responses," and that they then use some heuristic to "narrow down" a more precise response within that range. It is plausible that hypothetical bias could affect the first step, but not be so important for the second step. If that were the case, then a task that constrained the range of feasible responses, such as our ranking task that restricts the subjects to choose ranks between 1 and 12, might not suffer from hypothetical bias. On the other hand, a valuation task might plausibly elicit extreme responses in a hypothetical setting, as subjects note that they could just as easily say that they would pay nothing as say that they would pay a million dollars. In this setting, there is no natural constraint, such as comparing to one's budget to constrain feasible responses. Hence, the second stage of the posited decision process would be applied to different feasible ranges. Even if the second stage were roughly the same for hypothetical and real tasks, if the first stage were sufficiently different then the final response could be very different. This is speculation, of course. The experiment considered here does not provide any evidence for this specific thought process, but it does serve to rationalize the results.

5. MITIGATING HYPOTHETICAL BIAS

There are two broad ways in which one can try to mitigate hypothetical bias: by means of instrument calibration before the survey, or by means of statistical calibration after the survey.

5.1. Instrument Calibration

Much of the debate and controversy over "specifications" in the CV literature concerns the choice of words. The problem of "choosing the right words" in CV studies has assumed some importance through the result of judicial decisions. In 1989 the U.S. District Court of Appeals, in State of Ohio v. U.S. Department of the Interior (880 F.2nd. at 474), asserted that the "... simple and obvious safeguard against overstatement [of WTP], however, is more sophisticated questioning." (p.497). While we disagree that this process is "simple and obvious," it is apparent that one can only assess the improvement from different CV questionnaires if one has a way of knowing if any bias is being reduced. This mandates the use of some measure of the real economic commitment that a subject would make in the same setting as the hypothetical question. The laboratory is clearly one place where such measures can be readily generated.

CV research partially addresses these "wording issues" by employing focus groups to help guide the initial survey design and/or employing variations in the final survey design. With design variation, if survey results are similar across several different versions of a questionnaire, then there is some presumption that the hypothetical responses do not depend on the particular words chosen from this set. If the results are not similar across survey designs, then they provide some bounds on the hypothetical response. See, for example, Imber et al. (1991) and Rowe et al. (1991).

Of course, there is no claim in these studies that shows that any of these versions is any closer than the other to the real economic commitments that subjects would make. The only claim is that they all might give comparable hypothetical numbers or bounds on the hypothetical WTP. A pack of drunk rednecks agreeing that the UCF Golden Knights are the best college football team does not, sadly, make it so.

The increasing use of focus groups in CV research, in which subjects are directly asked to discuss their interpretation of CV questions (e.g., see Smith (1990, 1992) or Schkade and Payne (1993)), is a practical response to the concerns cognitive psychologists have long expressed about the importance of different ways of presenting valuation questions. For example, Fischoff and Furby (1988) and Fischoff (1991) correctly characterize many possible disparities between the way subjects perceive the CV valuation question and the way investigators perceive it. Useful as focus groups might be to help avoid misinterpretation of a survey instrument in some manner, how are focus groups to be judged effective in reducing bias? In the absence of comparable responses from real behavior, one can only speculate on the importance of what is learned from focus groups in demonstrating that any alternative wordings for a survey may reduce (or exacerbate) hypothetical bias.

The laboratory provides a simple metric by which one can test, in meaningful ways, the importance of different presentations of valuation questions. Because controlled laboratory experiments may be used to enforce real economic commitments, they provide benchmarks to which alternative scenario designs, or wording choices, may be evaluated in their effectiveness of reducing hypothetical bias. Thus, using laboratory experiments is likely to be more informative than the casual introspective nature of the literature on wording choice in survey design.[25] The problem of deciding which set of words is "best" might, in some instances,[26] be easily and directly tested using controlled laboratory experiments such as those presented earlier.

The idea of instrument calibration has already generated two important innovations in the way in which hypothetical questions have been posed: recognition of some uncertainty in the subject's understanding of what a "hypothetical yes" means (Blumenschein et al. (1998, 2001)), and the role of "cheap talk" scripts directly encouraging subjects to avoid hypothetical bias (Cummings et al. (1995a), Cummings and Taylor (1998), List (2001), Aadland and Caplan (2003) and Brown et al. (2003)).

The evidence for these procedures is mixed. Allowing for some uncertainty can allow one to adjust hypothetical responses to better match real responses, but presumes that one knows ex ante what threshold of uncertainty is appropriate to apply. Simply showing that there exists a threshold that can make the hypothetical responses match the real responses, once you look at the hypothetical and real responses, is not particularly useful unless that threshold provides some out-of-sample predictive power. Similarly, the effects of "cheap talk" appear to be context-specific, which simply means that one has to test its effect in each context rather than assume it works in all contexts.

5.2. Statistical Calibration

Can a decision maker calibrate the responses obtained by a hypothetical survey so that they more closely match the real economic commitments that the subjects would have been expected to make? A constructive answer to this question was offered by Blackburn et al. (1994). The essential idea underlying this approach is that the hypothetical survey provides an informative, but statistically biased, indicator of the subject's true WTP for the environmental good. The trick is how to estimate and apply such bias functions.[27] They propose doing so with the complementary use of field elicitation procedures that use hypothetical surveys, laboratory elicitation procedures that use hypothetical and nonhypothetical surveys, and laboratory elicitation procedures that use incentive-compatible institutions.[28]

The upshot of the statistical calibration approach is a simple comparison of the original responses to the hypothetical survey and a set of calibrated responses that the same subjects would have made if asked to make a real economic commitment in the context of an incentive-compatible procedure. This approach does not predetermine the conclusion that the hypothetical survey is "wrong." If the hypothetical survey is actually eliciting what its proponents say that it is, then the calibration procedure should say so. In this sense, calibration can be seen as a way of validating "good hypothetical surveys" and correcting for the biases of "bad hypothetical surveys."[29]

The statistical calibration approach can do more than simply pointing out the possible bias of a hypothetical survey. It can also evaluate the confidence with which one can infer statistics such as the population mean from a given survey. In other words, a decision maker is often interested in the bounds for a damage assessment that fall within prescribed confidence intervals. Existing hypothetical surveys often convey a false sense of accuracy in this respect. A calibration approach might indicate that the population mean inferred from a hypothetical survey is reliable in the sense of being unbiased, but that the standard deviation was much larger than the hypothetical survey would directly suggest. This type of extra information can be valuable to a risk-averse decision maker.

Consider the analogy of a watch that is always 10 minutes slow to introduce the idea of a statistical bias function for hypothetical surveys. The point of the analogy is that hypothetical responses can still be informative about real responses if the bias between the two is systematic and predictable. The watch that is always 10 minutes slow can be informative, but only if the error is known to the decision maker and if it is transferable to other instances (i.e., the watch does not get further behind the times over time).

Blackburn et al. (1994) define a "known bias function" as one that is a systematic statistical function of the socio-economic characteristics of the sample. If this bias is not mere noise then one can say that it is "knowable" to a decision maker. They then test if the bias function is transferable to a distinct sample valuing a distinct good, and conclude that it is. In other words, they show that one can use the bias function estimated from one instance to calibrate the hypothetical responses in another instance, and that the calibrated hypothetical responses statistically match those observed in a paired real elicitation procedure. Johannesson et al. (1999) extend this analysis to consider responses in which subjects report the confidence with which they would hypothetically purchase the good at the stated price, and find that information on that confidence is a valuable predictor of hypothetical bias.

There have been two variants on this idea of statistical calibration: one from the marketing literature dealing with the pooling of responses from hypothetical and real data processes, and one from the experimental literature dealing with in-sample calibration.

5.2.1. Pooling Responses From Different Mechanisms

Building on long-standing approaches in marketing, a different statistical calibration tradition seeks to recover similarities and differences in preferences from data drawn from various institutions. The original objective was "data enrichment," which is a useful way to view the goal of complementing data from one source with information from another source.[30] Indeed, the exercise was always preceded by a careful examination of precisely what one could learn from one data source that could not be learned from another, and those insights were often built into the design. For example, attribute effects tend to be positively correlated in real life: the good fishing holes have many of the positive attributes fishermen want. This makes it hard to tease apart the effects of different attributes, which may be important for policy evaluation. Adroit combination of survey methods can mitigate such problems, as illustrated by Adamowicz et al. (1994).

Relatively few applications of this method have employed laboratory data, such that there is at least one data generating mechanism with known incentive compatibility. One exception is Cameron et al. (2002). They implement 6 different hypothetical surveys, and one actual DC survey. All but one of the hypothetical surveys considered the same environmental good as the actual DC survey; the final hypothetical survey used a "conjoint analysis" approach to identify attributes of the good. Their statistical goal was to see if they could recover the same preferences from each data-generation mechanism, with allowances for statistical differences necessitated by the nature of the separate responses (e.g., some were binary, and some were open ended). They develop a mixture model, in which each data-generation mechanism contributes to the overall likelihood function defined over the latent valuation. Although they conclude that they were generally able to recover the same preferences from most of the elicitation methods, their results depend strikingly on the assumed functional forms.[31] Their actual DC response was only at one price, so the corresponding latent WTP function can only be identified if one is prepared to extrapolate from the hypothetical responses. The upshot is a WTP function for the actual response that has a huge standard error, making it hard to reject the null that it is the "same" as the other WTP functions. The problems are clear when one recognizes that the only direct information obtained is that only 27% of the sample would purchase the environmental good at $6 when asked for real, whereas 45% would purchase the good when asked hypothetically.[32] The only information linking the latent-WTP functions is the reported income of respondents, along with a raft of assumptions about functional form.

A popular approach to combining data from different sources has been proposed in the SC literature: see Louviere et al. (2000; ch. 8, 13) for a review. One concern with this approach is that it relies on differences in an unidentified "scale parameter" to implement the calibration. Consider the standard probit model of binary choice to illustrate. One common interpretation of this model is that it reflects a latent and random utility process in which the individual has some cardinal number for each alternative that can be used to rank alternatives. This latent process is assumed to be composed of a deterministic core and an idiosyncratic error. The "error story" varies from literature to literature,[33] but if one further assumes that it is normally distributed with zero mean and unit variance then one obtains the standard probit specification in which the likelihood contribution of each binary choice observation is the cumulative distribution function of a standard normal random variable evaluated at the deterministic component of the latent process. Rescaling the assumed variance only scales up or down the estimated coefficients, since the contribution to the likelihood function depends only on the cumulative distribution below the deterministic component. In the logit specification a comparable normalization is used, in which the variance is set to $\pi^2/3$. Most of the "data enrichment" literature in marketing assumes that the two data sources have the same deterministic component, but allows the scale parameter to vary. This has nothing to say about calibration as conceived here.

But an extension of this approach does consider the problem of testing if the deterministic components of the two data sources differ, and this nominally has more to do with calibration. The methods employed here were first proposed by Swait and Louviere (1993), and are discussed in Louviere et al. (2000; §8.4). They entail estimation of a model based solely on hypothetical responses, and then a separate estimation based solely on real responses. In each case the coefficients on the explanatory variables (e.g., sex, age) conditioning the latent process are allowed to differ, including the intercept on the latent process. Then they propose estimation of a "pooled" model in which there is a dummy variable for the data source. Implicitly the pooled model assumes that the coefficients on the explanatory variables other than the intercept are the same for the two data sources.[34] The intercepts implicitly differ if one thinks of there being one latent process for the hypothetical data and one latent process for the real data. Since the data are pooled, the same implicit normalization of variance is applied to the two data sources. Thus, one effectively constrains the variance normalizations to be the same, but allows the intercept to vary according to the data source. The hypothesis of interest is then tested by means of an appropriate comparison of likelihood values.

In effect, this procedure can test if hypothetical and real responses are affected by covariates in the same manner, but not if they differ conditional on the covariates. Thus,if respondents have the same propensity to purchase a good at some price, this method can identify that. But if men and women each have the same elevated propensity to "purchase" when the task is hypothetical, this method will not identify that.[35] And the overall likelihood tests will indicate that the data can be pooled, since the method allows the intercepts to differ across the two data sources. Hence claims in Louviere et al. (2000; ch.13) of widespread "preference regularity" across disparate data sources and elicitation methods should not be used as the basis for dismissing the need to calibrate hypothetical and real responses.[36]

On the other hand, the tests of preference regularity from the marketing literature are capable of being applied more generally than the methods of pooling preferences from different sources. The specifications considered by Louviere et al. (2000;

p.233-236) clearly admit the possibility of marginal valuations differing across hypothetical and real settings.[37] In fact, it is possible to undertake tests that some coefficients are the same while others are different, illustrated by Louviere et al. (2000; §8.4.2). This is a clear analogue to some parameters in a real/hypothetical experiment being similar (e.g. some marginal effects) but others being quite different (e.g. purchase intention), as illustrated by Lusk and Schroeder (2004). The appropriate pooling procedures then allow some coefficients to be estimated jointly while others are estimated separately, although there is an obvious concern with such specification tests leading to reported standard errors that understate the uncertainty over model specification.

5.2.2. Calibrating Responses Within-Sample

Fox et al. (1998) and List and Shogren (1998, 2002) propose a method of calibration which uses hypothetical and real responses from the same subjects for the same good.[38] But if one is able to elicit values in a nonhypothetical manner, then why bother in the first place eliciting hypothetical responses that one has to calibrate? The answer is that the relative cost of collecting data may be very different in some settings. It is possible in marketing settings to construct a limited number of "mock ups" of the potential product to be taken to market, but these are often expensive to build due to the lack of scale economies. Similarly, one could imagine in the environmental policy setting that one could actually implement policies on a small scale at some reasonable expense, but that it is prohibitive to do so more widely without some sense of aggregate WTP for the wider project. The local implementation could then be used as the basis for ascertaining how one must adjust hypothetical responses for the wider implementation.

These considerations aside, the remaining substantive challenge for calibration is to demonstrate feasibility and utility for the situation of most interest in environmental valuation, when the underlying target good or project is nondeliverable and one must by definition consider cross-commodity calibration. Again, the work that needs to be done is to better understand when statistical calibration works and why, not to just document an occasional "success here" or "failure there." The literature is replete with selective citations to studies that support one position or another; the greater challenge it to explain this disparity in terms of operationally meaningful hypotheses.

6. OPEN ISSUES

6.1. Advisory Referenda and Realism

One feature of hypothetical surveys in the field is not well captured by most experiments: the chance that the subject's hypothetical response might influence policy or the level of damages in a lawsuit. To the extent that we are dealing with a subjective belief, such things are intrinsically difficult to control perfectly. In some field surveys, however, there is a deliberate use of explicit language which invites the subject to view their responses as having some chance of affecting real decisions.

If one accepts that field surveys are successful in encouraging some subjects to take the survey for real in a subjectively probabilistic sense, then the natural question to ask is: "how realistic does the survey have to be in the eyes of respondents before they respond as if it were actually real?" In other words, if one can encourage respondents to think that there is some chance that their responses will have an impact, at what point do the subjects behave the way they do in a completely real survey? Obviously this question is well posed, since we know by construction that they must do so when the chance of the survey being real is 100%. The interesting empirical question, which we examine, is whether any smaller chance of the survey being real will suffice. This question takes on some significance if one can show that the subject will respond realistically even when the chance of the payment and provision being real is small.

6.1.1. Field Counterparts

Many field surveys are designed to avoid the problem of hypothetical bias. Great care is often taken in the selection of motivational words in cover letters, opening survey questions, and key valuation questions, to encourage the subject to take the survey seriously in the sense that their response will "count". It is not difficult to find many prominent examples of this pattern.

Consider the generic cover letter advocated by Dillman (1978; pp.165ff.) for use in mail surveys. The first paragraph is intended to convey something about the social usefulness of the study: that there is some policy issue which the study is attempting to inform. The second paragraph is intended to convince the recipient of their importance to the study. The idea here is to explain that their name has been selected as one of a small sample, and that for the sample to be representative they need to respond. The goal is clearly to put some polite pressure on the subject to make sure that their socio-economic characteristic set is represented.

The third paragraph ensures confidentiality, so that the subject can ignore any possible repercussion from responding one way or the other in a "politically incorrect" manner. Although seemingly mundane, this assurance can help the researcher interpret the subject's response as a response to the question at hand rather than to some uncontrolled and unknown (to the researcher) perceptions of repercussions. It also serves to mimic the anonymity of the ballot box.

The fourth paragraph builds on the preceding three to drive home the usefulness of the survey response itself, and the possibility that it will influence behavior:

The fourth paragraph of our cover letter reemphasizes the basic justification for the study -- its social usefulness. A somewhat different approach is taken here, however, in that the intent of the researcher to carry through on any promises that are made, often the weakest link in making study results useful, is emphasized. In {an example cover letter in the text} the promise (later carried out) was made to provide results to government officials, consistent with the lead paragraph, which included a reference to bills being considered in the State Legislature and Congress. Our basic concern here is to make the promise of action consistent with the original social utility appeal. In surveys of particular communities, a promise is often made to provide results to the local media and city officials (Dillman, 1978; p.171).

From our perspective, the clear intent and effect of these admonitions is to attempt to convince the subject that their response will have some probabilistic bearing on actual outcomes. We do not need to enter into any debate on whether this intent is realized.[39]

This generic approach has been used, for example, in the CV study of the Nestucca oil spill by Rowe et al. (1991). Their cover letter contained the following sentences in the opening and penultimate paragraphs:

Government and industry officials throughout the Pacific Northwest are evaluating programs to prevent oil spills in this area. Before making decisions that may cost you money, these officials want your input. [...] The results of this study will be made available to representatives of state, provincial and federal governments, and industry in the Pacific Northwest (emphasis added).

In the key valuation question, subjects are motivated by the following words:

Your answers to the next questions are very important. We do not yet know how much it will cost to prevent oil spills. However, to make decisions about new oil spill prevention programs that could cost you money, government and industry representatives want to learn how much it is worth to people like you to avoid more spills.

These words reinforce the basic message of the cover letter: there is some probability, however small, that the response of the subject will have an actual impact.

More direct connections to policy consequences occur when the survey is openly undertaken for a public agency charged with making the policy decision. For example, the Resource Assessment Commission of Australia was charged with making a decision on an application to mine in public lands, and used a survey to help it evaluate the issue. The cover letter, signed by the Chairperson of the Commission under the letterhead of the Commission, spelled out the policy setting clearly:

The Resource Assessment Commission has been asked by the Prime Minister to conduct an inquiry into the use of the resources of the Kakadu Conservation Zone in the Northern Territory and to report to him on this issue by the end of April 1991.[40] [...] You have been selected randomly to participate in a national survey related to this inquiry. The survey will be asking the views of 2500 people across Australia. It is important that your views are recorded so that all groups of Australians are included in the survey (Imber et al. , 1991, p.102).

Although no promise of a direct policy impact is made, the survey responses are obviously valued in this instance by the agency charged with directly and publicly advising the relevant politicians on the matter.

There are some instances in which the agency undertaking the study is deliberately kept secret to the respondent. For example, this strategy was adopted by Carson et al. (1992, 2003) in their survey of the Exxon Valdez oil spill undertaken for the Attorney General of the State of Alaska. They, in fact, asked subjects near the end of the survey who they thought had sponsored the study, and only 11% responded correctly (p.91). However, 29% thought that Exxon had sponsored the study. Although no explicit connection was made to suggest who would be using the results, it is therefore reasonable to presume that at least 40% of the subjects expected the responses to go directly to one or other of the litigants in this well-known case. Of course, that does not ensure that the responses will have a direct impact, since there may have been some (rational) expectation that the case would settle without the survey results being entered as evidence.

We conclude from these examples that even if field survey researchers would be willing to accept the claim that "hypothetical surveys are biased in relation to real surveys," they might deny that they actually conduct hypothetical surveys. Without entering into a debate about how realistic the surveys are as the result of direct or implied "social usefulness," their claim must be that a little bit of reality elicits the same responses as The Real Thing.

6.1.2. Experimental Results

Cummings et al. (1995b) and Cummings and Taylor (1998) report striking results with the design illustrated in Figure 2. The extreme bars on the left and right reflect the results from CEHM: subjects were either given a hypothetical referendum or a real one, and there was a large difference in observed behavior. The four intermediate bars reflect treatments in which subjects were told that there was some probability that their referendum responses would be binding on them, and that they would have to pay the stated amount if the majority voted "yes," or would forego the project if the majority voted "no."

As the probability of the real economic commitment being binding increased from 0% to 1% there was virtually no change in the fraction voting yes. In fact, it went up from 45% to 46%, and while that is not a statistically significant increase it is reminiscent of the effect of Light Cheap Talk: plausibly, the information that there was only a 1% chance that the referendum was to be binding served to remind some respondents that it was not real. As the chance of the referendum response being binding increases to 25%, 50% and 75%, the responses get closer and closer to those obtained when it was completely binding.

It remains an open question how subjects in the field might interpret the advisory nature of their responses. If a sample of 100 was contacted and told that their responses would be scaled up to the whole population and applied without fail, would that be interpreted by the subject as a 1% chance of the referendum response being binding or as a 100% chance if it being binding? The latter would be a sensible interpretation, but then the respondent must decide how likely it is that their response will be pivotal. And then the respondent needs to evaluate the chances of this survey sample being binding, given the nature of the political and litigation process. These issues of perception deserve further study. However, the results at hand do not suggest that by making the probability of the response binding by "epsilon" that responses will be exactly the same as if they were 100% binding.

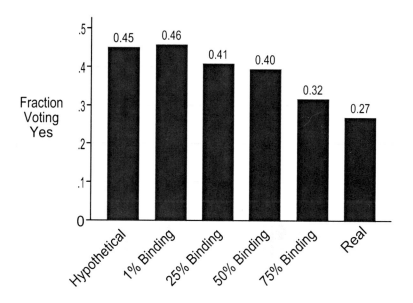

FIGURE 2. *Probabilistic Referenda in the Laboratory*
Source: Cummings et al. (1995)

6.1.3. Field Surveys

In 1993, a replication and extension of the ExxonValdez oil spill survey of Carson et al. (1992, 2003) was conducted. The replication was close, in the sense that essentially the same survey instrument was used from the original study and the same in-person survey method used.[41] Three treatments were added that make the

1993 replication particularly interesting for present purposes, since they arguably served to make the voting task more realistic to the subject. One treatment was the use of a "ballot box" in which the respondent could privately deposit their response, and did not have to reveal it to the interviewer. Another treatment was the addition of a "no vote" option, such that respondents could explicitly say whether they were "for," "against," "not sure" or "would not vote." And a third treatment was a cross of the last two: the "no vote" option was implemented with a ballot box. The overall sample was 1,182, with roughly 25% allocated at random to each version.[42]

Within each version, each subject was asked how they would vote if the cost to their household was a particular amount, chosen at random from $10, $30, $60 or $120. In the surveys that did not use the ballot box, respondents were asked a follow-up question based on their initial responses; we ignore these follow-up responses, since they were not common over all versions and have some problems of interpretation. Results from the 1993 replication were published in Carson et al. (1998) and Krosnick et al. (2002).

Figure 3 displays the raw responses in each of the four versions. To simplify, the light grey lines with a circle marker indicate responses "for" the proposed policy to avoid another oil spill over the next 10 years, and the black lines with square markers indicate responses "against" the policy. Gray dashed lines with diamond markers, as appropriate, indicate "no vote" responses when asked for. These responses have not been adjusted for any population weights, or complex survey sample design features; nothing of consequence here is affected by those corrections.

The top left panel of Figure 3 shows that respondents tend to favor the policy on balance when the tax price is lowest, and that this net vote for the policy diminishes as the tax price increases. These results would suggest that the largest tax price that would just receive a majority vote would be around $60. The exact determination of the point at which the "for" responses equal 50% would be determined by applying one or another statistical estimators to the raw responses. Although there is some debate over the best estimators to apply, for now we will simply use the piecewise linear estimates connecting the raw responses.[43]

The use of the anonymous ballot box, in the top right panel of Figure 3, reduces the positive and negative responses at the lowest tax price of $10, but otherwise has relatively little effect in relation to the "original recipe" used in version #1. As a consequence there is much less net support for the proposal at that $10 level, which might become an issue if one recognized sampling errors around these responses. But the main effect of the ballot box is to dampen enthusiasm for respondents that are for or against the proposal at the lowest tax price, suggesting that those responses may have been affected by the presence of an observer of the vote.

The raw responses with the explicit "no vote" option are shown in the bottom left panel of Figure 3. Compared to version #1, above it, there is a very slight increase in the "for" responses at $10, and a marked reduction in the "against" responses. The other large change is the reduction in the "against" responses at the $120 tax price. Although the fraction of "no vote" responses increases slightly with the tax price, from 9% at $10 to 11% at $120, it is relatively constant with respect to tax price. Taken together, these changes suggest that this treatment may be picking up respondents that originally voted against the proposal because they reject one or more aspects of the scenario presented in the survey referendum.

When the "no vote" and ballot box treatments are crossed, in version #4, shown in the bottom right panel of Figure 3, the fraction of "no vote" responses goes up to around 15% for the lowest tax prices and then 21% for the highest tax price. The direct "for" and "against" responses at the lowest tax price are akin to those observed for version #2, in which the ballot box was the sole treatment. However, both are lower due to the fraction siphoned off into a "no vote" response. In fact, the policy scenario barely survives a vote even at the lowest tax price level of $10.

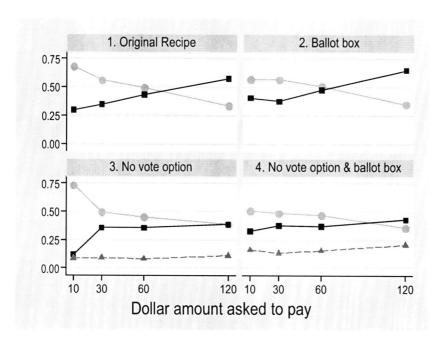

FIGURE 3. Raw Responses in 1993 Exxon Valdez CV Study

Figure 4 shows what the responses would be if we simply condition on voter turnout. When political elections are held, or real referenda voted on, nobody says very much about the "vote that might have been" if everyone had turned out.[44] Instead, what matters in law is simply the vote count based on those that chose to vote. The results for version #1 and version #2 are identical to those shown in Figure 3, of course, since they had no option not to vote. But the bottom panels in Figure 4 suggest that the policy has a much better chance of survival if the conditional vote is examined. All that is happening is that the votes "for" or "against" are both re-normalized by the same amount, so that the vote for the proposal equals or exceeds 50% for tax prices up to $60. Again, it should be noted that no standard errors are being placed around these responses, but the 2000 Presidential elections in the United States remind us that none need be as a matter of law.

Figures 5 and 6 examine the change in voting patterns due to the provision of the "no vote" option, varying by three different assumptions on how to interpret those that chose that option. In each case we show version #3 compared to version #1, and version #4 compared to version #2, since that makes the pure effect of the "no vote" treatment clear. The solid lines are the original responses, from Figure 3, and the dotted overlaid line is the set of responses from the treatment with the "no vote" option and the specific interpretation assumed. We also treat those that said that they were "not sure" as equivalent to not voting – they correspond to those that turn up to vote, go into the voting booth, and cast an invalid vote.[45]

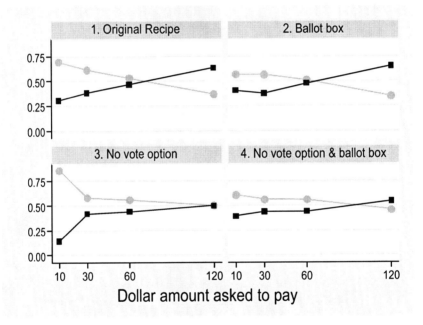

FIGURE 4. Responses Conditional on Voter Turnout

Figure 5 shows the effect of assuming that a "no vote" response means that the individual would not have turned up for the election, and hence that the referenda would stand or fall on the votes actually cast by those that did turn up. In effect, it overlays the bottom two panels of Figure 3 (the solid lines in Figure 5) with the bottom two panels of Figure 4 (the dotted lines in Figure 5).

The conclusion is that interpreting a "no vote" response in this manner significantly improves the chances of approval of this policy. The tax price at which the proposal is supported at the 50% level is either $120 or around $100, depending on the use of the ballot box.

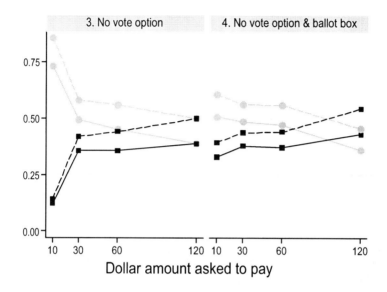

FIGURE 5. *Effect of Endogenous Voter Turnout if "No Vote" or "Unsure" Responses Mean "No Turnout"*

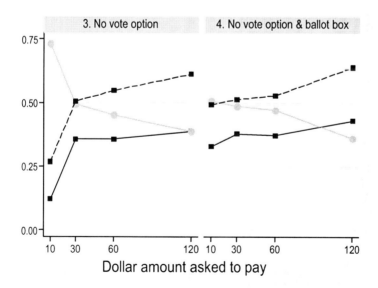

FIGURE 6. *Effect of Endogenous Voter Turnout if "No Vote" or "Unsure" Reponses Mean "Against"*

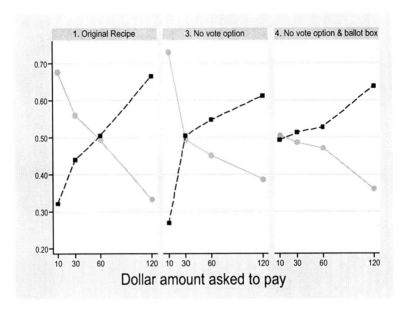

FIGURE 7. *Comparison Undertaken by Carson et al. (1997) Assuming "No Vote" or*
"Unsure" Responses Mean "Against"

Figure 6, on the other hand, paints a different outcome for the policy. In this case
the "no vote" responses are interpreted as voting "against" the proposal, and the
proposal fails at much lower tax prices. In the absence of a ballot box, the
referendum proposal barely passes at the $30 level, and with the ballot box it barely
survives at the $10 level.

These results indicate that for one of the most important survey referenda ever
mounted in the field of environmental valuation, the inferences are very sensitive to
how one interprets responses. How have previous studies interpreted these
responses?

Carson et al. (1997) consider version #1 only, and adopt (p.156) an agnostic
stance with respect to the "unsure" responses. They show the effects of interpreting
them as "against," as a separate category, and as being irrelevant (in the sense of
being deleted and allowing the existing votes to be re-normalized). In context, their
approach is appropriate, since they are only testing the temporal stability of the
responses from 1991 to 1993.[46]

Carson et al. (1998) consider version #1 and version #3 only, and adopt (p.336)
the interpretation of "no vote" responses employed in our Figure 6. Their
comparison is actually a hybrid of ones displayed here, so it is useful to visualize it
explicitly. Figure 7 does so, also including version #4 for good measure. The "for"
responses are the raw ones shown in Figure 3, so they are drawn with a solid line to
indicate the raw response. The "against" responses are the constructed responses
based on the raw responses as well as the assumption that "no vote" and "unsure" are

the same as an "against" vote. Carson et al. (1998) conclude that the two left-hand panels in Figure 7 are not statistically different. Since they look different to the naked eye, it is useful to go through the statistical tests they use to draw their conclusion.

The first test is a simple contingency table test of independence, where one treatment is the "for" or "against" response and the other treatment is the provision of a "no vote" option or not. They undertake these tests for each tax price. With the $10 tax price, for example, the 68% and 32% responses in the left panel (which are 59 individuals and 28 individuals) are compared to the 73% and 27% responses in the right panel (or 60 individuals and 22 individuals), using standard tests. The χ^2 statistic is 0.58 in this case, with a p-value of 0.45, so one cannot reject the null that these treatments are independent. Similarly for the other tax prices. The problem is that these tests have extremely low power at these sample sizes. Using a p-value of 5% for a two-tailed test, one would need samples of over 1500 per cell in order to reject the above null hypothesis with a power of 0.90 or greater. Alternatively, with the actual samples of only 87 and 82, the power for tests of this null hypothesis is only 0.086.

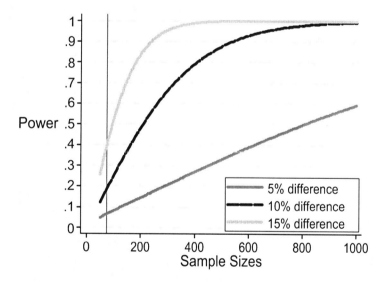

FIGURE 8. Power Curves for Test of Null Hypothesis of 50% "Yes" Responses

Figure 8 shows how bleak things are for any interesting hypothesis test using nonparametric tests such as the one just referred to. The null hypothesis in Figure 8 is that the "for" responses are 50% of the votes. The alternative hypotheses are that there is a 5, 10 or 15 percentage-point difference, to consider the range of practical interest here. The ability to detect a 5 percentage-point difference is very low indeed at samples of around 75, as indicated by the vertical line. Only when samples get well above 1,000 can one begin to believe that these tests are detecting such differences with any acceptable power. Of course, larger differences can be detected with greater power for the same sample sizes, but even 15 percentage-point differences will be detected with low power for samples sizes around 75.

One implication is that, since the sample sizes cannot be increased, we must be prepared to make some parametric assumptions about responses in order to detect differences due to these treatments. This is what Carson et al. (1998) do, by considering parametric statistical models of responses.

Returning to Figure 7, consider the effect of moving from version #1 to version #4: the referendum fails, or comes close to failing, at the lowest tax price of $10. It definitely fails at any higher tax price. No statistical tests are needed in this case to see that the interpretation of the CV, plus the use of different versions, makes a huge difference to the implied damages.

6.2. Scenario Ambiguity

One of the first "cultural" differences that strikes an experimental economist dipping his toes into the sea of CV and SC studies is how careful those studies are in their choice of language on some matters and how incredibly vague they are on other matters. The best CV studies spend a lot time, and money, on focus groups in which they tinker with minute details of the scenario and the granular resolution of pictures used in displays. But they often leave the most basic of the "rules of the game" for the subject unclear.

For example, consider the words used to describe the scenario in the Valdez study. Forget the simple majority-rule referendum interpretation used by the researchers, and focus on the words actually presented to the subjects. The relevant passages concerning the provision rule are quite vague.

How might the subjects be interpreting specific passages? Consider one hypothetical subject. He is first told,

> In order to prevent damages to the area's natural environment from another spill, a special safety program has been proposed. We are conducting this survey to find out whether this special program is worth anything to your household" (p.52).

Are the proposers of this program going to provide it no matter what I say, and then come for a contribution afterwards? In this case, I should free ride, even if I value the good. Or, are they actually going to use our responses to decide on the program? If so, am I that Mystical Measure-Zero Median voter whose response might "pivot" the whole project into implementation? In this case, I should tell the truth.

Actually, the subject just needs to attach some positive subjective probability to the chance of being the decisive voter. As that probability declines, so does the (hypothetical) incentive to tell the truth. So, to paraphrase Dirty Harry the interviewer, "do you feel like a specific order statistic today, punk?" Tough question, and presumably one that the subject has guessed at an answer to. I am just adding additional layers of guesswork to the main story, to make clear the extent of the potential ambiguity involved.

Returning to the script, the subjects are later told, "If the program was approved, here is how it would be paid for." But who will decide if it is to be approved? Me, or is that out of my hands as a respondent? As noted above, the answer matters for my rational response. The subjects were asked if they had any questions about how the program would be paid for (p. 55), and had any confusions clarified then. But this is no substitute for the control of being explicit and clear in the prepared part of the survey instrument.

Later in the survey the subjects are told, "Because everyone would bear part of the cost, we are using this survey to ask people how they would vote if they had the chance to vote on the program" (p.55). Okay, this suggests that the provision rule would be just like those local public school bond issues I always vote on, so the program will (hypothetically) go ahead if more than 50% of those that vote say "yes" at the price they are asking me to pay.[47] But I am bothered by that phrase "if they had the chance to vote." Does this mean that they are not actually going to ask me to vote and decide if the program goes ahead, but are just floating the idea to see if I would be willing to pay something for it after they go ahead with the program? Again, the basic issue of the provision rule is left unclear. The final statement of relevance does nothing to resolve this possible confusion: "If the program cost your household a total of $(amount) would you vote for the program or against it?" (p.56).

Is this just "semantics"? Yes, but it is not "just semantics." Semantics are relevant if we define it as the study of "what words mean and how these meanings combine in sentences to form sentence meanings" (Allen (1995; p.10)). Semantics, along with syntax and context, are critical determinants of any claim that a sentence in a CV instrument can be unambiguously interpreted. The fact that a unique set of words can have multiple, valid interpretations is generally well known to CV researchers. Nonetheless, it appears to have also been well forgotten in this instance, since the subject simply cannot know the rules of the voting game he is being asked to play.

More seriously, we cannot claim as outside observers of his survey response that we know what the subject is guessing at.[48] We can, of course, guess at what the subject is guessing at. This is what Carson et al. (1992) do when they choose to interpret the responses in one way rather than another, but this is still just a dressed-up guess. Moreover, it is a serious one for the claim that subjects may have an incentive to free ride, quite aside from the hypothetical bias problem.

The general point is that one can avoid these problems with more explicit language about the exact conditions under which the program would be implemented and payments elicited. I fear that CV researchers would shy away from such language since it would likely expose to the subject the truth about the hypothetical nature of the survey instrument. The illusory attraction of the frying pan again.

6.3. Salient Rewards

Experimental economics differentiates between nonsalient rewards and salient rewards. The former refer to rewards that do not vary with performance in the task, for example, an initial endowment of cash, or perhaps the show-up fee.[49] The latter refers to rewards that vary with performance in the task. In parallel to the distinction between fixed and variable costs, these might be called fixed rewards and variable rewards. The hypothetical setting for virtually all of the experiments considered here should be better referred to as experiments with nonsalient rewards, since subjects were typically rewarded for participating. The hypothetical surveys popular in the field rarely reward subjects for participating, although it has occurred in some cases. There could be a difference between the nonsalient experiments which are called "hypothetical" and "truly hypothetical" experiments in which there are no rewards (salient or nonsalient). More systematic variation in the nonsalient rewards provided in CV studies would allow examination of these effects.

7. CONCLUSIONS

There is no reliable way to trick subjects into thinking that something is in their best interests when it is not. Nonetheless, the literature on nonmarket valuation in environmental economics is littered with assertions that one can somehow trick people into believing something that is not true. One probably can, if deception is allowed, but such devices cannot be reliable more than once. The claims tend to take the form, "if we frame the hypothetical task the same way as some real-world task that is incentive compatible, people will view it as incentive compatible." The same view tends to arise in the SC literature, but is just a variant on a refrain that has a longer history.

There are some specifications which do appear to mitigate hypothetical bias in some settings, but such instances do not provide a general behavioral proof that can be used as a crutch in other instances. For example, there is some evidence that one can isolate hypothetical bias to the "buy or no-buy" stage of a nested purchase decision, and thereby mitigate the effects on demand for a specific product. Similarly, there is some evidence that one can avoid hypothetical bias by using ranking tasks rather than choice or valuation tasks. In each case there are interesting conjectures about the latent decision-making process that provide some basis for believing that the specific results might generalize. But we simply do not know yet, and the danger of generalizing is both obvious and habitually neglected in the environmental valuation literature. These possibilities should be explored, and evaluated in other settings, before relied on casually to justify avoiding the issue.

The only recommendation that can be made from experiments designed to test for incentive compatibility and hypothetical bias is that one has to address the issue head on. If one can deliver the commodity, which is the case in many SC applications in marketing, do so. If it is expensive, such as a beta product, then do so for a sub-sample to check for hypothetical bias and correct it statistically. If it is prohibitive or impossible, which is the case in many SC applications in environmental economics, use controlled experiments for a surrogate good as a complementary tool. That is, find some deliverable private or public good that has some of the attributes of the target good, conduct experiments to measure hypothetical bias using samples drawn from the same population, and use the results to calibrate the instrument and/or the responses. And explore the task specifications that appear to mitigate hypothetical bias. Above all, read with great suspicion any study that casually sweeps the problem under the rug.

---

8. ENDNOTES

I am grateful to Mark Dickie, Shelby Gerking, Michael Hanemann, Bengt Kriström, John List, J. Walter Milon, Elisabet Rutström and V. Kerry Smith for conversations and healthy debate. Financial support from the U.S. National Science Foundation under grant NSF/HSD 0527675 and grant NSF/SES 0616746 is gratefully acknowledged. Supporting data are stored at http://exlab.bus.ucf.edu.

[1] The MPL is now widely used in experimental economics, as discussed later. It has a longer history in the elicitation of hypothetical valuation responses in contingent valuation survey settings, discussed by Mitchell and Carson (1989, p. 100, fn. 14).

[2] Section 3 reviews the brief history of the experimental literature on hypothetical bias, and section 5 focuses more narrowly on varieties of choice tasks that are relevant for CV. More detail on the experimental literature is provided by Harrison and Rutström (2006a) and Harrison (2006b).

[3] A dictatorial mechanism is one in which the outcome always reflects the preferences of one specific agent, independent of the preferences of others.

[4] See Gibbard (1973) and Satterthwaite (1975) for the original statements of this theorem, and Moulin (1988) for an exposition.

[5] See Rasmussen (1989; p.161). The Epsilon Truthfulness assumption is used in formal mechanism design problems when the incentive constraints are defined so as to ensure that the expected utility to each agent from a truthful report is greater than *or equal to* the expected utility from any other feasible report.

[6] Kurz (1974; p.333) uses this assumption and notes clearly that it is not to be accepted lightly: "As innocent as it may look, [this assumption] is a very strong one and we hope to remove it in future work; however, some experimental results by Bohm (1972) suggest that this assumption may not be unreasonable." Bohm (1994) later argues that his 1972 results do *not* support such a conclusion. See Harrison (1989, 1992, 1994) for a debate on related methodological issues in experimental economics.

[7] The adoption of this assertion by DOI and NOAA is apparently based on a reference to the following statement that appears in an appendix to the NOAA Panel report of Arrow et al. (1993): "As already noted, such a question form [a dichotomous choice question posed as a vote for or against a level of taxation] also has advantage in terms of incentive compatibility" (p. 4612). This reference ignores, however, the text of the NOAA Panel's report which includes a lengthy discussion of the advantages and disadvantages of the referendum format used in the *hypothetical* setting of an application of the CV method (pp. 4606-4607), discussions which belie the later assertion of incentive compatibility. Among the disadvantages discussed by them are the respondent's reactions to a hypothetical survey, the fact that there can be no real implication that a tax will actually be levied, and the damage actually repaired or avoided. Thus, the NOAA Panel suggests that "...considerable efforts should be made to induce respondents to take the question seriously, and that the CV instrument should contain other questions designed to detect whether the respondent has done so" (1993; p.4606). Further, the NOAA Panel notes an additional problem that could detract from the reliability of CV responses: "A feeling that one's vote will have no significant effect on the outcome of the hypothetical referendum, leading to no reply or an unconsidered one...." (1993; p.4607).

[8] Free riding is said to occur when a subject does not make any contribution to the provision of a public good, assuming the subject has some positive value from the provision of the good.

[9] This point can be stated more formally by thinking of the choice study as a game between the surveyor and the respondent. There is a difference between complete information and common knowledge in strategic games that captures this distinction. Surveyors can tell subjects something that is true, but that is a not the same thing as knowing that subjects believe those things to be true. Linguistics has rich traditions that help us think about the everyday transition to common knowledge in these settings. Statistical approaches to the linguistic issue of how people resolve ambiguous sentences in natural languages are becoming quite standard. See, for example, Allen (1995; Ch.7, 10) and Schütze (1997; Ch.2), and the references cited there. Nonstatistical approaches, using axioms of conversation to disambiguate sentences, are proposed in another line of linguistic research by Grice (1989) and Clark (1992).

[10] Carson et al. (2001; p.191) appear to take issue with this claim, but one simply has to parse what they say carefully to understand it as actually in agreement: "For provision of private or quasi-public goods, a yes response increases the likelihood that the good will be provided, however, the actual decision to purchase the good need not be made until later. Thus, a yes response increases the choice set at no expense." They are not clear on the matter, so one has to fill in the blanks to make sense of this. If the DC involves a real commitment, such that the subject gets the private good if private money is given up, then the yes response does not increase the choice set for free. So Carson et al. cannot be referring to a real DC response in their statement. In the case of a hypothetical DC for private goods, it does not follow that the yes response increases the likelihood of the good being provided. Of course, subjects are entitled to hold whatever false expectations they want, but the explicit script in Cummings et al. (1995) contained nothing intended to lead them to that belief. Carson et al. (2001) then suggest how one can make this setting, which can only be interpreted as referring to a hypothetical DC, incentive compatible: "The desirable incentive properties of a binary discrete choice question can be restored in instances where the agent is asked to choose between two alternatives, neither of which represents a strict addition to the choice set." Their footnote 44 then explains what they mean: "It can be shown that what a coercive payment vehicle does is to effectively convert a situation whereby an addition to the choice set (e.g., a new public good) *looks like* a choice between two alternatives, neither of which is a subset of the other, by ensuring the extraction of payment for the good" (emphasis added). So this is just saying that one can make a hypothetical DC incentive compatible by requiring real payment, which is the point that Cummings, Harrison and Rutström (1995) viewed as apparent and hardly in need of notation and proof. The words "look like" are problematic to an experimental economist. They suggest that one must rely on subjects misunderstanding the hypothetical nature of the task in order for it to be incentive compatible. But if subjects misunderstand part of the instructions, how does one know that they have understood all of the rest? Circular logic of this kind is precisely why one needs stark experiments.

[11] Some researchers fall back defensively to notions of *weak* incentive compatibility, and seem content to use awkward double-negatives such as "the subjects had no incentive not to misrepresent their preferences, so I assume they told the truth." This ploy was reviewed earlier, in the context of a discussion by Rasmussen (1989; p.161) of the Epsilon Truthfulness assumption in game theory.

[12] Haab et al. (1999) argue for allowing the residual variance of the statistical model to vary with the experimental treatment. They show that such heteroskedasticity corrections can lead the *coefficients* on the experimental treatment to become statistically insignificant, if one looks only at the coefficient of the treatment on the mean effect. This is true, but irrelevant for the determination of the *marginal effect* of the experimental treatment, which takes into account the joint effect of the experimental treatment variable on the mean response and on the residual variance. That marginal effect remains statistically significant in the original setting they consider, which is the referendum experiments of CEHM.

[13] This is smaller than the difference estimated by Coller and Williams (1999; p. 120), although qualitatively consistent. As noted, their estimation sample included several treatment variations in the real subsample that could have confounded inferences about hypothetical bias.

[14] The coefficient estimate is 0.23, implying that the estimated standard error in the real task is only 23% of the standard error in the hypothetical task since we employ a multiplicative heteroskedasticity specification. The p-value on this estimate is 0.51, however.

[15] An additional treatment was to control for the order of presentation of the task within each MPL table.

[16] Alternative statistical specifications might be expected to lead to different estimates of risk attitudes, although one would not expect radically different estimates. On the other hand, alternative specifications that deviate from traditional expected utility theory (EUT), such as allowance for probability weighting, might lead to very different inferences about hypothetical bias.

[17] The use of clustering to allow for panel effects from unobserved individual effects is common in the statistical survey literature. Clustering commonly arises in national field surveys from the fact that physically proximate households are often sampled to save time and money, but it can also arise from more homely sampling procedures. For example, Williams (2000; p.645) notes that it could arise from dental studies that "collect data on each tooth surface for each of several teeth from a set of patients" or "repeated measurements or recurrent events observed on the same person." The procedures for allowing for clustering allow heteroskedasticity between and within clusters, as well as autocorrelation within clusters. They are closely related to the "generalized estimating equations" approach to panel estimation in epidemiology (see Liang and Zeger, 1986), and generalize the "robust standard errors" approach popular in econometrics (see Rogers, 1993).

[18] Harrison (2006a) also shows that these inferences about hypothetical bias are sensitive to non-EUT specifications. However, there is also evidence of hypothetical bias in the probability weighting function of (separable) prospect theory, when applied to these data.

[19] That is, one task is selected after all choices have been made, and the subject plays it out and receives the consequences. This avoids the potentially contaminating effects of changes in real income if one plays out all choices sequentially.

[20] As a procedural matter, experimental economists generally rely on physical randomizing devices, such as die and bingo cages, when randomization plays a central role in the mechanism. There is a long tradition in psychology of subjects second-guessing computer-generated random numbers, and the unfortunate use of deception in many fields from which economists recruit subjects makes it impossible to rely on the subject trusting the experimenter in such things.

[21] When subjects are indifferent over options, it does not follow that they will choose at random. They might use other heuristics to make choices which exhibit systematic biases. For example, concern with a possible left-right bias leads experimental economists looking at lottery-choice behavior to randomize the order of presentation.

[22] See List et al. (2006) for some evidence consistent with this conjecture.

[23] After removing subjects that failed to complete the survey in some respect, there are 91 remaining subjects.

[24] See Harrison and Rutström (2006b) for one review.

[25] This is not to disavow the use of casual introspection, particularly when it is prohibitively costly in terms of money or time to collect data in the laboratory. Many of the wording and logistical suggestions of Dillman (1978), for example, seem plausible and sensible enough a priori that one would not bother applying scarce research dollars testing them.

[26] The qualification here refers to the existence of a feasible and affordable laboratory procedure for eliciting valuations from subjects that are truthful. Such procedures clearly exist for private, deliverable goods. They also exist for public, deliverable goods under certain circumstances. They do not presently exist for nondeliverable goods.

[27] The possible use of estimated bias functions for public goods valuation was first proposed by Kurz (1974). A subsequent, and brief, discussion of the idea appears in Freeman (1979). Although restricted to the private goods experiments of CHR, Blackburn et al. (1994) appears to be the first application and test of the idea. Finally, the idea of bias function estimation was raised by Roy Radner at a public meeting into the use of CV method conducted under the auspices of the National Oceanic and Atmospheric Administration (1992). He asked one speaker, "... what would be a practical method, if any, of taking the results of the CVM [CV method] willingness to pay and adjusting them ... in order to come to a damage assessment? How would one go about that?" (p. 99), and later followed up with a related question: "... are there things that one can do when one does the CVM, if one were to do it, and that would minimize this bias and, secondly, enable one to estimate it?" (p. 100). The studies reviewed here attempt to provide answers to these questions.

[28] Related work on statistical calibration functions includes Fox et al. (1998), Johannesson et al. (1999), Harrison et al. (1999) and List and Shogren (1998, 2002).

[29] Mitchell and Carson (1989) provide a popular and detailed review of many of the traits of "bad hypothetical surveys." One might question the importance of some of these traits, but that debate is beyond the scope of this review.

[30] See Hensher et al.(1999) and Louviere et al. (2000; chs.8, 13) for reviews.

[31] Unfortunately the data from this study are not available for public evaluation (Trudy Cameron; personal communication), so one cannot independently assess the effects of alternative specifications.

[32] Using the acronyms of the original study, this compares the 0-ACT and 1-PDC treatments, which are as close as possible other than the hypothetical nature of the response elicited.

[33] In the SC literature they refer to unobserved individual idiosyncracies of tastes (e.g., Louviere et al. (2000; p.38)), and in the stochastic choice literature they also refer to trembles or errors by the individual (e.g., Hey, 1995).

[34] This is particularly clear in the exposition of Louviere et al. (2000; p. 237, 244) since they use the notation α^{RP} and α^{SP} for the intercepts from data sources RP and SP, and a common β for the pooled estimates.

[35] Interactions may or may not be identified, but they only complicate the already-complicated picture.

[36] Despite this negative assessment of the potential of this approach for constructive calibration of differences between hypothetical and real responses, the "data enrichment" metaphor that originally motivated this work in marketing is an important and fundamental one for economics.

[37] Louviere et al (2000; p. 233) use the notation α^{RP} and α^{SP} for the intercepts from data sources RP and SP, and β^{RP} and β^{SP} for the coefficient estimates.

[38] Fox et al. (1998; p.456) offer two criticisms of the earlier calibration approach of Blackburn et al. (1994). The first is that it is "inconclusive" since one of the bias functions has relatively large standard errors. But such information on the imprecision of valuations is just as important as information on the point estimates if it correctly conveys the uncertainty of the elicitation process. In other words, it is informative to convey one's imprecision in value estimation if the decision maker is not neutral to risk. The second criticism is that Blackburn et al. (1994) only elicit a calibration function for one price on a demand schedule in their illustration of their method, and that the calibration function might differ for different prices. This is certainly correct, but hardly a fundamental criticism of the method in general.

[39] Cummings et al. (1995a) and Cummings and Taylor (1999) demonstrate how one could evaluate such "cheap talk" in a controlled experimental manner.

[40] The cover letter was dated August 28, 1990.

[41] Carson et al. (1997) compare the original Exxon Valdez survey referendum and the 1993 replication, finding no statistical difference between the two. Carson et al. (1992; Table 5-5, p.95) report that the raw percentage vote for the proposal in the original referendum survey was 68%, 52%, 50% and 36%, respectively, at tax prices of $10, $30, $60 and $120. This compares with raw responses of 68%, 56%, 49% and 33% in the 1993 replication.

[42] In the end, sample sizes for versions 1 through 4 were 300, 271, 322 and 289, or 25.4%, 22.9%, 27.2% and 24.5%, respectively. Samples were drawn from 12 primary sampling units across the country.

[43] One could use a simple probit estimator, in which the tax price was an independent variable and the "for" responses the dependent variable. In this case the estimated tax price can be solved from the estimated equation, which could control for individual characteristics in the sample to ensure comparability across versions. Using such a model one calculates damages for versions 1 through 4 of $1.390 billion, $2.587 billion, $1.641 billion and $3.659 billion, respectively. These calculations employ synthetic tax prices between $1 and $500 in increments of $1.

[44] Actually, voter turnout is the main focus of party activists prior to elections, and can vary dramatically from election to election.

[45] Again, recall the Florida recount in the 2000 Presidential elections in the United States.

[46] The issue of temporal stability arose from the report of the NOAA Panel contained in Arrow et al. (1994). The concern was that public outrage soon after an oil spill might lead to relatively high valuations of damages compared to valuations conducted much later. Without further assumptions about the propriety of valuation differences, however, there is no reason for one to believe that valuations ought to be temporally stable, as Carson et al. (1997; p.159ff.) note. Moreover, there is little *a priori* reason to expect valuations elicited 22 months after the oil spill to be different from valuations elicited 39 months after. The real issue here is likely to involve comparisons much closer to the time of the spill, although even then there is nothing to say that such valuations should be the same as later valuations.

[47] Each household was given a "price" which suggested that others may pay a different "price." This is standard in such referendum formats, and could be due to the vote being on some fixed formula that taxes the household according to assessed wealth. Although the survey does not clarify this for the subjects, it would be an easy matter to do so.

[48] Statistical approaches to the linguistic issue of how people resolve ambiguous sentences in natural languages are becoming quite standard. See, for example, Allen (1995; Ch.7, 10) and the references cited there.

[49] The show-up fee is fixed conditional on the subject turning up and participating. It is definitely presumed to be salient with respect to the participation decision.

9. REFERENCES

Aadland, D. and A.J. Caplan, 2003, "Willingness to Pay for Curbside Recycling with Detection and Mitigation of Hypothetical Bias," *American Journal of Agricultural Economics*, 85: 492-502.

Adamowicz, W., J. Louviere and M. Williams, M., 1994, "Combining Stated and Revealed Preference Methods for Valuing Environmental Amenities," *Journal of Environmental Economics and Management*, 26: 271-292.

Afriat, S., 1967, "The Construction of a Utility Function from Expenditure Data," *International Economic Review*, 8: 67-77.

Allen, J., 1995, *Natural Language Understanding,* Redwood City, CA: Benjamin/Cummings, Second Edition.

Andersen, S., G.W. Harrison, M.I. Lau and E.E. Rutström, 2006a, "Elicitation Using Multiple Price Lists," *Experimental Economics*, forthcoming.

Andersen, S., G.W. Harrison, M.I. Lau, and E.E. Rutström, 2006b, "Valuation Using Multiple Price Lists," *Applied Economics*, forthcoming.

Arrow, K., R. Solow, P. Portney, E.E. Leamer, R. Radner and H. Schuman, 1993, "Report of the NOAA Panel on Contingent Valuation," *Federal Register*, 58(10): 4602-4614.

Binswanger, H.P., 1980 "Attitudes Toward Risk: Experimental Measurement in Rural India," *American Journal of Agricultural Economics*, 62: 395-407.

Blackburn, M., G.W. Harrison, and E.E. Rutström, 1994, "Statistical Bias Functions and Informative Hypothetical Surveys," *American Journal of Agricultural Economics*, 76(5): 1084-1088.

Blumenschein, K. , M. Johannesson, G.C. Blomquist, B. Liljas, and R.M. O'Coner, 1998, "Experimental Results on Expressed Certainty and Hypothetical Bias in Contingent Valuation," *Southern Economic Journal*, 65: 169-177.

Blumenschein, K., M. Johanneson, K.K Yokoyama and P.R. Freeman, 2001, "Hypothetical Versus Real Willingness to Pay in the Health Care Sector: Results from a Field Experiment," *Journal of Health Economics*, 20: 441-457.

Bohm, P., 1972, "Estimating Demand for Public Goods: An Experiment," *European Economic Review*, 3: 111-130.

Bohm, P., 1994, "CVM Spells Responses to Hypothetical Questions," Natural Resources Journal, 34(1): 37-50.

Bohm, P., J. Lindén and J. Sonnegård, 1997, "Eliciting Reservation Prices: Becker-DeGroot-Marschak Mechanisms vs. Markets," *Economic Journal*, 107: 1079-1089.

Boyce, R.R., T.C. Brown, G.H. McClelland, G. Peterson and W.D. Schulze, 1989, "Experimental Evidence of Existence Value in Payment and Compensation Contexts," in Western Regional Research Project W-133: Benefits and Costs in Natural Resources Planning, Interim Report 2, K.J. Boyle and T. Heekin, Eds., Department of Agricultural and Resource Economics, University of Maine, Orono, July 1, 1989.

Brown, T.C., I. Ajzen and D. Hrubes, 2003, "Further Tests of Entreaties to Avoid Hypothetical Bias in Referendum Contingent Valuation," *Journal of Environmental Economics and Management*, 46(2): 353-361.

Cameron, T.A., G.L. Poe, R.G. Ethier and W.D. Schulze, 2002, "Alternative Non-market Value-Elicitation Methods: Are the Underlying Preferences the Same?" *Journal of Environmental Economics and Management*, 44: 391-425.

Carlsson, F. and P. Martinsson, 2001, "Do Hypothetical and Actual Marginal Willingness to Pay Differ in Choice Experiments?" *Journal of Environmental Economics and Management*, 41: 179-192.

Carson, R.T., 1991, "Constructed Markets," in *Measuring the Demand for Environmental Quality*, J.B. Braden and C.K. Kolstad, Eds., Amsterdam: North-Holland.

Carson, R.T., 1997, "Contingent Valuation: Theoretical Advances and Empirical Tests Since the NOAA Panel," *American Journal of Agricultural Economics*, 79(5): 1501-1507.

Carson, R.T., N.E. Flores and N.F. Meade, 2001, "Contingent Valuation: Controversies and Evidence," *Environmental and Resource Economics*, 19: 173-210.

Carson, R.T, W.M. Hanemann, R.J. Kopp, J.A. Krosnick, R.C. Mitchell, S. Presser, P.A. Ruud and V.K. Smith, 1997, "Temporal Reliability of Estimates from Contingent Valuation," *Land Economics,* 73(2): 151-163.

Carson, R.T., W.M. Hanemann, J.A. Krosnick, R.C. Mitchell, S. Presser, P.A. Ruud and V.K. Smith, 1998, "Referendum Design and Contingent Valuation: The NOAA Panel's No-Vote Recommendation," *Review of Economics and Statistics,* 80(2): 335-338; reprinted with typographical corrections in *Review of Economics and Statistics,* 80(3).

Carson, R.T., R.C. Mitchell, W.M. Hanemann, R.J. Kopp, S. Presser, P.A. Ruud, 1992, "A Contingent Valuation Study of Lost Passive Use Values Resulting From the Exxon Valdez Oil Spill," Anchorage: Attorney General of the State of Alaska.

Carson, R.T. R.C. Mitchell, W.M. Hanemann, R.J. Kopp, S. Presser and P.A. Ruud, 2003, "Contingent Valuation and Lost Passive Use: Damages from the Exxon Valdez," *Environmental and Resource Economics,* 25: 257-286.

Clark, H.H., 1992, *Arenas of Language Use,* Chicago: University of Chicago Press.

Coller, M. and M.B. Williams, 1999, "Eliciting Individual Discount Rates," *Experimental Economics,* 2: 107-127.

Cummings, R.G. and G.W. Harrison, 1994, "Was the Ohio Court Well Informed in Their Assessment of the Accuracy of the Contingent Valuation Method?," *Natural Resources Journal,* 34(1): 1-36.

Cummings, R.G. and G.W. Harrison, 1995, "The Measurement and Decomposition of Nonuse Values: A Critical Review," *Environmental and Resource Economics,* 5: 225-247.

Cummings, R.G., S. Elliott, G.W. Harrison and J. Murphy, 1997, "Are Hypothetical Referenda Incentive Compatible?" *Journal of Political Economy,* 105(3): 609-621.

Cummings, R.G., G.W. Harrison and L.L. Osborne, 1995a, "Can the Bias of Contingent Valuation Be Reduced? Evidence from the Laboratory," Economics Working Paper B-95-03, Division of Research, College of Business Administration, University of South Carolina, (see http://www.bus.ucf.edu/gharrison/wp/).

Cummings, R.G., G.W. Harrison and L.L. Osborne, 1995b, "Are Realistic Referenda Real?" Economics Working Paper B-95-06, Division of Research, College of Business Administration, University of South Carolina.

Cummings, R.G., G.W. Harrison and E.E. Rutström, 1995, "Homegrown Values and Hypothetical Surveys: Is the Dichotomous Choice Approach Incentive Compatible?" *American Economic Review,* 85(1): 260-266.

Cummings, R.G. and L.O. Taylor, 1998, "Does Realism Matter in Contingent Valuation Surveys?" *Land Economics,* 74(2): 203-215.

Cummings, R.G. and L.O. Taylor, 1999, "Unbiased Value Estimates for Environmental Goods: A Cheap Talk Design for the Contingent Valuation Method," *American Economic Review,* 89(3): 649-665.

Davis, D.D. and C.A. Holt, 1993, *Experimental Economics,* Princeton, NJ: Princeton University Press.

Department of the Interior, 1994, "Proposed Rules for Valuing Environmental Damages," Federal Register, 59(85): 23098-23111.

Dillman, D.A., 1978, *Mail and Telephone Surveys: The Total Design Method,* New York: Wiley.

Fischoff, B., 1991, "Value Elicitation. Is there Anything in There?," *American Psychologist,* 46: 835-847.

Fischoff, B. and L. Furby, 1988, "Measuring Values: A Conceptual Framework for Interpreting Transactions with Special Reference to Contingent Valuations of Visibility," *Journal of Risk and Uncertainty*, 1: 147-184.

Fox, J.A., J.F. Shogren, D.J. Hayes, and J.B. Kliebenstein, 1998, "CVM-X: Calibrating Contingent Values with Experimental Auction Markets," *American Journal of Agricultural Economics*, 80: 455-465.

Freeman III, A.M., 1979, *The Benefits of Environmental Improvement*, Baltimore: Johns Hopkins Press.

Gibbard, A., 1973, "Manipulation of Voting Schemes: A General Result," *Econometrica*, 41: 587-601.

Grice, P., 1989, *Studies in the Way of Words,* Cambridge, MA: Harvard University Press.

Haab, T.C., J-C. Huang and J.C. Whitehead, 1999, "Are Hypothetical Referenda Incentive Compatible? A Comment," *Journal of Political Economy*, 107(1): 186-196.

Harrison, G.W., 1989, "Theory and Misbehavior of First-Price Auctions," *American Economic Review*, 79: 749-762.

Harrison, G.W., 1990, "Risk Attitudes in First-Price Auction Experiments: A Bayesian Analysis," *Review of Economics & Statistics*, 72: 541-546.

Harrison, G.W. 1992, "Theory and Misbehavior of First-Price Auctions: Reply", *American Economic Review*, 82: 1426-1443.

Harrison, G.W., 1994, "Expected Utility Theory and the Experimentalists," *Empirical Economics*, 19(2): 223-253.

Harrison, G.W., 2006a, "Hypothetical Bias Over Uncertain Outcomes," in *Using Experimental Methods in Environmental and Resource Economics*, J.A. List, Ed., Northampton, MA: Elgar.

Harrison, G.W., 2006b, "Experimental Evidence on Alternative Environmental Valuation Methods," *Environmental & Resource Economics,* 34: 125-162.

Harrison, G.W., R.L. Beekman, L.B. Brown, L.A. Clements, T.M. McDaniel, S.L. Odom and M. Williams, 1996, "Environmental Damage Assessment With Hypothetical Surveys: The Calibration Approach," in *Topics in Environmental Economics*, M. Boman, R. Brännlund and B. Kriström, Eds., Amsterdam: Kluwer Academic Press.

Harrison, G.W. and J. Hirshleifer, 1998, "An Experimental Evaluation of Weakest-Link/Best-Shot Models of Public Goods," *Journal of Political Economy*, 97: 201-225.

Harrison, G. W. and M.I. Lau, 2005, "Is the Evidence for Hyperbolic Discounting in Humans Just An Experimental Artefact?" *Behavioral & Brain Sciences*, 28: 657.

Harrison, G.W., M.I. Lau, and M.B. Williams, 2002, "Estimating Individual Discount Rates for Denmark: A Field Experiment," *American Economic Review*, 92(5): 1606-1617.

Harrison, G.W.; M.I. Lau, E.E. Rutström and M.B. Sullivan, 2005, "Eliciting Risk and Time Preferences Using Field Experiments: Some Methodological Issues," in *Field Experiments in Economics,* J. Carpenter, G.W. Harrison and J.A. List, Eds., Greenwich, CT: JAI Press, Research in Experimental Economics, Volume 10.

Harrison, GW., and J.A. List, 2004, "Field Experiments," *Journal of Economic Literature*, 42(4): 1013-1059.

Harrison, G.W., R.M. Harstad and E.E. Rutström, 2004, "Experimental Methods and Elicitation of Values," *Experimental Economics*, 7(2): 123-140.

Harrison, G.W. and E.E. Rutström, 2006a, "Experimental Evidence on the Existence of Hypothetical Bias in Value Elicitation Methods," in *Handbook of Experimental Economics Results*, C.R. Plott and V.L. Smith, Eds., Amsterdam: North-Holland.

Harrison, G.W. and E.E. Rutström, 2006b, "Eliciting Subjective Beliefs About Mortality Risk Orderings," *Environmental & Resource Economics,* 33: 325-346.

Harstad, R.M., 2000, "Dominant Strategy Adoption and Bidders' Experience with Pricing Rules," *Experimental Economics*, 3(3): 261-280.

Hayes, D.J., J. Shogren, S.Y. Shin and J.B. Kliebenstein, 1995, "Valuing Food Safety in Experimental Auction Markets," *American Journal of Agricultural Economics*, 77: 40-53.

Hensher, D., J. Louviere and J.D. Swait, 1999, "Combining Sources of Preference Data*," Journal of Econometrics*, 89: 197-221.

Hey, J.D., 1995, "Experimental Investigations of Errors in Decision Making Under Risk," *European Economic Review*, 39: 633-640.

Hoffman, E., D.J. Menkhaus, D. Chakravarti, R.A. Field and G.D. Whipple, 1993, "Using Laboratory Experimental Auctions in Marketing Research: A Case Study of New Packaging for Fresh Beef," *Marketing Science*, 12(3): 318-338.

Holt, C.A. and S.K. Laury, 2002, "Risk Aversion and Incentive Effects," *American Economic Review*, 92(5): 1644-1655.

Holt, CA. and S.K. Laury, 2005, "Risk Aversion and Incentive Effects: New Data Without Order Effects," *American Economic Review*, 95(3): 902-912.

Horowitz, J.K., 1991, "Discounting Money Payoffs: An Experimental Analysis," *Handbook of Behavioral Economics,* Greenwich, CT: JAI Press, Inc., v. 2B: 309-324.

Imber, D. G. Stevenson and L.A. Wilks, 1991, "A Contingent Valuation Survey of the Kakadu Conservation Zone," Canberra: Australian Government Publishing Service for the Resource Assessment Commission.

Johannesson, M., G.C. Blomquist, K. Blumenschein, P-O. Johansson, B. Liljas and R.M. O'Conner, 1999, "Calibrating Hypothetical Willingness to Pay Responses," *Journal of Risk and Uncertainty*, 8: 21-32.

Kagel, J.H., R.M. Harstad and D. Levin, 1987, "Information Impact and Allocation Rules in Auctions with Affiliated Private Values: A Laboratory Study," *Econometrica*, 55: 1275-1304.

Kahneman, D., J.L. Knetsch and R.H. Thaler, 1990, "Experimental Tests of the Endowment Effect and the Coase Theorem," *Journal of Political Economy*, 98: 1325-1348.

Krosnick, J.A., A.L. Holbrook, M.K. Berent, R.T. Carson, W.M. Hanemann, R.J. Kopp, R.C. Mitchell, S. Presser, P.A. Ruud, V.K. Smith, W.R. Moody, M.C. Green and M. Conaway, 2002, "The Impact of 'No Opinion' Response Options on Data Quality: Non-Attitude Reduction or an Invitation to Satisfice?" *Public Opinion Quarterly*, 66: 371-403.

Kurz, M., 1974, "Experimental Approach to the Determination of the Demand for Public Goods," *Journal of Public Economics*, 3: 329-348.

Liang, K-Y. and S.L. Zeger, 1986, "Longitudinal Data Analysis Using Generalized Linear Models," *Biometrika*, 73: 13-22.

List, J.A., 2001, "Do Explicit Warnings Eliminate the Hypothetical Bias in Elicitation Procedures? Evidence from Field Auctions for Sportscards," *American Economic Review*, 91(5): 1498-1507.

List, J.A. and J.F. Shogren, 1998, "Calibration of the Differences Between Actual and Hypothetical Valuations in a Field Experiment," *Journal of Economic Behavior and Organization*, 37: 193-205.

List, J.A. and J.F. Shogren, 1999, "Price Signals and Bidding Behavior in Second-Price Auctions with Repeated Trials," *American Journal of Agricultural Economics*, 81: 942-929.

List, J.A. and J.F. Shogren, 2002, "Calibration of Willingness-to-Accept," *Journal of Environmental Economics and Management*, 43(2): 219-233.

List, J.A., P. Sinha and M. Taylor, 2006, "Using Choice Experiments to Value Non-Market Goods and Services: Evidence from the Field," *Advances in Economic Analysis and Policy*, 6(2): Article 2; http://www.bepress.com/bejeap/advances/vol6/iss2/art2.

Loomes, G., C. Starmer and R. Sugden, Robert, 2003, "Do Anomalies Disappear in Repeated Markets?" *Economic Journal*, 113: C153-C166.

Loomis, J., A. Gonzalez-Caban, and R. Gregory, 1994, "Do Reminders of Substitutes and Budget Constraints Influence Contingent Valuation Estimates?" *Land Economics*, 70: 499-506.

Loomis, J., T. Brown, B. Lucero and G. Peterson, 1996, "Improving Validity Experiments of Contingent Valuation Methods: Results of Efforts to Reduce the Disparity of Hypothetical and Actual Willingness to Pay," *Land Economics*, 72(4): 450-461.

Louviere, J.J., D.A. Hensher, and J.D. Swait, 2000, *Stated Choice Methods: Analysis and Application*, New York: Cambridge University Press.

Lusk, J.L. and T.C. Schroeder, 2004, "Are Choice Experiments Incentive Compatible? A Test with Quality Differentiated Beef Steaks," *American Journal of Agricultural Economics*, 86(2): 467-482.

Schulze, W., G. McClelland, D. Waldman and J. Lazo, 1996, "Sources of Bias in Contingent Valuation," in *The Contingent Valuation of Environmental Resources: Methodological Issues and Research Needs*, D. Bjornstad and J. Kahn, Eds., Cheltenham, UK: Edward Elgar.

Milgrom, P.R. and R.J. Weber, 1982, "A Theory of Auctions and Competitive Bidding," *Econometrica*, 50(5): 1089-1122.

Mitchell, R.C. and R.T. Carson, 1989, *Using Surveys to Value Public Goods: The Contingent Valuation Method*, Baltimore: Johns Hopkins Press.

Moulin, H., 1988, *Axioms of Cooperative Decision Making*, New York: Cambridge University Press.

Murphy, J.J., T. Stevens and D. Weatherhead, Darryl, 2003, "An Empirical Study of Hypothetical Bias in Voluntary Contribution Contingent Valuation: Does Cheap Talk Matter?" Unpublished Manuscript, Department of Resource Economics, University of Massachusetts.

Nape, S.W., P. Frykblom, G.W. Harrison and J.C. Lesley, 2003, "Hypothetical Bias and Willingness to Accept," *Economic Letters*, 78(3): 423-430.

National Oceanic and Atmospheric Administration, 1992, "Contingent Valuation Panel, Public Meeting, Wednesday, August 12, 1992," Certified Official Transcript, 283 pp. plus attachments, Department of Commerce, Washington, DC.

National Oceanographic and Atmospheric Administration, 1994a, "Proposed Rules for Valuing Environmental Damages," *Federal Register*, 59(5): 1062-1191.

National Oceanic and Atmospheric Administration, 1994b, "Natural Resource Damage Assessments; Proposed Rules," *Federal Register*, 59(85), Part II.

Neill, H.R., R.G. Cummings, P.T. Ganderton, G.W. Harrison and T. McGuckin, 1994, "Hypothetical Surveys and Real Economic Commitments", *Land Economics*, 70(2): 145-154.

Rasmussen, E., 1989, *Games and Information: An Introduction to Game Theory*, New York: Basil Blackwell.

Rogers, W. H., 1993, "Regression standard errors in clustered samples," *Stata Technical Bulletin*, 13: 19-23.

Rowe, R.D., W.D. Schulze, W.D. Shaw, D. Schenk and L.G. Chestnut, 1991, "Contingent Valuation of Natural Resource Damage Due to the Nestucca Oil Spill," Final Report, RCG/Hagler, Bailly, Inc., Boulder.

Rutström, E.E., 1998, "Home-Grown Values and the Design of Incentive Compatible Auctions," *International Journal of Game Theory*, 27(3): 427-441.

Saha, A., 1993, "Expo-Power Utility: A Flexible Form for Absolute and Relative Risk Aversion," *American Journal of Agricultural Economics*, 75(4): 905-913.

Samuelson, P.A., 1938, "A Note on the Pure Theory of Consumer's Behavior," *Economica*, 5(17): 61–71.

Satterthwaite, M.A., 1975, "Strategy-proofness and Arrow's Conditions: Existence and Correspondence Theorems for Voting Procedures and Social Welfare Functions," *Journal of Economic Theory*, 10: 187-217.

Schkade, D.A. and J.W. Payne, 1993, "Where Do the Numbers Come From? How People Respond to Contingent Valuation Questions," in *Contingent Valuation: A Critical Appraisal*, J. Hausman, Ed., Amsterdam: North-Holland.

Schütze, H., 1997, *Ambiguity Resolution in Language Learning*, Stanford: CLSI Publications.

Shogren, J.F., 2004, "Experimental Methods and Valuation," in *Handbook of Environmental Economics. Volume 2: Valuing Environmental Changes,* K-G. Mäler and J Vincent, Eds., Amsterdam: North-Holland.

Shogren, J.F., S.Y. Shin, D.J. Hayes and J.B. Kliebenstein, 1994, "Resolving Differences in Willingness to Pay and Willingness to Accept," *American Economic Review*, 84(1): 255-270.

Shogren, J.F., J.A. List and D.J. Hayes, 2000, "Preference Learning in Consecutive Experimental Auctions," *American Journal of Agricultural Economics,* 82(4): 1016-1021.

Smith, V.L., 1982, "Microeconomic Systems as an Experimental Science," *American Economic Review*, 72(5): 923-955.

Smith, V.K., 1990, "Can We Measure the Economic Value of Environmental Amenities?," *Southern Economic Journal*, 56: 865-887.

Smith, V.K., 1992, "Arbitrary Values, Good Causes, and Premature Verdicts," *Journal of Environmental Economics and Management*, 22: 71-89.

Svedsäter, H. and O. Johansson-Stenman, 2001, "Choice Experiments and Self Image: Hypothetical and Actual Willingness To Pay," Unpublished Manuscript, Department of Economics, Gothenburg University.

Swait, J. and J. Louviere, 1993, "The Role of the Scale Parameter in the Estimation and Comparison of Multinomial Logit Models," *Journal of Marketing Research*, 30: 305-314.

Williams, R.L., 2000, "A Note on Robust Variance Estimation for Cluster-Correlated Data," *Biometrics*, 56: 645-646.

Varian, H.R., 1982, "The Nonparametric Approach to Demand Analysis," *Econometrica*, 50: 945-73.

Varian, H.R., 1983, "Non-Parametric Tests of Consumer Behavior," *Review of Economic Studies*, 50: 99-110.

CHAPTER 5

HOW AND HOW MUCH?

The Role of Information in Stated Choice Questionnaires

KRISTY E. MATHEWS

Veritas Economic Consulting, LLC, Cary, North Carolina, U.S.A.

MIRANDA L. FREEMAN

Triangle Economic Research, Cary, North Carolina, U.S.A.

WILLIAM H. DESVOUSGES

W.H. Desvousges & Associates, Inc., Raleigh, North Carolina, U.S.A.

1. INTRODUCTION

The type, quality, and quantity of information provided in a stated choice (SC) survey play a crucial role and directly affect the results: respondents base their answers on this information. Often, respondents interpret the information based on their own unique experiences and knowledge. Nevertheless, respondents must understand and accurately process the information provided so that survey results are valid. Survey information also may indirectly affect results because inadequate or vague information may cause respondent confusion. Moreover, too much information can cause respondent fatigue, leading to other concerns about the reliability of the results.

This chapter uses examples from actual surveys to illustrate the various roles that information can play. Some examples show the role of information in helping to establish context or background for the respondent. Examples range from those where people have substantial experience, such as recreational fishing, to those where people have little experience, such as valuing ecological services. The examples also show how information is used to define the commodity in a survey. It is especially important in SC surveys that respondents understand the specific

111

attributes included in the survey and their respective levels. In a SC survey about automobile preferences, for example, attribute levels can be categorical (the type of stereo system or color) or numerical (the number of doors or the horsepower), or they can indicate the presence or absence of an attribute (air conditioning). Thus, identifying the specific attributes and their levels is part of the information conveyed to respondents during the survey.

Deciding how to convey information and how much information to convey is inextricably linked with pretesting. During pretesting, researchers can determine the extent of respondent knowledge, whether the survey includes too much or too little information, and whether respondents interpret the survey terminology, instructions, and questions as the researchers intended. Finally, pretesting enables researchers to directly question respondents about their reactions to the survey while there is still an opportunity to make changes.

The hypothetical nature of SC responses amplifies the importance of the role of information. A SC survey collects data from respondents reacting to hypothetical scenarios. The results are not based on actual, observed behavior made by people in an economic market who face the consequences of their decisions.[1] While no amount of information is likely to eliminate hypothetical bias, respondent confusion attributable to information deficiencies can only exacerbate the situation. This chapter emphasizes the importance of including various types of evaluations within the survey to examine how respondents process and use the information provided.

2. PEOPLE MAKE THE WORLD GO AROUND

Survey research involves people. The heterogeneity of people makes it challenging to provide the right information in the right way. Many SC surveys are designed to be administered to the general population, which means that survey respondents will cover a wide spectrum of educational levels, technical backgrounds, and opinions. Some respondents will not be high school graduates. Moreover, some high school graduates may have limited reading comprehension. Even SC surveys targeting a narrower population (an angler study, for example) will include respondents who differ in how they process information and in their ability to comprehend new information.

Some of the cognitive difficulties can be solved by designing surveys to reflect an eighth-grade reading level. Writing short sentences and choosing simple words helps facilitate respondent comprehension. Pretesting also helps to ensure that respondents interpret questions in the way that the survey designer intends.

Nevertheless, surveys on environmental topics may present unique challenges. For example, such surveys often involve highly technical and unfamiliar information. Even well educated respondents are likely to be unfamiliar with information on the fate and transport of contaminated sediment in an estuarine system or the mechanics of groundwater hydrology. Moreover, the challenges associated with communicating health risks from environmental contamination have long been documented in the literature (Smith and Desvousges, 1987, Slovic, 1987). We expand on this topic later in the chapter.

In the absence of adequate or understandable information, respondents fill in the gaps themselves. Respondents have unique ideas that often can be elicited during pretesting.

- One respondent said that he was not worried about possible groundwater contamination beneath his house because he was sure he could re-engineer the flow of groundwater and divert it away from his house.

- Another respondent said that he would rather live near a facility with PCB contamination than farther away from it because PCBs are oil-based and everybody knew that oil and water did not mix. In his reasoning it was safer to live near the factory because the rain would wash PCBs away from properties closest to it.

- Another respondent in a recreational fishing study reported his rationale for keeping fish caught at a site that was clearly posted with a "do not eat" advisory. He said he had a large freezer at home, which he had been filling with fish from the river for some time. As soon as that sign came down, he was going to eat all the fish in his freezer because then it would be completely safe.

These stories underscore the challenges associated with providing information to respondents.

Another challenge relates to the mathematical abilities of respondents. For example, performing simple arithmetic calculations may be challenging for some respondents. We recommend avoiding a survey where respondents are expected or may be tempted to make calculations themselves. Provide the necessary numbers so that all respondents rely on the same numerical information.

An extension of this issue is how to convey measures of a good or service. It seems straightforward to simply state quantities as the levels of an attribute, but what terms should be used to describe the quantity? This becomes even more complex when dealing with a change in quantity, because the terms used to describe a quantity or a change can influence whether the amount seems large or small. The first option is to use absolute numbers (e.g., catch 1 more fish, save 1,000 birds). A second option is to use percentages (e.g., 20% more sunny days, increase water quality by 10%).

An example can help illustrate how the numerical terms used to describe something can influence the responses received. We designed a SC survey on salmon preservation in the Pacific Northwest. In the Salmon Preservation Study, respondents were asked to trade off job losses attributable to limitations on hydroelectric power necessary for increases in the wild salmon population.[2] The Salmon Preservation Study gave three levels for the attribute Jobs Lost: no jobs, 1,000 jobs, and 4,000 jobs. However, jobs total 4 million, so the percentage decreases associated with each of the Jobs Lost levels are 0 percent, 0.025 percent, and 0.1 percent, respectively. The change between levels seems much smaller in percentage terms than in absolute terms. Thus, we provided both absolute numbers and percentages to help respondents gain a better understanding of the proposed job losses.

Survey researchers recognize that there is a limit to the amount of information, however clear and concise, that respondents can process in any survey. Although some surveys provide incentive payments to respondents to compensate them for the time it takes to complete a questionnaire, researchers must be reasonable about the length of time respondents need to spend on the questionnaire. In most instances, we rely on their cooperation and good graces for data. Ultimately, determining how and how much information to provide in a questionnaire requires an explicit recognition of the human aspects of survey research. No formula works the same in every instance, and there is no substitute for thorough pretesting with respondents who are representative of the target population.

3. JUST THE FACTS, MA'AM

Survey research textbooks have long advocated that survey information presented to respondents must be neutral and factually based (Dillman, 1978). The survey literature offers many examples of the effects of nonneutral wording in biasing results (Rea and Parker, 1992, Rossi, Wright, and Anderson, 1983). Lack of neutrality can take the form of overtly leading questions or subtle implications of an acceptable answer (Schuman and Presser, 1981). Moreover, Schuman and Presser (1977) reasoned that poorly educated respondents would more likely be influenced by emotionally toned words, while better-educated respondents should more easily grasp the general point of a question or statement and not be as easily affected by emotionally charged words. Maintaining neutrality in context is just as important in a SC questionnaire as it is in any other questionnaire.

In addition to neutral wording in a survey, any information provided must be factually correct. In cases where accurately measuring the effect of environmental contamination is the issue under study, the commodity specified must match the facts of the actual contamination. This task can prove challenging when those facts are disputed at the time of questionnaire development. Nevertheless, if the survey instrument asks for values based on one set of facts when the real situation varies from those facts, the values given—setting aside any issues of hypothetical bias— will not be valid for assessing the impact of the contamination.

The importance of accurately reflecting the facts of the contamination in a damage assessment survey was recently affirmed in U.S. District Court. In *U.S. v. Montrose*, the government based its $0.5 billion natural resource damage claim on a contingent valuation (CV) survey (Carson et al., 1994) that government scientists later admitted misrepresented the actual effects of DDT and PCBs on wildlife. The judge excluded the CV results from evidence on the grounds that the CV scenario presented to respondents was not even consistent with the testimony of the trustees' own injury experts (Sidley and Austin, 2000).

One key aspect of the factual content is any uncertainty about the extent and effects of environmental contamination. The psychological literature shows that people have a difficult time answering questions when uncertainty is present. In particular, the literature shows that people's preferences are poorly formed and very sensitive to the way questions are framed and that people are unable to process probabilistic information (Tversky and Kahneman, 1981, Slovic, Fischoff, and Lichtenstein, 1982). One research finding particularly pertinent to SC (especially CV) questionnaires is the certainty effect, where people respond to questions quite differently when one of the options presented involves a certain outcome (Weinstein and Quinn, 1983, Tversky and Kahneman, 1981). Because we do not know everything about hazardous substances in the environment, SC questionnaires on environmental issues should identify any uncertainty associated with the alleged effects on contamination, the clean-up, or the restoration program.

In light of the potential hypothetical bias of SC (see Harrison, this volume), presenting complete information is equally as important as getting the facts right. Consider the recreational study conducted by McConnell et al. (1986) at New Bedford Harbor.[3] At the time of this study, the harbor contained many pollutants, one of them PCBs. The questionnaire asked residents of New Bedford how often they would visit the beaches if the PCBs were cleaned up. In 1987, a different set of researchers reframed the questionnaire to make it clear that only PCBs would be removed but other pollutants would remain in the harbor (Cicchetti, Dubin, and Wilde, 1991). In the revised version, 79 percent of the respondents changed their answers.

In a study we conducted as part of the Clark Fork River litigation, we evaluated a survey that John Duffield conducted on behalf of the State of Montana.[4] Dr. Duffield asked the following question to respondents in a telephone survey:

Suppose your household had a choice between being on a private well or the Butte municipal water system for your tap water. Say the water from the private well would be of better quality, as well as less expensive in the long run than the Butte water system. Which system would your household prefer, given these conditions?

Approximately 55 percent responded that they would prefer to have a groundwater well. Subsequently, we re-interviewed the same respondents and asked the same question as Dr. Duffield, but we added information about the typical cost of installing a well in Montana, shown in the question below.

Suppose your household had a choice between being on a private well or the Butte municipal water system for your tap water. Say the water from the private well would be of better quality, as well as less expensive in the long run than the Butte water system. Which system would your household prefer, given these conditions?

The total cost of installing a well is typically about $6,000. Would you prefer a well if you would have to pay $6,000 now to have a well installed?

When presented with the cost information, the percentage of respondents saying that they would have a well declined from 55 percent to 14 percent. These studies provide a striking example of how incomplete information can affect survey results.

4. A PICTURE IS WORTH A THOUSAND WORDS

Photographs, graphics, drawings, maps, and other illustrations can convey information more effectively and efficiently than text. They draw the reader's attention and add visual interest to the survey. Concepts such as geography, aesthetics, and quantitative differences are best described using pictures. Pictures can be used alone or in conjunction with text, depending on the complexity of the concept to be conveyed and on how well the picture meets the information needs.

In some cases, pictures may be the only way to convey the necessary information. For example, the Oregon Ocean Recreation Survey was intended to capture the aesthetic impact of a shipwreck located on a remote beach in Oregon. Given that shipwrecks are an uncommon sight for most people and that there is great variation among shipwrecks, it was simply not practical to try to describe the wreck using text. The only way to convey to respondents the aesthetics of the shipwreck was to show them a picture of it, reproduced in Figure 1. In this instance, we judged the photograph to be sufficiently descriptive and added only the brief caption "1999 Shipwreck."

FIGURE 1. Photograph of the New Carissa Shipwreck

As mentioned earlier, using pictures to convey geographic information is appropriate (Mitchell and Carson, 1989). Figure 2 shows a map that we provided to respondents in the Salmon Preservation Study. It would have been very tedious to describe the location of all 51 dams in the Columbia River Basin by using only words. The map in Figure 2, however, conveyed both the number and locations of dams.

FIGURE 2. *Hydroelectric Dams in the Columbia River Basin*

The Desvousges et al. (1992) CV survey (Birds Survey) provides an example of how text can be supplemented and combined with a map to convey both geography and quantity in more than one way.[5] The Birds Survey asked questions about migratory waterfowl and waste-oil holding ponds in the Central Flyway of the United States. Figure 3 shows the map used in the survey to show the location of the Central Flyway. Textual information about the size of the Central Flyway and the number of migratory waterfowl using the flyway is shown on the map and included in the text accompanying the map. Repeating the information in two different formats increases the likelihood that respondents will process the information.

In some cases, pictures may provide too much information and confuse respondents. In the Birds Survey, respondents were asked CV questions about proposed regulations requiring owners to cover waste-oil holding ponds in the Central Flyway with wire netting. Covering the holding ponds would prevent waterfowl from coming into contact with the oil. During pretesting, participants were shown drawings of the proposed wire-netting covers. However, rather than clarify what was proposed, the drawings actually confused respondents. The final questionnaire did not include the drawings and instead used a simple text description:

The best type of covering for these holding ponds is a heavy wire netting that prevents waterfowl from landing on the ponds and coming in contact with the oily wastes. The wire netting would be a very small mesh to prevent the waterfowl from getting entangled in the cover.

Thus, while pictures are often helpful in conveying information, they are not the best choice in every survey.

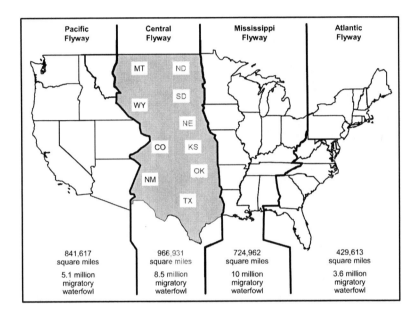

FIGURE 3. *Birds Survey Map Showing the Location of the Central Flyway*

5. RISKY BUSINESS

As we noted previously, surveys about risk present some of the greatest challenges in determining what information to provide and how to present it. The senior author of this chapter conducted some of the early SC work on this topic as part of a two-year project with the U.S. Environmental Protection Agency (Smith, Desvousges, and Freeman, 1985).[6] The study involved the use of various methods to evaluate the potential benefits of reducing the risks from the exposure to hazardous wastes. The surveys were conducted in the Boston area in the 1980s after extensive pretesting using focus groups and other techniques.

The results of the focus groups from that study, and subsequent work on nuclear risks, show that some people prefer verbal explanations, others prefer visual representation, and still others work best with mathematical representations such as probability (Desvousges and Frey, 1989). Further, this research showed that when multiple methods were used to convey the same concept, people gravitated toward the method they found most comfortable and ignored the others. The focus group results showed that when people were provided only with fractions to explain risk, they often calculated the implied percentages (Desvousges and Smith, 1988). As noted in the previous section, providing information in several different terms can prevent respondents from doing the conversions themselves (and hence the risk of mathematical errors) and gives a more complete picture of the magnitude of the amount and changes under evaluation.

Diagrams can also be used to communicate information. One example of a diagram is a ladder or scale that shows different levels. Figure 4 shows a risk ladder used in a SC survey conducted in the Boston area (Smith and Desvousges, 1987). The ladder establishes linkages between activities and risk and conveys information from a technical origin in an easy-to-follow manner. The respondent can see at a glance what activities are associated with each level of risk. The breaks in the ladder make it easier to accommodate the wide variation that is often found in communicating different kinds of risk. While this ladder was developed for CV, the same kind of ladder could be used to define the levels of risk in a SC format.

In addition, the ladder compares risks involving a range of characteristics to make it easier for people to think about their own situations. However, ladders like this should be used cautiously. For example, focus group participants reviewing a draft version of the ladder said that it was helpful for eliciting perceptions but it would not be useful to convince them to "accept" a certain level of risk because the risks were so diverse.

Risk circles also have been used to communicate risk information in surveys. See Figures 5 and 6. As noted above, focus groups and other pretesting methods played several important roles in developing the risk circles for the Hazardous Waste Risk Study. For example, focus group participants in the study emphasized the importance of using risk information based on hazardous wastes and not trying to use more simplified risk examples, such as lotteries or rain occurring, to help people evaluate different levels of risks.

Participants found the differences in context too confusing. In addition, the participants found the charts using three circles (Figure 6) to be more useful than trying to combine the information into just two circles (Figure 5). Because the study focused on reducing the risk of exposure to hazardous wastes, having the second circle showing the fixed conditional probability made it easier to see how reducing exposure subsequently reduced the risk of death.

Researchers can gain insights about the influence of the type and tone of information from the risk communication literature. For example, in a study designed to test the effectiveness of different ways to communicate risks, Smith et al. (1988, 1990) developed different versions of a brochure and administered them to a large sample of homeowners who had tested their homes for radon. The brochure systematically varied the use of qualitative and quantitative information using risk ladders (see Figure 7).[7]

Smith et al. found that if the objective was to help align subjective risk perceptions with objective risk measures, the quantitative version was more effective. However, the qualitative version performed better on other evaluation measures, such as improved learning and understanding about radon.

Finally, despite intensive efforts to help communicate risks to respondents in surveys, challenges remained. The psychological literature is replete with studies demonstrating the various heuristics that people use to process information involving risk. See Slovic (1987) and Payne (1982). These heuristics may or may not correspond to assumptions that economists routinely rely upon in valuing risk reductions. Moreover, some practical difficulties remain unsolved, especially in developing visual aids to show the low probabilities usually associated with environmental risks. Thus, communicating risks in SC surveys presents many challenges and few definitive answers.

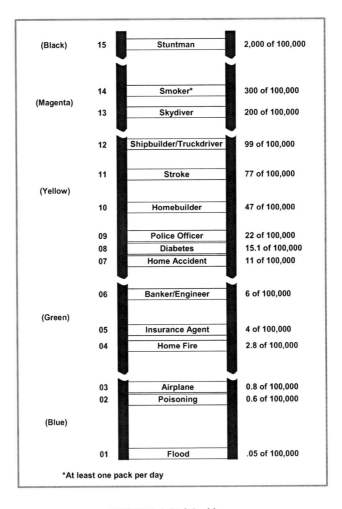

FIGURE 4. *Risk Ladder*

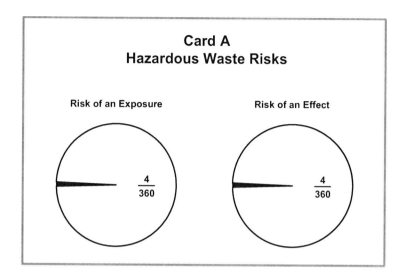

FIGURE 5. *Two Circles Depicting Hazardous Waste Risks*

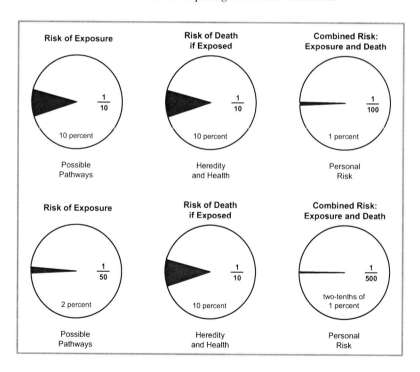

FIGURE 6. *Three Circles Depicting Hazardous Waste Risks*

Quantitative			Qualitative	
Radon Risk Chart			**Radon Risk Chart†**	
Lifetime exposure (picocuries per liter)	**Lifetime risk of dying from radon*** (out of 1,000)	**Comparable risks of fatal lung cancer** (lifetime or entire working life)	**Lifetime exposure** (picocuries per liter)	**Comparable risks of fatal lung cancer** (lifetime or entire working life)
75	214 – 554		75	
40	120 – 380		40	
20	60 – 210	Working with asbestos	20	Working with asbestos
10	30 – 120	Smoking 1 pack cigarettes/day	10	Smoking 1 pack cigarettes/day
4	13 – 50		4	
2	7 – 30	Having 200 chest X-rays per year	2	Having 200 chest X-rays per year
1	3 – 13		1	
02	1 – 3		02	

*U.S. Environmental Protection Agency lifetime risk estimates. The National Council on Radiation Protection has estimated lower risk, but it still considers radon a serious health concern.

†Colors are based on U.S. Environmental Protection Agency lifetime risk estimates. The National Council on Radiation Protection has estimated lower risk, but it still considers radon a serious health concern.

FIGURE 7. *Radon Risk Charts*

6. MAKING THE PORRIDGE

Is the information too little, too much, or just right? Unfortunately, survey researchers do not have Goldilocks to tell them how much information is just right. The process of determining the answer is an iterative one, with trial and error during pretesting providing some guidance. The ultimate answer to the question may be that various amounts and types of information are included in different versions of the questionnaire to assess the significance.

Respondents' background knowledge of the survey topic influences the amount of information needed in the survey. If respondents are familiar with and knowledgeable about the topic of the survey, providing a detailed explanation is both unnecessary and boring for respondents. For example, when surveying anglers about their saltwater fishing trips, it is unnecessary to spend several paragraphs describing a saltwater fishing trip. Anglers already know what fishing trips are like. On the other hand, if too little explanation is provided, particularly in terms of assumptions, respondents fill in the blanks themselves.

It also is useful to include questions in the survey that enable a researcher to differentiate among respondents with different levels of knowledge. In some cases, modifying the survey design to compare alternative information treatments may even be required. See Smith et al. (1990).

For less familiar and highly technical environmental commodities, respondents may have difficulty answering the questions if too little information is provided. In these instances, information plays an educational role. For example, in the Salmon Preservation Study, we did not expect the general public to be familiar with salmon migration, the dam system in the Pacific Northwest, and how preserving salmon could result in job loss. So, it was necessary to provide detailed background information in order for respondents to fully comprehend the survey and provide educated responses to the survey questions. Figure 8 shows an excerpt from the fact sheet provided to respondents as part of the Salmon Preservation Study.

Although some initial judgments about the appropriate level and amount of information to provide in a survey are needed, pretesting provides an opportunity to evaluate the accuracy of the guess and determine how effectively the information is performing. For example, large amounts of information can bore respondents, causing them to skip parts of the survey instructions, background, or even questions. This introduces uncertainty and potential bias into the results because there is no way to determine what information respondents processed and what was skipped.

During in-person pretests, asking respondents to read the survey out loud as they take it can help determine what they may skip. For example, during the pretest for the Oregon Ocean Recreation Survey, one respondent skipped the entire instructions page. Asking him why he skipped the instructions revealed that the text was too blocky and dense, intimidating the respondent. Minimizing the amount of text, adding bullets, and adding more white space between sentences helped make the instructions easier to read and less intimidating. Figure 9 shows the instructions before and after these changes.

Pretesting is particularly helpful for determining what information is missing from a survey. It is crucial to ensure that the survey provides enough information for respondents to make the same choices that they would make in a real-life situation. Suppose anglers choose where to fish based on the type of fish they want to catch, but the survey does not include fish species as an attribute when describing places to fish. Respondents will be unable to follow the same decision-making process in the survey as they would use in real life. Hence, they can be expected to provide different answers, introducing error into the survey results. Asking questions such as "Is there anything else you would want to know before making your choice?" can elicit feedback on what is missing in a survey. Listening to the thought process respondents use to answer the choice questions can also help determine if important attributes are missing.

Hatchery-Raised Salmon

To combat the decline in the salmon population, salmon hatcheries have been built along the Basin's rivers. In these hatcheries, salmon eggs are hatched, and young salmon are kept until they are old enough to make the journey downstream.

Each year, approximately 160 million hatchery-raised salmon are released into the Basin's rivers. Despite this large number, only a small proportion of hatchery-raised salmon return to spawn because they face many of the same obstacles as wild salmon. Currently, hatchery-raised salmon comprise 75 percent of all returning salmon (see Figure 5).

Some experts are concerned about the large percentage of hatchery-raised salmon because interactions between the hatchery-raised salmon and wild salmon may be contributing to the decline in the Basin's wild salmon.

For instance, hatchery-raised salmon compete with wild salmon for food and habitat. In addition, interbreeding between these groups dilutes the gene pool for wild salmon, which may weaken their survival instincts.

Causes of Salmon Decline

Although hatchery-raised salmon may contribute to the declining wild salmon populations, they are only one of several factors. Other factors contributing to the decline of salmon in Pacific Northwest are:

- construction and operation of hydroelectric dams,
- commercial fishing,
- the decline of wildlife habitat from agriculture, logging, and urbanization, and
- natural causes, such as drought

Wild Salmon (Salmon that are hatched in their natural environment)	**+**	**Hatchery-Raised Salmon** (Salmon that are hatched in hatcheries and released into the rivers and streams)	**=**	**Total Salmon**
25%		75%		100%

Source: Northwest Power Planning Council

FIGURE 8. Excerpt from Fact Sheet Used in the Salmon Preservation Study

Keep in mind that subtle differences in information, even the choice of a specific word, can matter. In some instances, a word choice can prevent the respondents from interpreting the survey information as intended. Researchers and respondents may interpret the survey terminology differently, leading to misinterpretation or confusion. For example, the Oregon Ocean Recreation Survey originally asked respondents about "coastal recreation." However, focus group respondents made it clear that to people who live on the Oregon Coast, "coastal recreation" includes everything from the ocean shore to the coastal mountain range. Changing the term to "ocean recreation" and explaining what it meant in the survey alleviated this confusion.

INSTRUCTIONS

Please Read Carefully

This survey asks questions about ocean recreation. Ocean recreation includes any activities you do on the ocean beach/rocks, on the sand dunes, or in the ocean itself. These activities include, but are not limited to, walking/hiking, beachcombing, fishing, driving, horseback riding, picnicking, and wildlife observation.

This survey asks questions about the features that are important to you when you decide where to go along the ocean. In the following questions you will be asked to choose between two ocean places, X and Y, for your next trip to the ocean. Each place will be described in terms of its features. The following list explains each feature.

Ocean View: What you see when you look at the ocean (open ocean, a lighthouse, rocks, a shipwreck).

Access: Whether the walk to the beach is easy (short or flat), or hard (long or steep).

Sand Dunes: Whether there are sand dunes at this place (yes or no).

People on Beach: Approximately how many other people you see on the beach (none, some, many).

Vehicles: Whether vehicles or ATVs are allowed on the beach or dunes (yes or no).

Please assume:

You can do your favorite ocean recreation activities at either place
There is no fee for visiting either place
It takes the same amount of time to drive to both places from your home
It is a typical summer day with good weather.

On the next page is an example of the type of questions you will be asked to answer. Suppose that for your next trip to the ocean, you had to choose between Place X and Place Y. Place X is described in the second column, and Place Y is described in the third column. Read the features of each place, and think about which place you would rather go to. At the bottom, circle the place you would choose to visit. Finally, when choosing a place to visit, please consider the choices on each page separately.

INSTRUCTIONS

Please Read Carefully

This survey is about ocean recreation. Ocean recreation includes any activities you do on the ocean shore, on the sand dunes, or in the ocean itself. These activities include, but are not limited to:

- walking, running, or hiking
- watching the waves
- beachcombing
- fishing
- driving on the beach or dunes
- surfing
- camping
- watching wildlife.

You will be asked to choose between two places, X and Y, for your next visit to the ocean. Each place will be described in terms of its features. The features are:

Ocean View: What you see when you look at the ocean (such as rocks or a shipwreck).

Walk to Beach: What the walk to the beach is like (short and flat, or long and steep).

Sand Dunes: Whether there are sand dunes at this place (yes or no).

People on Beach: Approximately how many other people you see on the beach (none, some, many).

Vehicles: Whether vehicles, including ATVs, are allowed on the beach and dunes (allowed, not allowed).

Please assume:

- **Place X and Place Y are the only places you can go for your next visit.**
- **There is a wide, sandy beach at both places**
- **There is no fee to visit either place**
- **It takes the same amount of time to drive to both places from your home**
- **It is a typical summer day with good weather**

Please answer each question as if it is the **ONLY** question.

Please read the example on the opposite page before answering the questions.

FIGURE 9. *Instructions to the Oregon Ocean Recreation Survey Before and After Pretesting*

However, pretesting showed that the explanation also had to be very carefully worded. The pretest screener survey asked the following question to recruit ocean recreators:

> Our study focuses on ocean recreation. By ocean recreation, I mean activities you do on the ocean beaches or rocks, on the sand dunes, or in the ocean. How many adults in your household, including yourself, participate in ocean recreation? Please include all adults in your household who participate in ocean recreation, even if it is only occasional recreation.

During the pretest, several respondents revealed that all they do at the ocean is watch the waves, so they did not feel they were really ocean recreators. The researchers had intended to include people who participated in passive recreation such as watching the waves, but respondents had a different, more active definition of "ocean recreation." To make the meaning clearer, researchers amended the question with the italicized text:

> Our study focuses on ocean recreation. By ocean recreation, I mean activities you do on the ocean beaches or rocks, on the sand dunes, or in the ocean. *This includes walking on the beach and watching the ocean waves.* How many adults in your household, including yourself, participate in ocean recreation, even occasionally?

7. A RECIPE FOR DESIGN

Once the background and context of the environmental issue have been provided to respondents, the actual SC questions follow. Information plays a role in the composition and presentation of the specific attributes and levels. In a SC study context, it is impossible to use every possible characteristic as an attribute and every possible level of each attribute as a level. Thus, it falls to the researcher to determine what the specific attributes and levels are, keeping in mind that what is salient to the researcher may not be meaningful to respondents. The number of attributes and levels themselves comprise the experimental design (see Johnson et al., this volume). In this chapter, we limit discussion to deciding what the attributes should be and how to explain them to survey respondents.

Admittedly, selecting the attributes and levels requires a degree of judgment. Once some preliminary decisions are made, however, it is critical to re-evaluate them. One way to evaluate the design choices is to ask respondents what attributes are least important to them when answering the choice questions. Attributes that are consistently identified as unimportant can be eliminated. Pretesting is undoubtedly the best tool available for identifying the most meaningful attributes and levels. Based on our experience, we recommend that the researcher first develop a list of possible attributes and corresponding levels and then use pretesting to narrow and refine the list. In addition, use pretesting to explore how to most effectively communicate the attributes and levels.

In the Salmon Preservation study, we used a separate survey to select the attributes that were most meaningful to respondents. Based on our review of technical documentation and reports on salmon preservation, we began with a list of more than 10 attributes to describe the commodity. After using focus groups to eliminate some attributes, we then administered a brief questionnaire to a convenience sample that mirrored the target population. In this questionnaire, respondents were asked to rate each potential attribute on a scale from 0 to 4 in terms of its importance to them. Analysis of the results revealed that the overall rating of some attributes were statistically higher than the overall rating of other attributes. For the final questionnaire, we chose the attributes with the highest levels of statistical difference. Fries and Gable (1997) provide more information on this separate survey to determine attributes for our Salmon Preservation Study.

In a saltwater angler study, we used pretesting to select the levels of attributes, specifically the number of fish caught. This study was part of a combined revealed preference/SC survey we designed and administered to anglers near the central Gulf Coast of Texas.[8] We had originally focused on trying to express catch as a rate (2 fish per hour). What we learned in pretesting, however, was that the strict bag limits for a highly sought after species made the higher levels of catch rate nonsensical. Based on the feedback we received from anglers in our pretesting, we modified the "catch" attribute in the final questionnaire to correspond to a number of fish combined with a specific species (1 red drum, 10 flounder, etc.).

Sometimes the refinements to information that come from pretesting seem small but are still significant in terms of the specific wording chosen to convey attributes or levels. For example, in the Oregon Ocean Recreation Survey, one of the attributes is whether or not vehicles are allowed to be driven on the beach. The pretest survey had two levels for this attribute, yes and no, and the attribute was described in the question simply as "Vehicles." However, between reading the attribute description in the instructions and actually answering the questions, some respondents became confused about what "yes" and "no" meant. Some respondents interpreted the vehicle attribute to indicate parking availability. Others assumed that "yes" meant that there actually were vehicles on the beach, not merely that they were allowed on the beach. To clarify this attribute, the levels were changed to "Allowed" and "Not Allowed."

Finally, pictures can also be used to make a survey convey attributes and levels. For example, Figure 10 shows how the Wisconsin Outdoor Recreation Survey used small drawings to illustrate the attribute levels, mostly in conjunction with text descriptions.[9] The view from the recreation site is depicted only with drawings, which were defined in the survey instructions. Choice A shows a "developed" view, Choice B shows a "somewhat developed" view, and Choice C shows an "undeveloped" view. For this attribute, the drawings conveyed more about the view than the words "developed," "somewhat developed," and "undeveloped." However, for the other attributes, the pictures simply made the survey more interesting for respondents.

8. THE PROOF IS IN THE PUDDING

A logical extension of the role of information in SC surveys is confirming that respondents understand and correctly interpret the information provided. Although respondent comprehension might be a lesser issue for a well-understood commodity (such as a fishing trip), respondent comprehension for more complex or unfamiliar commodities is of great importance. The researchers have failed in their quest to provide the right information if respondents do not understand and process the information. Thus, including a method to measure and reinforce respondent comprehension is particularly important.

One option available for testing whether or not the information has been successfully absorbed by respondents is to incorporate quiz questions into the questionnaire. For example, the Salmon Preservation Study contained five multiple-choice questions. These questions reinforce key facts about the salmon/job trade-offs presented in the survey overview section. When respondents answered the quiz question correctly, the computer program informed them that they selected the

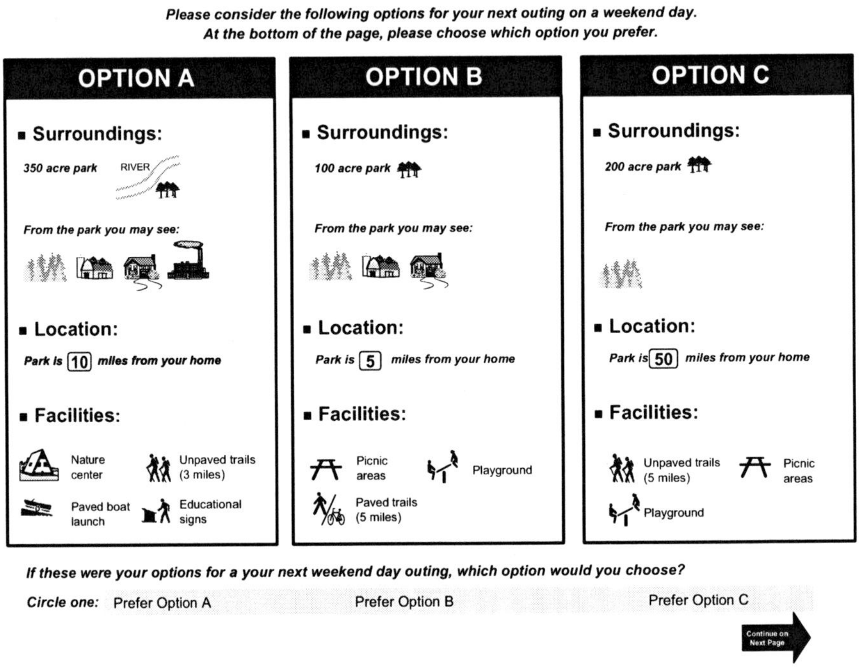

Please consider the following options for your next outing on a weekend day.
At the bottom of the page, please choose which option you prefer.

If these were your options for a your next weekend day outing, which option would you choose?

Circle one: Prefer Option A   Prefer Option B   Prefer Option C

FIGURE 10. Question from Wisconsin Outdoor Recreation Survey

correct answer. When respondents answered incorrectly, the computer program provided the "best" (i.e., correct) answer. These quiz questions provide a way to gauge the respondent's initial comprehension of the bundled commodity being valued in this study. In Mathews and Johnson (1999), we present analysis that explains how the quiz scores can be used as an explanatory variable in our model. Moreover, our analysis shows that including the quiz score helps to control for "noise" in the model and improve model performance.

Similarly, Johnson, Desvousges, and Ruby (1997) used quizzes in a SC survey to help enhance respondent comprehension about the potential health endpoints associated with exposure to air pollution. Specifically, the researchers conducted the survey in centralized locations using a computerized interview. In addition, respondents were given a brief brochure developed by Health Canada that explained the various health conditions. After respondents read the brochure, the questionnaire required them to answer questions based on the content of the brochure. The computer program provided further reinforcement of the information by telling people immediately whether their answers were correct, or if not, providing them with the correct answer. As in the Salmon Preservation Study, the quiz scores provided useful data for the subsequent econometric analysis.

Finally, the researcher can consider using a study design that is amenable to testing the consistency in SC responses. Because SC surveys collect multiple observations for each respondent, it is possible to test a variety of hypotheses about the consistency of SC responses with basic economic principles. If responses violate basic tenets of economic theory, then the results cannot represent valid economic values. For example, suppose that a respondent's responses are completely random, or that inattentive respondents simply choose the same response for every question as a simple way to get through the questionnaire. Obviously, either series of evaluations provides no useful information about the value of the commodity.

From SC data, three types of tests are possible:

- Monotonic—holding costs constant, individuals should prefer more to less of any normal good
- Transitive—if a subject prefers A to B, and B to C, then individual also should prefer A to C
- Stable—preferences do not change over the course of the survey.

Tests for these characteristics can be incorporated into the study with careful design of the pairs seen by respondents.[10] One test for monotonicity uses a dominant-pair comparison where all the attributes of one profile in a choice set are unambiguously better than all the attributes of the other profile in the comparison. For monotonicity to hold, respondents must always choose the dominant profile within the pair.

Careful structuring of the pairs that respondents see can also test for transitivity. For example, suppose a respondent sees Option A versus Option B and Option B versus Option C. If so, a comparison of Option A versus Option C provides the ability to check transitivity. If the study design permits, preference stability can be tested in either graded-pairs or choice formats by including questions at the beginning of the series that are repeated at the end. Preference stability is tested by comparing responses from the SC questions at the beginning of the series to the identical questions later in the series.

Johnson and Mathews (2001), Johnson and Bingham (2001), and Johnson, Mathews, and Bingham (2000) demonstrate that some SC responses do not conform to basic economic tenets. For example, Johnson and Mathews reveal that in the Salmon Preservation Study, more than 25 percent of the respondents did not select the dominant pair in a graded-pair comparison question. Johnson and Mathews also reveal that some respondents' answers violate both transitivity and preference stability tests. In some cases, these departures from basic economic principles result in substantially different willingness-to-pay estimates for the good or service in the study.

9. IN A NUTSHELL

To summarize our experience, we provide the following "ten top" pieces of advice to SC researchers:

1. Pretesting is a crucial part of getting the information aspects of a SC survey right. We cannot stress enough how important pretesting is. For surveys that are predominantly research-oriented (e.g., not intended to withstand the scrutiny of litigation), informal or convenience-based pretesting is better than no pretesting at all.

2. The survey results can be useful to the issue at hand only if the factual information is correct. Part of getting the facts right includes acknowledging any uncertainty that may exist in the consequences of environmental degradation or the proposed environmental restoration.

3. Pictures and graphics can go a long way in accurately and efficiently conveying information, provided that they are factually accurate.

4. Successfully communicating risks can be a significant challenge. There is a wealth of information in the risk communication and risk perception literature. Take advantage of these lessons learned but recognize that there are no easy answers or bright lines to follow.

5. Respondents' previous knowledge of the issue at hand is a key determinant to finding the balance between too little and too much information.

6. Do not overlook the fact that information is an inherent part of the specific attributes and levels. Effectively communicating those elements is just as important as conveying background information.

7. The hypothetical nature of SC data amplifies the role of information in a SC survey. Nevertheless, hypothetical bias remains a significant concern.

8. The use of quizzes, particularly in computerized surveys, can help gauge and even enhance respondent comprehension.

9. Consider using consistency tests as part of the study design. Incorporating these tests may produce more robust models.

10. Finally, remember that researchers and respondents are people. Explicitly acknowledging the "human element" of survey research is a trait of a good survey researcher. It is this human element that makes survey research simultaneously challenging and rewarding.

---

10. ENDNOTES

[1] For further discussion on hypothetical bias, particularly in CV studies, see Braden, Kolstad, and Miltz (1991); Smith (1986); Imber, Stevenson and Wilkes (1991); and Silberman, Gerlowski, and Williams (1992).

[2] See Dunford et al. (1995) and Mathews and Johnson (1999) for more information on the Salmon Preservation Study.

[3] This study can best be described as a contingent behavior study where respondents are presented with information and then asked what they would do. The hypothetical nature of this format makes it sufficiently similar to CV and SC to be relevant.

[4] See Duffield (1995) and Desvousges (1995) for a more complete discussion of the surveys.

[5] See Desvousges et al. (1992) and Desvousges et al. (1993) for more information about the survey.

[6] Kerry Smith, who was at Vanderbilt University at the time, and Rick Freeman were the other two principal investigators for this work, reported in 1985.

[7] These risk ladders differ from the early ones used in the Hazardous Waste Risk Study. Note that all the risks involve similar health outcomes and that people used the ladder to place the radon reading in context.

[8] For more information on this study, see Ruby, Johnson and Mathews (2002) and Mathews, Gribben and Desvousges (2002).

[9] Although the view from the recreation site attribute under "Surroundings" does not include a text description, the levels depicted with drawings are defined in the survey instructions. For more information on this survey, see Desvousges, MacNair and Smith (2000).

[10] Of course, including some of these types of tests affects the experimental design. See Johnson, et al. (this volume) for a discussion.

11. REFERENCES

Banzhaf, M.R., F.R. Johnson and K.E. Mathews, 2001, "Opt-Out Alternatives and Anglers' Stated Preferences," in *Choice Modelling Approach to Environmental Evaluation,* J. Bennett and R. Blemey, eds, Northampton, MA: Edward Elgar Publishing.

Braden, John B., Charles Kolstad and David Miltz, Eds., 1991, "Introduction," in *Measuring the Demand for Environmental Quality,* Amsterdam: Elsevier Science Publishers B.V. (North-Holland).

Carson, Richard T., W. Michael Hanemann, Raymond J. Kopp, Jon A. Krosnick, Robert C. Mitchell, Stanley Presser, Paul A. Ruud and V. Kerry Smith, 1994, *Prospective Interim Lost Use Value Due to DDT and PCB Contamination in the Southern California Bight,* Report prepared for the National Oceanic and Atmospheric Administration, September 30, La Jolla, CA: Natural Resource Damage Assessment, Inc.

Cicchetti, Charles J., Jeffrey A. Dubin and Louis L. Wilde, 1991, "The Use and Misuse of Surveys in Economic Analysis: Natural Resource Damage Assessment Under CERCLA," California Institute of Technology Social Science Working Paper 786.

Desvousges, W.H., 1995, *Volume V: Report on Potential Economic Losses Associated with Groundwater,* Submitted to United States District Court, District of Montana, Helena Division in the matter of *State of Montana v. Atlantic Richfield Company,* Case No. CV-83-317-HLN-PGH.

Desvousges, W.H. and J.H. Frey, 1989, "Integrating Focus Groups and Surveys: Examples from Environmental Risk Studies," *Journal of Official Statistics* 5(4):349–363.

Desvousges, W.H., F.R. Johnson, R.W. Dunford, K.J. Boyle, S.P. Hudson and K.N. Wilson, 1992, *Measuring Nonuse Damages Using Contingent Valuation: An Experimental Evaluation of Accuracy,* Monograph 92-1, Prepared for Exxon Company, USA., Research Triangle Park, NC: Research Triangle Institute.

Desvousges, W.H., F.R. Johnson, R.W. Dunford, K.J. Boyle, S.P. Hudson and K.N. Wilson, 1993, "Measuring Natural Resource Damages With Contingent Valuation: Tests of Validity and Reliability," in *Contingent Valuation: A Critical Assessment*, J.A. Hausman, Ed., pp. 91–164, Amsterdam: Elsevier.

Desvousges, W.H., D.J. MacNair and G.A. Smith, 2000, *Lower Fox River and Bay of Green Bay: Assessment of Potential Recreational Fishing Losses and Restoration Offsets*, Durham, NC: Triangle Economic Research.

Desvousges, W.H. and V.K. Smith, 1988, "Focus Groups and Risk Communication: The 'Science' of Listening to Data," *Risk Analysis* 8(4):479–484.

Dillman, Don, 1978, *Mail and Telephone Surveys: The Total Design Method*, New York: John Wiley and Sons.

Duffield, John W., 1995, *Literature Review and Estimation of Municipal and Agricultural Values of Groundwater Use in the Upper Clark Fork River Drainage*, Report prepared for the State of Montana Natural Resource Damage Program, January, Missoula, MT: Bioeconomics, Inc.

Dunford, R.W., K.E. Mathews, A.R. Gable, E.E. Fries, F.R. Johnson and W.H. Desvousges, 1995, *Nonuse Values for Nonenvironmental Commodities: Preliminary Conjoint Valuation Results for Avoiding Job Losses*, Prepared for the U.S. Department of Energy, Durham, NC: Triangle Economic Research.

Fries, E.E. and A.R. Gable, 1997, "Defining Commodities in Stated Preference Experiments: Some Suggestions," *AERE Newsletter*, 17(1):14-18.

Imber, David, Gay Stevenson and Leanne Wilks, 1991, *A Contingent Valuation Survey of the Kakadu Conservation Zone*, Resource Assessment Commission Research Paper No. 3, Vol. 1, Canberra: Australian Government Publishing Service.

Johnson, F.R. and M.F. Bingham, 2001, "Evaluating the Validity of Stated-Preference Estimates of Health Values," *Swiss Journal of Economics and Statistics*, 137(1):49–64.

Johnson, F.R., W.H. Desvousges and M.C. Ruby, 1997, "Valuing Stated choices for Health Benefits of Improved Air Quality: Results of a Pilot Study," The Annual W-133 Meeting, Portland Oregon.

Johnson, F.R. and K.E. Mathews, 2001, "Sources and Effects of Utility-Theoretic Inconsistency in Stated-Preference Surveys," *American Journal of Agricultural Economics*, 83(5):1328–1333.

Johnson, F.R., K.E. Mathews and M.F. Bingham, 2000, "Evaluating Welfare-Theoretic Consistency in Multiple-Response, Stated-Preference Surveys," TER Technical Working Paper No. T-0003, Durham, NC: Triangle Economic Research.

Mathews, K.E., K.J. Gribben and W.H. Desvousges, 2002, "Integration of Risk Assessment and Natural Resource Damage Assessment: A Case Study of Lavaca Bay," in *Human and Ecological Risk Assessment: Theory & Practice*, Dennis J. Paustenbach, Ed., New York: John Wiley and Sons.

Mathews, Kristy E. and F. Reed Johnson, 1999, "Dammed if You Do and Dammed if You Do not: Nonuse Stated choices in Salmon-Preservation Policy," Technical Working Paper T-9903, Durham, NC: Triangle Economic Research.

McConnell, Kenneth E. and Industrial Economics, Inc., 1986, *The Damages to Recreational Activities from PCBs in New Bedford Harbor*, Report prepared for Ocean Assessment Division, National Oceanic and Atmospheric Administration, Rockville, MD.

Mitchell, Robert Cameron and Richard T. Carson, 1989, *"Using Surveys to Value Public Goods: The Contingent Valuation Method,"* Washington DC: Resources for the Future, Inc.

Payne, J.W., 1982, "Contingent Decision Behavior," *Psychological Bulletin*, 92(2):382–402.

Rea, Louis M. and Richard A. Parker, 1992, *Designing and Conducting Survey Research: A Comprehensive Guide,* San Francisco: Jossey-Bass Publishers.

Rossi, P.H., J.D. Wright and A.B. Anderson, 1983, *Handbook of Survey Research,* Orlando: Academic Press, Inc.

Schuman, H. and S. Presser, 1977, "Question Wording as an Independent Variable in Survey Analysis," *Sociologic Methods and Research,* 6(2):151–170.

Schuman, H. and S. Presser, 1981, *Questions and Answers in Attitude Surveys,* New York: Academic Press.

Sidley & Austin Environmental Advisory, 2000, "Court Rejects Contingent Valuation Study in *Montrose* Case," June, www.sidley.com.

Silberman, Jonathan, Daniel A. Gerlowski and Nancy A. Williams, 1992, "Estimating Existence Value for Users and Nonusers of New Jersey Beaches," *Land Economics,* 68(2):225–236.

Slovic, P., 1987, "Perception of Risk," *Science,* 236(4799):280–285.

Slovic, Paul, Baruch Fischhoff and Sarah Lichtenstein, 1982, "Facts versus Fears: Understanding Perceived Risks," in *Judgment Under Uncertainty: Heuristics and Biases,* D. Kahneman, P. Slovic and A. Tversky, Eds., Cambridge: Cambridge University Press.

Smith, V. Kerry, 1986, "To Keep or Toss the Contingent Valuation Method," in *Valuing Environmental Goods: An Assessment of the Contingent Valuation Method,* Ronald G. Cummings, David Brookshire and William D. Schulze, Eds., Totowa, NJ: Rowman and Allanheld.

Smith, V.K. and W.H. Desvousges, 1987, "An Empirical Analysis of the Economic Value of Risk Changes," *Journal of Political Economy,* 95(1):89–114.

Smith, V.K., W.H. Desvousges, A. Fisher and F.R. Johnson, 1988, "Learning About Radon's Risk," *Journal of Risk and Uncertainty,* 1:233–258.

Smith, V.K., W.H. Desvousges and A.M. Freeman, 1985, *Valuing Changes in Hazardous Waste Risks: A Contingent Valuation Analysis,* Washington, DC: U.S. Environmental Protection Agency.

Smith, V.K., W.H. Desvousges, F.R. Johnson and A. Fisher, 1990, "Can Public Information Programs Affect Risk Perceptions?" *Journal of Policy Analysis and Management,* 9(1):41–59.

Tversky, Amos and Daniel Kahneman, 1981, "The Framing of Decisions and the Psychology of Choice," *Science,* vol. 211, January 30:453–458.

Weinstein, M.C. and R.J. Quinn, 1983, "Psychological Considerations in Valuing Health Risk Reductions," *Natural Resources Journal,* 23(3):659–673.

CHAPTER 6

ATTRIBUTE PROCESSING IN CHOICE EXPERIMENTS AND IMPLICATIONS ON WILLINGNESS TO PAY

DAVID A. HENSHER

Institute of Transport and Logistics Studies, School of Business,
Faculty of Economics and Business, University of Sydney, Sydney, Australia

1.   INTRODUCTION

There is a growing interest in understanding the rules respondents invoke to deal with the information presented in stated choice (SC) studies. Although the impetus for this focus appears to have been motivated by an interest in cognitive burden, research by Hensher and DeShazo (amongst others) has found that the real issue is not the amount of information respondents are expected to process, otherwise known as 'complexity', but rather the relevance of the information. This discovery opened up the possibility that a study of the implications on choice response of the amount of information provided in a choice experiment should be investigated in the context of the broader theme of what rules individuals bring to bear when assessing the information. These rules may be embedded in prejudices that have little to do with the amount of information in the experiment; rather they may be rational coping strategies that are used in everyday decision making. There is an extensive literature on information processing, which includes prospect theory (Kahnemann and Tversky, 1979), case-based decision theory (Gilboa and Schmeidler, 2001), and nonexpected utility theory (Starmer, 2000). This literature has not yet been integrated into the modeling of the SC process.

This chapter promotes the case for increasing our knowledge of the roles played by (i) the dimensionality of a SC experiment, (ii) the framing of SC design profiles relative to an experience profile (a reference base) and (iii) aggregating attributes. If these factors influence choices made, then it is important to understand how. It is also important to account for these influences, both with respect to the resulting willingness to pay (WTP) estimates and in any use of model outputs in prediction on hold out samples.

B.J. Kanninen (ed.), Valuing Environmental Amenities Using Stated Choice Studies, 135–157.

In the following, we discuss various ways that the information in a SC experiment may be processed. Specifically, we find that there are two issues to explore: the dimensionality of the SC experiment, and the substantial heterogeneity in processing strategies of individuals in sample. We suggest that failure to take into account the relevancy of the information offered in the evaluation process, no matter how 'simple' or 'complex' a design is, will contribute to biases in preference revelation. The great majority of researchers and practitioners ignore this aspect of SC methods, assuming, instead, that attributes offered are all relevant to some degree.

This chapter is organized as follows. We begin with an overview of a range of behavioral perspectives on information processing promoted in the theoretical literature. We then use two case studies to illustrate some of the ways in which we can identify sources of systematic variation associated with the SC setting that influence attribute processing (particularly inclusion and exclusion rules) and how we might accommodate attribute processing rules in model estimation. We conclude with a summary of our findings and suggestions for future applications.

2. HOW DOES A RESPONDENT ASSESS STATED CHOICE TASKS?

Imagine that you have been asked to review the following choice screen and indicate which alternative is your preferred (Figure 1). There is a lot of information in this screen that you have to *attend to*, in deciding what influences your decision (what we refer as *relevant* information). There are likely to be many implicit and often subconscious rules being adopted to process the attributes and alternatives that are used, possibly to cope with the amount of information to assess (what we refer to as a *coping* strategy). The screen, for example, may be regarded as too *complex* in terms of the amount of information presented and its content. Whether one invokes a specific set of *processing rules* to cope with complexity, or whether these are a subset of the rules you have built up over time and draw on from past experiences, may be unclear. What we do suspect is that there is a large number of processing rules (what we call heterogeneity in information processing) being used throughout any sampled population, and that individuals are using them to handle mixtures of relevancy and cognitive burden. Indeed, it may be reasonable to suggest that relevancy is in part a natural response to cognitive burden.

It is reasonable to propose that individuals do have a variety of AP styles, including the *simplifying* strategy of ignoring certain attributes (for whatever reason). Heterogeneity in AP strategies is widely reported in consumer research (see for example Hensher, 2004, DeShazo and Fermo, 2002, 2004) and its existence in choice experiments is supported by observation of lexicographic choice behavior in segments of respondents completing SC surveys (see for example, Saelensminde, 2002).[1] When researchers fail to account for such an AP strategy, they are essentially assuming that all designs are comprehensible, all design attributes are relevant (to some degree) and the design has accommodated the relevant amount of 'complexity' necessary to make the choice experiment meaningful (Hensher et al., 2005).

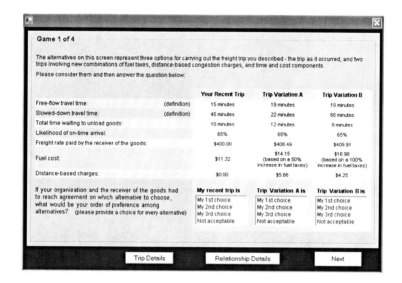

FIGURE 1. *Example of a Stated Choice Screen*

The (implicit) assumption in SC studies that all attributes are processed by all respondents has been challenged by a number of researchers (e.g., DeShazo and Fermo, 2004, Hensher, 2004, in press a, Hensher et al., 2005) who argue that it is more likely that individuals react to increasingly 'complex' choice situations by adopting one of two AP strategies, broadly defined by the rival *passive-bounded rationality* and *rationally-adaptive* behavioral models. Under the passive-bounded rationality model, individuals are thought to continue assessing all available attributes, however, they do so with increasing levels of error as choice complexity increases (de Palma et al., 1994). The rationally-adaptive model assumes that individuals recognize that their limited cognition may have positive opportunity costs and react accordingly. As DeShazo and Fermo (2004) state: "Individuals will therefore allocate their attention across alternative-attribute information within a choice set in a rationally-adaptive manner by seeking to minimize the cost and maximize the benefit of information evaluation" (p. 3).

It is important to recognize that simplistic designs may also be 'complex' in a perceptual sense. Individuals may expect more information than was given to them, thinking such information would be relevant in a real market setting.[2]

The development of a SC experiment, supplemented with questions on how an individual processed the information, enables the researcher to explore sources of systematic influences on choice. Examples of such questions are shown in the two screens below (Figures 2 and 3).

There is a substantial extant literature in the psychology domain about how various factors affect the amount of information processed in decision tasks. Recent evidence demonstrates the importance of such factors as time pressure (e.g., Diederich, 2003), cognitive load (e.g., Drolet and Luce, 2004), and task complexity

(Swait and Adamowicz, 2001). There is also a great deal of variability in decision strategies employed in different contexts, and this variability adds to the difficulties of understanding the behavioral mechanisms. A recent attempt to define a typology of decision strategies (e.g., Payne et al., 1992) has been particularly useful.

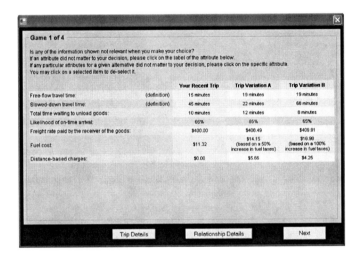

FIGURE 2. *Attribute and Alternative-Specific Processing Rules*

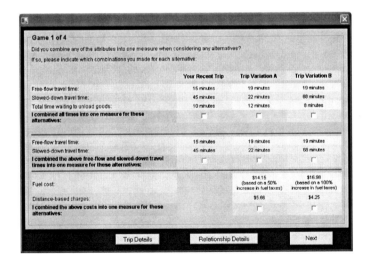

FIGURE 3. *Inter-related Attribute Processing Rules*

Payne et al. (1992) characterized decision strategies along three dimensions: basis of processing, amount of processing, and consistency of processing. Decision strategies are said to differ in terms of whether or not many attributes within an alternative are considered before another alternative is considered (*alternative-based* processing) or whether values across alternatives on a single attribute are processed before another attribute is processed (*attribute-based* processing). Strategies are also said to differ in terms of the amount of information processed (i.e. whether any information is ignored or not processed before a decision may be made). Finally, decision strategies can be grouped in terms of whether the same amount of information for each alternative is examined (*consistent* processing) or whether the amount of processing varies depending on the alternative (*selective* processing).

On the basis of this typology, Payne et al. (1992) identified six specific decision strategies, three of which are attribute-based and three alternative-based approaches. The attribute-based approaches included the elimination-by-aspects (EBA), lexicographic choice (LEX), and majority of confirming dimensions (MCD) strategies. The alternative-based approaches included the weighted additive (WADD), satisficing (SAT), and equal-weight (EQW) strategies. These strategies are further described in Table 1 below. The main argument posited by Payne et al. (1992) was that individuals construct strategies depending on the task demands and the information they are faced with.

TABLE 1. Typology of Decision Strategies

Strategy	Attribute or Alternative-based	Amount of Information	Consistency
EBA	Attribute-based	Depends on values of alternatives and cut-offs	Selective
LEX	Attribute-based	Depends on values of alternatives and cut-offs	Selective
MCD	Attribute-based	Ignores probability or weight information	Consistent
WADD	Alternative-based	All information processed	Consistent
SAT	Alternative-based	Depends on values of alternatives and cut-offs	Selective
EQW	Alternative-based	Ignores probability or weight information	Consistent

The status quo in SC modeling is the WADD strategy, since it assumes that all information is processed. Elimination by aspects (See Starmer, 2000) involves a determination of the most important attribute (usually defined as the attribute with the highest weight/probability) and the cut-off value for that attribute (i.e., a threshold). An alternative is eliminated if the value of its most important attribute falls below this cut-off value. This process of elimination continues for the second most important attribute, and so on, until a final alternative remains. Thus, the EBA strategy is best characterized as a *'threshold'* attribute processing strategy. The LEX strategy, in its strictest sense, involves a direct comparison between alternatives on the *most important* attribute. In the event of a tie, the second most important attribute is used as a comparison, and so on until an alternative is chosen. The LEX strategy is thus best characterized as a *'relative comparison'* strategy. Thus, we can clearly differentiate two classes of attribute processing strategies: threshold and relative comparison.

A major deficiency of these strategies is that although they assume selectivity in attribute processing across different decision task contexts, they assume consistency in attribute strategy within the same decision context. In other words, once a strategy is selected for a given task (or choice), it does not change within the task. This issue is further complicated by psychological theory, which identifies two main stages in the decision process. Differentiation and Consolidation Theory, developed by Svenson (1992), assumes that decision-making is a goal-oriented task, which incorporates the pre-decision process of differentiation and the post-decision process of consolidation. This theory is crucial in encouraging a disaggregation of the entire decision process.

The two issues discussed above, namely the *adaptive* nature of strategies and the *disaggregation* of the decision process, are issues that can only be assessed realistically within a paradigm that relaxes the deterministic assumption of most models of decision-making. A preferred approach would involve a stochastic specification of attribute processing that is capable of accommodating the widespread consensus in the literature that decision-making is an active process which may require different decision making strategies in different contexts and at different stages of the process (e.g., Stewart et al., 2003). As the relevance of attributes in a decision task changes, so too must our approach to modeling the strategies individuals employ when adapting to such changes. Specifically we need a flexible framework within which we can accommodate the influence of one or more of the processing strategies on choice making across the sampled population.

3. HOW DO ANALYSTS ACCOUNT FOR HETEROGENEOUS ATTRIBUTE PROCESSING?

How is the attribute processing strategy (APS) of each individual best represented within the SC modeling framework? The editing stage of prospect theory (see Starmer, 2000, Kahnemann and Tversky, 1979) is a useful theoretical setting; in this stage, agents use heuristics to make a decision setting optimally tractable. The APS can be partitioned into: (i) processes associated with decision making in real markets, and (ii) processes invoked to accommodate the information load introduced by the SC survey instrument.

Hensher (2004) has shown that the two processes are not strictly independent. The processing on a SC experiment has some similarity to how individuals process information in real markets.[3] The APS may be hypothesized to be influenced by relevant information sources resident in the agent's memory bank, either processing instructions or knowledge sources. Specific processing instructions can include:

(i) reference dependency,[4] (ii) event and attribute splitting, (iii) attribute re-packaging, (iv) degree of information preservation, and (v) the role of deliberation attributes. Knowledge sources can include the macro-conditioners as defined above.

We can view the treatment of process via one or more rules, as a deterministic or stochastic specification. In Hensher et al. (2005), for example, we treated the exogenous information of attribute inclusion/exclusion deterministically. We assumed that the analyst knows for certain which attributes are used by which respondents. It is probably more realistic, however, for the exogenous information to point to the correct likelihood specification, so that the likelihood for a respondent is a probabilistic mixture of likelihoods. We illustrate this idea in Section 4.2.

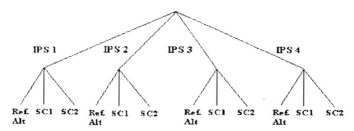

FIGURE 4. *Individual-specific Decision Structure for SC Assessment*

Since the choice made by an individual is conditioned on the APS, and given the two-stage decision process promoted in prospect theory, it is desirable to re-specify the choice model as a two-stage processing function wherein each individual's choice of alternative is best represented by a joint choice model involving the individual's choice conditional of the APS and the (marginal) choice of APS (Figure 4). We then have to decide which set of influences reside in the APS utility expression and in the choice utility expression. We anticipate that it is the processing rules that reside in the APS expressions (e.g., equation 1) and the attributes of alternatives that reside in the choice utility expressions. The contextual interactions may reside in both sets of utility expressions. The APS utility expression might be:

$$U_{aps\_i} = \alpha + \beta_1 AddAtts_i + \beta_2 \#IgnAtts_i + \beta_3 RefDepX_{1i} + \beta_4 RefDepX_{2i} + \beta_5 IV_i \quad (1)$$

where AddAtts is a dummy variable taking the value 1 if the attributes are aggregated and zero otherwise; #IgnAtts is the number of attributes ignored in processing; RedDepXj i is the difference between the ith attribute level for the reference alternative and the SC alternative j; and IV_i is the expected maximum utility associated with the choice process at the lower level of the tree structure proposed in Figure 4, similar to the theoretical link established within a nested-logit model. This model recognizes that the information processing strategy is influenced by the actual information setting within which the preferred contract outcome is selected by an agent.

Defining the choice set of AP strategies is also important and is a little-studied issue. Hensher (2004) investigated one AP strategy, where the alternatives were defined in terms of the number of attributes that are not ignored (i.e., that are attended to). This is appealing in the sense that individuals, when evaluating alternatives in a choice set, have in front of them information from the attributes (number, levels and range). The individual then processes this information by invoking a series of rules that appear to be linked to the processing instructions given above.[5] The case study below develops such an APS 'choice' model. The approach described above implies a specific experimental design strategy.

All individuals are given a single design specification in terms of the constituent attribute dimensions (number of attributes, number of levels of each attribute, attribute range) plus a fixed number of alternatives. For each choice task, a choice is made and then supplementary questions establish how the choice task is processed in terms of the invoking of one or more of the processing instructions listed above.

Alternatively, we might establish the APS more directly through the first stage of a two-stage choice experiment. In stage 1 we might offer a number of pre-designed choice experiments with varying numbers, levels and range of attributes across two alternatives, plus a reference alternative (from the agent's memory bank). These attributes can be structured in each design (in accordance with D-optimality conditions of experimental design) under rules of preservation, attribute re-packaging and relativity to the reference alternative.[6] Individuals would be asked to evaluate each design and to indicate their preferred design in terms of the information that matters to them (i.e., relevancy). We could then identify, across all designs, what information is irrelevant for behavioral processing and what is ignored to avoid cognitive burden. We can also establish the extent to which specific alternatives are seen as similar to prior accumulated experience resident in the memory bank of the individual, which are recalled as an aid in AP (since this links nicely to the notion of similarity-weighted utility in choice-based decision theory).[7]

4. EMPIRICAL EXAMPLES

To illustrate the presence of systematic sources of influence on how individuals process choice experiments we draw on a unique data set collected by the author in 2002, that has 16 SC designs embedded in the full data set. The motivation of the empirical study was the desire to establish what influence the dimensionality of SC experiments has on the WTP for specific attributes, or more precisely, the value of travel time savings for car commuter trips. The richness of the data is still being tapped, but a number of papers are available that focus on specific aspects of the relationships among three factors: design dimensionality, processing rules and valuation (see Hensher, 2004, in press a, in press b). The material presented below is not a complete analysis of the results, and interested readers should consult the papers by the author listed in the references.

The choice set assessed by each respondent involved a current commute trip and two SC alternatives, all defined as unlabelled routes. The candidate attributes have been selected based on earlier studies (see Hensher, 2004). They are: free-flow time (FFT), slowed-down time (SDT), stop/start time (SST), trip-time variability (TTV), toll cost (TLC), and running cost (RC) (based on c/litre, litres/100km). For the different choice set designs, we selected the following combinations of the six attributes:

- *designs with three attributes:* total time (free flow + slowed down + stop/start time), trip-time variability, total costs (toll + running cost)
- *designs with four attributes:* free-flow time, congestion time (slowed down + stop/start), trip-time variability, total costs
- *designs with five attributes:* free-flow time, slow-down time, stop/start time, trip-time variability, total costs
- *designs with six attributes:* free-flow time, slow-down time, stop/start time, trip-time variability, toll cost, running cost

All attribute levels of the two SC alternatives are pivoted off the values given for the current trip. The attribute profiles across all designs are summarized in Table 2. An example of a SC screen is shown as Figure 5.

Questions additional to the SC experiment and current trip attribute profile are shown below in Figure 6. Note especially, the deterministic information used to identify the chosen attribute processing strategy.

***TABLE 2**. Attribute Profiles for the Entire Design*

(units = %)	Base range			Wider range			Narrower range		
Levels:	2	3	4	2	3	4	2	3	4
Free-flow time	± 20	-20, 0, +20	-20, -10, +10, +20	-20, +40	-20, +10, +40	-20, 0, +20, +40	± 5	-5, 0, +5	-5, -2.5, +2.5 +5
Slow down time	± 40	-40, 0, +40	-40, -20, +20, +40	-30, +60	-30, +15, +60	-30, 0, +30, +60	± 20	-20, 0, +20	-20, -2.5, +2.5, +20
Stop/start time	± 10	10, 0, +40	-40, -20, +20, +40	-30, +60	-30, +15, +60	-30, 0, +30, +60	± 20	-20, 0, +20	-20, -2.5, +2.5, +20
Slow down-stop/start time	± 40	-40, 0, +40	-40, -20, +20, +40	-30, +60	-30, +15, +60	-30, 0, +30, +60	± 20	-20, 0, +20	-20, -2.5, +2.5, +20
Total travel time	± 40	-40, 0, +40	-40, -20, +20, +40	-30, +60	-30, +15, +60	-30, 0, +30, +60	± 20	-20, 0, +20	-20, -2.5, +2.5, +20
Uncertainty of travel time	± 40	-40, 0, +40	-40, -20, +20, +40	-30, +60	-30, +15, +60	-30, 0, +30, +60	± 20	-20, 0, +20	-20, -2.5, +2.5, +20
Running costs	± 20	-20, 0, +20	-20, -10, +10, +20	-20, +40	-20, +10, +40	-20, 0, +20, +40	± 5	-5, 0, +5	-5, -2.5, +2.5 +5
Toll costs	± 20	-20, 0, +20	-20, -10, +10, +20	-20, +40	-20, +10, +40	-20, 0, +20, +40	± 5	-5, 0, +5	-5, -2.5, +2.5 +5
Total costs	± 20	-20, 0, +20	-20, -10, +10, +20	-20, +40	-20, +10, +40	-20, 0, +20, +40	± 5	-5, 0, +5	-5, -2.5, +2.5 +5

4.1. Assessing Sources of Influence on the Number of Attributes Processed

In this section, we parameterize an ordered mixed-logit model to investigate the role of five classes of influences on respondent's inclusion or exclusion of specific attributes within a choice set:

1.   The dimensionality of the SC task;
2.   The deviation of the design attribute levels from the reference alternative;
3.   The use of 'adding up' attributes when feasible;

4. The number of choice sets to be evaluated; and
5. The socio-economic characteristics of the respondent.

The dependent variable is the stated number of attributes that are ignored (or not attended to), with zero defining the inclusion of all attributes. Final ordered mixed-logit (OML) models for each of the four settings are given in Table 3 with marginal effects in Table 4. A marginal effect is the influence a one unit change in an explanatory variable has on the probability of selecting a particular outcome, *ceteris paribus*.[8] The marginal effects need not have the same sign as the model parameters. Hence, the statistical significance of an estimated parameter does not imply the same significance for the marginal effect.

The evidence identifies a number of statistically significant influences on the amount of information processed, given the maximum amount of information provided. Individuals clearly self-select information to process in SC studies, just as they do in real markets where the (transaction) costs of seeking out, compiling and assessing large amounts of (potentially useful) information is often seen as burdensome and/or as not producing sufficient benefits.

While the evidence herein cannot establish whether an information reduction strategy is *strictly* linked to behavioral relevance or to a coping strategy, both of which are legitimate paradigms in real markets, it does provide important signposts on how information provided within a specific context is processed to reflect what we broadly call the relevancy paradigm. Something is relevant either because it does influence a choice in a real sense of inherent preference and/or in discounting its potential role as a coping mechanism. We do this daily in most decisions we make and hence it could be argued that this information processing strategy is not unique to SC studies, but a commonly practiced AP strategy. Taking a closer look at the OML model, there are some important empirical outcomes. In the following, we highlight the lessons learned in a summary manner and refer the interested reader to Hensher (in press b) for more details.

4.1.1. Design Dimensions
The statistical significance of each of the three dimensions of a choice set is high. For the number of levels per attribute and attribute range, the negative marginal effects for zero and one levels of the response variable and the positive marginal effects for levels two and three suggests that the probability of preserving more (or all, in case of the zero response) attributes from the offered set increases *dramatically* as the number of levels per attribute declines and the attribute level range widens. What this may indicate is that *if each attribute across the alternatives in a choice set provides less variability over a wider range, then a respondent may find it useful to preserve the information content of all attributes when considering a response.* Furthermore, as we increase the number of alternatives to evaluate, the importance of maintaining more (including all) attributes increases, again as a possible mechanism for ensuring greater clarity of differentiation among the alternatives.

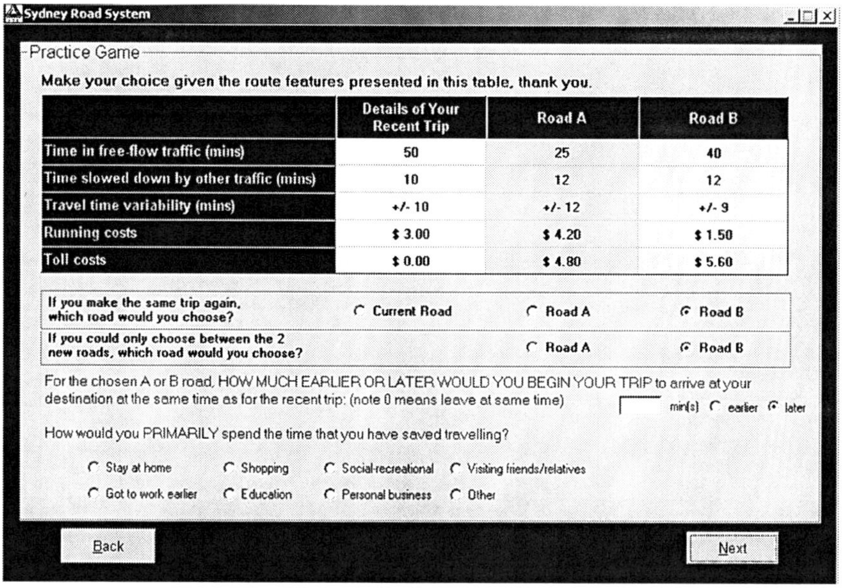

Sydney Road System

Practice Game

Make your choice given the route features presented in this table, thank you.

	Details of Your Recent Trip	Road A	Road B
Time in free-flow traffic (mins)	50	25	40
Time slowed down by other traffic (mins)	10	12	12
Travel time variability (mins)	+/- 10	+/- 12	+/- 9
Running costs	$ 3.00	$ 4.20	$ 1.50
Toll costs	$ 0.00	$ 4.80	$ 5.60

If you make the same trip again, which road would you choose? ○ Current Road ○ Road A ● Road B

If you could only choose between the 2 new roads, which road would you choose? ○ Road A ● Road B

For the chosen A or B road, HOW MUCH EARLIER OR LATER WOULD YOU BEGIN YOUR TRIP to arrive at your destination at the same time as for the recent trip: (note 0 means leave at same time) [ ] min(s) ○ earlier ● later

How would you PRIMARILY spend the time that you have saved travelling?

○ Stay at home ○ Shopping ○ Social-recreational ○ Visiting friends/relatives
○ Got to work earlier ○ Education ○ Personal business ○ Other

Back   Next

FIGURE 5. An Example of a Stated Choice Screen

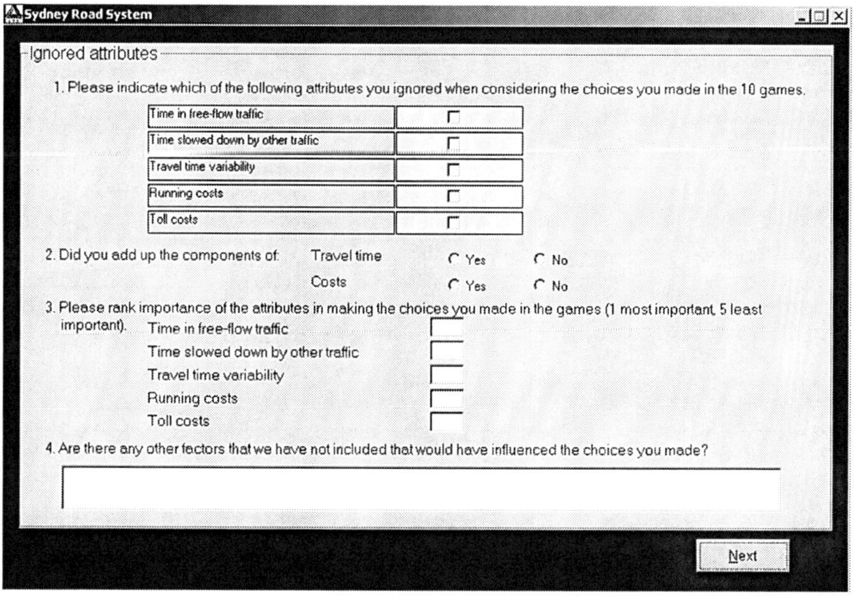

Sydney Road System

Ignored attributes

1. Please indicate which of the following attributes you ignored when considering the choices you made in the 10 games.

Time in free-flow traffic	□
Time slowed down by other traffic	□
Travel time variability	□
Running costs	□
Toll costs	□

2. Did you add up the components of: Travel time ○ Yes ○ No
   Costs ○ Yes ○ No

3. Please rank importance of the attributes in making the choices you made in the games (1 most important, 5 least important). Time in free-flow traffic [ ]
   Time slowed down by other traffic [ ]
   Travel time variability [ ]
   Running costs [ ]
   Toll costs [ ]

4. Are there any other factors that we have not included that would have influenced the choices you made?

Next

FIGURE 6. CAPI Questions on Attribute Relevance

TABLE 3. *Ordered Mixed-Logit Models for IPS models with 6,5,4 and 3 attributes per alternative*
RPL = random parameter, FP = fixed parameter

Attribute	Units	OML6 (0-3)	OML5	OML4	OML3
Constant		4.0372 (4.75)	7.494 (5.51)	5.1041 (8.44)	-2.244 (-4.24)
NonRandom Parameters:					
No. of choice sets	Number	-	-	-	-.3305 (-5.1)
Number of levels	Number	RPL	RPL	RPL	2.7935 (5.84)
Narrow attribute range	1,0	1.1129 (6.60)	2.4602 (3.91)	.7829 (2.16)	-
No. of alternatives	Number	-.8036 (-3.27)	-1.7753 (-5.04)	RPL	RPL
Adding travel time components	1.0	-.3951 (-3.10)	-1.1360 (-5.3)	.5976 (4.05)	N/A
Free-flow time for Base (total time for OML3) minus SC alternative	Minutes	0.0173 (2.19)	0.0262 (3.10)	-.0068 (-.76)	-.0089 (-1.43)
Congested time for Base (total time for OML3) minus SC alternative	Minutes	0.0140 (2.08)	-.0207 (-2.50)	.0121 (1.83)	N/A
Personal income	$000s	-.0052 (-3.13)	-.01873 (-5.3)	-.0052 (-3.63)	-.0110 (-4.5)
Random Parameters:					
No. of levels	Number	0.4824 (3.64)	-.1645 (-1.80)	-.0851 (-.74)	FP
No. of alternatives	Number	FP	FP	-.7948 (-4.0)	-1.1426 (-4.8)
Scale Parameters					
No. of levels	Number (normal)	0.5539 (7.22)	0.4508 (4.15)	.4904 (7.56)	FP
No. of alternatives	Number (normal)	FP	FP	.0604 (.16)	.5985 (4.0)
Threshold Parameters:					
Mu1		1.7088 (13.60)	4.6264 (10.60)	3.762 (15.33)	6.2020 (6.47)
Mu2		3.6897 (14.16)	-	6.548 (16.21)	-
Log-Likelihood		-4523.64	-1834.76	-3926.26	-2136.92

TABLE 4. *Marginal Effects Derived from Ordered Mixed-Logit Models for IPS models with 6, 5, 4 and 3 attributes per alternative*

Attribute	OML6				OML5		
	0	1	2	3	0	1	2
No. of levels	-.0814 (-3.76)	-.0343 (-2.55)	0.078 (1.61)	.0370 (.85)	.0402 (1.9)	-.039 (-1.8)	-.0012 (-.97)
Narrow attribute range	-.143 (-4.87)	-.128 (-20.8)	.1478 (0.53)	0.123 (5.85)	-.547 (-59.7)	.520 (44.6)	.0271 (7.57)
No. of alternatives	0.136 (3.38)	.0571 (2.38)	-.131 (-1.42)	-.062 (-0.92)	.433 (5.1)	-.421 (-5.1)	-.013 (-.86)
Adding travel time components	0.0919 (11.2)	.0538 (3.45)	-.063 (-.90)	-.034 (-.33)	.276 (20.5)	-.264 (-21.8)	-.0121 (-.50)
Free-flow time for Base minus SC alternative	-.0029 (-2.23)	-.0012 (-1.90)	0.003 (1.70)	0.001 (0.67)	-.006 (-3.1)	.006 (3.1)	.0002 (.77)
Congested time for Base minus SC alternative	-.0024 (-2.10)	-.0010 (-1.90)	0.002 (1.72)	0.001 (0.66)	0.005 (2.5)	-.005 (-2.5)	-.0001 (-.74)
Personal income	0.0009 (3.26)	0.0004 (2.28)	-0008 (-.78)	-.0004 (-.74)	.005 (7.7)	-.004 (-7.7)	-.0001 (-.97)
Attribute	OML4				OML3		
	0	1	2	3	0	1	2
Number of choice sets					.077 (5.7)	-.077 (-5.6)	-.0003 (-1.8)
No. of levels	.010 (.74)	-.0004 (-.20)	-0088 (-.66)	-.0008 (-.47)	-.650 (-6.5)	.647 (6.5)	.003 (1.7)
Narrow attribute range	-.077 (-3.2)	-.029 (-2.28)	.097 (1.6)	.0049 (6.8)			
No. of alternatives	.093 (4.0)	-.0004 (-.20)	-0823 (-5.5)	-.007 (-1.1)	.266 (5.3)	-.265 (-5.3)	-.0013 (-1.8)
Adding travel time components	-.080 (-2.9)	.0219 (1.3)	.054 (1.3)	.0045 (4.8)			
Free-flow time for Base (total time for OML3) minus SC alternative	.0008 (.76)	-.00003 (-.20)	-0007 (-.71)	-.00006 (-.53)	.002 (1.5)	.002 (-1.43)	.00001 (-1.1)
Congested time for Base minus SC alternative	-.0014 (-1.82)	.00006 (.21)	.0012 (1.73)	.0001 (.85)			
Personal income	.0006 (3.9)	.000024 (-.22)	-0005 (-2.5)	-.00005 (-.88)	.003 (4.7)	-.2646 (-5.3)	-.00001 (-1.9)

This evidence adds further support to the view that a narrower attribute range tends to decrease the probability of preserving all or most attributes. Another way of stating this is that if an analyst continues to include, in model estimation, an attribute across the entire sample that is not marked for preservation, then there is a much greater likelihood of biased parameter estimates in circumstances where the attribute range is narrow rather than wide. This has interesting implications for the growing evidence that WTP for an attribute tends to be greater when that attribute is offered over a wider range. Simply put, the greater relevance in preserving the attribute content under a wider range will mean that such an attribute is relatively more important to the outcome than it is under a narrow range specification, and hence a higher WTP is inferred.

Greater differentiation within the attribute set (levels and range) is preferred as the number of alternatives to evaluate increases.[9] This is an important finding that runs counter to some views that individuals will tend to ignore increasing amounts of attribute information as the number of alternatives increases. *Our evidence suggests that the AP strategy is dependent on the nature (i.e. profile) of the attribute information and not strictly on the quantity.*

Overall, we see a picture emerging that design dimensionality seems to have less of an influence on the AP strategy when we have fewer items to process. This makes good sense but should not be taken to imply that designs with fewer items are preferred. It is more the case that preference heterogeneity in invoking an AP strategy appears to decline substantially as the information content declines, for real or spurious reasons. Contrariwise, individuals appear to increasingly invoke a relevancy strategy as the amount of information to process increases. The need to account for this growing heterogeneity in AP strategies is clear and may be captured through the inclusion of an APS 'selectivity correction' variable in the behavioral choice models.

4.1.2. Framing around the Base

The theoretical argument promoted for reference points is supported by our empirical evidence. We have framed two attributes relative to the experienced, recent car commute as (i) free-flow time for current (or base) minus the level associated with that of each SC alternative and (ii) the congested (or nonfree flow) travel time for the base also minus the level associated with each SC alternative. Where the travel time attribute is total time (free flow plus nonfree flow), we have used it as a single framing attribute.

The evidence indicates that reference dependence is a significant influence on the AP strategy. When the difference in attribute magnitude increases, the probability of including more attributes in the selection process decreases across all AP response levels for free flow. The probability, however, changes direction for congested time for all AP response levels that remove attributes.[10]

Looking more closely at free-flow time, the evidence supports the role played by all (or most) attributes in narrowing down the choices, but importantly highlights how much easier it is to process information where the relativities are much greater. As the attribute magnitudes move closer, individuals appear to use some approximation paradigm in which closeness suggests similarity and hence ease of eliminating specific attributes.[11] This contrast can draw on regret theory (Loomes and Sugden, 1987) in which large differences between what you get from a chosen alternative and what you might have obtained from an alternative, give rise to disproportionately large regrets. This leads to individuals preferring greater certainty in the distribution of regret by choosing the alternative with which they have experience. This is the same as staying with the 'safe bet.'

4.1.3. Attribute Packaging

The event-accumulation rule in stage 1 editing under prospect theory is consistently strong for the aggregation of travel time components across all models (excluding the three-attribute model where travel time is a single attribute).[12] The mean parameter estimate is negative for six and five attributes and positive for four attributes, producing positive marginal effects for the zero response level for the six- and five-attribute and negative marginal effects for the four-attribute model.

For the six-attribute model, the statistically significant positive marginal effect applies to response levels zero and one, which suggests that if a respondent wishes to preserve the information content of all or most attributes, then the probability of processing them through an aggregation rule increases. The effect is strongest when no attributes are excluded. Indeed, it appears from other research (see Hensher, 2004) that evaluating components and aggregating them is not strictly equivalent to adding up attributes and then evaluating the aggregated attribute.

The four-attribute model produces the opposite directional impact, suggesting that when the travel time components are added up (in this case only two attributes: free flow and the pre-aggregated components of congestion time), the probability of preserving all but one attribute decreases. Checking the data shows that the attribute removed was trip-time variability, reducing the assessment to a comparison on total time and total cost. This may suggest that when one gets down to so few attributes, there is a sense of simplicity being imposed on the respondent.

There is clear evidence that a relevant simplification rule is re-packaging of the attribute set, where possible, through addition. This is not a cancellation strategy but a rational way of processing the information content of component attributes and then weighting this information (in some unobserved way) when comparing alternatives.

4.2. Influence of SC Design on Attributes Attended to and Implications for WTP

This section uses another data set and develops a mixed-logit model of the choice amongst attribute packages with the purpose of estimating WTP for travel time savings under alternative assumptions about how attributes are attended to. The data is drawn from a study undertaken in Sydney, Australia in 2004, in the context of car driving noncommuters making choices from a range of service packages defined in terms of travel times and costs, including a toll where applicable. The sample of 223 effective interviews, each responding to 16 choice sets, resulted in 3,568 observations for model estimation.

Three specifications of mixed-logit were estimated in which we (i) did not account for the presence or absence of one or more attributes in attribute processing (M1); (ii) removed an attribute if the individual stated that they ignored it in the assessment of the alternatives (M2); and (iii) introduced a stochastic specification (M3) which assumes that the analyst does not know for certain which attributes are used by which respondents. For case (iii), we can only establish, up to probability, what attribute mix a sampled individual attends to, drawing inferences from the distribution across the sampled population.

The stated incidence of not attending to one or more attributes is summarized in Table 5. This is the attribute processing choice set for the sample. We focus the analysis on four attributes – free-flow time, slow-down time, running costs and toll cost.

TABLE 5. Incidence of Mixtures of Attributes Processed

Attribute Processing Profile	Sample no. of observations=3568
All attributes attended to (v1)	1856
Attributes not attended to:	
Running cost (v2)	640
Running and toll cost (v3)	192
Toll Cost (v4)	96
Slow-down time (v5)	192
Free flow and slow-down time (v6)	304
Free-flow time (v7)	112
Slow-down time and running cost (v8)	64
Free flow and slow-down time and toll cost (v9)	48

In developing M3, we account for the assumption that the analyst is not able to identify the attribute processing strategy for a specific individual by inferring the attention to attributes up to probability. We have estimated a separate model to establish the probability of a sampled individual drawn from a population choosing a specific attribute processing strategy in terms of the portfolio of attributes that are attended and not attended to. Table 5 defines the choice set of nine alternatives for estimating an attribute inclusion/exclusion processing model. The estimated parameters are used to derive, for each individual, an index of the expected maximum utility (EMU) associated with the portfolio of attending to strategies for an individual drawn from the sampled population, calculated as the usual logsum formula in a nested-logit model (i.e. $\ln \sum_{i=1}^{9} \exp V_i$). This index is a function of the attribute levels for free-flow time, slow-down time, running cost and toll cost, as well as the respondent's age and household income. The utility expressions for each of the nine attribute processing rules are given in Table 6. Importantly, the attribute processing rule recognizes the role of the *level* of each attribute in influencing an individual's AP rule. An EMU for each sampled individual is introduced (sequentially) into the mixed-logit model M3 (see Table 7) as a way of conditioning the marginal utility of the attributes of each alternative. The presence of estimated parameters in EMU is accounted for through an assumption of additive (common) error with the η_q, although we might reasonably assume that the difference between the true and estimated parameters in EMU is small relative to the preference heterogeneity captured in η_q attributable to other influences.

TABLE 6. *Utility expressions for attribute attention profiles, estimated as multinomial logit*

v1=2.0909+.02872*age-.01088*income-.03606*ff+.11071*sdt+.1969*cost+.06767*toll

v2=1.7487+.019159*age-.011466*income-.03545*ff+.10151*sdt+.17557*cost+.06932*toll

v3=-1.49000+.01978*age-.001379*income-.00194*ff+.13364*sdt+.07899*cost+.01865*toll

V4=-3.055+.01147*age+.01349*income-.020047*ff+.1175*sdt+.20619*cost+.07678*toll

V5=0.82309+.03845*age-.01994*income-.01032*ff-.05525*sdt+.33109*cost+.00305*toll

V6=1.68608+.01397*age-.02204*income-.061966*ff+.126399*sdt+.2674*cost+.0999*toll

V7=1.5842-.02523*age-.003078*income-.017136*ff+.07665*sdt+.14232*cost-.016056*toll

V8= -4.10832+0.07469*age-.0112178*income-.03349*ff+.12575*sdt+.23752*cost-.00806*toll

V9=0

Pseudo-R^2 = 0.179, bolded= statistically insignificant at 95 percent confidence level

The random parameters in the mixed-logit models in Table 7 have a triangular distribution, which is constrained to ensure that the WTP for travel time savings was nonnegative.

The values of travel time savings (VTTS) are reported in Table 7. In our example, we see some similarities and some differences in the distributions of VTTS under the different attribute processing assumptions. Most notably, the mean VTTS varies from $7.21 to $7.95 for free-flow time and from $8.86 to $10.65 for slow-down time. We find great similarity in free-flow time between the specifications that assume all attributes are attended to and the deterministic inclusion/exclusion rule. The stochastic specification displays greater preference heterogeneity across the sample. For slow-down time, there are greater differences in the mean and standard deviations for VTTS. Specifically the model that assumes all attributes are attended to delivers a lower mean VTTS and a lower standard deviation, except for free-flow time where the standard deviation is virtually the same as the deterministic AP rule.

In order to test for differences in the variances of the free flow and slow-down time VTTS distributions over the three models (i.e., M1, M2 and M3), Brown and Forsyth (1974) tests for homogeneity of variances were conducted. We reject the null hypothesis of homogeneity of variances and conclude that the variances for the VTTS distributions are significantly different from one another over the three models (i.e., M1, M2 and M3).

This evidence suggests a deflating effect on VTTS when one ignores the attribute processing strategy and assumes that all attributes are attended to. While the differences do not appear to be large at the mean for free flow, they are sizeable for slow-down time, and when converted to time savings benefits in road projects could make a substantial difference in terms of total user benefits.

5. CONCLUSIONS

This chapter has promoted the case for increasing our knowledge on the role of (i) the dimensionality of a SC experiment, (ii) the framing of SC design profiles relative to an experience profile (a reference base) and (iii) aggregating attributes, in conditioning the processing of information associated with specific numbers of attributes across a choice set. The empirical assessment provides evidence on sources of systematic influence on how many attributes are processed relative to the full set offered.

Accounting for the inclusion vs. exclusion of an attribute in an individual's decision calculus does appear to impact the behavioral outputs of a discrete choice model; in our example the behavioral value of travel time savings distribution and its associated moments appear to be influenced by the assumptions made about how attributes are processed. This, in turn, can mean a sizable impact on estimated project benefits.

The findings in Sections 4.1 and 4.2 suggest some additional elements of SC modeling in future applications. The most appropriate elements are:

1. A series of questions to establish which attributes were ignored, either after each choice task or after completing all choice tasks. To date we have adopted the latter approach and current research is assessing the merits of identifying the attribute processing rule after each task, in part to see if the attribute level matters.

2. Effort to establish whether or not specific attributes are added up, in cases when such addition makes sense.

3. Recognition of the role of reference points, which provide the pivot for actual attribute levels shown to a respondent. The reference package is related to respondent experience and is not included in the design of the experiment. It may or may not be included in the actual survey instrument, although we tend to add it in since it appears to assist respondents in assessing the SC alternatives. If it is included, we suggest that the analyst obtain two choice responses, one in the presence of the reference alternative and the other in its absence.

4. The treatment of ignored attributes, which is best handled through a stochastic specification along the lines of the calculation of an expected maximum utility expression, similar to that obtained when linking nests in a nested-logit model.

5. Tailoring to each respondent's circumstance. Computer aided personal interviews (with an interviewer) is the preferred approach, although internet surveys are appealing where budget is a concern and /or when interviewee security is at risk in a face to face setting.

TABLE 7. *Mixed-Logit Choice Models with alternative information processing conditions (3,568 observations). Time is in minutes, cost is in dollars (500 Halton draws).*

Attribute	All attributes assumed to be attended to M1	Deterministic attribute exclusion M2	Stochastic attribute exclusion M3
Mean of random parameters			
Free-flow time	-0.0755 (-16.3)	-0.0758 (-15.1)	-0.1676 (-10.1)
Slow-down time	-0.0928 (-16.8)	-0.1034 (-15.9)	-0.1249 (-9.78)
Toll-route quality bonus*	0.6624 (4.52)	0.0998 (0.74)	0.6849 (4.94)
Standard deviations of random parameters:			
Free-flow time	0.0755 (16.3)	0.0758 (15.1)	0.1676 (10.1)
Slow-down time	0.0928 (16.8)	0.1034 (15.9)	0.1249 (9.78)
Toll-route quality bonus	2.397 (3.45)	3.6910 (5.49)	
Heterogeneity around mean:			
Free-flow time x expected maximum utility from attending to specific attributes			0.01550 (5.99)
Slow-down time x expected maximum utility from attending to specific attributes			0.00396 (2.75)
Non Random Parameters			
Running cost	-0.3321 (-12.7)	-0.3619 (-12.12)	-0.3444 (-13.4)
Toll cost	-0.6282 (-14.0)	-0.5824 (-12.03)	-0.62501 (-17.9)
Model Fits			
Pseudo-R^2	0.300	0.292	0.307
Log-Likelihood	-2739.65	-2772.62	-2714.5
Number of respondents who ignored this attribute			
Free flow excluded		496	
Slow-down time excluded		624	
Running cost excluded		976	
Toll cost excluded		304	

*The toll-route quality bonus, defined as a dummy variable to account for the relative benefits of a tolled route (compared to a free route) after accounting for the levels of service engendered in the measured attributes.

TABLE 8. *Values of travel time savings*
($ per person hour car noncommuter driver)
time = random parameter, cost = fixed parameter

Attribute	All attributes assumed to be attended to		Deterministic attribute exclusion		Stochastic attribute exclusion	
	Sample mean	Sample Std dev	Sample mean	Sample Std dev	Sample mean	Sample Std dev
Free-flow time	7.21	0.44	7.81	0.46	7.95	3.59
Slow-down time	8.86	0.54	10.65	0.67	9.91	1.22
Ratio slowed to free-flow time	1.23	1.22	1.36	1.46	1.25	0.69
Sample Size	3568		3071/2944*		3568	

* 3,071 relates to free flow and 2,944 to slow-down time.

---

6. ENDNOTES

The contributions of my colleagues John Rose, Tony Bertoia, Sean Puckett, Andrew Collins and Mike Bliemer are recognized and embedded in the material herein. I alone, however, am responsible for any specific errors of omission.

[1] Significant research effort has been expended on how to optimize the outputs derived from these single design plans using statistical design theory (e.g., Bunch et al., 1994, Huber and Zwerina, 1996, Kanninen, 2002, Kuhfeld et al., 1994, Lazari and Anderson, 1994, Sandor and Wedel, 2001), whilst minimizing the amount of cognitive effort required of respondents (e.g., Louviere and Timmermans, 1990, Oppewal et al., 1994, Wang et al., 2001, Bliemer and Rose, 2005).

[2] There is widespread evidence in the psychology literature concerning the behavioral variability, unpredictability and inconsistency regularly demonstrated in decision making and choices (e.g., Gonzales-Vallejo, 2002, Slovic, 1995), reflecting an assumption that goes back at least to Thurstone's law of comparative judgment (1927). One of the particularly important advantages of using a stochastic representation of decision strategies, as promoted herein, is that it enables a more behaviorally realistic analysis of variation in decision strategies.

[3] The main difference is that the stated choice experiment provides the information to be processed, in contrast to real markets where more effort is required to search for relevant information. We recognize, however, that the amount of information in the SC experiment may be more than what an individual would normally use in making a choice. Yet that is precisely why we have to establish the APS of each individual to ensure that the offered information is represented appropriately in model estimation. For example, if an attribute is ignored, we need to recognize this and not assume it is processed as if it is not ignored.

[4] Defined empirically by the relative distance between the attribute levels in the SC alternative and levels that an individual is familiar with (i.e., a case-based-decision-theoretical memory set that actually has been experienced as defined herein by the base alternative – a recent or a most-experienced alternative). Reference dependency is a member of the broader class of the similarity condition of CBDT in which it is

suggested that individuals choose acts based on their performance in similar problems in the past. The review and assessment of a choice task is defined as a *problem* in CBDT.

[5] Importantly, in order to establish the full dimensionality of an agent's APS, we must show them the full attribute design and establish how they choose to process it. This is essential for each choice set if we are to assess the influence of reference dependency as defined by the levels of attributes in each SC alternative relative to the reference alternative (i.e., experienced or memory-based).

[6] The range of possible IPS's would be established in prior in-depth interviews with stakeholders. The advantage of this two-stage approach is that each design (conditioned on the IPS) will be D-optimal.

[7] Establishing how similarity from memory is built into the estimation of the choice model is challenging. As a global condition, it can be treated as an exogenous adjustment through a discrete-continuous choice specification. For example, we might estimate a similarity model where the dependent variable is some measure of 'similarity,' and then use the predicted similarity indicator as a multiplicand of the utility estimate attached to each alternative in the discrete choice model prior to deriving the choice probabilities.

[8] This holds for continuous variables only. For dummy (1,0) variables, the marginal effects are the derivatives of the probabilities given a change in the level of the dummy variable.

[9] Up to the number evaluated in this study. In studies with a greater number of attributes, there may be a threshold beyond which additional attributes are not preserved.

[10] For congested time, the sign change for the marginal effects is not statistically significant (as reported for OML6).

[11] This result reinforces the evidence on the influence of the number of levels and range of attributes in the SC design.

[12] Hensher (in press a) presents the data set in detail. We find that over 80% of the sample who evaluated the 6, 5 and 4 attribute designs added up components of travel time.

7. REFERENCES

Bliemer, M.C. and J.M. Rose, 2005, "Efficient Designs for Alternative Specific Choice Experiments, Institute of Transport and Logistics Studies," University of Sydney.

Brown, M.B. and A.B. Forsythe, A.B., 1974, "Robust Tests for Equality of Variances," *Journal of American Statistical Association,* 69: 264-267.

Bunch, David S., Jordan J. Louviere, and Donald A. Anderson, 1996, "A Comparison of Experimental Design Strategies for Choice-Based Conjoint Analysis with Generic-Attribute Multinomial Logit Models," Working Paper, Graduate School of Management, University of California, Davis.

DePalma, Andre, Gordon M. Meyers, and Yorgos Y. Papageorgiou, 1994, "Rational Choice Under an Imperfect Ability to Choose," *American Economic Review,* 84: 419-440.

De Shazo, J.R. and G. Fermo, 2002, "Designing Choice Sets for Stated Preference Methods: The Effects of Complexity on Choice Consistency," *Journal of Environmental Economics and Management,* 44: 123-143.

DeShazo, J.R. and G. Fermo, 2004, "Implications of Rationally-adaptive Pre-choice Behavior for the Design and Estimation of Choice Models, Working Paper, School of Public Policy and Social Research, University of California at Los Angeles.

Diederich, A., 2003, "MDFT Account of Decision Making Under Time Pressure," *Psychonomic Bulletin & Review*, 10: 157-166.

Dosman, D. and W. Adamowicz, 2003, "Combining Stated and Revealed Preference Data to Construct an Empirical Examination of Intrahousehold Bargaining," Department of Rural Economy, University of Alberta.

Drolet, A. and M.F. Luce, 2004, "The Rationalizing Effects of Cognitive Load on Emotion-based Trade-off Avoidance," *Journal of Consumer Research*, 31: 63-77.

Gilboa, I. and D. Schmeidler, 2001, *A Theory of Case-Based Decisions*, Cambridge University Press, Cambridge.

Gilboa, I., D. Schmeidler and P. Wakker, 2002, "Utility in Case-based Decision Theory," *Journal of Economic Theory*, 105: 483-502.

González-Vallejo, C., 2002, "Making Trade-offs: A Probabilistic and Context-sensitive Model of Choice Behavior," *Psychological Review*, 109: 137-155.

Greene, W.H., D.A. Hensher and J. Rose, In Press, "Accounting for Heterogeneity in the Variance of Unobserved Effects in Mixed Logit Models, *Transportation Research B*.

Hensher, D.A., 2004, "Accounting for Stated Choice Design Dimensionality in Willingness to Pay for Travel Time Savings, *Journal of Transport Economics and Policy*, 38 (2): 425-446.

Hensher, D.A., In Press a, "Revealing Differences in Behavioral Response Due to the Dimensionality of Stated Choice Designs: An Initial Assessment, *Environment and Resource Economics*.

Hensher, D.A., In Press b, "How do Respondents Handle Stated Choice Experiments? Attribute Processing Strategies Under Varying Information Load, *Journal of Applied Econometrics*.

Hensher, D.A., J. Rose and W. Greene, 2005, *Applied Choice Analysis: A Primer*, Cambridge University Press, Cambridge.

Hensher, D.A., J. Rose, and W. Greene, 2005, "The Implications on Willingness to Pay of Respondents Ignoring Specific Attributes," *Transportation*, 32(2): 203-222.

Huber, Joel Klaus Zwerina, 1996, "The Importance of Utility Balance and Efficient Choice Designs, *Journal of Marketing Research*, 33 (3): 307-317.

Kahnemann, D. and Tversky, A., 1979, "Prospect Theory: An Analysis of Decisions Under Risk," *Econometrica*, 47 (2): 263-91.

Kanninen, Barbara J., 2002, "Optimal Design for Multinomial Choice Experiments," *Journal of Marketing Research*, 39 (2): 214-217.

Kuhfeld, Warren F., Randal D. Tobias and Mark Garratt, 1994, Efficient Experimental Design with Marketing Research Applications," *Journal of Marketing Research*, 21 (4): 545-557.

Lazari, Andreas G. and Donald A. Anderson, 1994, "Designs of Discrete Choice Experiments for Estimating Both Attribute and Availability Cross Effects," *Journal of Marketing Research*, 31 (3): 375-383.

Loomes, G. and R. Sugden, R., 1987, "Some Implications of a More General Form of Regret Theory, *Journal of Economic Theory*, 41 (2): 270-87.

Louviere, Jordan J. and Harry J.P. Timmermans, 1990, "Hierarchical Information Integration Applied to Residential Choice Behavior, *Geographical Analysis*, 22: 127–145.

Louviere, J.J., D.A. Hensher and J.F. Swait, 2000, *Stated Choice Methods and Analysis*, Cambridge University Press, Cambridge.

Oppewal, Harman, Jordan J. Louviere amd Harry J.P Timmermans, 1994, "Modeling hierarchical information integration processes with integrated conjoint choice experiments," *Journal of Marketing Research*, 31: 92–105.

Payne, J.W., J.R. Bettman and E.J. Johnson, 1988, "Adaptive Strategy Selection in Decision Making," *Journal of Experimental Psychology: Learning, Memory, and Cognition*, 14: 534-552.

Payne, J.W., J.R. Bettman, E. Coupey and E.J. Johnson, 1992, "A Constructive Process View of Decision Making: Multiple Strategies in Judgment and Choice," *Acta Psychologica*, 80: 107-141.

Sælensminde, Kjartan, 1994, "The Impact of Choice Inconsistencies in Stated Choice Studies," *Environmental & Resource Economics*, 23 (4): 403-420.

Sandor, Zsolt and Michel Wedel, 2001, "Designing Conjoint Choice Experiments Using Managers' Prior Beliefs," *Journal of Marketing Research*, 38 (4): 430-444.

Slovic, P., 1995, "The Construction of Preference," *American Psychologist*, 50: 364-371.

Starmer, C., 2000, "Developments in Non-expected Utility Theory: The Hunt for a Descriptive Theory of Choice Under Risk," *Journal of Economic Literature*, XXXVIII: 332-382.

Stewart, N., N. Chater, H.P. Stott and S. Reimers, 2003, "Prospect Relativity: How Choice Options Influence Decision Under Risk," *Journal of Experimental Psychology: General*, 132: 23-46.

Svenson, O., 1992, "Differentiation and Consolidation Theory of Human Decision Making: A Frame of Reference for the Study of Pre-and Post-decision Processes," *Acta Psychologica*, 80: 143-168.

Swait, J. and W. Adamowicz, 2001, "The Influence of Task Complexity on Consumer Choice: A Latent Class Model of Decision Strategy Switching," *Journal of Consumer Research*, 28: 135-148.

Thurstone, L. L., 1927, "A Law of Comparative Judgment," *Psychological Review*, 23: 273–286.

Tversky, A., 1972, "Elimination by Aspects: A Theory of Choice," *Psychological Review*, 79: 281-299.

Wang, Donggen, Jiuqun Li and Harry J.P. Timmermans, 2001, "Reducing Respondent Burden, Information Processing and Incomprehensibility in Stated Preference Surveys: Principles and Properties of Paired Conjoint Analysis, *Transportation Research Record*, 1768: 71–78.

CHAPTER 7

EXPERIMENTAL DESIGN FOR STATED CHOICE STUDIES

F. REED JOHNSON

RTI International, Research Triangle Park, North Carolina, U.S.A.

BARBARA KANNINEN

Arlington, Virginia, U.S.A.

MATTHEW BINGHAM

Veritas Economic Consulting, Cary, North Carolina, U.S.A.

SEMRA ÖZDEMIR

RTI International, Research Triangle Park, North Carolina, U.S.A.

1. INTRODUCTION

People's time and cognitive resources are valuable and collecting data is costly. No matter how well researchers plan and prepare a survey, eventually they have to ask a large number of people to donate (or sell) some of their time to answer questions. The greater the burden, the more likely some potential subjects will either refuse to participate or provide inaccurate or ill-considered responses. Researchers should therefore do everything in their power to minimize the time and effort required to respond fully and accurately to their survey. In particular, it is important to minimize the number of questions we ask, given the goal of obtaining information[1] that is both reliable and statistically efficient.

The idea behind experimental design is that researchers, in our field and others, have the ability to control certain factors within their study. These factors, in turn, affect parameter identification, model flexibility, and the statistical efficiency of resulting estimators.[2] In this chapter, we are specifically concerned with designing choice tasks for stated choice (SC) surveys. SC tasks may involve binary choices: two alternatives, where the respondents are asked to pick the more–preferred one; or

B.J. Kanninen (ed.), Valuing Environmental Amenities Using Stated Choice Studies, 159–202.

multinomial choices: more than two alternatives, where respondents are asked to pick the most-preferred.[3]

For each alternative in a choice task, researchers must describe the attributes that define the commodity, or commodities, of interest. Attributes are such features as color, size, brand name, risk characteristics, location, aesthetic qualities, comfort, or price, to name several examples. Some of these features are qualitative variables, coded into the dataset as either dummy (zero/one) variables or effects codes, and some are quantitative, coded at their numerical levels. How these attributes vary within and between alternatives, across choice tasks within a survey, and across surveys, will affect the quality of the information ultimately garnered from the survey.

This chapter summarizes our current understanding of the field of experimental design for SC studies. We begin with a simple example to illustrate some basic principles of experimental design and then move on to larger problems, providing examples of approaches that use readily available catalog designs, tried-and-true formulaic techniques, and computer algorithms. Throughout, we interweave the topic of optimal design, the study of ways to improve an experimental design so that parameter estimates are more precise.

2. FACTORIAL DESIGNS

We begin with a very simple example using soup recipes.[4,5] Suppose you have three kinds of ingredients (attributes) for soup: meat, noodles, and vegetables. There are two kinds (levels) of meat: chicken or beef. You can include or not include noodles, and you can include or not include vegetables. Table 1 summarizes the different choices of soup ingredients.

In Table 1, there are three attributes, each with two levels. The total possible number of ingredient combinations then, is $2^3 = 2 \times 2 \times 2 = 8$. Design names, such as 2^3, or, as another example, $2^2 3$, take a moment to digest. The full sized numbers refer to the number of levels each attribute takes, while the exponent represents the number of different attributes that can take those levels. Multiplying out the terms gives the total number of possible combinations in the full-factorial design (attributes are called factors in design theory). The full-factorial list of all eight possible soup recipes is shown in Table 2.

Let us define a utility function that describes an individual's utility for different kinds of soup:

$$U(\text{Soup}) = \beta_o + \beta_m \text{ Beef} + \beta_n \text{ Noodles} + \beta_v \text{ Vegetables}$$
$$+ \beta_{mn} \text{Beef} \cdot \text{Noodles} + \beta_{mv} \text{Beef} \cdot \text{Vegetables} + \beta_{nv} \text{Noodles} \cdot \text{Vegetables}$$
$$+ \beta_{mnv} \text{Beef} \cdot \text{Noodles} \cdot \text{Vegetables} \qquad (1)$$

where $\beta_o = U(\text{Chicken, No Noodles, No Vegetables})$. Thus the recipe for "vegetable beef soup" offers a utility equal to $\beta_o + \beta_m \text{ Beef} + \beta_v \text{ Vegetables} + \beta_{mv} \text{Beef} \cdot \text{Vegetables}$. Note that this utility function contains linear terms for each of the attribute levels (beef, noodles and vegetables) as well as three two-way interactive terms (beef·noodles, beef·vegetables, noodles·vegetables) and one three-way interactive term (beef·noodles·vegetables).

TABLE 1. *Attribute Table for Soup Recipes*

<table>
<tr><td rowspan="3">LEVELS</td><td colspan="3">ATTRIBUTES</td></tr>
<tr><td>MEAT</td><td>NOODLES</td><td>VEGETABLES</td></tr>
</table>

<table>
<tr><td>LEVELS</td><td>Chicken</td><td>Yes</td><td>Yes</td></tr>
<tr><td></td><td>Beef</td><td>No</td><td>No</td></tr>
</table>

TABLE 2. *Full-factorial List of Soup Recipes*

Soups	MEAT	NOODLES	VEGETABLES
1	Chicken	Yes	Yes
2	Chicken	Yes	No
3	Chicken	No	Yes
4	Chicken	No	No
5	Beef	Yes	Yes
6	Beef	Yes	No
7	Beef	No	Yes
8	Beef	No	No

To estimate this function using stated choice, a researcher would have to ask a number of respondents to express their preferences for the various soup recipes. Importantly, if the researchers are interested in estimating all of the coefficients in equation 1, they will have to obtain some sort of reading on each of the possible soup recipes in the full-factorial (Table 2). By correctly mixing all the possibilities in the full factorial into different choice tasks, researchers should be able to estimate the full model.

Table 3 presents the 2^3 full-factorial design of Table 2 in a different way. Renaming the soup terminology as attributes A, B, and C, the table indicates the presence (+1) or absence (-1) of each attribute under Main Effects.[6] The other columns indicate whether the interaction effects between and among the attributes are positive or negative. This approach to coding the data is called effects coding. If the attributes each had three levels rather than two, the corresponding effects codes would be +1, 0, and -1.[7] With this coding, we can investigate the concept of orthogonality.

A matrix is said to be orthogonal when every pair of columns within it are orthogonal to each other. Two columns are orthogonal to each other when there is no correlation between their elements. Geometrically, this occurs when two vectors are perpendicular to each other; they, basically, have nothing in common. Algebraically, orthogonality occurs when vector multiplying two columns gives a result of zero. Looking at attributes A and B: A'B = (-1)·(-1) +(-1)·(+1) +(+1)·(-1) +(+1)·(+1) +(-1)·(-1) + (-1)·(+1) +(+1)·(-1) +(+1)·(+1) = 0, and thus, these two columns are orthogonal. We will discuss more about orthogonality later in this section.

TABLE 3. Full-Factorial, 2^3 Design

Combi-nation	Main Effects			Two-Way Interactions			Three-Way Interaction
	A	B	C	A·B	A·C	B·C	A·B·C
1	-1	-1	+1	+1	-1	-1	+1
2	-1	+1	-1	-1	-1	+1	+1
3	+1	-1	-1	-1	+1	-1	+1
4	+1	+1	+1	+1	+1	+1	+1
5	-1	-1	-1	+1	+1	+1	-1
6	-1	+1	+1	-1	+1	-1	-1
7	+1	-1	+1	-1	-1	+1	-1
8	+1	+1	-1	+1	-1	-1	-1

As mentioned above, our soup example is a very simple one. Often, researchers are interested in a larger set of attributes. If we wanted to look at six soup ingredients, for example, we would have to collect utility information about 64 different recipes. If we wanted to look at eight ingredients, we would have 256 different recipes. Needless to say, the numbers quickly get unwieldy.[8] Therefore, researchers often rely on fractional-factorial designs. These smaller designs provide enough information for researchers to estimate coefficients for the "main effects," but do not allow estimation of all the interaction effects. This is a trade-off that researchers generally have to accept, given the limited research resources available to them.[9]

The first four rows of Table 3 are a principal fraction of the full 8-row factorial. A main-effects design that uses only these first four rows (and the first three columns) is orthogonal and balanced.

The sacrifice of information when using fractional-factorial designs is immediately apparent. In Table 3, the first four rows for A are -1, -1, 1, 1, which are identical to the corresponding rows for A·C. Thus, the effect that A has on utility cannot be separated from the effect that the interactive effect, A·C, has. The same is true for B and B·C, and for C and A·B. The following models are therefore statistically equivalent.[10]

$$Y = \beta_1 \cdot A + \beta_2 \cdot B + \beta_3 \cdot C$$
$$Y = \beta_1 \cdot A \cdot C + \beta_2 \cdot B \cdot C + \beta_3 \cdot A \cdot B$$

(2)

When modeling utility, then, we cannot tell whether our estimate of β_1 represents the marginal utility of A or of A·C. Looking at the soup example, we would not know whether our estimate for β_1 represents the main effect of including vegetables in the soup or the interactive effect of having beef and noodles together. Note, though, that we are able to estimate the main effect for beef and the main effect for noodles. The confounding occurs only with the interactive effects for these two ingredients. We can get rid of this confounding by assuming that beef and noodles only enter the utility function as independent effects. That is, we allow the main effects, βm and βn, to fully describe the impact on utility of including beef and noodles in the recipe and assume that $\beta_{mn} = 0$. Fractional-factorial designs require that we make such assumptions.

It is important to understand what is being sacrificed when we set up a design that confounds different effects. Interaction effects occur when one factor's main effect is not the same for different levels of another factor (Keppel, 1973). For example, in a laboratory, a simple one-factor experiment might have one set of outcomes when the temperature in the lab is 58 degrees F and a different set of outcomes when the lab is 72 degrees. If the change in temperature alters the outcome in ways that are not fully explained by the main effect of temperature alone, then there is also some type of interaction between temperature and the other factor under study. Not accounting for this will bias the results of the experiment.

However, to make our designs and samples reasonably sized, we often have to ignore interactive effects. Louviere (1988) argues that main-effects designs tend to account for as much as 80% of the explained variance in choice models, so ignoring interactive effects is like settling on a first-order approximation of the true model. We generally believe that simple, main-effects designs predict choices fairly well. However, it is prudent to carefully consider other options. It may be possible to incorporate at least a few interactions that you consider potentially important. Valid welfare calculations depend on the assumption of unbiased parameter estimates; omitted variables are a well-known source of bias. At the very least, researchers should have a clear conceptual or empirical rationale for excluding interactive effects.

The question of how to effectively combine alternatives into choice tasks is a difficult one and is discussed in the next section. First, for background, we need to address the simpler question of how to design open-ended experiments: those where subjects actually provide utility responses for all possible soup recipes. In other words, we assume that respondents know (with some error) the dependent variable, utility, and that they are willing to state it directly. This assumption allows us to cover some of the principles of traditional experimental and optimal design theory. Later, we will see that some of the principles that are sacred to traditional experimental design do not cross over to the situation of designing choice sets, while others do.

We generally express utility as:

$$U_i = X_i \beta + e_i \tag{3}$$

where U_i is the utility a respondent experiences from a choice scenario or alternative i, X is a row vector of K attributes that describe the alternative, β is a Kx1 vector of marginal utilities, and e_i is an error term that is independently and identically distributed normal with mean 0 and variance σ^2. (We suppress the respondent-specific subscript for simplicity.)

Our goal is to find ways to construct designs that provide the most statistical information possible, while, of course, also keeping matters such as respondent cognitive burden in check (see Hensher, this volume). A common expression of statistical information is the Fisher information matrix, which for the β coefficients in equation 2, is equal to $(1/\sigma^2)$ X'X. The information matrix turns out to be the inverse of the asymptotic covariance matrix of the maximum likelihood estimates (see Alberini et al., this volume, and Swait, this volume). This is an important result and shows the fundamental relationship between the Fisher information matrix and our general design goal: we would like to obtain estimates that have low variances and covariances and this goal, in some sense, is inversely correlated with the idea of *maximizing* the statistical information provided by the information matrix.

The field of optimal design is the study of "best" designs based on specific criteria. Optimal design researchers generally believe that maximizing the determinant of the Fisher information matrix will offer the best design when the goal is to jointly estimate the β parameters as well as possible. This design criterion is referred to in the literature as D-optimality.

We can draw a couple of basic conclusions about best designs for a linear model such as equation (2) based on the expression for the information matrix above. Maximizing $| (1/\sigma^2) $ X'X $ |$ with respect to the dataset (X) is the same as maximizing $|$ X'X $|$. The maximum $|$ X'X $|$ occurs when the diagonal components of the X'X matrix are as large as possible and the off-diagonal components are as small in absolute value as possible; in other words, as close to zero as possible. This occurs when the levels of the attributes in X are at their most extreme points (both positive and negative) and when the columns of the X matrix are *orthogonal*.

Let's look first at the "extreme points" part of that statement. Since two points define a line, researchers only need to collect responses to two different attribute levels to estimate linear main effects. By looking at a simple one-variable example, it is not hard to see that by placing those two data points far from each other, researchers have a better basis for identifying the regression line than if the two data points had been placed close together. This result, of course, requires researchers to fully believe in the linearity of the effect. It also requires understanding what respondents regard as a reasonable range of values. A daily pass at a state park, for example, should not be offered at $100. "Extreme" here refers to the upper (lower) bound or maximum (minimum) value that would reasonably define a linear segment of utility.

Now, turning to orthogonality: looking at our example in Table 2, defining yes·yes and no·no as equal to 1 and yes·no and no·yes as equal to zero, we find that the columns for Noodles and Vegetables are orthogonal to each other. Making similar assumptions and calculations, we find the other two column pairings to be orthogonal as well. This turns out to be exactly what we need to obtain D-optimality. The off-diagonal terms of the information matrix are the cross-products of the data vectors and we'd like to get them as close to zero as possible.

Orthogonality has long been an important property for experimental design, even before the days of optimal design. Back when statisticians ran analyses of variance on their hand-held calculators, they needed zero correlation between and among their experimental variables so that sums-of-squares statistics would be easy to calculate. Today, we have these traditional roots, as well as the optimality results for the linear model upholding the importance of orthogonality. It has become the gold standard of design.

Another design feature that is considered important for statistical efficiency is level balance. In Table 2, for example, each of the attribute levels occur the same number of times across the matrix. Chicken occurs four times, for example, and Beef occurs four times. Noodles and No Noodles and Vegetables and No Vegetables are also included four times each. Level balance provides an equal number of observations for each attribute level. This, essentially, ensures that we obtain the most information possible about each individual parameter. Any imbalance we might introduce would increase the information we obtain about one particular parameter at the expense of another.

3. CHOICE SET DESIGN

Until now, what we have discussed is fairly standard experimental design material. Under the assumption of a linear model with a continuous dependent variable, the best designs are orthogonal and balanced and cover enough of the various possibilities to identify the parameters of interest. We now turn to the problem that makes our field of study different from others: the problem of constructing choice sets. This turns out to be difficult territory and to date there is no generally established theory to guide us. Instead, we have a literature that has provided a variety of approaches, from simple and straightforward (but not always the best) to more time-consuming, sophisticated procedures. We present the various options below. First, however, we briefly review the choice model.

As discussed in Alberini et al. (this volume) and Swait (this volume), the choice model takes equation 2 and assumes that the error term is independently and identically distributed according to the Gumbel distribution. Following McFadden (1974), the probability that a respondent will choose alternative i from a choice set C_n is:

$$P_{in}(C_n, \beta) = \frac{\exp(x_{in}\beta)}{\sum_{j \in C_n} \exp(x_{jn}\beta)}$$

(4)

$\hat{\beta}$ is derived by the method of maximum likelihood.

Alberini et al. (this volume) show how the multinomial choice model is, in fact, a function of attribute differences, rather than absolute attribute levels. In other words, when different levels of an attribute are assumed to offer the same marginal utility, individuals are assumed to evaluate a choice between, say, an attribute taking levels 0 and 1 as equivalent to the choice between the same attribute taking levels 3 and 4. In both cases, the attribute difference is 1. If this assumption is thought to be a problem, the researcher can specify separate β's for different levels of the attribute, to allow for different marginal utilities as the attribute level changes. The question of "same beta versus separate betas" on each attribute is an important modeling decision that will affect the design. In the following, we generally assume "same beta," but this assumption is easy to relax. If the researcher prefers separate betas, the attribute is essentially sectioned into two or more separate attributes (with only one of the sections appearing in each alternative).

Assuming binary choices, the Fisher information matrix is now:

$$I = X_0'P'[(I - P)X_0]$$
(5)

where P is a $N \times N$ diagonal matrix with diagonal elements equal to the expected probability p_i of respondents preferring the particular alternative, i, and X_0 is the $N \times K$ data matrix of attribute level differences between alternative i and the second alternative. Looking at the details of the matrix:

$$I = \begin{pmatrix} \sum w_i x_{01i}^2 & \sum w_i x_{01i} x_{02i} & \cdots & \sum w_i x_{0Ki} \\ & \sum w_i x_{02i}^2 & \cdots & \sum w_i x_{01} x_{0Ki} \\ \bullet & & \ddots & \vdots \\ & & & \sum w_i x_{0Ki}^2 \end{pmatrix}$$
(6)

where $w_i = p(1 - p)$ for all i.[11]

A simple and straightforward approach to generating choice pairs is to use a random strategy. The researcher might start with the first four rows of the full factorial and then sample without replacement from the remaining rows: five through eight. To remain true to the randomized approach, the researcher could write the four remaining row numbers on slips of paper, turn them over, mix them up, and draw them one at a time and match them up with the first four rows.

Table 4A shows one possible outcome of this random process. For simplicity, we pretended to draw rows five through eight in order. This is just as likely an outcome as any other, and is based on the particular ordering we provided for the full factorial in Table 3. The discussion that follows is relevant to any particular ordering one might obtain from a truly random process.

The first thing that probably becomes apparent in Table 4A is that every choice set has not one, but two overlaps in attributes. Overlap means that an attribute level is the same for both alternatives in the choice set. When attributes do not vary in a choice set, the researcher does not obtain any information about respondent trade-off preferences from that observation. Clearly, this is not a good feature for choice set design, and we will generally want to minimize its occurrence.

Looking back at the expression for the Fisher Information matrix, we also see that a choice set that results in one alternative being very attractive (getting a response probability near 1) versus an alternative that is very unattractive (getting a response probability near 0), would give a $p(1-p)$ close to zero. Such a choice set would provide practically no statistical information to the researcher. From an intuitive standpoint, one alternative is dominated, or nearly dominated, by the other. If we understand some basic things about preferences (for example, that low prices are preferred to high prices), then we can reduce the number of dominant or near-dominant choice sets in the design.

Looking at Table 4A, suppose we know that +1 is always preferred to -1 for attribute C (+1 might represent higher quality than -1). In this case, we would rule out pairing profile 1 with profile 5, since all levels of profile 1 are at least as good, or better, than all levels of profile 5. All attentive subjects will prefer alternative 1 to alternative 5 and we learn nothing about their willingness to accept trade-offs among attributes.

TABLE 4A. *Arbitrary Choice-Set Pairs, 2^3 Design*

	Alternative 1				Alterative 2			
Choice Sets	Profiles	A_1	B_1	C_1	Profiles	A_2	B_2	C_2
1	1	-1	-1	+1	5	-1	-1	-1
2	2	-1	+1	-1	6	-1	+1	+1
3	3	+1	-1	-1	7	+1	-1	+1
4	4	+1	+1	+1	8	+1	+1	-1

TABLE 4B. *Foldover Choice-Set Pairs, 2^3 Design*

	Alternative 1				Alterative 2			
Choice Sets	Profiles	A_1	B_1	C_1	Profiles	A_2	B_2	C_2
1	1	-1	-1	+1	8	+1	+1	-1
2	2	-1	+1	-1	7	+1	-1	+1
3	3	+1	-1	-1	6	-1	+1	+1
4	4	+1	+1	+1	5	-1	-1	-1

Table 4B uses a better strategy for arranging profiles into choice sets: it uses foldovers. A foldover replaces an attribute level with its opposite. Each -1 in Alternative 1 is paired with a corresponding +1 in Alternative 2, and vice versa. This choice-set formulation strategy works particularly well with binary choices because it guarantees that the resulting choice sets will have no overlap.

Table 5 summarizes the overlap and dominance patterns for the choice sets in both Table 4A and Table 4B, assuming that +1 is preferred to -1 for each of the attributes. All the pairs in Table 4A have two overlaps each. This leaves only one attribute in each pair with contrasting levels. Even more seriously, one member of the pair is clearly better than the other in every case. This design provides no information on preferences!

In contrast, the foldover design has no overlaps (by construction) and only one dominated pair. Note that no matter how we rearrange our assumptions about +1 and -1 being preferred for each attribute, there will always be one pair in this design that is dominant. Interestingly, then, if we chose to drop this final choice set from the design, it would not affect the amount of statistical information collected. Dropping this observation, however, results in a non-orthogonal dataset! So, it turns out that with choice sets, the traditional rules for experimental design do not work the same way they do for linear models. Clearly, since that last choice set would offer no information to us, we would save time and money by eliminating it from the design. In general, we have found that perfect orthogonality, the gold standard of the linear model, does not necessarily work with choice models – at least not when you have enough prior knowledge to identify dominated choice sets.

TABLE 5. Overlap and Dominance in Choice Sets

	Overlap	Dominance
Table 4A Choice Sets		
1, 5	2	Yes
2, 6	2	Yes
3, 7	2	Yes
4, 8	2	Yes
Table 4B Choice Sets		
1, 8	0	No
2, 7	0	No
3, 6	0	No
4, 5	0	Yes

Here's another example. Suppose we know that all of our sample respondents prefer beef to chicken, having vegetables to not having them, and having noodles to not having them. The foldover choice sets for the soup example are shown in Table 6. Each choice set is "difficult" for subjects because it contrasts recipes that contain both more desirable and less desirable components. The choice task requires subjects to weigh the relative importance of the positive and negative features. The resulting pattern of choices reveals these weights for the overall sample.

Even though we use most of the full factorial to generate choice sets, this design only allows us to estimate the main-effects. This is because the design gives no variation among the interactions. The foldover pattern gives $A_1 \cdot B_1 = \{ +1, -1, -1 \} = A_2 \cdot B_2$, that is, overlap in all the two-way interactions. An experimental design that ensures variation in the interaction effects requires other choice-set construction strategies.

TABLE 6. *Foldover Choice-Set Pairs, Soup Example*

Choice Sets	Alternative 1			Alterative 2		
	A_1	B_1	C_1	A_2	B_2	C_2
1	Chicken	No Noodles	Vegetables	Beef	Noodles	No Vegetables
2	Chicken	Noodles	No Vegetables	Beef	No Noodles	Vegetables
3	Beef	No Noodles	No Vegetables	Chicken	Noodles	Vegetables

This example demonstrates that, with very simple design spaces, it is possible to manually construct choice sets that work from simple, full-factorial design matrices. Unfortunately, small designs like this rarely occur in practical research problems. For one thing, people's preferences are complicated. The idea behind traditional experimental design is to control for as many variables that affect outcomes as possible. Even preferences for a movie might be affected by many different attributes. Certainly, when we are addressing preferences for healthcare provision or natural resource amenities, we are likely to have to consider a reasonably large array of attributes.

In these cases, issues of orthogonality, balance, overlap and dominance are much harder to control for and they sometimes conflict with each other. Developing designs can be challenging. Design researchers have devised several methods for finding workable designs, however. We consider several such approaches below.

4. CATALOG-BASED DESIGNS

Tables of orthogonal main-effects designs (OMEDs) are widely available (see, for example, Cochran and Cox, 1957, Addelman, 1962, Lorenzen and Anderson, 1993, Sloane, 2004, or Warren Kuhfeld's online catalog: http://support.sas.com/techsup/technote/ts723.html). These catalog plans provide efficient flat designs (full- or fractional-factorial matrices) from which to construct choice sets. The foldover approach described in the previous section is effective for two-level attributes, but does not work for problems involving attributes with three or more levels. Chrzan and Orme (2000) suggest three methods for deriving choice sets from flat catalog designs: rotation or shifting (Bunch, et al., 1994), mix-and-match (Louviere, 1988), and L^{MA} (Louviere, et al., 2000).

4.1. Rotation Method

Table 7 illustrates the rotation approach. We begin with a 4x3x2 OMED with 16 rows (which could be drawn from a catalog).[12] Without loss of generality, we can assign attribute A levels of {-2, -1, 1, 2}, attribute B levels of {-1, 0, 1}, and attribute C levels of {-1,1}. Construct choice sets with the rotation method as follows:

1.   Use the 16 original OMED rows as the first alternative in each of the 16 choice sets.

2.   Place three new columns next to the original OMED columns. Column 4 is just column 1 shifted, or rotated, one place over to the right or wrapped around to the beginning of the sequence: -2 in column 1 becomes -1 in column 4, -1 becomes 1, 1 becomes 2, and 2 wraps around to -2. The levels in column 5 are the levels in column 2 shifted in the same way. Likewise, column 6 is a rotation of column 3. Attribute C is a two-level attribute, so the rotation in column 6 is simply the foldover of column 3.

3.   The three columns 4-6 become the second profile in each of the 16 choice sets. The procedure ensures that the new alternative is orthogonal and has no overlap in any choice set.

4.   You can repeat step 2, rotating the values in columns 4-6 to create a third alternative (though attribute C in the third alternative would overlap with alternative 1).

5.   Replace the level numbers with category labels or continuous variable numbers for the final design.

Although the rotated choice-set alternatives have zero overlap and are orthogonal, they are not necessarily undominated. You have to check to make sure all the levels of one alternative in a choice set are not better than corresponding levels in another alternative. In addition, the imbalance in Attribute C creates mild correlation in the level differences between alternatives equal to -0.17. Thus, orthogonality in each alternative does not ensure orthogonality in the choice sets. Finally, rotated choice sets are not flexible enough to deal with interactions, profile restrictions, and other complications.

4.2. Mix-and-Match Method

One downside of the rotation method is that it follows a set pattern throughout so that every choice set contains the same type of incremental difference. The mix-and-match method starts with the same approach but adds a randomizing (shuffling) step.

1.   Use the three columns from the 4x3x2 OMED to create a candidate set of 16 profiles.

2.   Follow the rotation method to create a second set of profiles.

3. If desired, repeat step 2 to create a third or fourth candidate set of profiles.
4. Shuffle each of the candidate sets separately.
5. Draw one profile from each shuffled candidate set. These become choice set 1.
6. Repeat, drawing without replacement until all the profiles are used up and 16 choice sets have been created.

TABLE 7. Two-Alternative Choice Sets, Rotation Method

Choice Set	4x3x2 OMED			Rotated Alternative		
	A_1	B_1	C_1	A_2	B_2	C_2
1	-2	-1	-1	-1	0	1
2	-1	-1	1	1	0	-1
3	1	-1	-1	2	0	1
4	2	-1	1	-2	0	1
5	-2	0	1	-1	1	-1
6	-1	0	-1	1	1	1
7	1	0	1	2	1	-1
8	2	0	-1	-2	1	1
9	-2	1	-1	-1	-1	1
10	-1	1	1	1	-1	-1
11	1	1	-1	2	-1	1
12	2	1	1	-2	-1	1
13	-2	-1	1	-1	0	-1
14	-1	-1	-1	1	0	1
15	1	-1	1	2	0	-1
16	2	-1	-1	-2	0	1

Although mixing and matching should preserve orthogonality, it does not prevent either overlap or dominated pairs. It may be necessary to experiment with the level exchanges and randomization to minimize such undesirable properties.

4.3. L^{MA} Method

The L^{MA} method requires starting with a symmetric OMED, that is a flat design with the same number of levels L for each attribute. Find a catalog OMED with MxA columns, where A is the number of attributes and M is the number of alternatives in each choice set. Suppose we have 4 attributes with 3 levels each and 2 alternatives in each choice set. We need a 38 OMED, which has 27 rows. The eight columns give us the two groups of four attributes each that we need to make the 27 choice sets. Again, while orthogonality is ensured here, there are no guarantees about overlap or dominated pairs.

While catalog methods have the advantages of simplicity and orthogonality, they do not necessarily maximize the statistical information obtainable from a design. Their statistical efficiency is particularly affected by balance problems, overlap, and dominated pairs, but also by the implied fixed, upfront assumption about the levels the attributes may take. In the next section, we relax this assumption and look at recent research in the field of optimal design.

5. THE CHOICE-PERCENTAGES APPROACH TO OPTIMAL CHOICE-SET DESIGN

The assumption behind optimal design is that researchers have a specific goal in mind when they conduct a study and they would like to generate a design that most helps them achieve that goal. As mentioned in Section 2, one such goal is D-optimality, the maximization of the determinant of the Fisher information matrix. While pursuit of this goal alone would be single-minded (researchers often have a variety of goals in mind when they conduct a study) we believe, when all other bases are covered (model identification, flexibility, hypothesis tests of interest), understanding D-optimality can only help researchers improve their designs.

A number of marketing researchers have considered ways of improving the information efficiency of choice sets, including Bunch et al. (1994), Anderson and Wiley (1992), Huber and Zwerina (1996), Kuhfeld et al. (1994) and Sàndor and Wedel (2001). The earlier of these studies tended to draw on what we know about optimal design with the linear model: that is, they emphasized concepts such as orthogonality and balance. Later studies employed computer searches for better designs. We will look at some of these techniques in the next section. Here, we summarize the design results that Kanninen (2001, 2002, 2005) derived. Kanninen took a different approach from the studies listed above. She allowed attributes to be continuous, rather than pre-specified at certain levels, and solved, using numerical optimization, for the optimal attribute levels and placements.

Kanninen drew two important conclusions. First, she found that, just as with the standard, linear model of equation 2, most attribute levels are best placed at their extreme points according to an orthogonal, main effects design matrix. In other words, researchers obtain the most information about an attribute's effects when the attribute levels being compared are very different from each other. Further, in the case of binary choices, choice sets should be generated using the foldover procedure.

Kanninen's second conclusion is quite new to the literature. She found that, once all attributes, except one, are placed according to the main effects, orthogonal array, the final attribute (Kanninen recommends price, but it could be any attribute) should be used to control choice percentage outcomes. Here is how the procedure works, starting with a 2^{K-1} flat design, assuming there are K attributes in the design and price is the continuous variable used to control choice percentages.

- Find the appropriate 2^{K-1} design (examples are in Appendix A). Use the foldover approach illustrated in Table 4B to set up the choice sets for K-1 of the attributes. When possible, replace each +1 with the reasonable upper-bound (for continuous attributes) or best category for each attribute. Replace each -1 with the reasonable lower-bound (for continuous variables) or worst category for each attribute.

- Even though your initial information on preferences may be limited, try to assign price levels that will be likely to produce the optimal choice percentages for the two alternatives in each choice set. Table 8 shows optimal choice percentages for models with between two and eight two-level attributes. Note that these optimal percentages range from about a one-fifth/four-fifths split to a two-thirds/one third split.[13] Note also that, by definition, this procedure does not allow dominated alternatives.

- Collect data in a large pretest or halt the survey partway through to reassess. Compare the observed choice percentages with the optimal ones. Adjust price levels to move empirical choice percentages toward the optimal ones. Update the design as many times as possible throughout the experiment.

TABLE 8. *Optimal Main-Effects 2^{K-1} Designs, Two-Alternatives*

Number of Attributes (K)	Number of Unique Choice Sets in Design	Design Array for Attributes 1 through K-1	Optimal Choice-Percentage Split for Two-Alternative Model
2	2	{-1, 1}	.82 / .18
3	4	Table A-1	.77 / .23
4	4	Table A-2	.74 / .26
5	8	Table A-3	.72 / .28
6	8	Table A-4	.70 / .30
7	8	Table A-5	.68 / .32
8	8	Table A-6	.67 / .33

Steffens et al. (2002) apply Kanninen's approach empirically. In their case, the price attribute reached its assumed boundary points before the optimal choice percentages were achieved. Steffens et al. suggest that, when this occurs, researchers try adjusting a second attribute to reach the desired choice percentages.

Kanninen (2002) provides optimal designs for larger choice sets. Table A-8 is the optimal design for four-attribute models with three alternatives. Table A-9 is the optimal design for four attributes and five alternatives. Note how the probability splits focus on two alternatives in each choice set. The additional alternatives carry low probabilities and have overlap. This is an interesting finding. It says that, even with larger choice sets, the "difficult" choice should be between two particular alternatives, while the remaining alternatives serve to stretch the information out toward the tails. This would be an intriguing design strategy to test in practice. It seems like it would not only be optimal from a statistical perspective, but probably an easier choice task for respondents.

Though it works in theory, the optimal choice-percentage approach is not always practical. For one thing, researchers may not be comfortable allowing price or other attributes to vary to the extent needed to get this procedure to work. Also, if prior information is poor, it is not practical to think of obtaining the optimal choice percentages. Finally, some design plans are complicated, with large numbers of attributes or attribute levels all taking separate main and interactive-effect terms, making the idea of deriving optimal choice percentages unrealistic. At this point, it appears that when design plans are complicated and prior information is diffuse, the only feasible approach to improving one's design is to use a computer algorithm. Computers are particularly good at randomizing or swapping choices around and testing a large number of design arrays. By their nature, computer searches tend to be inelegant in execution, but because they can work so fast and test so many options, they do offer a way to improve one's design when the standard approaches mentioned above do not apply.

6. SEARCHING FOR D-OPTIMAL EXPERIMENTAL DESIGNS

6.1. A D-Optimal Search Algorithm

Given one or more criteria for measuring design efficiency, we can use search algorithms to evaluate thousands of potential designs to find one that comes closest to a conceptually ideal design. Various authors have proposed search methods (Bunch et al., 1994, Huber and Zwerina, 1996, Kuhfeld et al., 1994, Lazari and Anderson, 1994), but we summarize the method first suggested by Zwerina et al. (1996) and currently implemented in a set of SAS macros.[14] Figure 1 outlines the necessary steps.

We can start the search for D-optimal choice designs either with a catalog OMED flat design, a fractional-factorial design, or the full factorial. The dimensions of the flat candidate design are determined by the number of rows and columns needed to estimate the parameters of the choice model. The OMED assures orthogonality, while using the full factorial sacrifices some degree of orthogonality, but generally yields designs with higher D-efficiency scores (measures of proximity to full D-optimality). A fractional-factorial design strikes a compromise between these two alternatives and converges more quickly than using the full factorial. The search algorithm uses a modified Fedorov procedure (Fedorov, 1972, Cook and Nachtsheim, 1980) to optimize the expected variance matrix.

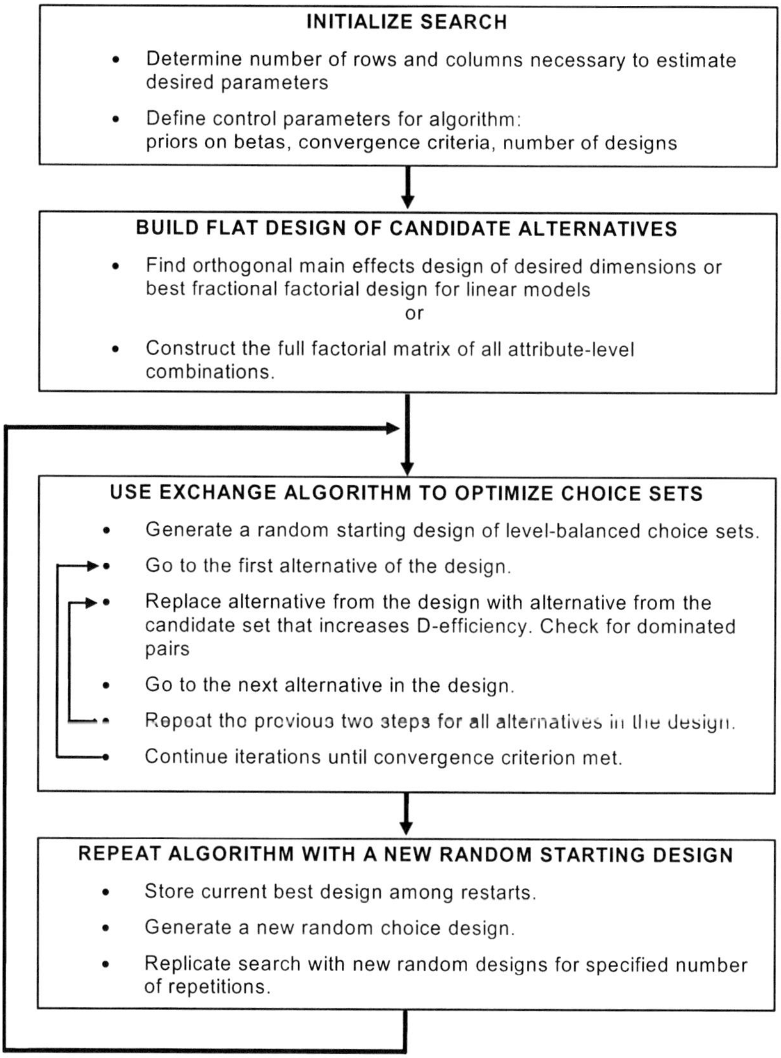

INITIALIZE SEARCH

- Determine number of rows and columns necessary to estimate desired parameters

- Define control parameters for algorithm:
  priors on betas, convergence criteria, number of designs

BUILD FLAT DESIGN OF CANDIDATE ALTERNATIVES

- Find orthogonal main effects design of desired dimensions or best fractional factorial design for linear models
  or

- Construct the full factorial matrix of all attribute-level combinations.

USE EXCHANGE ALGORITHM TO OPTIMIZE CHOICE SETS

- Generate a random starting design of level-balanced choice sets.

- Go to the first alternative of the design.

- Replace alternative from the design with alternative from the candidate set that increases D-efficiency. Check for dominated pairs

- Go to the next alternative in the design.

- Repeat the previous two steps for all alternatives in the design.

- Continue iterations until convergence criterion met.

REPEAT ALGORITHM WITH A NEW RANDOM STARTING DESIGN

- Store current best design among restarts.

- Generate a new random choice design.

- Replicate search with new random designs for specified number of repetitions.

FIGURE 1. Search Algorithm for D-Optimal Design

TABLE 9. *Minimum Sample Sizes for Two-Alternative Choice Designs*

Number of choice task repetitions:	6	8	10	12	14
Maximum number of levels for any one attribute:	Number of Respondents >=				
3	125	94	75	63	54
4	167	125	100	83	71
5	208	156	125	104	89
6	250	188	150	125	107
7	292	219	175	146	125
8	333	250	200	167	143

6.2. Using the SAS Market Research Macros to Construct Practical Designs: Three-Alternative Fish-Advisory Design

Before constructing an experimental design, it is necessary to determine how many attributes, how many levels for each attribute, how the data will be analyzed (which determines how many parameters and thus how many degrees of freedom the analysis requires), and how large the respondent sample size will be. Given a desired list of attributes and associated levels, Orme (1998) suggests the following rule of thumb for determining adequate sample sizes for choice surveys.

$$N = 500 \cdot \frac{NLEV}{NALT \cdot NREP} \qquad (7)$$

where N is the respondent sample size, NREP is the number of choice questions per respondent, NALT is the number of alternatives per choice set, and NLEV is the largest number of levels in any attribute, including interactions. Table 9 shows minimum sample sizes for these various considerations.

Thus, minimum sample sizes generally range between 100 and 300 for two-alternative designs with typical numbers of attributes and levels. Obviously, larger sample sizes provide greater statistical power for testing hypotheses.

Suppose we are interested in estimating willingness to pay (WTP) to avoid fish advisories. Fish advisories are warnings about how much fish caught at a particular site can safely be eaten due to PCB or mercury contamination. After conducting focus groups, suppose we determine that anglers are most concerned about the features listed in Table 10.

The experimental design requires five attributes with three levels each, so the full factorial is $3^5 = 243$. If we estimate a model that treats all levels as categorical, we need a minimum of $5*(3-1)+1 = 11$ degrees of freedom, which corresponds to 11 choice sets. This is called a "saturated" design. Bigger designs are generally preferred to improve model flexibility and statistical power.

TABLE 10. Fish Advisory Study Attributes and Levels

Factor	Attribute	Levels
X1	Distance	20 miles 50 miles 100 miles
X2	Expected Catch	0 – 1 2 – 4 5 – 7
X3	Amenities	None Dock, pit toilet Dock, flush toilet, bait shop, gas station
X4	Congestion	Low Moderate High
X5	Fish Advisory	No limitation Eat no more than 2 per month Don't eat

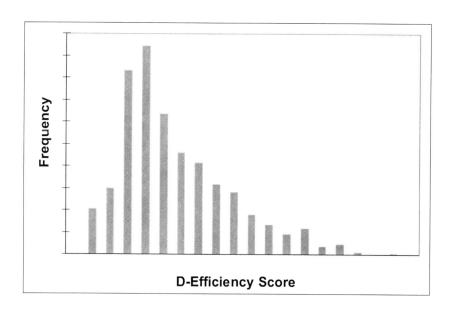

FIGURE 2. Distribution of D-Efficiency Scores for Random Draws on the Full Factorial

We decide to use three site alternatives in each choice set. A pretest indicates that respondents appear to be willing to answer up to nine choice questions. Thus, we can have 6*3 = 18 site profiles for the design. We will use this example to illustrate use of the SAS experimental-design macros.[15]

We first ask SAS to determine what OMED or fractional-factorial flat candidate designs are available using the following command:

```
title 'Fish Advisory Design';
%mktruns(3 ** 5);
```

The syntax (3 ** 5) indicates five three-level attributes. (3 3 3 3 3) would be an equivalent way to express this. This code produces the following output:

Fish Advisory Candidate Designs

Design Summary

Number of Levels	Frequency
3	5

Saturated = 11

Full Factorial = 243

Some Reasonable Design Sizes	Violations	Cannot Be Divided By
18 *	0	
27 *	0	
36 *	0	
12	10	9
15	10	9
21	10	9
24	10	9
30	10	9
33	10	9
11	15	3 9

* * - 100% Efficient Design can be made with the MktEx Macro

n	Design		Reference
18	2 ** 1	3 ** 7	Orthogonal Array
18	3 ** 6	6 ** 1	Orthogonal Array
27	3 ** 13		Fractional-Factorial
27	3 ** 9	9 ** 1	Fractional-Factorial
36	2 ** 11	3 ** 12	Orthogonal Array

36	2 ** 10	3 ** 8	6 **1	Orthogonal Array
36	2 ** 4	3 ** 13		Orthogonal Array
36	2 ** 3	3 ** 9	6 ** 1	Orthogonal Array
36	2 ** 2	3 ** 12	6 ** 1	Orthogonal Array
36	2 ** 2	3 ** 5	6 ** 2	Orthogonal Array
36	2 ** 1	3 ** 8	6 ** 2	Orthogonal Array
36	3 ** 13	4 ** 1		Orthogonal Array
36	3 ** 12	12 ** 1		Orthogonal Array
36	3 ** 7	6 ** 3		Orthogonal Array

Candidate OMED or fractional-factorial designs with 18, 27 or 36 rows can be used to construct efficient designs. Other design sizes will result in some level-balance violations.

The output table lists various catalog flat designs that could be used for the flat candidate design. For example, there is an 18-row OMED consisting of one two-level column and seven three-level columns that could be used. Since we need only five three-level columns, the surplus columns would be deleted. Alternatively, we could generate a design from the relatively small 243-row full factorial. As indicated previously, the full factorial places the fewest restrictions on the search for a D-optimal design, so we will use that.

The candidate set must indicate site profiles that may be used for each alternative. The %MktEx macro uses "flag" variables to indicate alternatives, designated here as f1, f2, and f3. The flag variable for each alternative consists of ones for profiles that may be included for that alternative and zeros for profiles that may not be included for that alternative. The candidate set may contain one profile that is only used for the last, constant alternative. This reference condition may be a status-quo alternative (such as the last site or usual site visited) or a no-trip or opt-out alternative (would not go fishing if these were the only alternatives available). In this case, we allow any site profile to appear in any alternative, which effectively forces the angler to choose a site, even if none is particularly appealing. We will discuss the role of the opt-out condition later.

The following code creates the full-factorial candidate design. The Output dataset is called FINAL.

```
%mktex(3 ** 5, n=243)
%mktlab(data=design, int=f1-f3)
proc print data=final(obs=27); run;
```

Here are the first 20 rows of the candidate design saved in the output data set.

Obs	f1	f2	f3	x1	x2	x3	x4	x5
1	1	1	1	1	1	1	1	1
2	1	1	1	1	1	1	1	2
3	1	1	1	1	1	1	1	3

(cont.)

4	1	1	1	1	1	1	2	1
5	1	1	1	1	1	1	2	2
6	1	1	1	1	1	1	2	3
7	1	1	1	1	1	1	3	1
8	1	1	1	1	1	1	3	2
9	1	1	1	1	1	1	3	3
10	1	1	1	1	1	2	1	1
11	1	1	1	1	1	2	1	2
12	1	1	1	1	1	2	1	3
13	1	1	1	1	1	2	2	1
14	1	1	1	1	1	2	2	2
15	1	1	1	1	1	2	2	3
16	1	1	1	1	1	2	3	1
17	1	1	1	1	1	2	3	2
18	1	1	1	1	1	2	3	3
19	1	1	1	1	1	3	1	1
20	1	1	1	1	1	3	1	2

The next step is to search for a near-optimal design of the desired dimensions from this full-factorial set of candidate profiles. The following command sets up the search.

```
%choiceff(data=final, model=class(x1-x5), nsets=9, maxiter=100,
     seed=121, flags=f1-f3, beta=zero);
```

where FINAL is the input file, model=class(x1-x5) indicates we intend to model the attributes as categorical variables, nsets indicates the number of choice sets, and maxiter is the number of designs the macro will search for. The macro will save the design with the highest D-efficiency score[16] out of 100 designs. Seed sets the randomization seed to ensure we get the same result every time we run the macro, flags indicates the columns that assign profiles to alternatives, and beta=0 indicates that we are not conditioning the search on assumed coefficient values for the choice model. (If we had pretest results, we might use estimates for the betas here, which would allow the routine to optimize under the assumption that we know something about preferences.)

The SAS documentation provides little guidance on the question of how many iterations are advisable to be sure the search results in a design reasonably close to D-optimal. We performed an experiment to calculate the distribution of D-optimality scores for 1,000 draws on the full-factorial flat design. Our results are displayed in Figure 2. The distribution of D-efficiency outcomes appears to be approximately lognormal with high D-efficiency scores occurring in small numbers. This indicates the importance of doing a large number of draws to ensure that the routine captures these high-end designs.

The SASmacro produces a record of the search progress for each of the 100 designs. For example, the intermediate output for the first design is:

Design	Iteration	D-Efficiency	D-Error
1	0	0.352304	2.838455
	1	0.946001	1.057081
	2	1.001164	0.998838
	3	1.041130	0.960494
	4	1.044343	0.957540

The particular scale of the D-efficiency score is specific to the problem setup and is only useful for comparing efficiencies across designs generated in the same way. D-error is just 1/D-efficiency. In this case, Design 34 had the best efficiency as described in the final results:

Final Results

Design	34
Choice Sets	6
Alternatives	3
D-Efficiency	1.154701
D-Error	0.866025

The data set BEST contains the final design, which is printed out with:

title 'Fish Advisory Design';
Proc print; by set; id set; run;

Notice that each level occurs exactly once in each attribute and choice set, so there is no overlap.

Fish Advisory Design

Set	x1	x2	x3	x4	x5
1	1	3	3	1	2
	2	2	1	3	3
	3	1	2	2	1
2	3	3	1	2	2
	1	2	2	1	3
	2	1	3	3	1
3	1	2	3	3	1
	3	3	2	1	3
	2	1	1	2	2
4	3	2	1	1	1
	1	1	2	3	2
	2	3	3	2	3

(cont.)

5	2	1	2	1	3
	1	2	1	2	2
	3	3	3	3	1
6	1	3	2	2	1
	3	1	1	3	3
	2	2	3	1	2
7	1	1	3	2	3
	3	2	2	3	2
	2	3	1	1	1
8	2	3	2	3	2
	3	2	3	2	3
	1	1	1	1	1
9	1	3	1	3	3
	2	2	2	2	1
	3	1	3	1	2

While we were able to construct a tractable design with nine choice questions in this example, practical designs involving more attributes, more levels, or more interactions often require more than the 8-12 repetitions of the choice task often used in empirical work. In such instances, we can reduce the burden to individual respondents by dividing the choice sets into blocks. For example, we could divide an 18-choice set design into three 6-set blocks and have three different versions of the survey. To ensure that the block designs are balanced and orthogonal, we simply use a blocking factor, an additional attribute with number of levels equal to the desired number of blocks. Optimization theoretically ensures that the blocking factor will be orthogonal to the attribute levels within blocks. SAS provides a macro that sorts the sets into blocks to ensure we have not induced any confounding at the block level.

%mktblock(nblocks=3, factors=x1-x5, seed=292)

The output file from this procedure is called "blocked." The practical importance of using a blocking factor may not be great. If parameter estimates will be obtained with conditional logit analysis of the stacked data without reference to respondent-level panel effects, any potential block-level or within-subject correlation effects are ignored. Efficient blocking could be more important, however, if the analysis includes panel modeling or individual-specific parameter estimates (see Swait, this volume). It is difficult to sort sets into blocks to maintain the same level balance achieved in the overall design, and the macro often fails to find the balance necessary to ensure orthogonality. An alternative to using a blocking factor is simply to randomize set assignment to blocks, then check for approximate balance, as well as for any odd sequences that might inadvertently affect respondent evaluations.

6.3. Three Alternatives with Opt-Out Reference Condition

While there may be circumstances where respondents are already "in the market" and thus a forced-choice format is appropriate, in many cases accurate welfare estimation requires that respondents be allowed to select a "no-purchase," status-quo, or opt-out alternative in each choice set. The following code sets up the candidate profile data set with a constant alternative.

```
title 'Fish Advisory Design';
%mktex(3 ** 5, n=243);
data advise(drop=i);
set design end=eof;
retain f1-f3 1 f4 0;
output;
if eof then do;
array x[9] x1-x5 f1-f4;
do i = 1 to 4; x[i] = 2; end;
x[5] = 3;
x[9] = 1;
output;
end;
run;
proc print data=advise(where=(x1 eq x3 and x2 eq x4 and x3 eq x5 or f4)); run;
```

Here are some profiles in the candidate set.

Fish Advisory Design

Obs	x1	x2	x3	x4	x5	f1	f2	f3	f4
1	1	1	1	1	1	1	1	1	0
31	1	2	1	2	1	1	1	1	0
61	1	3	1	3	1	1	1	1	0
92	2	1	2	1	2	1	1	1	0
122	2	2	2	2	2	1	1	1	0
152	2	3	2	3	2	1	1	1	0
183	3	1	3	1	3	1	1	1	0
213	3	2	3	2	3	1	1	1	0
243	3	3	3	3	3	1	1	1	0
244	2	2	2	2	3	0	0	0	1

The first 243 profiles are the full factorial, which may be used for any of the first three alternatives. The last profile has flag 4 turned on, indicating it can only be used for the fourth alternative. In this example, the constant alternative is composed of the mean effects of each of the site attributes, except for the fish-advisory policy attribute, which is set at the worst level. All alternatives are then equal to or better than the reference condition in terms of the policy variable. The macro code to initiate the search for the D-optimal design and print the results is:

```
title 'Fish Advisory Design';
%choiceff(data=advise, model=class(x1-x5), nsets=9, maxiter=100,
seed=121, flags=f1-f4, beta=zero);
proc print; by set; id set; run;
```

Alternatives to specifying a constant hypothetical reference site include using the features of the respondent's most recent or usual trip or specifying the alternative as "no trip on this choice occasion." The no-trip or opt-out alternative is specified as an alternative-specific constant, possibly modeled as interacted with angler-specific characteristics. In either case, the experimental design is no different than the forced-choice case, since the constant alternative has no effect on design efficiency.

6.4. Comparing Empirical Efficiency of Alternative Design Strategies

Setting up the search for a suitable experimental design requires a number of judgments, including the dimensions of the design, whether to do a simple assignment of a catalog OMED to choice sets or search for a D-optimal design, how many choice questions to ask each respondent, and how many alternatives to include in each choice set. There is limited information on the relative importance of such judgments on the statistical efficiency and cognitive burden of resulting designs. However, researchers have begun to explore this question and we summarize several recent studies.

Huber and Zwerina (1996) argue that the variance of parameter estimates (the inverse of the Fisher information matrix) depends on actual parameter values (through the w terms in equation 6). Thus, design efficiency can be improved if researchers have, and use, any kind of prior information to generate choice sets.

Carlsson and Martinsson (2003) conducted a simulation experiment to evaluate the effect of using or not using accurate prior information on parameter values. They also compared OMED and D-optimal designs. Their results indicate that mean squared error (MSE) varies substantially according to the design used. An optimal design, which relies on the use of priors for the parameter values, gives a lower MSE than other approaches. The optimal designs provide unbiased estimates even at low sample sizes. Importantly, Carlsson and Martinsson find that the penalty for assuming incorrect prior parameter values is small. They even find that D-optimal designs based on zero priors for the betas performed better than orthogonal designs in two out of three experiments.

Although statistically efficient designs are important for obtaining precise, unbiased parameter estimates, measurement error resulting from respondents' failure to absorb information about the evaluation task or to complete the task accurately may be a much larger source of error. Simple designs may improve respondent performance but potentially at the expense of statistical efficiency. Hensher (this volume) examines these issues. He finds that:

- increasing the range of attribute levels reduces mean WTP,
- narrow-range attributes produce the largest variability in WTP estimates,
- the number of alternatives and the number of attribute levels do not have significant effects on estimates,
- the differential variance across the alternatives increases as the number of attributes increases, and
- an overall measure of complexity is significant in explaining variability in WTP estimates.

DeShazo and Fermo (2002) evaluate the effect of survey-design features on WTP estimates for management policies in an undeveloped national park. They vary the number of alternatives in the choice sets, the number of attributes associated with each alternative, the degree to which attributes within an alternative are correlated with one another, i.e., attribute levels may be all high, all low, or mixed for an alternative, and the degree of correlation of all attributes across alternatives in the choice set. These variations systematically affect the cognitive complexity of respondents' evaluation task.

The authors find that all complexity factors significantly affect choice consistency. For example, increasing the quantity of information and the degree of negative correlation among the attributes and alternatives generally increases choice variance. However, the relationship between the number of alternatives and the variance is quadratic; increasing the number of alternatives in a choice set reduces the variance up to a threshold number and thereafter increases it. Increasing the variation of attributes in an alternative has a significantly larger impact on choice consistency than any other factor.

The authors suggest that problems related to design complexity can be minimized by choosing the optimal number of alternatives and carefully selecting attributes and correlation structures. This suggestion potentially implies compromising the statistical efficiency of an orthogonal or D-optimal design. Second, at the estimation stage, economists should identify, parameterize, and properly control for complexity econometrically to mitigate the impacts on welfare estimates.

7. AN ALTERNATIVE TO FIXED EXPERIMENTAL DESIGNS

Sawtooth Software offers a popular alternative to constructing experimental designs on the basis of statistical principles called Adaptive Conjoint Analysis (ACA).[17] ACA avoids constructing experimental designs by using an algorithm to update a set of relative importance weights based on a linear model after each question a respondent answers.

The ACA procedure consists of two stages. In the first stage, respondents indicate the relative importance of attributes. In the second stage, respondents answer conjoint questions. However, the conjoint questions administered at this point are quite different from those of a traditional experimental design in that they are not predetermined. Rather, these questions are based on information gathered in the first stage and prior answers to conjoint questions. The algorithm then uses the updated parameter vector to determine what pair of profiles is likely to be most informative in improving parameter estimates. Personal computers allow ACA to adapt the conjoint task to the individual respondent.

To simplify the problem of updating utility weights, ACA displays only partial profiles, meaning that respondents see only a subset of the attributes for each question. Table 11 compares important features of ACA and traditional (not optimal) conjoint designs.

As table 11 indicates, an important limitation of ACA is that it must be computer-administered. This is because the interview adapts to respondents' previous answers. Some researchers, such as Johnson (1989) have noted that the computer-based adaptive nature of ACA may provide an advantage over traditional choice designs. In this case, the advantage cited is that ACA is less likely to suffer from systemic design problems, for example, the relative importance of attributes can be influenced by the order in which the attributes are presented. While the computer-based nature of ACA provides for easy randomization of attributes, effects of this nature can also be eliminated through randomization of the order in which attributes are presented from a traditional design and/or accounted for through appropriate modeling techniques.

TABLE 11. Adaptive and Conventional Designs

	Adaptive Conjoint Design	Conventional Choice Design
Administration Mode	Computer	Any
Number of Attributes	More	Fewer
Orthogonality	Lower	Higher
Utility Balance	Higher	Lower

Table 11 indicates another ACA advantage: it can measure more attributes than a traditional design can. This is because ACA respondents do not evaluate all attributes at the same time. Finkbeiner and Platz (1986) compared ACA with the traditional method in a study involving six attributes and obtained similar predictive validities. Green and Srinivasan (1990) also recommend traditional experimental designs when this number of attributes are being considered but recommend ACA when there are ten or more attributes being considered.[18]

Table 11 also indicates that there is a trade-off between orthogonality and utility balance between adaptive conjoint and traditional designs. This trade-off occurs because the ACA approach makes choices successively more difficult (moving toward the 50/50 point of indifference) for each individual.

The statistical properties of the pattern of ACA trade-off tasks are unobserved and endogenous to each respondent. While this procedure can yield individual-level parameter estimates, it is not possible to model the features of the endogenous designs or to estimate more complex models involving interactions and alternative-specific constants.

8. CONCLUDING COMMENTS

This chapter has covered a number of approaches to generating SC designs. The reader is probably left wondering, "so what am I to do now?" Our answer, not surprisingly, is "it depends."

It depends first on the size of your study. If your numbers of attributes and attribute levels fit, or nearly fit, the examples in our tables, you can use those designs to good effect. You can also start with the designs presented here (or in other catalogs, such as: http://support.sas.com/techsup/technote/ts723.html) and combine them with a rotation or mix-and-match approach to generate more alternatives or choice sets. If possible, our preferred method from Section 4 is the L^{MA} method. If your design is small, you may have the flexibility to include some, but not all, interactive terms. Careful manipulation will allow you to identify those terms you believe to be important.

From there, you have to think about how much you know about preferences. If you truly know nothing, then you should go with the orthogonal design you just generated. If you know something (and you probably at least know the signs of the coefficients) then you can deal with dominated alternatives. These can be dropped without losing any information, but you do have to consider whether your design provides enough statistical variation to still identify model parameters, given what you know.

The next question is whether you can use your prior information to improve your design even more, using optimal design principles. With Kanninen's results in mind, we have found that binary choice sets that end up with less than 10% or more than 90% expected, percentage-response rates are very uninformative. In these cases, designs can be improved by manually manipulating attribute levels to move the expected probabilities inward. Of course, if your prior information is good, or if you have the chance to update your design part way through the data collection process, we do recommend attempting to manipulate attribute levels to achieve the optimal ones shown in Table 8.

Finally, when problems are large, we have found that computer algorithms, such as those described above, work quite well.

---

9. ENDNOTES

[1] We use the term "information" here in a broad sense: referring to both the model parameter estimates and willingness-to-pay estimates, as well as the ability to conduct valid hypothesis tests and make inferences regarding estimators of interest. Obtaining information efficiently requires an understanding of the statistical properties of experimental designs, as well as an understanding of people's cognitive ability to evaluate complex choice scenarios. Other chapters in this volume (Harrison, Hensher, Mathews et al.) explore various aspects of how to ask stated-preference questions. This chapter focuses on how to combine commodity attributes and levels into a statistically helpful sequence of choice tasks.

[2] The early literature on experimental design focused on the ability to conduct meaningful analyses of variance, particularly in the area of agriculture and biology (Fisher, 1990, Box et al., 1978, Winer et al.,

1991). One of the main concerns of this literature was to identify unintended experimental effects. For example, if an experiment were conducted over the course of a day, laboratory equipment might get mucked up so that the same treatment, tested earlier in the day and later, might produce different outcomes. Such effects, if identified beforehand, can be specifically addressed and estimated by blocking: conducting qualitatively identical experiments under each suspected block effect.

[3] There are other types of choice tasks, for example ranking, but we do not consider them here because, as far as we know, no experimental design research has been conducted for them. See Train (2003) for a few examples.

[4] We are grateful to Jordan Louviere for suggesting this example.

[5] We focus in this chapter on so-called generic or unlabeled designs; these are designs where the specific ordering of alternatives within a choice task does not carry meaning. In other words, respondents would see Alternative A versus Alternative B as the identical choice task to Alternative B versus Alternative A. These types of designs are common in environmental and health applications. Branded or labeled designs are more common in market research, where the specific alternatives may be consistently labeled as, for example, Ford versus Chrysler. They may also be used in environmental or health applications, however, and the basic results presented here can be adapted to these situations.

[6] The +1 for presence and -1 for absence could be reversed and the same set of 8 alternatives would occur, just in different order.

[7] Dummy variable and effects codes for a three-level attribute, where the third level is the omitted category would be:

	Dummy 1	Dummy 2	Effects Code 1	Effects Code 2
Level 1	1	0	1	0
Level 2	0	1	0	1
Level 3	0	0	-1	-1

[8] As discussed in Alberini (this volume), multinomial logit models are based on attribute-level *differences*, rather than the actual attribute levels. So, depending on the spacing of attribute levels, the number of combinations required to estimate the full model might larger or smaller than the numbers we supply here. In most cases, we expect the number to be larger.

[9] Street et al. (2001), Burgess and Street (2003), and Street and Burgess (2003) have made progress in this area, finding designs that are smaller than traditional designs, yet still address interactive effects.

[10] Because the coefficient for the omitted effects-coded category is the negative sum of the included category, effects-coded models do not require a constant term.

[11] Note that equations 2 and 3 look a lot like the Fisher Information matrix for the linear model, except for the w_i terms. We discussed maximizing $|X'X|$ in Section 2. If we are interested in maximizing the determinant of equation 3, we might think the solution is related to that of maximizing the w_i terms alone. It turns out that the w_i terms are always maximized for $p = 1 - p = .50$: in other words, at probability response rates of 50%. This concept is known as utility-balance (Huber and Zwerina, 1996). Under utility balance, respondents would be offered choices for which they were completely indifferent. As shown in Section 5, D-optimal designs for stated choice experiments do not generally have this property.

[12] Although the OMED is orthogonal, it is not balanced because we are combining attributes with both even and odd numbers of levels. Attribute A has four levels, which each appears four times and Attribute C has two levels, each of which appears eight times in the 16 rows. Attribute B has three levels and is unbalanced in the matrix. The first level appears twice as often as the other two levels. Imbalance in asymmetric designs is an inherent problem with the catalog approach. Louviere, et al. (2000) advise against using asymmetric designs because the imbalance results in variation in statistical power among

attribute levels and/or between attributes. In practice, however, researchers often have limited control over numbers of attribute levels they need to include.

[13] The utility model can include an alternative-specific term. If it does, the alternative-specific term counts toward the total number of attributes (the number of columns in the X matrix) in determining the appropriate optimal choice percentages in Table 8. Also, if a column of ones is part of the X matrix, the optimal choice percentages have to match up with a different orthogonal column. For example, if there are seven attributes plus a constant term, assign attributes 2 through 7 to the second through seventh columns in Table 2. Assign attribute 1 according to column 1 in Table 2, going for a response rate of .67 for the first four observations in that table (where +1 appears in column 1) and .33 for the last four (where –1 appears in column 1).

[14] Appendix B contains the IML code for the basic algorithm. Kuhfeld has adapted and updated this procedure in a set of SAS macros (Kuhfeld, 2004). Hensher et al. (2004, Chapter 5) discuss constructing designs using procedures in SPSS.

[15] This example was adapted from Kuhfeld (2004), pp. 314-342. See this document for additional information on using SAS market-research macros to construct D-optimal choice designs.

[16] D-efficiency is defined as: $100 \times (1 / N|X'X^{-1}|^{1/K})$. (See Kuhfeld, 1997.)

[17] The first version of ACA, released in 1985, was Sawtooth Software's first conjoint product. Sawtooth also offers modules for traditional conjoint surveys and choice-format surveys. Their website also provides a large number of helpful technical documents on stated-preference surveys. (See http://www.sawtoothsoftware.com/technicaldownloads.shtm.)

[18] Partial-profile designs can address this issue. In such designs, each choice question includes a subset of the attributes being studied. These attributes are randomly rotated into the profiles, allowing each respondent to consider all attributes and levels.

10. REFERENCES

Addelman, Sidney, 1962, "Orthogonal Main Effects Plans for Asymmetrical Factorial Experiments," Technometrics, 4: 21-46.

Anderson, D.A. and J.B. Wiley, 1992, "Efficient Choice Set Designs for Estimating Cross-Effects Models," Marketing Letters, 3: 357-70.

Box, George E.P., William G. Hunter and J. Stuart Hunter, 1978, Statistics for Experimenters: An Introduction to Design, Data Analysis and Model Building, New York: John Wiley and Sons.

Bunch, David S., Jordan J. Louviere and Don Anderson, 1994, "A Comparison of Experimental Design Strategies for Multinomial Logit Models: The Case of Generic Attributes," Working paper, UCD-GSM-WP# 01-94, Graduate School of Management, University of California, Davis.

Bunch, David S., Jordan J. Louviere and Don Anderson, 1996, "A Comparison of Experimental Design Strategies for Choice-Based Conjoint Analysis with Generic-Attribute Multinomial Logit Models," Working Paper, Graduate School of Management, University of California, Davis.

Burgess, Leonie and Deborah Street, 2003, "Optimal Designs for 2 Choice Experiments," Communications in Statistics – Theory and Methods, 32.

Carlsson, Fredrik and Peter Martinsoon, 2003, "Design Techniques for Stated Preference Methods in Health Economics," Health Economics, 12(4):281-94.

Chrzan, Keith and Bryan Orme, 2000, "An Overview and Comparison of Design Strategies for Choice-Based Conjoint Analysis," Sawtooth Software Technical paper, http://www.sawtoothsoftware.com/techpap.shtml.

Cochran, W.G. and G.M. Cox, 1957, Experimental Designs, Second Edition, New York: John Wiley & Sons.

Cook, R. Dennis and Christopher J. Nachtsheim, 1980, "A Comparison of Algorithms for Constructing Exact D-Optimal Designs," Technometrics, 22(3): 315-324.

Cook, R. Dennis and Christopher J. Nachtsheim, 1989, "Computer-Aided Blocking of Factorial and Response-Surface Designs," Technometrics, 31(3): 339-346.

Carlsson, Fredrik and Peter Martinsson, 2003, "Design Techniques for Stated Preference Methods in Health Economics," Health Economics, 281-294.

DeShazo, J. R. and G. Fermo, 2002, "Designing Choice Sets for Stated Preference Methods: The Effects of Complexity on Choice Consistency," Journal of Environmental Economics and Management, 44(1): 123-143.

Fedorov, V.V., 1972, Theory of Optimal Experiments, translated and edited by W.J. Studden and E.M. Klimko, New York: Academic Press.

Finkbeiner, Carl T. and Patricia J. Platz, 1986, "Computerized Versus Paper and Pencil Methods: A Comparison Study," paper presented at the Association for Consumer Research Conference, Toronto, October.

Fisher, R.A., 1990, Statistical Methods, Experimental Design, and Scientific Inference: A Re-issue of Statistical Methods for Research Workers, The Design of Experiments, and Statistical Methods and Scientific Inference, in J.H. Bennett and F. Yates, Eds., Oxford: Oxford University Press.

Green, Paul E. and V. Srinivasan, 1990, "Conjoint Analysis in Marketing Research: New Developments and Directions," Journal of Marketing, 54 (October): 3-19.

Huber, J. and Zwerina K., 1996, "The Importance of utility Balance and Efficient Choice Designs," Journal of Marketing Research, 33 (August): 307-317.

Hensher, David A., John M. Rose, and William H. Greene, 2004, Applied Choice Analysis: A Primer, Cambridge University Press: New York.

Johnson, Richard M., 1989, "Assessing the Validity of Conjoint Analysis," Sawtooth Software Conference Proceedings, Ketchum, ID: Sawtooth Software, June, 273-80.

Kanninen, Barbara, 2001, "Optimal Design of Choice Experiments for Nonmarket Valuation," Paper presented at EPA's Environmental Policy and Economics Workshop, "Stated Preference: What do we know? Where do we go?" held in Washington, D.C, 2000.

Kanninen, Barbara, 2002, "Optimal Design for Multinomial Choice Experiments," Journal of Marketing Research, XXXIX: 214-227.

Kanninen, Barbara, 2005, "Optimal Design for Binary Choice Experiments with Quadratic or Interactive Terms," Paper presented at the 2005 International Health Economics Association conference, Barcelona, July.

Keppel, Geoffrey, 1973, Design and Analysis: A Researcher's Handbook, Englewood Cliffs, New Jersey: Prentice-Hall, Inc.

Kuhfeld, Warren F., 1997, "Efficient Experimental Designs Using Computerized Searches," Sawtooth Software Research Paper Series, SAS Institute, Inc.

Kuhfeld, Warren F., undated, "Orthogonal Arrays," SAS Technical Document TS-723, http://support.sas.com/techsup/technote/ts723_Designs.txt.

Kuhfeld, Warren F., 2004, "Marketing Research Methods in SAS: Experimental Design, Choice, Conjoint, and Graphical Techniques." SAS Technical Document TS-694, http://support.sas.com/techsup/technote/ts694.pdf .

Kuhfeld, Warren F., Randall D. Tobias, and Mark Garratt, 1994, "Efficient Experimental Design with Marketing Research Applications," Journal of Marketing Research, XXXI(November): 545-557.

Lazari, Adreas G. and Donald A. Anderson, 1994, "Designs of Discrete Choice Set Experiments for Estimating both Attribute and Availability Cross Effects," Journal of Marketing Research, XXXI(August): 375-383.

Lorenzen, T.J. and V. L Anderson, 1993, Design of Experiments: A No-Name Approach, New York: Marcel Dekker.

Louviere, Jordan J., 1988, "Analyzing Decision Making: Metric Conjoint Analysis," Sage University Paper Series on Quantitative Applications in the Social Sciences, 07-67, Sage Publications, Newbury Park, CA.

Louviere, Jordan J., David A. Hensher, and Joffre D. Swait, 2000, Stated Choice Methods: Analysis and Application, New York: Cambridge University Press.

McFadden, Daniel, 1974, "Conditional Logit Analysis of Qualitative Choice Behavior," in Frontiers of Econometrics, P. Zarembka, Ed., New York: Academic Press, 105-42.

Minkin, S., 1987, "Optimal Designs for Binary Data," Journal of the American Statistical Association, 82(400): 1098-1103.

Mitchell, Toby J., 1974, "An Algorithm for the Construction of 'D-Optimal' Experimental Designs," Technometrics, 16(2): 203-210.

Montgomery, D.C., 1991, Design and Analysis of Experiments, New York: John Wiley and Sons.

Orme, Bryan, 1998, "Sample Size Issues for Conjoint Analysis Studies," Sawtooth Software Technical Paper, http://www.sawtoothsoftware.com/technicaldownloads.shtml#ssize.

Sándor, Z. and M. Wedel, 2001, "Designing Conjoint Choice Experiments Using Managers' Prior Beliefs," Journal of Marketing Research, 38(November).

Silvey, S.D., 1980, Optimal Designs, London: Chapman & Hall.

Sloane, N.J.A., 2004, "A Library of Orthogonal Arrays," http://www.research.att.com/~njas/oadir/index.html.

Snee, Ronald D., 1985, "Computer-Aided Design of Experiments—Some Practical Experiences," Journal of Quality Technology, 17(4): 222-236.

Steffens, K., F. Lupi, B. Kanninen and J. Hoehn, 2002, "A Sequential Updating Approach to the Experimental Design of a Binary Choice Model," mimeo.

Street, Deborah, David Bunch and Beverley Moore, "Optimal Designs for 2k Paired Comparison Experiments," Communications in Statistics – Theory and Methods, 30: 2149-2171.

Street, Deborah and Leonie Burgess, 2003, "Optimal and Near-Optimal Pairs for the Estimation of Effects in 2-Level Choice Experiments, Journal of Statistical Planning and Inference, forthcoming.

Train, Kenneth E., 2003, Discrete Choice Methods with Simulation, Cambridge: Cambridge University Press.

Winer, B.J., D.R. Brown and K.M. Michels, 1991, Statistical Principles in Experimental Design, Third Edition, New York: McGraw-Hill, Inc.

Zwerina, Klaus, Joel Huber, and Warren F. Kuhfeld, 1996, "A General Method for Constructing Efficient Choice Designs." SAS Technical DocumentTS-694, http://support.sas.com/techsup/technote/ts694e.pdf.

11. APPENDIX 1: CATALOG ORTHOGONAL MAIN EFFECTS DESIGNS

TABLE A-1. 2^3

	Attributes		
Rows	A	B	C
1	-1	-1	-1
2	-1	+1	+1
3	+1	-1	+1
4	+1	+1	-1

TABLE A-2. 2^4

	Attributes			
Rows	A	B	C	D
1	-1	-1	-1	-1
2	-1	+1	+1	-1
3	+1	-1	+1	-1
4	+1	+1	-1	-1
5	+1	+1	+1	+1
6	+1	-1	-1	+1
7	-1	+1	-1	+1
8	-1	-1	+1	+1

TABLE A-3. 2^5

Rows	Attributes				
	A	B	C	D	E
1	-1	-1	-1	-1	-1
2	+1	-1	-1	+1	+1
3	-1	+1	-1	+1	-1
4	-1	-1	+1	-1	+1
5	+1	+1	-1	-1	+1
6	+1	-1	+1	+1	-1
7	-1	+1	+1	+1	+1
8	+1	+1	+1	-1	-1

TABLE A-4. 2^7

Rows	Attributes						
	A	B	C	D	E	F	G
1	-1	-1	-1	-1	-1	-1	-1
2	+1	-1	+1	-1	+1	-1	+1
3	-1	+1	+1	-1	-1	+1	+1
4	+1	+1	-1	-1	+1	+1	-1
5	-1	-1	-1	+1	+1	+1	+1
6	+1	-1	+1	+1	-1	+1	-1
7	-1	+1	+1	+1	+1	-1	-1
8	+1	+1	-1	+1	-1	-1	+1

TABLE A-5. 2^8

Rows	Attributes							
	A	B	C	D	E	F	G	H
1	-1	-1	-1	-1	-1	-1	-1	-1
2	-1	+1	-1	+1	-1	+1	-1	+1
3	-1	-1	+1	+1	-1	-1	+1	+1
4	-1	+1	+1	-1	-1	+1	+1	-1
5	-1	-1	-1	-1	+1	+1	+1	+1
6	-1	+1	-1	+1	+1	-1	+1	-1
7	-1	-1	+1	+1	+1	+1	-1	-1
8	-1	+1	+1	-1	+1	-1	-1	+1
9	+1	+1	+1	+1	+1	+1	+1	+1
10	+1	-1	+1	-1	+1	-1	+1	-1
11	+1	+1	-1	-1	+1	+1	-1	-1
12	+1	-1	-1	+1	+1	-1	-1	+1
13	+1	+1	+1	+1	-1	-1	-1	-1
14	+1	-1	+1	-1	-1	+1	-1	+1
15	+1	+1	-1	-1	-1	-1	+1	+1
16	+1	-1	-1	+1	-1	+1	+1	-1

TABLE A-6. 3^4

	Attributes			
Rows	A	B	C	D
1	-1	-1	-1	-1
2	-1	0	0	1
3	-1	1	1	0
4	0	-1	0	0
5	0	0	1	-1
6	0	1	-1	1
7	1	-1	1	1
8	1	0	-1	0
9	1	1	0	-1

TABLE A-7. Full Factorial Design, One 3-Level and Two 2-Level Attributes

Main Effects			Two-way Interactions			Three-way Interactions
A	B	C	A·B	A·C	B·C	A·B·C
-1	+1	+1	-1	-1	+1	-1
0	+1	+1	0	0	+1	0
+1	+1	+1	+1	+1	+1	+1
-1	-1	-1	+1	+1	+1	-1
0	-1	-1	0	0	+1	0
+1	-1	-1	-1	-1	+1	+1
-1	+1	-1	-1	+1	-1	+1
0	+1	-1	0	0	-1	0
+1	+1	-1	+1	-1	-1	-1
-1	-1	+1	+1	-1	-1	+1
0	-1	+1	0	0	-1	0
+1	-1	+1	-1	+1	-1	-1

TABLE A-8. *Optimal Main-Effects 2^{4-1} Design, Three Alternatives*
U = Upper bound, L = Lower bound

Choice Set	Alternative	A	B	C	Choice %
1	1	U	U	U	.63
1	2	L	U	L	.06
1	0	L	L	L	.31
2	1	U	U	U	.06
2	2	L	U	L	.63
2	3	U	L	U	.31
3	1	L	L	U	.63
3	2	U	L	L	.06
3	0	U	U	L	.31
4	1	L	L	U	.06
4	2	U	L	L	.63
4	0	L	U	U	.31

TABLE A-9. *Optimal Main-Effects 2^{4-1} Design, Five Alternatives*
U = Upper bound, L = Lower bound

Choice Set	Alternative	A	B	C	Choice %
1	1	U	U	U	.51
1	2	L	U	L	.04
1	3	L	L	U	.04
1	4	U	L	L	.04
1	0	L	L	L	.37
2	1	U	U	U	.04
2	2	L	U	L	.51
2	3	L	L	U	.04
2	4	U	L	L	.04
2	0	U	L	U	.37
3	1	U	U	U	.04
3	2	L	U	L	.04
3	3	L	L	U	.51
3	4	U	L	L	.04
3	0	U	U	L	.37
4	1	U	U	U	.04
4	2	L	U	L	.04
4	3	L	L	U	.04
4	4	U	L	L	.51
4	0	L	U	U	.37

12. APPENDIX B

SAS Program to generate initial linear design and effects-code it

```
* Program to generate an efficient flat design using OPTEX;
* Add blocking factor for version

* Create full-factorial design;
proc plan ordered;
          factors x1=2 x2=3 x3=6 x4=2 x5=2 x6=4 x7=2 x8=2/ noprint;
          output out=candidat;

proc transreg design data=candidat;
  model class(x1-x8 / effects);
  output out=designx;

data sub2f;
  set designx;

proc print;
```

GAUSS program to implement choice-experiment design algorithm [g:\gssfiles\design\lavaca.prg]

```
@ Program to construct choice-experiment design. Based on SAS/IML program
  in Zwerina, Huber, and Kuhfeld, "A General Method for Constructing
  Efficient Choice Designs," 1996.          @

new;
output file = lavaca.out reset;
outwidth 150;
"OPTIMAL CHOICE EXPERIMENT DESIGN      lavaca.prg ";
print;

nalts = 2;      @ number of alternatives @
nsets = 15;     @ number of choice sets @
ndesigns = 20;
nblocks=2;

format /rd 5,0;
"Number of alternatives =  " nalts ;
"Number of choice sets =   " nsets;
"Number of designs constructed = " ndesigns;
print;
```

```
load sasdat[]=sas4c.txt;
sasdat=reshape(sasdat,rows(sasdat)/9,9);
attrib=sasdat[1,.]';
attrib=trimr(attrib,1,1);
sasdat=trimr(sasdat,1,0);
block=sasdat[.,cols(sasdat)];
sasdat=trimr(sasdat',1,1)';
nrows=rows(sasdat);

levels="0";
ncols=0;
i=0;do while i<cols(sasdat);i=i+1;
 z=unique(sasdat[.,i],0);
 ncols=ncols+rows(z)-1;
 levels=levels|z;
 z=varput(z,attrib[i]);
endo;
levels=trimr(levels,1,0);

@ Construct effect codes @
cand0=zeros(nrows,1);
k=0;
label=" ";
i=0;do while i<rows(attrib);i=i+1;
 z=varget(attrib[i]);      @ get labels @
 if i==2;
  k=k+1;
  cand0=cand0~recode(sasdat[.,i],sasdat[.,i].$==z',15|30|5);
  label=label|"Dist";
 else;
  j=0;do while j<rows(z)-1;j=j+1;
   k=k+1;
   cand0=cand0~(sasdat[.,i].$==z[j]);
   cand0[.,cols(cand0)]=
    substute(cand0[.,cols(cand0)],sasdat[.,i].$==z[rows(z)],-1);
   label=label|z[j];
  endo;
 endif;
endo;
label=trimr(label,1,0);
cand0=trimr(cand0',1,0)';

DEFF0 = 100/(NROWS*DET(INV(CAND0'CAND0))^(1/COLS(CAND0)));
print;
print "   Design  D-Efficiency D-Error";
```

```
print "  ===================================";
desnum="Linear Model";
 __fmtnv = { "*.*lf" 13 4};
 __fmtcv[2 3] = 13~18;
mask=1~1;
" Linear Model";;call printfmt(deff0~(1/deff0),mask);


@ delete last category for each attribute @
let beta = { 0      @ Type @
   0     @ Distance @
   0 0 0 0 0   @ Species/Catch @
   0     @ View @
   0     @ Congestion @
   0 0 0    @ Amenities @
   0 };    @ Advisory @
beta=beta';


@ ---------------- Begin Efficient Design Search --------------------- @
b=0;do while b<nblocks;output on;print;print;
format /rd 1,0;b=b+1;"BLOCK #";;b;output off;
 cand=selif(cand0,block.==b);

utils = exp(cand*beta);     @ exp(alternative utilities) @
np = 1/cols(cand);        @ exponent applied to determinant @
imat = eye(nalts);       @ identity matrix @
nobs = nsets * nalts;      @ total n of alts in choice design @
ncands = rows(cand);      @ number of candidates @
fuzz = eye(cols(cand))*1e-8;   @ X'X ridge factor, avoid singular @

proc center(x,exputil);    @ probability centering subroutine @
 local i, k, p, z;
 i=0;do while i<rows(x)/nalts;i=i+1;  @ do for each choice set @
 k = seqa((i-1)*nalts+1,1,nalts); @ choice set index vector @
 p = exputil[k,.];    @ probability of choice @
 p = p./sumc(p);
 z = x[k,.];     @ get choice set @
 x[k,.] = (z - sumc(z.*p)').*sqrt(p); @ center choice set, absorb p's @
 endo;
 retp(x);
endp;


@ ------------- Create Designs with Different Random Starts ----------- @
fn randomize(m,n)=submat(rankindx(rndu(n,1),1),seqa(1,1,m),1);
```

```
desnum=0;do while desnum<ndesigns;desnum=desnum+1;
indvec = randomize(ncands,ncands); @ Sample without replacement @
des = cand[indvec,.];   @ indvec points to sample rows @
des = center(des,utils[indvec,.]); @ Probability center @
currdet = det(des'des);   @ Initial determinants, eff's @
maxdet = currdet;
oldeff = currdet^np;
fineff = oldeff;
iter=0;
derr=0;
if fineff <= 0;
 derr = miss(derr,derr);
else;
 derr = 1/fineff;
endif;

format /rz 13,4; print;
print "  Design  Iteration D-Efficiency  D-Error";
print
"============================================================";
print desnum iter fineff derr ;

@ ----------------- Internal Iterations --------------------- @
converge=0;
iter=0;do while converge==0;iter=iter+1;

@ ----- Consider Replacing Each Alternative in the Design ------ @
desi=0;do while desi<nobs;desi=desi+1; @ Process each alt in design @
 ind = ceil(desi/nalts);
 ind = seqa((ind-1)*nalts+1,1,nalts);
 besttry = des[ind,.];
 des[ind,.] =
   zeros(rows(ind),cols(des));
 xpx = des'des;
 d = det(xpx);
 if d<0;goto continue;endif;

 i=-1;d=0;do while d^np<1e-8;i=i+1;
  xpx = des'des + fuzz*i^2; @ X`X, ridged if necessary @
  d = det(xpx);   @ Determinant, if 0 then X`X will @
 endo;        @ be ridged to make it nonsingular @
 xpxinv = inv(xpx);   @ Inverse (all but current set) @
 indcan = indvec[ind];   @ Indvec for this choice set @
 alt = ((desi-1)%nalts) + 1; @ Alternative number   @

@-------------Loop Over All of the Candidates---------------@
```

```
candi=0;do while candi<ncands;candi=candi+1;
 indcan[alt] = candi;  @ Update indvec for this candidate @
 tryit = cand[indcan,.];  @ Candidate choice set   @
 tryit = center(tryit,  @ Probability center   @
   utils[indcan,.]);
 currdet = d *    @ Update determinant   @
  det(imat + tryit * xpxinv * tryit');

@--------Store Results When Efficiency Improves----------@

 if currdet > maxdet;
  maxdet = currdet;   @ Best determinant so far  @
  indvec[desi] = candi;  @ Indvec of best design so far @
  besttry = tryit;   @ Best choice set so far  @
 endif;
endo;

continue:
des[ind,.] = besttry;  @ Update design with new choice set@

endo;

@----------Evaluate Efficiency/Convergence, Report Results------@
neweff = maxdet^np;    @ Newest efficiency  @

converge = ((neweff - oldeff) / @ Less than 1/2 percent  @
  maxc(oldeff|1e-8) < 0.005); @ improvement is convergence @
oldeff = neweff;     @ Store for use in next iteration @
fineff = det(des'des)^np;   @ Efficiency at end of iteration @

if fineff <= 0;
 derr = miss(derr,derr);
else;
 derr = 1/fineff;
 print desnum iter fineff derr ;
endif;
endo;

@--Store Efficiency, Index of Efficient Design, Covariance Matrix--@

if desnum==1;
 final = desnum~fineff~derr~indvec';
 cov = reshape(desnum,cols(des),1)~inv(des'des);
else;
 final = final | desnum~fineff~derr~indvec';
 cov = cov |reshape(desnum,cols(des),1)~inv(des'des);
```

```
 endif;
endo;
 @-------------------- Save Results --------------------@

final = sortc(final,3);
output on;
 print;
 print "   Design D-Efficiency D-Error";
 print "  =======================================";
desnum=ftocv(final[.,1],1,0);
__fmtnv = { "*.*lf" 13 4};
__fmtcv[2 3] = 13~4;
mask=0~1~1;
call printfmt(desnum~final[.,2 3],mask);

print;format /rd 7,0;
"Best Design:";
"------------";
designi=trimr(final[1,.]',3,0);
optdesign=cand[designi,.];
setib=seqa(1,1,nsets);
setib=vecr(setib[.,ones(1,nalts)]);
if b==1;seti=setib;else; seti=maxc(seti)+setib;endif;

k=0;
design=zeros(nrows/nblocks,1);
i=0;do while i<rows(attrib);i=i+1;
 z=varget(attrib[i]);     @ get labels @
 if i==2;
  k=2;
  colk=optdesign[.,k];
  design=design~recode(colk,colk.==(15~30~5),z);
 else;
  k=seqa(maxc(k)+1,1,rows(z)-1);
  colk=optdesign[.,k];
  nextcol=zeros(rows(colk),1);
  j=0;do while j<cols(colk);j=j+1;
   hit=indnv(colk[.,j],1|0|-1);
   nextcol=recode(nextcol,hit.==1,z[j]);
   nextcol=recode(nextcol,hit.==3,z[rows(z)]);
  endo;
  design=design~nextcol;
 endif;
endo;
design=trimr(design',1,0)';
```

```
design=seti~design;
format /rd 8,0;
print " Choice";
print "  Set";;$attrib';
  __fmtnv = { "*.*lf" 8 0};
  __fmtcv = { "*.*lf" 9 8};
mask=1~zeros(1,cols(design)-1);
call printfmt(design,mask);

if b==1;
 alldesign=design;
 allcov=cov;
else;
 alldesign=alldesign|design;
 allcov=allcov|cov;
endif;
 output off;

endo;

save alldesign,allcov;
end;
```

CHAPTER 8

BASIC STATISTICAL MODELS FOR STATED CHOICE STUDIES

ANNA ALBERINI

Department of Agricultural and Resource Economics, University of Maryland, College Park, Maryland, U.S.A. and Fondazione ENI Enrico Mattei, Italy

ALBERTO LONGO

University of Bath, Bath, UK

MARCELLA VERONESI

Department of Agricultural and Resource Economics, University of Maryland, College Park, Maryland, U.S.A.

1. INTRODUCTION

Stated choice (SC) studies are a survey-based technique used to investigate the tradeoffs that people are prepared to make between different goods or policies. In a typical SC survey, respondent are shown alternative variants of a good described by a set of attributes, and are asked to rank these alternatives, to rate them or to choose their most preferred (Hanley et al., 2001). In the latter case, the technique is sometimes termed "conjoint choice" or "conjoint choice experiments." The alternatives differ from one another in the levels taken by two or more of the attributes. Statistical analyses of the responses obtained in any one of these ways can be used to obtain the marginal values of the attributes and the willingness to pay (WTP) for any alternative of interest.

The purpose of this chapter is to present the basic statistical models for SC studies. The chapter is organized as follows. Section 2 describes the random-utility model underlying SC questions, derives the conditional logit model and discusses its properties. It also describes how to compute the value of a good or project and the

B.J. Kanninen (ed.), Valuing Environmental Amenities Using Stated Choice Studies, 203–227.
© 2006 *Springer.*

marginal prices of attributes. We provide an application using the data collected from a recent survey of Venice residents about urban regeneration projects. Section 3 is dedicated to contingent valuation (CV). We define WTP and willingness to accept (WTA), present the most popular models of the responses to dichotomous-choice payment questions, and discuss difficulties and possible remedies.

2. MODEL AND ECONOMETRIC ANALYSES OF THE RESPONSES

2.1. The Random-Utility Model

In a SC exercise, respondents are shown a set of alternative representations of a good and are asked to pick their most preferred. The responses can be used to estimate the marginal rates of substitution between attributes. If one of the attributes is cost, it is possible to calculate the marginal price of each attribute. If the "do nothing" or status quo option is included in the choice set, the experiments can be used to estimate the full value (WTP) of each alternative. SC has the advantage of simulating real market situations, where consumers face two or more goods characterized by similar attributes, but different levels of these attributes, and have the option of choosing to buy some, one, or none of the goods. Another advantage is that the choice tasks do not require as much effort by the respondent as rating or ranking alternatives do.

To motivate the statistical analysis of the responses to conjoint choice questions, it is assumed that the choice between the alternatives is driven by the respondent's underlying utility. The respondent's indirect utility is broken down into two components. The first component is deterministic, and is a function of the attributes of alternatives, characteristics of the individuals, and a set of unknown parameters, while the second component is an error term. Formally,

$$V_{ij} = \overline{V}(\mathbf{x}_{ij}, \boldsymbol{\beta}) + \varepsilon_{ij} \tag{1}$$

where the subscript i denotes the respondent, the subscript j denotes the alternative, $\mathbf{x}$ is the vector of attributes that vary across alternatives (or across alternatives *and* individuals), and ε_{ij} is an error term that captures individual- and alternative-specific factors that influence utility, but are not observable to the researcher. Equation (1) describes the random-utility model (RUM).

In many applications, it is further assumed that $\overline{V}$, the deterministic component of utility, is a linear function of the attributes and of the respondent's residual income, $(y - C)$:

$$V_{ij} = \beta_0 + \mathbf{x}_{ij}\boldsymbol{\beta}_1 + (y_i - C_{ij})\beta_2 + \varepsilon_{ij}, \tag{2}$$

where y is income and C is the cost of the alternative program to the respondent. Clearly, the coefficient β_2 is the marginal utility of income.

As mentioned, respondents are assumed to choose the alternative in the choice set that results in the highest utility. Because the observed outcome of each choice task is the selection of one out of K alternatives, the appropriate econometric model is a discrete choice model expressing the probability that alternative k is chosen. Formally,

$$\pi_{ik} = \Pr\left(V_{ik} > V_{i1}, V_{ik} > V_{i2}, ..., V_{ik} > V_{iK}\right) = \Pr(V_{ik} > V_{ij}) \quad \forall j \neq k, \tag{3}$$

where π_{ik} signifies the probability that option k is chosen by individual i. This means that:

$$\pi_{ik} = \Pr(\beta_0 + \mathbf{x}_{ik}\boldsymbol{\beta}_1 + (y_i - C_{ik})\beta_2 + \varepsilon_{ik} > \beta_0 + \mathbf{x}_{ij}\boldsymbol{\beta}_1 + (y_i - C_{ij})\beta_2 + \varepsilon_{ij}) \, \forall j \neq k, \tag{4}$$

from which follows that:

$$\pi_{ik} = \Pr[(\varepsilon_{ij} - \varepsilon_{ik}) < (\mathbf{x}_{ik} - \mathbf{x}_{ij})\boldsymbol{\beta}_1 - (C_{ik} - C_{ij})\beta_2) \quad \forall j \neq k. \tag{5}$$

Equation (5) shows that the probability of selecting an alternative no longer contains terms in (2) that are constant across alternatives, such as the intercept and income. It also shows that the probability of selecting k depends on the differences in the levels of the attributes across alternatives, and that the negative of the marginal utility of income is the coefficient on the difference in cost or price across alternatives.

2.2. The Conditional Logit Model

If the error terms ε are independent and identically distributed and follow a standard type I extreme-value distribution, one can derive a closed-form expression for the probability that respondent i picks alternative k out of K alternatives.

Since the cdf of the standard type I extreme-value distribution is $F(\varepsilon) = \exp(-e^{-\varepsilon})$, and its pdf is $f(\varepsilon_i) = \exp(-\varepsilon_i - e^{-\varepsilon_i})$, choosing alternative k means that $\varepsilon_k + V_k > \varepsilon_j + V_j$ for all j≠k, which can be written as $\varepsilon_j < \varepsilon_k + V_k - V_j$. The probability of choosing k is, therefore:

$$\pi_{ik} = \Pr(\varepsilon_{ij} < \varepsilon_{ik} + V_{ik} - V_{ij}) \text{ for all } j \neq k$$
$$= \int_{-\infty}^{+\infty} \prod_{j \neq k} F(\varepsilon_{ik} + V_{ik} - V_{ij}) \cdot f(\varepsilon_{ik}) d\varepsilon_{ik} \cdot \tag{6}$$

Expression (6) follows from the assumption of independence, and the fact that ε_k is an error term and not observed, so that it is must be integrated out of $F(\varepsilon_{ik} + V_{ik} - V_{ij})$. The product within expression (6) can be re-written as:

$$\prod_{j \neq k} F(\varepsilon_{ik} + V_{ik} - V_{ij}) \cdot f(\varepsilon_{ik}) = \prod_{j \neq k} \exp(-e^{-\varepsilon_{ik} - V_{ik} + V_{ij}}) \exp(-\varepsilon_{ik} - e^{-\varepsilon_{ik}})$$

$$= \exp\left[-\varepsilon_{ik} - e^{-\varepsilon_{ik}} \left(1 + \sum_{j \neq k} \frac{e^{V_{ij}}}{e^{V_{ik}}} \right) \right]. \qquad (7)$$

Now write[1]

$$\lambda_{ik} = \log\left(1 + \sum_{j \neq k} \frac{e^{V_{ij}}}{e^{V_{ik}}} \right) = \log\left(\sum_{j=1}^{K} \frac{e^{V_{ij}}}{e^{V_{ik}}} \right), \qquad (8)$$

which allows us to rewrite (6) as

$$\int_{-\infty}^{+\infty} \exp(-\varepsilon_{ik} - e^{-(\varepsilon_{ik} - \lambda_{ik})}) d\varepsilon_{ik} = \exp(-\lambda_{ik}) \int_{-\infty}^{+\infty} \exp(-\varepsilon_{ik}^* - e^{-\varepsilon_{ik}^*}) d\varepsilon_{ik}^*, \qquad (9)$$

where $\varepsilon_{ik}^* = \varepsilon_{ik} - \lambda_{ik}$. The integrand in expression (9) is the pdf of the extreme-value distribution and is, clearly, equal to 1. Equation (9) thus simplifies to $\exp(-\lambda_{ik})$, which by (8) is in turn equal to $\exp(V_{ik}) / \sum_{j=1}^{K} \exp(V_{ij})$.

Recalling (2), the probability that respondent i picks alternative k out of K alternatives is:

$$\pi_{ik} = \frac{\exp(\mathbf{w}_{ik}\boldsymbol{\beta})}{\sum_{j=1}^{K} \exp(\mathbf{w}_{ij}\boldsymbol{\beta})} \qquad (10)$$

where $\mathbf{w}_{ij} = \begin{bmatrix} \mathbf{x}_{ij} \\ C_{ij} \end{bmatrix}$ is the vector of all attributes of alternative j, including cost, and $\boldsymbol{\beta}$ is equal to $\begin{bmatrix} \boldsymbol{\beta}_1 \\ -\beta_2 \end{bmatrix}$.[2]

Equation (10) is the contribution to the likelihood in a conditional logit model. The full log likelihood function of the conditional logit model is:

$$\log L = \sum_{i=1}^{n} \sum_{k=1}^{K} y_{ik} \cdot \log \pi_{ik} \quad , \tag{11}$$

where y_{ik} is a binary indicator that takes on a value of 1 if the respondent selects alternative k, and 0 otherwise. The coefficients are estimated using the method of Maximum Likelihood.

We can further examine the expression for π_{ik} in equation (10) to show that π_{ik} depends on the differences in the level of the attributes between alternatives. To see that this is the case, we begin by re-writing (10) as:

$$\pi_{ik} = \frac{\exp(\mathbf{w}_{ik}\boldsymbol{\beta})}{\sum_{j=1}^{K} \exp(\mathbf{w}_{ij}\boldsymbol{\beta})} = \left[\frac{\exp(\mathbf{w}_{ik}\boldsymbol{\beta})}{\exp(\mathbf{w}_{i1}\boldsymbol{\beta}) + \ldots + \exp(\mathbf{w}_{ik}\boldsymbol{\beta}) + \ldots + \exp(\mathbf{w}_{iK}\boldsymbol{\beta})} \right], \tag{12}$$

which is equal to:

$$= \left[\frac{\exp(\mathbf{w}_{i1}\boldsymbol{\beta}) + \ldots + \exp(\mathbf{w}_{ik}\boldsymbol{\beta}) + \ldots + \exp(\mathbf{w}_{iK}\boldsymbol{\beta})}{\exp(\mathbf{w}_{ik}\boldsymbol{\beta})} \right]^{-1} , \tag{13}$$

and thus to :

$$= \left\{ \exp\left[(\mathbf{w}_{i1} - \mathbf{w}_{ik})\boldsymbol{\beta}\right] + \ldots + 1 + \ldots + \exp\left[(\mathbf{w}_{ik} - \mathbf{w}_{iK})\boldsymbol{\beta}\right] \right\}^{-1} . \tag{14}$$

For large samples and assuming that the model is correctly specified, the maximum likelihood estimates $\hat{\beta}$ are normally distributed around the true vector of parameters $\boldsymbol{\beta}$, and the asymptotic variance-covariance matrix, Ω, is the inverse of the Fisher information matrix. The information matrix is defined as:

$$I(\beta) = \sum_{i=1}^{n} \sum_{k=1}^{K} \pi_{ik} (\mathbf{w}_{ik} - \overline{\mathbf{w}}_i)(\mathbf{w}_{ik} - \overline{\mathbf{w}}_i)' , \tag{15}$$

where $\overline{\mathbf{w}}_i = \sum_{k=1}^{K} \pi_{ik} \mathbf{w}_{ik}$.

2.3. Goodness-of-fit Tests

The easiest approach to testing goodness-of-fit is to compare the log likelihood function of the full model with that of a model that restricts the coefficients of the attributes to be equal to zero, while allowing for a free intercept term. In what follows, let $\log L_U$ be the log likelihood function of the full (unrestricted) model and $\log L_R$ be the log likelihood function of the model with all slopes restricted to zero.

We can thus build the likelihood ratio test of the null that all slope coefficients are equal to zero. The test statistic is $-2 \cdot [\log L_R - \log L_U]$, which under the null hypothesis is distributed as a chi square with q degrees of freedom, denoted χ^2_q, where q is the number of slope coefficients being tested. If the test statistic rejects the null, we would conclude that the attributes of the alternatives do explain choice.

It should be noted that under this null hypothesis, the probability of choosing alternative k is equal to 1/K, where K is the dimension of the choice set. In other words, any alternative in the choice set is just as likely to be selected as the others. $\log L_R$ is, therefore, equal to $\sum_{i=1}^{n} \log \frac{1}{K} = \text{nlog}(1/k).$[3]

These full and restricted log likelihoods can also be used to create the likelihood ratio index, a measure of goodness of fit first suggested by McFadden (1974). This index is defined as $LRI = 1 - \log L_U / \log L_R$, and can be interpreted as the percentage improvement in the log likelihood function due to the inclusion of the regressors in the model.

Since $|\log L_U| \leq |\log L_R|$ and the log likelihood is always negative, the LRI is bounded between 0 and 1. If all the slope coefficients are truly zero, then adding the attributes to the model does not improve the likelihood (i.e., $\log L_U = \log L_R$), and the LRI is equal to zero. If, on the other hand, the model predicts the respondents' observations perfectly, the likelihood function at the estimated parameters L_U is one and so $\log L_U$ is zero, making LRI equal to one.

These cases are, however, extremes, and in practice the LRI will typically take values between 0 and 1. Unfortunately, as pointed out by Greene (2003) and Train (2003), the values between the extremes of zero and one have no natural interpretation. If we consider two models estimated using the same data and with the same set of alternatives, the model with the higher LRI is concluded to fit the data better, but it is not possible to compare models on different samples or different sets of alternatives using the LRI (Train, 2003).

Another goodness-of-fit measure that is sometimes used in empirical work is the percent of correctly predicted observations. If K = 2, which means that the conditional logit is simplified to a binary logit model, we use the model to compute the predicted probability $\hat{p}_i$ that $y_i = 1$, given the explanatory variables, x_i. The outcome variable y_i is predicted to be a one if $\hat{p}_i$ is greater than 0.5, and zero if $\hat{p}_i$

≤ 0.5. The percentage of times the predicted y_i matches the actual y_i is the percent correctly predicted.

If $K > 2$, then it is necessary to compute the probability that the decision maker selects each of the possible alternatives. The predicted choice is the one for which the model gives the highest estimated probability. The percentage of correct predictions is, again, the number of times out of the total number of observations when the prediction matches the observed choice. Train (2003, p.73) recommends against using the percentage of correctly predicted observations as a measure of fit because "the statistic is based on the idea that the decision maker is predicted by the researcher to choose the alternative for which the model gives the highest probability. However, [...], the researcher does not have enough information to predict the decision maker's choice. The researcher has only enough information to state the probability that the decision maker will choose each alternative." In many cases it is easy to predict one particular outcome and much harder to predict other outcomes, in which case the percent correctly predicted can be misleading as a goodness-of-fit statistic.

2.4. Marginal Prices and WTP

Once model (11) is estimated, the rate of tradeoff between any two attributes is the ratio of their respective β coefficients. The marginal value of attribute l is computed as the negative of the coefficient on that attribute, divided by the coefficient on the price or cost variable:

$$MP_l = -\frac{\hat{\beta}_l}{\hat{\beta}_2} \cdot \tag{16}$$

The WTP for a commodity is computed as:

$$WTP_i = -\frac{\mathbf{x}_i \hat{\boldsymbol{\beta}}_1}{\hat{\beta}_2} , \tag{17}$$

where $\mathbf{x_i}$ is the vector of attributes describing the commodity assigned to individual i. It should be kept in mind that a proper WTP can only be computed if the choice set for at least some of the choice sets faced by the individuals contains the "status quo" (in which no commodity is acquired, and the cost is zero). Expression (17) is obtained by equating the indirect utility associated with commodity $\mathbf{x}_i$ and residual income $(y_i - C)$ with the indirect utility associated with the status quo (no commodity) and the original level of income y_i, and solving for C.

When reporting the estimates of the marginal prices of the attributes and the WTP, it is important to report the standard errors around these estimates. As shown in (16) and (17), marginal prices and WTP are the ratios of variables that in large samples are jointly normally distributed. This means that standard errors around them must be computed using the delta method (Greene, 2003, p. 193), or, alternatively, simulation-based procedures.

To apply the delta method to get the standard error around the estimate of the marginal price of attribute l, let $g = -\dfrac{\beta_l}{\beta_2}$. The variance around marginal price (16) is thus:

$$Var(MP_l) = \frac{\partial g}{\partial \boldsymbol{\beta}'} \boldsymbol{\Omega} \frac{\partial g}{\partial \boldsymbol{\beta}} , \qquad (18)$$

where $\dfrac{\partial g}{\partial \boldsymbol{\beta}'}$ is a vector of zeros, except for the l-th element, which is $(-1/\beta_2)$, and the last element, which is β_l/β_2^2. The quantity $\boldsymbol{\Omega}$ is the variance-covariance matrix of the beta vector. In practice, all of the parameters in the expression for g and in (18) will be replaced with their estimates. The standard error is the square root of (18).

When we use the delta method to produce the variance around WTP for the alternative (equation (17)), we still use expression (18), but $\dfrac{\partial g}{\partial \boldsymbol{\beta}'}$ is in this case equal to $\left[-\mathbf{x}_i / \beta_2 \quad \mathbf{x}_i \boldsymbol{\beta}_1 / \beta_2^2 \right]$.

Alternatively, it is possible to adopt the method suggested by Krinsky and Robb (1986), which is based on simulations. To illustrate how this method would work for the marginal price, one would conduct a large number S of replications, where each replication is a random draw from a multivariate normal, with vector of means equal to $\hat{\boldsymbol{\beta}}$ and variance-covariance matrix equal to the estimated variance-covariate matrix between the coefficient estimates, $\hat{\boldsymbol{\Omega}}$.

Let $\boldsymbol{\beta}_S$ denote the vector of values for draw s, $s = 1, 2, ..., S$, which is comprised of β_{1s} and β_{2s}. For each draw s, one computes - β_{1s} / β_{2s}, obtaining in this fashion a total of S vectors of marginal prices. The calculated standard deviation of S marginal prices for each attribute is then assumed to be the standard error around the estimate (16) of the marginal price for that attribute. This approach is easy to implement, given appropriate software resources, but may be sensitive to very small or very large draws for β_2.

2.5. Heterogeneity and IIA

The conditional logit model described by equations (10)-(11) is easily amended to allow for heterogeneity among the respondents. Specifically, one can form interaction terms between individual characteristics, such as age, gender, education, etc., and all or some of the attributes, and enter these interactions in the indirect utility function. For example, if it was believed that the marginal utility of the attributes of, say, an air quality improvement program varies with the health of the individual, one might specify utility as:

$$V_{ij} = \beta_0 + \mathbf{x}_{ij}\boldsymbol{\beta}_1 + (y_i - C_{ij})\beta_2 + (\mathbf{x}_{ij} \times H_i)\boldsymbol{\beta}_3 + \varepsilon_{ij} , \qquad (19)$$

where H is a dummy denoting, for example, that the individual suffers from certain respiratory ailments. The interaction term ($\mathbf{x}_{ij} \times H_i$) varies across the alternatives (j), and one retains the ability to estimate the coefficients $\boldsymbol{\beta}_3$. The marginal utilities of the attributes are thus $\boldsymbol{\beta}_1$ for healthy individuals, and $(\boldsymbol{\beta}_1 + \boldsymbol{\beta}_3)$ for individuals with respiratory illnesses.

Whether or not interaction terms are included, implicit in the conditional logit model is the assumption of Independence of Irrelevant Alternatives (IIA), which states that the ratio of the odds of choosing any two alternatives depends only on the attributes of the alternatives being compared, and is not affected by the attributes of other alternatives. Formally,

$$\frac{\Pr(k)}{\Pr(h)} = \frac{\exp(\mathbf{w}_{ik}\boldsymbol{\beta})/\sum_j \exp(\mathbf{w}_{ij}\boldsymbol{\beta})}{\exp(\mathbf{w}_{ih}\boldsymbol{\beta})/\sum_j \exp(\mathbf{w}_{ij}\boldsymbol{\beta})} = \frac{\exp(\mathbf{w}_{ik}\boldsymbol{\beta})}{\exp(\mathbf{w}_{ih}\boldsymbol{\beta})} . \qquad (20)$$

An implication of the IIA is that, as shown in equation (20), adding another alternative, or changing the characteristics of a third alternative, does not affect the relative odds between alternatives k and h. IIA generally imposes restrictive substitution patterns among the alternatives. To illustrate, when we change the level of the lth attribute of alternative k, the marginal change in the probability of choosing k is:

$$\Pr(k) \cdot [1 - \Pr(k)] \cdot \beta_l , \qquad (21)$$

whereas changing the level of the lth attribute of another alternative—alternative j—, implies that the marginal change in the likelihood of choosing k is:

$$- \Pr(k) \cdot \Pr(j) \cdot \beta_l . \qquad (22)$$

A change in the attributes of one alternative, therefore, changes the probabilities of the other alternatives proportionately to satisfy the conditional logit's requirement that the ratio of these probabilities remains the same (Train, 1999). This implies that conditional logit is not well suited for alternatives that individuals perceive as close substitutes of one another.[4] Researchers are thus advised to test for violations of this assumption using the appropriate Hausman test, and to consider models that relax it, such as the multinomial probit and mixed logit models (see Swait, this volume).

To construct the Hausman test of IIA, Hausman and McFadden (1984) suggest creating an artificial choice subset containing J alternatives, of which one is the alternative the individual actually chose, and the other (J-1) are selected at random among the remaining alternatives in the original choice set. They reason that if IIA holds, omitting alternatives from this artificial choice subset will not change parameter estimates systematically. Exclusion of the omitted alternatives will be inefficient, but will not lead to inconsistency. By contrast, if the remaining odds ratios are not truly independent from these alternatives (i.e., if IIA does not hold), then the parameter estimates obtained when these choices are included will be inconsistent.

The null hypothesis of the Hausman test is that the IIA assumption holds, while the alternative hypothesis states that IIA does not hold. The statistic is:

$$h = \left(\hat{\beta}_r - \hat{\beta}_f\right)'\left[V(\hat{\beta}_r) - V(\hat{\beta}_f)\right]^{-1}(\hat{\beta}_r - \hat{\beta}_f) , \qquad (23)$$

where $\hat{\beta}_r$ is the estimator based on the restricted choice subset, $\hat{\beta}_f$ is the estimator based on the full set of choices, and $V(\hat{\beta}_r)$ and $V(\hat{\beta}_f)$ are the respective estimates of the asymptotic covariance matrices. Under the null hypothesis, the statistic has a limiting chi-squared distribution with degrees of freedom equal to the rank of the matrix $[V(\hat{\beta}_r) - V(\hat{\beta}_f)]$.

2.6. Respondent-Specific Effects

Since in many applications of SC the same respondent is faced with multiple choice tasks, it is reasonable to worry whether the error terms associated with the different choice occasions are correlated within the same respondent. All of the models here considered—the conditional logit, the random-coefficient logit, and the multinomial probit—can be amended to allow for random effects, whereby all error terms for a respondent share a common component. This component is fixed within the respondent, but varies across respondents, and is supposed to capture idiosyncratic, unobservable factors that can influence utility.

In practice, we have seen limited use of random-effects models to accommodate correlation within a respondent. One example is Haefele and Loomis (2001), who compare models with Respondent-Specific random effects with the conventional model using conjoint rating responses (which implies that the base model is an ordered probit). On inspecting their regression results (Table 1, p. 1235), it appears that using the random-coefficient model does change both coefficients and t statistics relative to the model that treats the observations within a respondent as independent of one another. Haefele and Loomis point out that the random-coefficient model results in a more efficient, and hence statistically significant, estimate of the coefficient on the variable measuring expected change in commercial timber harvest.

FIGURE 1. *Survey Screen with Photos and an Ancient Map of the Venice Arsenale*

2.7. Application

We illustrate the analysis of SC responses using data from a recent survey conducted by Alberini et al. (2004) to study the preferences of residents for urban regeneration alternatives for the Arsenale, the historical shipbuilding yard in Venice (see Figure 1). Our interest in the Arsenale was motivated by the fact that it is a large, underutilized area with a strong symbolic significance for the city of Venice, which was founded in the 12th century and quickly developed into an early assembly-line style production system for turning out battle and merchant ships.

We constructed alternative hypothetical regeneration scenarios defined by six attributes: (i) land use, (ii) presence/absence of a marina with capacity for 200 boats within the Arsenale for use by the residents of the city, (iii) construction of new buildings in the Northeast Arsenale, (iv) presence/absence of fast transportation links, (v) number of jobs created through reuse, and (vi) cost to the taxpayer.

Attribute (i) had a total of 4 levels, each of which is a combination of land uses (for example, research area, modern shipbuilding, homes) distributed over the land area of the Arsenale. We used two-dimensional and three-dimensional images to show the land uses and the possible changes in the architectural volume implied by any new construction. Attributes (ii)-(iv) are binary (presence/absence); attribute (v), the number of jobs, takes one of three possible levels (150, 250, and 350 permanent jobs); and the tax ranges from €25 to €150.

Each choice set was comprised of two hypothetical regeneration projects plus the status quo (keeping the Arsenale as it is at no extra cost to the taxpayer), which means that K=3.

Our respondents self-administered the survey questionnaire at the computers at the Palazzo Querini Stampalia library, and engaged in four choice questions each. We obtained a total of 168 completed questionnaires. After we cleaned the sample to eliminate the observations provided by the respondents who in debriefing questions admitted to having chosen at random, focused on only one attribute, or took either a very short or a very long time to complete the survey, we were left with a total of 472 usable responses to the choice questions.

We report the results of the conditional logit model for these responses in Table 1. The regressors are dummies for the land use (the default being the status quo, for which all attributes are coded as zeros), and 0/1 dummies or continuous variables for all of the other attributes. The results suggest that reuse alternatives are generally no less preferred than the status quo. The only exception is LANDUSE3, which calls for hotels to be built in the northeastern portion of the Arsenale, and office buildings to be established at the heart of the Arsenale, in its most ancient part. The negative coefficient on this regeneration dummy implies that people would rather hold on to the current use rather than implement a modern development form of land use. Although the coefficients on the land use dummies are individually insignificant, a likelihood ratio test (58.94, P value < 0.0001) rejects the null that they are jointly equal to zero.

Our respondents appreciate mooring spaces for the residents, alternatives with new construction in the northeastern Arsenale, the availability of fast transportation links, and jobs. As expected, the coefficients on the tax variable are negative and significant, implying that more expensive projects are deemed less attractive. The model as a whole is significant: The LR test of the null that all slopes are different from zero is 252.08 (p value < 0.0001), and the likelihood ratio index is 0.24 (see Section 2.3).

It is also possible to compute the marginal value of each attribute using equation (16). For example, our respondents are willing to pay a one-time tax of €46 for every 100 jobs generated through the regeneration of the Arsenale, and of €131 to secure fast transportation links with the mainland, the airport, and other parts of the city and the Lagoon. The overall value of a regeneration option with land use equal to land use 2 (housing, research labs and museums, but no shipbuilding or hotels), fast transportation links, no marina, 250 jobs, and new construction is €419.

For specification search purposes, we also estimated models with interactions between the attributes and selected individual characteristics of the respondents, but found that these interactions did not improve the fit of the model. We found limited evidence in favor of random coefficients, which seem to be limited to the transportation links attribute.

TABLE 1. Conditional logit model of the responses to the choice questions

Variable	Coefficient	t statistic
MOORINGS	0.3411*	2.066
NEW CONSTRUCTION	0.3716*	2.035
TRANSPORTATION LINKS	1.1021**	7.062
JOBS	0.0039*	2.297
TAXES	-0.0084**	-3.746
LANDUSE1	0.2067	0.400
LANDUSE2	0.5027	1.234
LANDUSE3	-1.0745^	-1.904
LANDUSE4	0.6049	1.124
log likelihood	-392.504	

^ = significant at the 10% level; * = significant at the 5% level; ** = significant at the 1% level.

3. CONTINGENT VALUATION

3.1. Willingness to Pay and Willingness to Accept

SC boils down to CV when K=2 and one of the two alternatives in the choice set is the status quo (current situation and no payment). CV asks people to directly report their WTP to obtain a specified good, or willingness to accept (WTA) to give up a good.[5]

The goal of CV is to measure the compensating or equivalent variation.[6] Both compensating and equivalent variation can be elicited by asking a person to report a WTP amount: the person may be asked to report his or her WTP to obtain the good, or to avoid the loss of the good. Formally, WTP is defined as the amount that must be taken away from the person's income while keeping utility constant. Suppressing individual subscripts, we have:

$$V(y-WTP, p, q_1; \mathbf{Z}) = V(y, \mathbf{p}, q_0; \mathbf{Z}) \qquad (24)$$

where V denotes the indirect utility function, y is income, $\mathbf{p}$ is a vector of prices faced by the individual, and q_0 and q_1 are the alternative levels of the good or quality indexes (with $q_1 > q_0$, indicating that q_1 refers to improved environmental quality). $\mathbf{Z}$ is a vector of individual characteristics.

WTA is defined as the amount of money that must be given to an individual experiencing a deterioration in environmental quality to keep his utility constant:

$$V(y + WTA, p, q_2; \mathbf{Z}) = V(y, p, q_0; \mathbf{Z}) \qquad (25)$$

where q_2 indicates a deterioration in quality compared to the status quo, q_0.

In equations (24) and (25), utility is allowed to depend on a vector of individual characteristics influencing the tradeoff that the individual is prepared to make between income and environmental quality. An important consequence of equations (24) and (25) is that WTP or WTA should, therefore, depend on (i) the initial and final level of the good in question (q_0 and q_1); (ii) respondent income; (iii) all prices faced by the respondent, including those of substitute goods or activities; and (iv) other respondent characteristics. Internal validity of the WTP responses can be checked by regressing WTP on variables (i)-(iv), and showing that WTP correlates in predictable ways with socio-economic variables.[7]

3.2. Dichotomous-Choice Contingent Valuation

The most widely used approach to eliciting information about the respondent's WTP is the so-called dichotomous-choice format. A dichotomous choice payment question asks the respondent if he would pay $X to obtain the good in question. A frequently used wording of the payment question is whether the respondent would vote in favor of the proposed plan or policy if approval of the plan would cost his household $X (for example, in the form of extra taxes, higher prices of products). There are only two possible responses to a dichotomous choice payment question: "yes," or "no" (or, "vote for" or "vote against"). The dollar amount $X is varied across respondents, and is usually termed the bid value.

The dichotomous choice approach mimics behavior in regular markets, where people usually purchase, or decline to purchase, a good at the posted price. It also closely resembles people's experience with political markets and propositions on a ballot. The dichotomous choice approach has been shown to be incentive-compatible: provided that respondents understand that provision of the good depends on the majority of votes, and the respondent's own vote in itself cannot influence such provision, truth-telling is in the respondent's best interest (Hoehn and Randall, 1987; see Harrison, this volume, for an alternative viewpoint on this issue). In addition to mimicking the behavior of people in regular marketplaces or voting situations, the dichotomous choice approach is also credited with reducing the cognitive burden placed on the respondent.

When dichotomous choice questions are used, the researcher does not observe WTP directly: at best, he can infer that the respondent's WTP amount is greater than the bid value (if the respondent is in favor of the program) or less than the bid amount (if the respondent votes against the plan), and form broad intervals around the respondent's WTP. To estimate the usual welfare statistics, it is necessary to fit binary data models.

The simplest such models assume that an individual's response to the WTP question is motivated by an underlying, and unobserved, WTP amount, which is normally (or logistically) distributed. Formally, let WTP* be the unobserved WTP:

$$WTP_i^* = \mu + \varepsilon_i \, , \tag{26}$$

where μ is both mean and median WTP, ε is a zero-mean normal (logistic) error with mean zero. The model is completed by specifying the mapping from the latent variable to the observables:

$$
\begin{aligned}
WTP_i \quad &= 1 \; \textit{iff} \quad WTP_i^* > B_i \text{ and} \\
&= 0 \; \textit{iff} \quad WTP_i^* \le B_i \, ,
\end{aligned}
\tag{27}
$$

where B_i is the bid that was assigned to respondent i, WTP = 1 means that the response to the payment question is a "yes," and WTP = 0 means that the response is a "no."

Because we observe discrete outcomes, we must derive the probabilities of "yes" and "no" responses. When attention is restricted to a normal latent WTP, the probability of a "yes" response is:

$$
\begin{aligned}
\Pr(yes \mid B_i) = \Pr(WTP_i = 1 \mid B_i) &= \Pr(WTP_i^* > B_i) \\
= \Pr(\varepsilon_i > B_i - \mu) &= \Pr\left(\frac{\varepsilon_i}{\sigma} > \frac{B_i}{\sigma} - \frac{\mu}{\sigma} \right) .
\end{aligned}
\tag{28}
$$

Because ε/σ is a standard normal variate, $\left[1 - \Phi\left(\frac{B_i}{\sigma} - \frac{\mu}{\sigma} \right) \right] = \Phi\left(-\frac{B_i}{\sigma} + \frac{\mu}{\sigma} \right)$ where $\Phi(\cdot)$ is the standard normal cdf. If we define $\alpha = \mu / \sigma$ and $\beta = -1/\sigma$, the probability of a yes response can be rewritten as:

$$\Pr(yes \mid B_i) = \Phi(\alpha + \beta \cdot B_i) \, . \tag{29}$$

Equation (29) is the contribution to the likelihood of a yes observation (or a one) in a probit model with the intercept and one regressor—the bid. As long as β is identified and estimable—which requires that the bid amount be varied to the respondents in the survey, so that it becomes a legitimate regressor in the probit model—mean/median WTP is estimated as:

$$\hat{\mu} = -\hat{\alpha} / \hat{\beta} \, , \tag{30}$$

while the standard deviation of WTP is estimated as:

$$\hat{\sigma} = -1/\hat{\beta} . \qquad (31)$$

The same formulae produce estimates of mean/median WTP and of the scale parameter of WTP from the logit coefficient if WTP is assumed to be a logistic variate (Cameron and James, 1987; Cameron, 1988).[8,9]

A standard probit routine will automatically produce standard errors for $\hat{\alpha}$ and $\hat{\beta}$, but not for $\hat{\mu}$ and $\hat{\sigma}$.[10] To obtain the variances of the latter estimates, researchers have resorted to a variety of techniques. The most straightforward is, once again, the delta method, illustrated for dichotomous choice CV data by Cameron (1991). To obtain the covariance matrix of $\hat{\mu}$ and $\hat{\sigma}$, one first needs the covariance matrix of $\hat{\alpha}$ and $\hat{\beta}$ produced by the probit routine, here denoted as $\mathbf{V}$. The expression for $\mathbf{V}$ is:

$$\mathbf{V} = \left\{ \sum_{i=1}^{n} w(z_i) \begin{bmatrix} 1 & B_i \\ B_i & B_i^2 \end{bmatrix} \right\}^{-1}, \qquad (32)$$

where $z_i = \hat{\alpha} + \hat{\beta} \cdot B_i$, and $w(z_i) = \phi^2(z_i) / \{\Phi(z_i)[1 - \Phi(z_i)]\}$, with $\phi(\bullet)$ the standard normal pdf. Next, it is necessary to compute the matrix $\mathbf{G}$, with $\mathbf{G} = \begin{bmatrix} -1/\hat{\beta} & 0 \\ \hat{\alpha}/\hat{\beta}^2 & 1/\hat{\beta}^2 \end{bmatrix}$. The final step requires calculating the matrix product $\mathbf{V_1} = \mathbf{G'} * \mathbf{V} * \mathbf{G}$, with $\mathbf{V_1}$ the covariance matrix of $\hat{\mu}$ and $\hat{\sigma}$.

If WTP is assumed to be a logistic variate, the steps required for the delta method are the same, except that $w(z)$ in expression (32) is equal to $\{\exp(z_i) / [1 + \exp(z_i)]^2\}$.

The above listed steps show clearly that the variances and covariance of $\hat{\mu}$ and $\hat{\sigma}$ depend crucially on three factors: (i) the distribution of WTP (normal or logistic), (ii) the true parameters of that distribution, μ and σ, and (iii) the sets of bid amounts used in the survey (see Kanninen, 1993; Alberini, 1995, and Cooper, 1993).

A second approach relies on the asymptotic distribution of $\hat{\alpha}$ and $\hat{\beta}$, which is a bivariate normal with means α and β and covariance matrix approximated by $\mathbf{V}$. A large number (S) of draws from the above bivariate normal distribution are taken, and for each draw (consisting of two values, one for $\hat{\alpha}$ and one for $\hat{\beta}$) $\hat{\mu}$ and $\hat{\sigma}$ are calculated. Finally, one averages all of the values of $\hat{\mu}$ and $\hat{\sigma}$ thus obtained, and computes the standard deviations of those values. The standard deviations thus calculated provide the standard errors for $\hat{\mu}$ and $\hat{\sigma}$. Confidence limits can be calculated using these standard errors, or by sorting $\hat{\mu}$ and $\hat{\sigma}$ in ascending order, and identifying the 2.5th percentile and the 97.5th percentile of each set (assuming that the desired confidence interval is 95 percent), although bias corrections to this interval may be appropriate (Cooper, 1994).

It should be pointed out that in some studies, depending on the frequencies of the "yes" and "no" responses to the payment questions, formula (30) produces a negative mean/median WTP figure. When Johannesson et al. (1997) queried a sample of Swedes about their WTP for a reduction in their risk of dying over the next year using dichotomous choice payment questions, they observed the frequency of "yes" responses displayed in Figure 2.

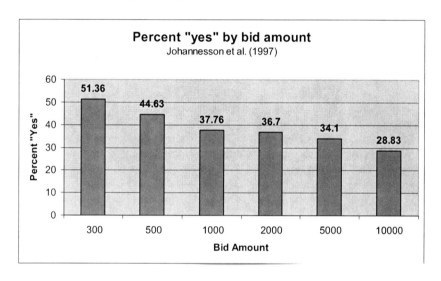

FIGURE 2.

When a probit model is fit to these responses, the intercept is pegged at -0.3485 and the slope at -0.00002, which imply that $\hat{\mu}$ is equal to -2096.08 Swedish Kroner (SEK). Similar results are found if a logit model is fit, in which case $\hat{\mu}$ is estimated to be -2007.75 SEK. Johannesson et al. get around this problem by computing mean WTP as $= \int_{0}^{\infty} [1 - G(\hat{\alpha} + \hat{\beta}y)]dy$, where $G(\bullet)$ is the standard logistic cdf, which is simplified to $\left(-1/\hat{\beta}\right)\ln[1 + \exp(\hat{\alpha})]$ and results in an estimate of mean WTP equal to 6300 SEK.

We remind the reader that the mean of a random variable is defined as $\int zf(z)dz$, which can be shown to be equal to $\int [1 - F(z)]dz$, where $f(\ )$ and $F(\ )$ are the pdf and cdf of the variate, respectively. The difference between this definition and the approach used by Johanesson et al. is in the limit of integration, which Johannesson et al. restrict to be from zero to infinity. Hanemann (1984) also advocated the approach used by Johannesson et al., but we do not agree. The approach chooses to ignore negative WTP values while the initial estimation approach allowed them.

Perhaps a better way to avoid this problem is to work with a WTP distribution that is defined only over the positive semi-axis. The Weibull and the lognormal are examples of such distributions. The cdf for a Weibull with parameters θ ($\theta>0$) and σ is $F(y) = 1 - e^{-(y/\sigma)^{\theta}}$. Mean WTP is $\sigma \cdot \Gamma\left(\dfrac{1}{\theta}+1\right)$, where $\Gamma(\bullet)$ is the gamma function, while median WTP is equal to $\sigma \cdot [-\ln(0.5)]^{1/\theta} = \sigma \cdot [\ln(2)]^{1/\theta}$. These expressions show that mean and median are generally different from one another.

If its shape parameter θ is less than 3.6, a Weibull random variable is positively skewed, which means that mean WTP is greater than median WTP. If the shape parameter θ is about 3.6, then the Weibull density is symmetric, which implies that mean and median WTP will be approximately equal. Finally, if the shape parameter θ is greater than 3.6, the Weibull is negatively skewed, so that its mean is less than its median.

The advantage of working with the Weibull distribution is that the value of θ is inferred directly from the data through maximum likelihood estimation. In our experience, the distribution of WTP is usually positively skewed, so in most applications we would expect θ to be less than 3.6, and mean WTP to exceed median WTP, sometimes by a factor of two or three, or even more. For example, Carson et al. (1994) report that in a survey of US households to elicit nonuse values of the natural resources of Prince William Sound, the estimates of mean and median WTP based on the Weibull model are \$94.41 and \$30.91 per household, respectively.

With dichotomous-choice responses and a Weibull WTP, the log likelihood function of the sample,

$$\sum_{i=1}^{n}\left[WTP_i \cdot \log(1 - F(B_i;\theta,\sigma)) + (1 - WTP_i) \cdot \log F(B_i;\theta,\sigma)\right], \qquad (33)$$

where F is the cdf of the Weibull with parameters θ and σ evaluated at the bid amount, takes the following expression:

$$\sum_{i=1}^{n}\left[WTP_i \cdot \log\left(\exp(-(B_i/\sigma)^{\theta})\right) + (1 - WTP_i) \cdot \log\left(1 - \exp(-(B_i/\sigma)^{\theta})\right)\right]. \qquad (34)$$

It is also possible to assume that WTP is a lognormal with parameters μ and σ, which produces the following log likelihood function:

$$\sum_{i=1}^{n} \left[WTP_i \cdot \log \Phi(\alpha + \beta \log B_i) + (1 - WTP_i) \cdot \log\left(1 - \Phi(\alpha + \beta \log B_i)\right) \right],$$

(35)

where, as before, $\alpha = \mu / \sigma$ and $\beta = -1/\sigma$. Mean WTP is equal to $\exp(-\alpha / \beta + 0.5 \cdot (1/\beta)^2)$ and median WTP is $\exp(-\alpha / \beta)$, which means that the former is larger than the latter.

Yet another possibility is to assume that the distribution of WTP is a log-logistic, which means that the logarithmic transformation of WTP is a logistic. The corresponding empirical model is a logit where the dummy response indicator is regressed on an intercept and on the logarithmic transformation of the bid. Median WTP is equal to $\exp(-\alpha / \beta)$, and mean WTP is $\exp(-\alpha / \beta) \cdot \Gamma(1 - 1/\beta) \cdot \Gamma(1 + 1/\beta)$. The problem with the log-logistic distribution is that if $|\beta| < 1$, mean WTP is infinity.

We conclude this presentation of asymmetric distributions by pointing out that median WTP is generally regarded as a robust, and conservative, welfare statistic associated with the good or proposed policy. It is usually estimated more precisely than mean WTP, and is interpreted as the value at which 50% of the respondents would vote in support of the program, and hence the cost at which the majority of the population would be in support of it. It is thus frequently reported by researchers as a robust lower-bound estimate of WTP. Mean WTP, however, is the classic welfare measure most appropriate for benefit-cost analyses, where the benefits are equal to WTP per beneficiary multiplied by the relevant population size.

3.3. Follow-up Question and Double-Bounded Estimation

To improve the precision of the WTP estimates, researchers have introduced follow-up questions to the dichotomous choice payment question (e.g., Hanemann, et al., 1991). To illustrate, consider a respondent who states he is not willing to pay $10 for a proposed plan. A follow-up question might ask him if he would pay $5. If the respondent answers "no" to both questions, it is assumed that his WTP amount falls between 0 and $5. If the respondent answers "no" to the initial question, and "yes" to the follow-up questions, it is assumed that his WTP amount falls between $5 and $10. The bid level offered in the follow-up question will be greater than that offered in the initial payment question if the answer to the initial payment question is "yes."

In choosing the bid level to be assigned to the respondent in the follow-up question, it is important that this follow-up bid be sufficiently different from the initial bid (so that it could be justified to the respondent as two different engineering estimates of the cost of the project), but not so different as to compromise the credibility of the survey. If the initial question was $25, it makes little sense to query the respondent about $26 or $2000.

If elicitation is based on an initial dichotomous choice question, followed by one dichotomous choice follow-up question (the "double-bounded" approach), a likelihood function based on interval data must be specified. To write out the likelihood function, first notice that four possible pairs of responses to the payment questions are possible: (a) yes, yes; (b) yes, no; (c) no, yes; and (d) no, no. Since the follow-up bid amount, B2, is greater than the first for those respondents who answered "yes" to the initial payment question (lower for those respondents who answered "no" to the initial payment question), the pairs identify intervals in which the respondents' WTP amount is assumed to fall.

Specifically, WTP is greater than B2 for "yes, yes" respondents; it lies between B1 and B2 for "yes, no" respondents, and between B2 and B1 for "no, yes" respondents. Finally, WTP is less than B2 for "no, no" respondents. This yields the log likelihood function:

$$\log L = \sum_{i=1}^{n} \log \left[F(WTP^{H};\boldsymbol{\theta}) - F(WTP^{L};\boldsymbol{\theta}) \right] \qquad (36)$$

where WTP^{H} and WTP^{L} are the upper and lower bound of the interval around WTP defined above, $F(\cdot)$ is the cdf of WTP, and $\boldsymbol{\theta}$ denotes the vector of parameters that index the distribution of WTP. (Notice that for respondents who give two "yes" responses, the upper bound of WTP may be infinity, or the respondent's income; for respondents who give two "no" responses, the lower bound is either zero (if the distribution of WTP admits only non-negative values) or negative infinity (if the distribution of WTP is a normal or a logistic.))[11]

Researchers have recently experimented with yet another approach, the so-called One-and-One-Half-Bound (OOHB) dichotomous choice CV model. Respondents are first informed that the bid will be somewhere in a range between "bid low" and "bid high" and they do not know the precise amount that will be asked. Then, one of the bids is selected at random by the interviewer, and the respondent is asked if she is willing to pay that amount. One advantage of this approach is that it eliminates the element of surprise in the follow-up offer. Cooper et al. (2002) derive the optimal bid design under this approach, showing that most of the statistical efficiency gains in the estimation of mean WTP come from the first follow-up question.

3.4. Internal Validity of the WTP Responses

After WTP responses have been collected through the survey, it is important to test for internal validity, i.e., to estimate models of WTP that relate the respondents' WTP amounts to the commodity being valued, the mode of provision of the commodity, and to individual characteristics of the respondents (See Krupnick and Adamowicz, this volume). Formally, the underlying regression equation is:

$$WTP_{i}^{*} = \mathbf{x}_{i}\boldsymbol{\beta} + \mathbf{z}_{i}\boldsymbol{\gamma} + \varepsilon_{i} \qquad (37)$$

where WTP* represents the (unobserved) WTP amount, x is a $k \times 1$ vector of indicators and continuous variables representing aspects of the commodity or of the provision mechanism that have been varied to respondents in the survey, as defined by the experimental design, and z is an $m \times 1$ vector of individual characteristics of the respondents. β and γ are vectors of unobservable coefficients, and ε is the econometric error term.

If respondents have been asked to value commodities of different size and quality, one would expect WTP to increase with the size and the quality of the commodity being valued. In the CV literature, this expectation is termed the "scope" effect. It can be empirically tested by checking that the coefficients on the variables capturing size and quality are statistically significant and of the appropriate sign. The size and quality of the commodity can be expressed in a number of ways, such as the number of species affected by a wildlife management or recovery program, the geographical area affected by the program, etc. If the commodity being valued is an episode of illness, WTP should be increasing in the severity of illness, measured as the number of sick days, the total number of symptoms, whether the illness will be severe enough for the respondent to seek professional health care and/or stay home from work, and the presence of specific symptoms (Alberini et al., 1997a). In a survey eliciting WTP to reduce mortality risks, the scope test implies checking that WTP increases with the size of the risk reduction being valued—and ideally, is strictly proportional with it (Hammitt and Graham, 1999).

If the mode of provision of the commodity or the payment vehicle is varied across respondents, dummy variables should be included in the right-hand side of the WTP equation to check whether WTP changes with these aspects of the scenario. Researchers have also investigated whether the amount of information provided to respondents about the commodity, and/or the way it was presented to them (Magat and Viscusi, 1992) has an impact on WTP.

The vector z usually includes individual characteristics such as age, education, gender, income, measures of attitude towards the commodity being valued (e.g., in the case of environmental resources, whether the respondent considers himself or herself an environmentalist), past behaviors that could explain WTP, and other conditions that could influence WTP (health).

With single-bounded dichotomous-choice CV and assuming that the distribution of WTP is normal (logistic), one can run a probit (logit) regression of the indicator of the "yes" (1) or "no" (0) responses on the desired regressors. The original intercept and slopes in (37) can be recovered with the usual procedure of dividing all probit (logit) coefficients by the coefficient of the bid (Cameron and James, 1987).

4. CONCLUSIONS

In this chapter, we have presented the basic statistical models for SC questions and have illustrated their use with a study on the public's preferences for re-use of a historical site in the city of Venice, the Arsenale. We have then discussed models for dichotomous choice questions, highlighting the advantages and disadvantages of the possible approaches. Recent developments that are covered in this chapter include mixed logit models, discrete mixture models, and non-parametric techniques. The reader is referred to Swait (this volume) for more on the former, and to Cooper (2002) for the latter.

---

5. ENDNOTES

[1] Note that "log" is the natural logarithm.

[2] The intercept in equation (2) is not identified and is therefore normalized to zero.

[3] In many SC studies, respondents are asked to engage in a series of M choice tasks. In this case, the restricted likelihood function is $n \cdot M \cdot \log \dfrac{1}{K}$ and the unrestricted likelihood function is $\sum_{i=1}^{n} \sum_{m=1}^{M} \sum_{k=1}^{K} y_{imk} \cdot \log \pi_{imk}$.

[4] An example of a situation where the IIA would not be plausible is the blue bus/red bus example due to McFadden (1974). Consider commuters initially choosing between two modes of transportation: car and red bus. Suppose that a consumer chooses between the car and bus with equal probability, 0.5, so that the ratio in equation (16) is one. Now suppose a third mode, blue bus, is added. IIA implies that the probability of consumers choosing each mode is 1/3; therefore, the fraction of commuters taking a car would have to fall from 1/2 to 1/3, a nonsensical result. While this example is admittedly extreme (in practice, one would group the blue bus and red bus into the same category), it indicates that the IIA property can impose unwanted restrictions on the conditional logit model (Wooldridge, 2002). [To grasp how the introduction of a new alternative might alter the odds between choosing two existing alternatives, consider the following example based on the presidential elections. Suppose than an individual prefers candidate A over candidate B. When asked to indicate his preference, clearly, this individual would vote for candidate A. Suppose now that a third candidate, C, is added that appears to have a stronger chance of winning than A, and is preferred to B, but less preferred than A. Strategic considerations might lead the individual to pick C, even though he is the second-best candidate, in an effort to avoid the victory of the least preferred candidate, B.]

[5] If market data are available about quantities exchanged and prices, one can derive an estimate for WTP by first estimating the demand function, and then computing the area under the inverse demand curve up to the current price. Estimation of demand functions is generally not easy, so that—absent hypothetical biases and other undesirable response effects (see Mitchell and Carson, 1989)—it would be easier to obtain directly people's WTP for a specified good.

[6] Compensating variation is the appropriate measure when the person experiences a utility gain, such as with an improvement in environmental quality. Equivalent variation is appropriate if the person faces a potential loss of the good, as he would if a proposed policy results in the deterioration of environmental quality.

[7] In theory, absent income effects and when WTP is a small fraction of income, WTP and WTA for a given commodity should be approximately equal. However, a number of CV studies have found that WTA is often much larger than WTP for the same commodity. Various explanations are possible for this finding. One explanation is that the difference between WTP and WTA depends on the elasticity of substitution between the commodity to be valued (a public good) and private substitutes. The lower such elasticity, and the fewer the available substitutes, the greater the difference between WTP and WTA (Hanemann, 1991). Another explanation—the theory of prospects—is that individuals value losses more

heavily than gains. It is also possible that individuals react to their perception of who has the property rights over the commodity in question. If the proposed policy contradicts their perception of the existing property rights, individuals might express their rejection of the scenario through high WTA values. This might happen if, for example, individuals believe that they are entitled to clean air, and are outraged at a proposed degradation in air quality. In practice, some or all of these alternative explanations may coexist. Carson (1991) suggests that WTP should be used whenever the individual might incur benefits from the proposed policy, and Mitchell and Carson (1989) offer ways to frame the payment question to elicit WTP.

[8] We remind the reader that the variance of the logistic distribution is $\sigma^2 \pi^2 / 3$.

[9] Cameron and James (1987) and Cameron (1988) work within the WTP context, while Hanemann (1984) derives the same results in the context of the random-utility model. McConnell (1990) reconciles the two approaches, showing that the deterministic models considered by Cameron and Hanemann are dual to one another.

[10] SAS is an exception: its probit routine prints out standard errors for the intercept and slope, as well as the variances and covariance of $\hat{\mu}$ and $\hat{\sigma}$.

[11] Recent studies (see for instance Alberini et al., 1997b) have examined WTP for government programs, finding that mean WTP estimated after the follow-up questions can be lower than that implied by the responses to the initial payment question. A possible explanation for this finding is that some respondents may treat the suggested cost of the project as a signal for the quality of the program and/or might erroneously believe that the program to be valued in the follow-up is different from the initial one. In other studies where the good to be valued is a private non-market good (days of illness) estimated WTP remains very stable over the rounds of follow-ups (Alberini et al., 1997a). Herriges and Shogren (1996) raise doubts about whether the follow-up payment question elicits information about the original WTP amount. They propose that respondents update their original WTP amount with information about the cost of the program, as revealed by the initial bid. The amount underlying the response to the follow-up bid, therefore, would be a weighted average of the original WTP and the initial bid amount. In many CV studies, researchers have found that the majority of the responses to the initial and follow-up payment questions are of the "yes"-"yes" and "no"-"no" variety, with fewer respondents offering one positive and one negative answer. DeShazo (2002) spells out the predicted probabilities of the various response categories under four distinct theories (the framing model, which derives from prospect theory; the cost expectation model; the strategic behavior model; yea-saying; and anchoring, or starting point bias) and uses data from three CV studies to empirically discriminate between these competing hypotheses.

6. REFERENCES

Alberini, A., 1995, "Optimal Designs for Discrete Choice Contingent Valuation Surveys: Single-bound, Double-bound and Bivariate Models," *Journal of Environmental Economics and Management*, 28, 187-306.

Alberini, A., M. Cropper, T.-T. Fu, A. Krupnick, J.-T. Liu, D. Shaw and W. Harrington, 1997a, "Valuing Health Effects of Air Pollution in Developing Countries: The Case of Taiwan," *Journal of Environmental Economics and Management*, 34, 107-26.

Alberini, A., B. Kanninen and R.T. Carson, 1997b, "Modeling Response Incentive Effects in Dichotomous Choice Contingent Valuation Data," *Land Economics*, 73(3), 309-24.

Alberini, A., P. Riganti and A. Longo, 2004, "Public Preferences and Urban Regeneration: Land Use Changes and Aesthetics at the Venice Arsenale," draft report to Fondazione Eni Enrico Mattei, Venice, October.

Cameron, T.A., 1988, "A New Paradigm for Valuing Non-market Goods Using Referendum Data: Maximum Likelihood Estimation by Censored Logistic Regression," *Journal of Environmental Economics and Management*, 15(3), 355-79.

Cameron, T.A., 1991, "Interval Estimates of Non-Market Resource Values from Referendum Contingent Valuation Surveys," *Land Economics,* 67(4), 413-21.

Cameron, T.A. and M.D. James, 1987, "Efficient Estimation Methods for 'Closed-Ended' Contingent Valuation Surveys," *Review of Economics and Statistics,* 69(2), 269-76.

Carson, R.T., 1991, "Constructed Markets," in John Braden and Charles Kolstad, eds., *Measuring the Demand for Environmental Commodities*, Amsterdam: North-Holland).

Carson, R.T., R.C. Mitchell, M.W. Hanemann, R.J. Kopp, S. Presser and P.A. Ruud, 1994, "Contingent valuation and lost passive use: Damages from the Exxon Valdez," Resources for the Future Discussion paper QE94-18, Washington, DC.

Cooper, J.C., 1993, "Optimal Bid Selection for Dichotomous Choice Contingent Valuation Surveys," *Journal of Environmental Economics and Management*, 24, 25-40.

Cooper, J.C., 1994, "A Comparison of Approaches to Calculating Confidence Intervals for Benefit Measures from Dichotomous Choice Contingent Valuation Surveys," *Land Economics*, 70(1), 111-22.

Cooper, J.C., 2002, "Flexible-form and Semi-nonparametric Estimation of Willingness to Pay Using Dichotomous Choice Data," *Journal of Environmental Economics and Management,* 2, 267-79.

Cooper, J.C., W.M. Hanemann and G. Signorello, 2002, "One and One-Half Bound Dichotomous Choice Contingent Valuation," *Review of Economics and Statistics*, 84(4), 742-50.

DeShazo, J.R., 2002, "Designing Transactions without Framing Effects in Iterative Question Formats," *Journal of Environmental Economics and Management*, 43, 360-85.

Greene, W.H., 2003, *Econometric Analysis*, 4th edition, Upper Saddle River, NY: Prentice Hall.

Haefele, M.A. and J.B. Loomis, 2001, "Improving Statistical Efficiency and Testing Robustness of Conjoint Marginal Valuation," *American Journal of Agricultural Economics*, 83(5,) 1321-327.

Hammitt, J.K. and J.D. Graham, 1999, "Willingness to Pay for Health Protection: Inadequate Sensitivity to Probabilities?" *Journal of Risk and Uncertainty*, 18(1), 33-62.

Hanemann, W.M., 1984, "Welfare Evaluations in Contingent Valuation Experiments with Discrete Responses," *American Journal of Agricultural Economics*, 66(3), 332-41.

Hanemann, W.M., 1991, "Willingness to Pay and Willingness to Accept: How Much Can They Differ?" *American Economic Review*, 81(3), 635-47.

Hanemann, W.M., J. Loomis and B.J. Kanninen, 1991, "Statistical Efficiency of Double-Bounded Dichotomous Choice Contingent Valuation," *American Journal of Agricultural Economics* 73(4), 1255-263.

Hanley, N., S. Mourato and R.E. Wright, 2001, "Choice Modelling Approaches: A Superior Alternative for Environmental Valuation?" *Journal of Economic Surveys*, 15(3), 435-62.

Hausman, J. and D. McFadden, 1984, "A Specification Test for the Multinomial Logit Model," *Econometrica*, 52, 1219-240.

Herriges, J.A. and J.F. Shogren, 1996, "Starting Point Bias in Dichotomous Choice Valuation with Follow-up Questioning," *Journal of Environmental Economics and Management*, 30, 112-31.

Hoehn, J.P and A. Randall, 1987, "A Satisfactory Benefit Cost Indicator from Contingent Valuation," *Journal of Environmental Economics and Management*, 14, 226-47.

Johannesson, M., Per-Olov Johansson and Karl-Gustav Löfgren, 1997, "On the Value of Changes in Life Expectancy: Blips Versus Parametric Changes," *Journal of Risk and Uncertainty*, 15, 221-39.

Kanninen, B.J., 1993, "Optimal Experimental Design for Double-Bounded Dichotomous Choice Contingent Valuation," *Land Economics*, 69, 138-46.

Krinsky, I. and A. Robb, 1986, "Approximating the Statistical Properties of Elasticities," *Review of Economics and Statistics*, 68, 715-19.

Magat, W.A. and W.K. Viscusi, 1992, *Informational Approaches to Regulation*, Cambridge: MIT Press.

McConnell, K.E., 1990, "Models for Referendum Data," *Journal of Environmental Economics and Management*, 18, 19-34.

McFadden, D.L., 1974, ''Conditional Logit Analysis of Qualitative Choice Analysis,'' in *Frontiers in Econometrics*, ed. P. Zarembka. New York: Academic Press, 105-42.

Mitchell, R.C. and R.T. Carson, 1989, *Using Surveys to Value Public Goods: The Contingent Valuation Method*, Washington, DC: Resources for the Future.

Train, K.E., 1999, "Mixed Logit Models for Recreation Demand," Chapter 4 in Joseph A. Herriges and Catherine L. Kling, eds., *Valuing Recreation and the Environment. Revealed Preference Methods in Theory and Practice*, Cheltenham, UK: Edward Elgar Publishing.

Train, K.E., 2003, *Discrete Choice Models with Simulations*, Cambridge: Cambridge University Press.

Wooldridge, J., 2002, *Econometrics Analysis of Cross Section and Panel Data*, Cambridge, MA: MIT Press.

CHAPTER 9

ADVANCED CHOICE MODELS

JOFFRE SWAIT

Advanis Inc. and Faculty of Business, University of Alberta, Alberta, Canada

1. INTRODUCTION

In Alberini et al. (this volume), an overview of the workhorse model (the Multinomial Logit, or MNL) for discrete choice analysis was presented from its conception to its practical use in predicting behavior and evaluating welfare impacts. Its highly nonlinear nature allows the MNL to capture a wide variety of compensatory attribute-based tradeoffs and has made this model specification a useful tool for economists, engineers and marketers. Allied to its flexibility is the fact that many general statistical analysis programs, as well as more specialized tools, straightforwardly implement estimation of the MNL model. And it doesn't hurt that the MNL's likelihood function is globally concave, implying that the output of these programs are guaranteed to be the maximum likelihood estimates (this is no small advantage in the realm we are about to enter).

This chapter deals with a number of interesting extensions to the basic MNL model. These more complex model forms are motivated by a number of MNL's shortcomings. Differently from other presentations of such material, however, I would like to motivate a certain order of presentation of these advanced choice models. So bear with me as I wander down some lanes that may at first seem unrelated to the chapter's main purpose; I believe that these digressions will help us tie these models together in a particularly useful form.

In many ways, the MNL model has served for discrete choice data the analogous role to the ordinary least squares or OLS model for continuous data. Despite the obvious differences between these models, there are important parallels between the two model forms concerning the assumptions made about their respective stochastic model components: (1) both assume independent and identically distributed error terms (in the MNL model, between both alternatives and persons; in the OLS model, between persons); (2) both assume homoscedastic error terms (in the MNL, iid

229

B.J. Kanninen (ed.), Valuing Environmental Amenities Using Stated Choice Studies, 229–293.
© 2006 *Springer.*

Gumbel, or Type I Extreme Value with mode zero and common variance $\sigma^2 = \pi^2/6\mu^2$, where $\mu > 0$ is a scalar; in the linear model, iid normal with mean zero and variance σ^2). In this way, then, MNL can be seen as a certain constrained (by the single choice among J objects) simultaneous-equation generalization of the simple linear model, with independent, identically distributed and homoscedastic error terms.

But this very constraint tying the J utility functions together via the single choice, allied to the fact that these utility functions are latent (i.e., unobservable, since we observe only the single choice made by the decision maker), complicates matters significantly for the MNL model *vis-à-vis* the linear when assumptions are violated. When the latter model does not evince homoscedasticity, it is well known that the maximum likelihood estimators of the unknown parameters are nonetheless consistent, albeit inefficient. In the case of the MNL model, violation of this assumption concerning the variance of the error terms is far more serious: Yatchew and Griliches (1984) show that in models of the logit/probit form, loss of homoscedasticity leads to far more harmful results, namely, biased parameter estimates, and that this bias increases as the heteroscedasticity is itself a function of the independent variables in the utility functions.

This bundling together of the utility functions through the single choice also introduces an additional complication in the MNL model: it is possible that the assumption of *error independence* is violated in a given empirical context. That is to say, the error terms are not independent, but instead exhibit some pattern of correlation among themselves that are ignored by the MNL model. Another way to think of this is that the independence assumption across alternatives leads to the "infamous" Independence of Irrelevant Alternatives (IIA) characteristic of the MNL model: the relative odds of alternative i over j depends only on the relative attractiveness of i and j, and is completely unaffected by the attractiveness of any third alternative k. (See Ben-Akiva and Lerman, 1985, pp. 108-111, for a discussion of IIA violations in the context of the so-called Red Bus/Blue Bus paradox.) Note that the MNL is not unique in exhibiting IIA: any choice model assuming independence among error terms will lead to the same property.

Early on in the development of discrete choice econometrics, several disciplines (particularly transportation and econometrics) were greatly interested in extensions to the MNL framework that would circumvent IIA violations. Beginning with early work such as Ben-Akiva (1973), who explored consistent ways of aggregating utilities to account for error term correlations, many authors ultimately contributed to the development of Nested MNL (NMNL) models (Daly and Zachary, 1976, Ben-Akiva and Lerman, 1977, Williams 1977, McFadden, 1978). The NMNL represented a straightforward generalization of the MNL by repeatedly applying the model in a certain tree structure reflecting the assumed correlations causing IIA violations. McFadden (1978) showed that the MNL and NMNL are actually members of a (potentially) large group of models called Generalized Extreme Value (GEV) choice models, all arising from a common super error-distribution that he derived in the paper. He also provided a most useful generating theorem that provides a mechanism for postulating new GEV models. A parallel literature, stymied early on due to computational difficulties, attempted to account for possible IIA violations by introducing the Multinomial Probit (MNP) model (e.g., Daganzo,

1979, Manski and Lerman, 1981); until the early 1990s this stream of research had been dormant, but computational developments in simulation estimation removed the MNP from its relative obscurity.

Lately, great interest has been shown in the extension of the MNL (and other choice models, for that matter) to account for other behavioral constructs than those reflected in stochastic utility assumptions – to wit, taste heterogeneity. Historically, to my best knowledge, Formann (1992) first extended the polytomous logit model to account for taste heterogeneity via the use of latent classes (S groups in the population are assumed to have homogeneous within-group tastes); the conditional logit model saw this extension a little earlier and contemporaneously in marketing (e.g., Kamakura and Russell, 1989, with scanner panel,[1] repeated measure data, and no classification variables; Swait, 1994, with cross-sectional, revealed preference data, using covariates for classification; Gupta and Chintagunta, 1994, with scanner panel data, also using covariates for classification model identification). The assumption of homogenous sub-populations is very appealing to marketing, so latent class models were quite popular in that discipline during the 1990s. Econometricians, however, tended to shy away from the finite support point assumption of the latent class models and preferred to take the route of assuming tastes were distributed in the population according to some known, continuous distribution. McFadden and Train's (2000) Mixed MNL model is perhaps the most well known and widely disseminated member of this class of models. The basic form of the Mixed MNL assumes that tastes are distributed Multivariate Normal (MVN) in the population with a certain mean and covariance matrix, which are estimable from the same data used for the common MNL. This model, because (1) it is such a straightforward conceptual generalization of the MNL, (2) computational advances in simulation estimation techniques have made its estimation practical, and (3) it is known to be capable of arbitrarily closely capturing any pattern of IIA violations (see McFadden and Train, 2000), has proven to be quite popular in various literatures (e.g., among many, many others, Train, 1999, Revelt and Train, 1999, Swait and Andrews, 2003).

I've outlined above something of a historical view of major developments in choice modeling in the last 30 years or so: from the simple MNL to workarounds of IIA (correlations) to introduction of taste heterogeneity to treatment of heteroscedasticity. But with the benefit of hindsight, I'd like to suggest what I believe is a more fruitful way of conducting an exploration of advanced choice models.

Let us return for a moment to the origins of what we're trying to accomplish: we are trying to identify the total utility associated with a good characterized by a bundle of attribute values. We admit up front that we know (or are willing to assume we know) something about the choice process through the systematic component of utility, but simultaneously admit our ignorance of the totality of sources giving rise to full utility by defining a stochastic utility to account for what we don't know. We purport to know/specify this random variable up to a density function, whose parameters are to be determined empirically.

With any random variable, we know that its characterization is most useful when we start with its first moment, then proceed up the line to higher-order moments. So, back to stochastic utility: we have, by assumption and without loss of generality, set its first moment (i.e., the mean) to be zero; then let us consider the second moment (i.e., the variance) of the stochastic utility; and lastly, let us consider the co-variation existing between pairs of stochastic utilities. This preference for first dealing with variances over covariances seems sensible because any valid covariance matrix must be diagonal dominant to be positive definite or semi-definite. Secondly, mis-specification of the model by ignoring heteroscedasticity will create biased estimates, just as would ignoring IIA violations. Hence, it seems that the specification of choice models should proceed, in broad strokes, as follows:

1. We should do as good a job as possible in specifying the systematic component of utility, thus reducing the importance of the stochastic utility components in the first place.
2. We should then specify a covariance matrix that gives preference to identifying the diagonal elements (variances) over the covariances.
3. Finally, if we still have identifiable parameters, we should look to the covariances. Here we can be guided by "tree-like" thinking to achieve parsimonious representations.

So, with these initial meanderings, it is now possible to more clearly outline the scope of this chapter and the models that will be presented. As with Alberini et al.'s chapter (this volume), we continue to limit ourselves to the case of a single choice out of a finite choice set of J categorical objects; we omit ordinal discrete or count dependent variables from further consideration. Most presentations of advanced choice models follow the historical pattern of presenting first the Nested MNL and related models, motivated by dealing with the IIA property. I have argued above, however, that it is just as important, and perhaps even more basic, to deal with the issue of heteroscedasticity in the error terms. Thus, we will first discuss generalizations of the MNL that deal with heteroscedasticity, then we shall deal with models whose purpose is to capture IIA violations reflected in the error terms (both the GEV family and the MNP models will be covered here). Then we shall turn our attention away from the stochastic components of the model and address the issue of taste heterogeneity in the systematic utility component (both finite and continuous support models will be presented). This will be followed by a limited discussion of several interesting and quite specialized topics: choice set formation, heuristics and the impact of complexity on choice. Finally, an empirical application comparing several model forms will be presented.

2. ASSUMPTIONS ABOUT ERROR TERMS

Let us consider this relatively general utility function representation:

$$U_{in} = V_{in} + \varepsilon_{in}, \ \forall i \in C_n, \tag{1}$$

where U_{in} is the total utility of alternative i for decision maker n, V_{in} is the systematic (or known by the analyst up to parameters) component of utility, ε_{in} is the stochastic component of utility (theoretically known to the decision maker, but not to the analyst except in distribution), and C_n is the choice set of J objects. This additive decomposition, though certainly not unique, is quite flexible enough for our present purposes.

Probabilities of choice can be derived from (1), once we specify the distributions for the ε's. Take, for instance, the binary case ($C=\{i,j\}$), for which the probability of individual n choosing i is given by:

$$P_{in} = \Pr(U_{in} > U_{jn}) = \Pr(V_{in} + \varepsilon_{in} > V_{jn} + \varepsilon_{jn}) = \Pr(\varepsilon_{jn} - \varepsilon_{in} < V_{in} - V_{jn})$$
$$= \Pr(\varepsilon_{i:j,n}^{*} < V_{in} - V_{jn}) .$$

$$(2)$$

Thus, the probability of choosing i from C is determined by the relative systematic attractiveness of i versus j, as well as by a new random variable $\varepsilon_{i:j,n}^{*}$, defined as the *difference* in stochastic utility between the alternatives. From the distribution functions of the individual error terms it is possible to derive the distribution function of $\varepsilon_{i:j,n}^{*}$, and from that the specific model form for the choice probability. This method generalizes to the case of three or more alternatives, as shown in the derivation by Ben-Akiva and Lerman (1985, 104-107) of the MNL model with an arbitrary number of alternatives in C and iid Gumbel[2] error terms with scale factor μ:

$$P_{in} = \frac{\exp(\mu V_{in})}{\sum_{j \in C} \exp(\mu V_{jn})} .$$

$$(3)$$

As pointed out in many references (e.g., Ben-Akiva and Lerman, 1985, Swait and Louviere, 1993, Louviere, Hensher and Swait, 2000), when the systematic utility function is linear-in-parameters ($V_{in}=\beta'X_{in}$, where β is the unknown taste vector and X_{in} is a conformable vector of attributes) it is not possible to separately identify the impact of the scale factor from that of tastes; in fact, we identify only the product ($\mu\beta$). Traditionally, we assume the normalizing condition $\mu\equiv1$ to allow identification of the taste vector.

But the insight about (2) that I wish to convey here can be obtained with somewhat less analytical effort. Consider the random variable $\varepsilon_{i:j,n}^{*}$, and calculate its variance, like so:

$$Var(\varepsilon_{i:j,n}^{*}) = Var(\varepsilon_{in}) + Var(\varepsilon_{jn}) - 2 \cdot Cov(\varepsilon_{in}, \varepsilon_{jn}) .$$

$$(4)$$

Therefore, the choice probability for alternative i depends on a random variable whose variance is a function of the variances of the stochastic utilities as well as the covariance between them. From expression (4) it is possible to see that if we're dealing with iid stochastic utilities (as in the MNL model, for example), all component variances on the RHS of (4) will be equal because of homoscedasticity, and the covariance will necessarily be zero because of independence. Thus, if the component stochastic utilities are homoscedastic and independent, the choice probabilities will be determined by random variables that are also homoscedastic.

What happens when the component stochastic utilities are heteroscedastic, though still independent? Does this lead to another model form? We investigate this case in the following section.

2.1. Heteroscedastic Models: $Var(\varepsilon_i) \neq Var(\varepsilon_j)$, $Cov(\varepsilon_i, \varepsilon_j)=0$

2.1.1. Case 1: Heteroscedasticity Across Decision Makers

For reasons that will become clearer later on, we first consider the case of heteroscedasticity based on decision maker or decision context characteristics (e.g., income, education, private versus public consumption context). As in the basic MNL model, we assume that the stochastic utilities are independent across decision makers and alternatives, that they are identically Gumbel distributed across the alternatives of a decision maker, but that they are not identically distributed across individuals. Specifically, let decision maker n have scale factor $\mu_n > 0$. Since the error terms in (1) are still homoscedastic within decision maker, choice probabilities will be exactly the MNL choice probability given in (3), but duly augmented by the decision-maker specific scale factor:

$$P_{in} = \frac{\exp(\mu_n V_{in})}{\displaystyle\sum_{j \in C_n} \exp(\mu_n V_{jn})} \ . \tag{5}$$

What have we gained by this development? Actually, quite a bit, as we shall see below. Figure 1 shows the behavior of a binary logit model of the form given in expression (5), drawn as a family of curves that are a function of different scale factors. For a given scale factor, the choice probability for alternative i rises as the systematic component of this alternative grows compared to that of j. But note that, for the exact same difference in systematic utilities, the choice probability of i is higher for decision makers that have a higher scale factor. In this particular example, at a systematic utility difference of $+2$, the choice probabilities vary from 0.55 with $\mu_n = 0.1$ to essentially unity at $\mu_n = 4$; this represents an 82% difference in choice probability for the very same difference in systematic utility advantage of i over j. Thus, the scale factor has an important role to play in determining choice probabilities. As scale (variance) approaches zero (infinity), expression (5) indicates that all choice probabilities will approach the value $1/J$, where J is the number of alternatives in C; as scale (variance) approaches infinity (zero), if the utility difference between alternatives is positive the choice probability shoots up to unity, and if the difference is negative the choice probability plunges to zero – that is, the choice probability approaches a perfectly discriminating step function.

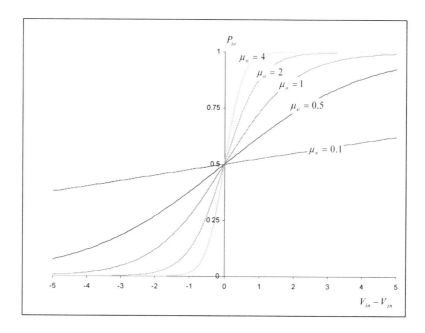

FIGURE 1. Behavior of Heteroscedastic MNL Model With Respect to Scale Factor Differences

Behaviorally, what does all this mean? Let us hark back to what the scale factor μ_n represents: in the Gumbel distribution, the scale factor captures the degree of spread, if you will, in the distribution. The larger (smaller) the scale factor, the smaller (larger) the variance of the distribution. Hence, if scale varies across individuals, it implies that there is variation in the degree to which the total utility of an alternative is reflected in the systematic component V_{in} compared to the stochastic utility component ε_{in}. In deriving model (5), we have postulated that some decision makers' total utilities are more nearly captured in V compared to ε (i.e., those with large scale factors), while for other decision makers their total utilities are in greater part reflected in ε than in V (i.e., those with small scale factors). Since scale factors are constant across alternatives for an individual, we have imposed the restriction that the distribution of stochastic utility is the same, thus arriving at the modified MNL model shown in expression (5).

Identification of the scale factor μ_n is still not possible unless we introduce exogenous information that separates tastes from scale. Specifically, we can use data in vector Z_n (i.e., person- or context-specific characteristics – these must *not* vary across alternatives) to identify the scale:

$$\mu_n = h(Z_n; \theta), \tag{6}$$

where θ is a parameter vector; forms for $h()$ must maintain the nonnegativity of the scale factor, so suitable functions might be

$$\mu_n = (\theta' Z_n)^2, \text{ or } \mu_n = \exp(\theta' Z_n). \tag{7}$$

Swait and Adamowicz (2001) used model (5) to introduce the impact of context complexity in stated choice (SC) tasks into the estimation of a discrete choice model. They reflect the impact of the number of attributes and alternatives in the SC task through the scale factor, by parametrizing μ_n as a function of the context entropy H_n.[3] They find that variance is a quadratic function of entropy, indicating that as entropy grows to a certain point of complexity the stochastic utility component's portion of total utility increases (i.e., variance grows), whereas after that level of complexity the role of the stochastic component begins to decrease (i.e., variance decreases). They postulate that this is due to the existence of an effort budget on the part of subjects. (For further discussion of this model, see Section 4.2. See also Hensher, this volume.)

It is instructive to note that the literature on data fusion (e.g., Morikawa, 1989, Louviere, Hensher and Swait, 2000, chapters 8 and 13), which considers the problem of estimating common taste parameters using two or more choice data sources that have (potentially) different scale factors, is essentially using model (5). The Z's become simply a set of dummy variables indicating decision maker membership in the different data sources.

Another interesting observation to be made concerning this model is that the products $(\mu_n V_{in})$ constitute interactions of the attributes with the heteroscedasticity corrections in the person-specific scale factor. This is, therefore, functionally identical to interacting a composite function of socio-demographic variables (in the scale function) with all the attributes in the systematic utility function. Intuitively, this should lead to very flexible functional forms that fit well to empirical data.

If we form the odds ratio of alternative i compared to alternative j using model (5), we will see that this model continues to exhibit the IIA property, just as the MNL model does. This ratio is:

$$\frac{P_{in}}{P_{jn}} = \exp[\mu_n(V_{in} - V_{jn})], \, i, j \in C_n. \tag{8}$$

Essentially, this property is the result of the independence of the error terms, so the presence of other alternatives seems to be irrelevant to this comparison. However, a subtle means exists for circumventing the IIA in this model: if μ_n contains explanatory variables which introduce the characteristics of alternatives other than i and j, then this ratio will be sensitive to characteristics of other goods. Thus, if heteroscedasticity is only a function of decision maker characteristics (e.g., income, education), the model will exhibit IIA; if, however, context variables (e.g., the entropy measure employed by Swait and Adamowicz, 2001) are used in the scale functions, then it is possible to capture non-IIA behavior with this model.

2.1.2. Case 2: Heteroscedasticity Across Alternatives Within Decision Maker

We now make the obvious extension of the prior model, and allow the scale factor to vary by alternative. Unfortunately, the Gumbel error terms of the J utility functions are no longer identically distributed. This makes this highly intuitive generalization of the MNL model a rather tricky step to take, since the derivation of the MNL depends crucially on the identical distribution of the error terms. What to do?

We'll have to perform a bit of "sleight-of-hand" to continue. Essentially, we must transform the non-iid Gumbel errors to iid Gumbel errors. Associated with ε_{in} is the scale factor μ_{in}. Now multiply both left and right hand sides of (1) by this scale factor to obtain

$$\mu_{in}U_{in} = \mu_{in}V_{in} + \mu_{in}\varepsilon_{in}, \ \forall i \in C_n. \tag{9}$$

The random variable $(\mu_{in}\varepsilon_{in})$ will be Gumbel distributed with the same mode as ε_{in}, and scale factor equal to unity (see Property 4 of the Gumbel distribution, Ben-Akiva and Lerman, 1985, pp. 104-105: if x is Gumbel distributed with scale μ, then αx will also be Gumbel, but with scale μ/α). That is to say, the transformed utilities in (9) are all independent Gumbel variates with unit scale ... so we're back to the iid Gumbel distributions across all alternatives in the choice set, but with systematic utilities $(\mu_{in}V_{in})$. Hence, the choice model now is:

$$P_{in} = \frac{\exp(\mu_{in}V_{in})}{\sum_{j \in C_n} \exp(\mu_{jn}V_{jn})} \ . \tag{10}$$

The trick to deriving the model above was to assume that the choice probabilities are determined by differences in the transformed utilities $(\mu_{in}U_{in})$, rather than the original utilities. From a behavioral perspective, the model seems to require the further "as-if" assumption that the decision maker "normalizes" utilities to allow comparison across alternatives with differing levels of idiosyncratic factors that affect their respective attractiveness. I am not entirely convinced the subtle mathematical operation applied above is innocuous; perhaps others can clarify this issue for the literature. However, let me assure the reader that (10) is a perfectly valid probabilistic choice model. It may not, however, be a member of the GEV family of models: McFadden's (1978) GEV choice model Generation Theorem (more on this subsequently) seemingly cannot be used to derive model (10) once the scale factors become alternative-specific; the actual impossibility of this application implies that model (10) does not belong to the same family of models as the ordinary MNL and model (5) presented above.

Nonetheless, there is much to commend in model (10) from a behavioral and empirical perspective: it allows alternative-specific characteristics to account for the differential importance of systematic versus stochastic utilities across alternatives. Specifically, scale factors can now be a function of exogenous vectors Z_{in}, which may include quality and price attributes, in addition to the socio-demographic and context effects permitted in model (5). Forms such as (7) can be used for the scale factor functions. Empirically, this is a powerful tool to explore and explain choice behavior.

For example, Dallaert et al. (1999) used model (10) to show that decision makers in a SC bus tour task (two alternatives, plus a None alternative described by five attributes including price) behaved consistently with the assumption of heteroscedastic stochastic utilities. These alternative-specific scale factors were found to be functions of own-price (varies by alternative) and price difference (a context effect, hence fixed across alternatives). As both of these variables increased, they found that scale decreased; hence, as absolute price levels increased and/or price differences between bus tours increased, scale decreased and stochastic utility was shown to play a larger role in explaining observed behavior. Conversely, at lower prices and/or smaller price differences, scale increased and systematic utility played a relatively larger role than stochastic utility in explaining behavior. The price differential was found to have the larger effect of the two variables included in the scale function.

As with model (5), model (10) is also capable of capturing non-IIA behavior depending upon the inclusion of variables among the Z_{in}'s that include quality- and price-based context effects. Additionally, it should be noted that J-1 alternative-specific constants can be identified in the scale function; any one alternative must be assigned unit scale for identification purposes.

2.1.3. Case 3: Heteroscedastic Extreme Value Model

Bhat (1995) took a somewhat different course than above to derive a choice model that allows for heteroscedasticity in the utility functions. He assumed that the stochastic utility terms are independent Gumbel (or Type I Extreme Value, or EV) variates, but are differently distributed with alternative-specific scale parameters μ_i.[4] While this set of assumptions is identical to those made for expression (10) above, the implementation is slightly different and leads to a different model form, which Bhat (1995) called the Heteroscedastic Extreme Value (HEV) model. Not surprisingly, it shares many of the same characteristics as the Heteroscedastic MNL just presented.

The standard EV ($\mu \equiv 1$) distribution and cumulative distribution functions are given respectively by (see Johnson et al., 1995)

$$\lambda(t) = \exp(-t)\exp(-\exp(-t)) \text{ and } \Lambda(t) = \exp(-\exp(-t)), \ -\infty < t < \infty. (11)$$

Thus, the error term ε_i in (1) has pdf and cdf as given below:

$$f_i(z) = \mu_i \lambda(\mu_i z) \text{ and } F_i(z) = \int_{-\infty}^{z} f_i(z)dz = \Lambda(\mu_i z), \ -\infty < z < \infty. \ (12)$$

Since the individual stochastic utility components are independent, it is a standard result of probability theory that their joint pdf and cdf will be the product of these individual functions. With these error term characterizations, the choice probability can be specified as follows:

$$P_{in} = \Pr(U_{in} > U_{jn}, j \neq i, \forall j \in C_n) = \Pr(\varepsilon_{jn} < V_{in} - V_{jn} + \varepsilon_{in}, j \neq i, \forall j \in C_n)$$

$$= \int_{\varepsilon_{in}=-\infty}^{\infty} \left(\prod_{\substack{j \in C \\ j \neq i}} \Lambda \left[\mu_{in} \left(V_{in} - V_{jn} + \varepsilon_{in} \right) \right] \right) \mu_{in} \lambda(\mu_{in} \varepsilon_{in}) d\varepsilon_{in}$$

$$(13)$$

Model (13) looks quite different from (10), though it is substantively equivalent to the Heteroscedastic MNL in its roots. Both models explicitly allow heteroscedasticity in the stochastic utility component, thus permitting inclusion of the types of effects previously discussed. In addition, both models allow interactions via the scale factors between systematic utility determinants (i.e., attributes and socio-demographics) and heteroscedasticity determinants (e.g., socio-demographics, context variables, and attributes), leading to very flexible model specifications. In both cases, it is possible to parametrize the scale factors in behaviorally informative ways using functional forms such as expressions (7). Finally, both models can reflect non-IIA behavior through the scale factors.

Computationally, model (13) is much more burdensome than (10) because the former does not have a convenient closed-form expression. In fact, calculation of the probability of choosing an alternative requires evaluation of a single dimensional integral over the stochastic utility component in question. As suggested by Bhat (1995), most implementations of the HEV employ the Laguerre Gaussian Quadrature formula to evaluate the integral. This procedure is certainly more onerous than the evaluation of a straightforward expression like that of choice probability (10), but the cost is not excessive.

Besides Bhat's (1995) initial formulation and testing of this model (using intercity mode choice revealed preference data), applications of this model have been carried out by Allenby and Ginter (1995), Hensher (1997, 1998a,b) and Louviere, Hensher and Swait (2000), among others. Computational details can be found in Louviere, Hensher and Swait (2000), Appendix B6.

2.2. Models With Correlated Error Terms: $Cov(\varepsilon_i, \varepsilon_j) \neq 0$

In the last section I presented three models (two heteroscedastic variants of the MNL model, and the HEV) that circumvented the IIA property of the MNL model by allowing the stochastic utility components of different alternatives to be independent but *not* identically distributed. Such models yield changes in the variances of utility differences (see expression 4) via differences in the individual variances, even while maintaining that the covariances are zero (the essence of the independence assumption). From (4) it is clear that the same result can be achieved in a second way: even when the individual variances are equal (i.e., homoscedasticity holds), utility difference variances can be heterogeneous due to nonzero covariances.

Historically, allowing for nonzero covariances between alternatives was the original method used to circumvent structural IIA. This led to the Nested MNL model (see Daly and Zachary, 1976, Ben-Akiva and Lerman, 1977, Williams, 1977, McFadden, 1978), which produced a more flexible model than the MNL model by postulating that nonzero correlations among error terms arose in accordance to a specification given by a tree arrangement of the alternatives. McFadden (1978) systematized the relationship between the MNL and Nested MNL models through the GEV (Generalized Extreme Value) Generation Theorem, which in fact lays out the framework for an entire class of related choice models that have the MNL at its core. A parallel interest in the Multinomial Probit (MNP) model (see Daganzo, 1979, Manski and Lerman, 1981), which allowed nonzero correlations between pairs of stochastic utility components in the more traditional format of a covariance matrix, had to await further computational developments to become practical.

In the following sections, I present the GEV Generation Theorem, then examine some specific GEV models that implement nonzero covariances, and finally, show the MNP model.

2.2.1. The GEV Generation Theorem

<u>GEV Generation Theorem:</u>

Suppose $G(y_1,...,y_J)$ is a nonnegative, homogenous-of-degree-μ (where $\mu \geq 0$) function of $(y_1,...,y_J) \geq 0$. Suppose $\lim G()=\infty$ as $y_i \to \infty$, for $i=1,...,J$. Suppose for any distinct $\{i_1,...,i_k\} \subseteq \{1,...,J\}$, $\partial^k G()/\partial y_{i1} \cdots \partial y_{ik} \geq 0$ if k is odd and ≤ 0 if k is even. Then,

$$P(i) = \frac{y_i G_i(y_1,...,y_J)}{\mu G(y_1,...,y_J)},$$ (14a)

where $G_i = \partial G/\partial y_i$. The corresponding multivariate cdf of the error vector ε_{Jx1} is given by

$$F(\varepsilon) = \exp(-G(\exp(-\varepsilon_1),...,\exp(-\varepsilon_J))), \quad -\infty < \varepsilon < \infty.$$ (14b)

<u>Proof.</u> See McFadden (1978).[5]

To my mind, this theorem is the most elegant result available in discrete choice analysis. Simply put, if one can define a function $G()$ of the systematic utilities y that satisfies the conditions of the theorem, then expressions (14a,b) specify the choice probability model and joint multivariate GEV error cumulative distribution function for the stochastic utility components. For example, the function

$$G(y_1,...,y_J) = \sum_{j=1}^{J} y_j^{\mu} , \mu \geq 0,$$ (15)

can be shown to satisfy the requirements of the GEV Theorem, and will produce the MNL choice probabilities in expression (3), after substituting $y_i = \exp(V_i), i = 1,...,J$, with V_i a latent variable without sign restrictions, to guarantee the nonnegativity of the arguments of $G()$. This shows that the MNL model is a member of the GEV family of choice models.

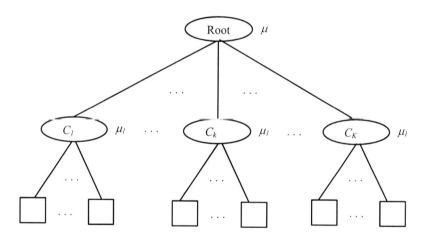

FIGURE 2. *A Two-Level Nested MNL Model*

2.2.2. The Nested MNL and Tree Extreme Value Models

A somewhat more complex $G()$ than (15) gives rise to the Nested MNL model. To make these concepts concrete, I will work below with the specific tree of depth two shown in Figure 2. Let

$$G(y_1,\dots,y_J) = \sum_{k=1}^{K}\left(\sum_{j\in C_k} y_j^{\mu_l}\right)^{\mu/\mu_l}, \tag{16}$$

where sets C_k, $k=1,\dots,K$, are mutually exclusive and collectively exhaustive subsets of $M=\{1,\dots,J\}$, $\mu,\mu_l\geq0$.[6] The sets C_k are called "clusters" or "nests" of alternatives, hence the name of the model. In Figure 2 the elemental (or observable) alternatives are shown in rectangles, whereas the "construct" (or latent) objects or groupings of alternatives are depicted as ellipses. The scale factors μ and μ_l are related, respectively, to the root and second level nodes of the tree in Figure 2. The former reflects the overall variability level of the data and the latter captures the degree of similarity (or correlation) in the stochastic component of utility of the alternatives in each cluster. Note that all Nested MNL models assume that:

(1)   the errors are homoscedastic,
(2)   the correlation among alternatives is the same in all nests with equal
           scale factors, and
(3)   the correlation is zero between alternatives in different nests.

Function (16) results in choice probabilities of the form:

$$P(i) = P(i|C_{(i)})Q(C_{(i)}), \qquad i=1,\dots,J, \tag{17a}$$

$$P(i|C_{(i)}) = \frac{\exp(\mu_1 V_i)}{\sum_{j\in C_{(i)}}\exp(\mu_1 V_j)} \tag{17b}$$

$$Q(C_{(i)}) = \frac{\exp(\mu I_{(i)})}{\sum_{k=1}^{K}\exp(\mu I_k)} \tag{17c}$$

$$I_k = \frac{1}{\mu_1}\ln\left(\sum_{j\in C_k}\exp(\mu_1 V_j)\right), \qquad k=1,\dots,K, \tag{17d}$$

where $C_{(i)}$ is the nest that contains alternative i, I_k is called the "inclusive value" of cluster k, and $I_{(i)}$ is the inclusive value of the cluster containing i. It can be shown that the inclusive value of a nest of alternatives with iid Gumbel (or Type I Extreme Value) error terms is equal to the expectation of the maximum utility of the alternatives in the nest (see Ben-Akiva and Lerman, 1985, pages 300-304). Thus, the attractiveness of latent construct set $C_{(i)}$ is endogenously defined by a monotonic transform of the utilities of the elemental alternatives; hence, the probability of choosing an alternative belonging to $C_{(i)}$ is endogenously determined by a two-stage transition (see 17a) that's a function of the relative attractiveness of the nests, then of the relative attractiveness of the elemental alternative *vis-à-vis* its nest siblings. (Though the final choice probability is indeed the product of this sequence of conditional probabilities, it is not necessary for the analyst to assume that decision makers are actually using this decision sequence.) This endogenous determination of the attractiveness of construct nodes is a general characteristic of GEV models. Note that when $\mu_1 \equiv \mu$ in Figure 2 (see expressions 17), this Nested MNL model collapses down to a MNL model. In fact, this is a general characteristic of the GEV class: for some configuration of parameters, all GEV choice models will simplify to the MNL. This forms the basis for convenient tests of the IIA property in empirical settings.

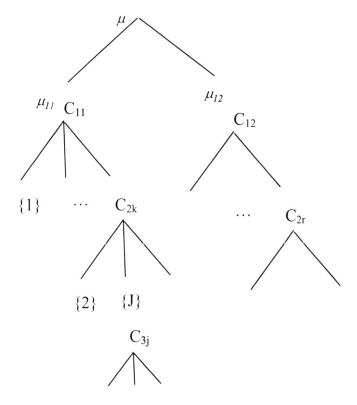

FIGURE 3. *A General Tree Extreme Value Correlation Tree Diagram*

The reader familiar with the Nested MNL model will note that expressions (17) seem oddly different from the usual way of defining these models in the literature. In fact, a plethora of forms for presenting these models exist, and we have chosen that of Ben-Akiva and Lerman (1985, ch. 10), which is consistent with our use of scale factors throughout this chapter. Other authors have defined "inclusive value" θ

($\equiv 1/\mu$) or "similarity" σ ($\equiv 1-\theta=(\mu-1)/\mu$) parameters; fundamentally, however, results are identical whatever form is adopted.

McFadden (1981) showed that the Nested MNL can be further generalized to what he termed the Tree Extreme Value (TEV) model. (His motivation: to formulate a model that mimicked EBA – Elimination by Aspects – choice probabilities; see Tversky, 1972.) This formulation does not require equal scale factors at the same level of the tree; the Nested MNL makes this requirement. The TEV extension to the example in Figure 2 would allow each construct node at the second level of the tree to have different scale values (μ_1, μ_2, ..., μ_K). In addition, TEV models tend to have more general trees depicting the covariational structure of the error terms (e.g., see Figure 3).

The TEV model particularly emphasizes the transition probability structure of GEV models. Let

T   = a preference tree characterizing the relationships between elemental and construct alternatives by indicating the predecessor (or parent) node of each alternative, equal to $C \cup E$;
E   = The set of elemental nodes (i.e., real alternatives);
C   = The set of construct alternatives, composed of $\forall a \in T$-E plus the root node (designated node 0);
D(a) = The parent node of $a \in T$; and
S(a) = The alternatives in the subnest of node $a \in T$, including a.

Let the conditional choice probability $\ell(a, S(a))$ of any node a among its siblings $S(a)$ be given by a MNL model, like so:

$$\ell(a, S(a)) = \frac{\exp(\mu_{D(a)}\tilde{V}_a)}{\sum_{j \in S(a)}\exp(\mu_{D(a)}\tilde{V}_j)}, \qquad (18)$$

where $\tilde{V}_a$ is an average attractiveness measure[7] defined as

$$\tilde{V}_a = \begin{cases} V_a(X_a;\beta) & \text{if } a \in E \\ \frac{1}{\mu_a}\ln\left(\sum_{j \in S(a)}\exp(\mu_{D(j)}\tilde{V}_j)\right) & \text{if } a \in C \end{cases}. \qquad (19)$$

In the expressions above, the scale factors $\mu_{D(a)}$ refer to the scale associated with the subset of alternatives whose parent is the same as the parent of node a; β is a vector of attribute importances. Given these two definitions, the unconditional choice probability of the elemental alternatives $i \in E$ is given by:

$$P_i = \prod_{a \in K(i)} \ell(a, S(a)) \tag{20}$$

where $K(i)$ is the path of nodes from i to the root of T, that is, $K(i) = \{i \rightarrow D(i) \rightarrow D(D(i)) \rightarrow ... \rightarrow r_0\}$, where r_0 is a node that has the root (0) as its parent, i.e., $D(r_0)=0$. The recursive nature of (19) was first recognized by Daly (1987), who formulated the TEV in the form shown above (though he used inclusive value coefficients rather than the scales employed here). Note that the original model form given by Daly (1987) contains a small but significant difference that makes his model inconsistent with the GEV Generation Theorem; his is a valid probabilistic choice model, but is not the TEV model as claimed. The reader should employ the form given above for the TEV model.

   With respect to the parameters of the systematic utility function, the same identification conditions hold as required by the MNL model. Certain identifying conditions pertain to the scale factors in the Nested MNL and TEV models.

1.   The scale factor of one node must be held constant for identification of the remainder; this reflects the fact that in actuality we can identify scale ratios, not the absolute scale factors. It is usual to set the root node scale to unity to accomplish this normalization.
2.   It is also required that scale factors be monotonically increasing as one traverses down a tree from the root (if inclusive value coefficients are used, it is required that they be *decreasing* as one descends in the tree).

   The intuition for this second condition comes from the expression for the correlation between a pair of alternatives (i,j) within a nest S (Ben-Akiva and Lerman, 1985, p. 289):

$$\rho_{i,j} = 1 - \left(\frac{\mu_{D(S)}}{\mu_S} \right)^2, \tag{21}$$

where μ_S and $\mu_{D(S)}$ are, respectively, the scales of the nest S and its parent node $D(S)$. If $\mu_{D(S)} \le \mu_S$, then (21) yields a valid correlation in the range $[0,+1]$ (i.e., in GEV models, products are substitutes, hence positively correlated); if $\mu_{D(S)} > \mu_S$, the correlation will conceivably be greater than unity in absolute value, therefore not a valid correlation. More generally, if this requirement with respect to the scale factors is met empirically, it signals that the choices being modeled are consistent with utility maximizing behavior (clearly, within the bounds of the assumptions of the model). Thus, when welfare analysis is a principal goal of a modeling exercise, the researcher should be well aware of these restrictions and select between models accordingly.

What happens, however, if the scales are not monotonically increasing as one goes deeper into the tree? It should first be noted that the resulting model is a perfectly valid probabilistic choice model: the predicted probabilities will be in the interval [0,1], and they will sum to one. So, for predictive purposes, it may be fine to continue to use such a model. Nonetheless, the reader should note that such a model is incompatible with utility maximizing behavior, hence not useful for welfare analysis. It is also my experience that such model behavior might be indicative that the proposed tree is perhaps not well specified; some deeper thought may generate alternative trees that are utility consistent. It is a good idea anyway to generate and estimate multiple trees for any given set of choice behaviors, so this outcome places no additional onus on the analyst. Sometimes "mis-behaving" trees are only marginally so; in such cases, judicious constraint of scale factors within the tree may bring it back into alignment with desirable theoretical restrictions.

There have been myriad applications of the Nested MNL models, particularly in the transportation planning field. Many applications were published in the literature in the 1970s, and the reader is directed to Ben-Akiva and Lerman (1985), particularly chapter 10, for references. Other fields have also used the Nested MNL model extensively: Schwabe et al. (2001) – evaluation of changes in deer hunting season length; Kamakura et al. (1996) – household selection of canned tuna in supermarkets, are some very few references of the application of these models in non-transportation settings. It has been somewhat less common to see applications of the Tree Extreme Value models: Swait and Bernardino (2000) study airline choice behavior in three routes and use TEV models in a relatively unique fashion to perform taste homogeneity tests between routes.

To conclude this section, I would like to point out that GEV models are not simply about the covariational structure of the stochastic utility components. In the mid 1990s and early 2000s, something of a renaissance occurred in the formulation and testing of new members in the GEV family. To name but a few developments: the Paired Combinatorial Logit (Chu, 1989, Koppelman and Wen, 2000); Generalized Nested Logit (Wen and Koppelman, 2001); Choice Set Generation Logit (Swait, 2001); Finite Mixture GEV (Swait, 2003). The reader is referred to these papers for other GEV models that have appeared in the literature.

2.2.3. The Multinomial Probit Model

As I indicated in my introductory remarks, the fact that the MNL model necessarily exhibited the IIA property led to an early interest in the Multinomial Probit (MNP) model (see, e.g., Daganzo, 1979, Manski and Lerman, 1981). Computational difficulties severely curtailed the application of this model for many years, until simulation estimation methods were developed in the early 1990s (see the review in Hajivassiliou, 1993). Despite its current feasibility, however, the MNP model has never really seen widespread use, for reasons to be discussed.

It has been customary in the literature to present this model with vector notation, one of the reasons being ease of exposition. Let us stack the J utility functions (and subcomponents) for alternatives in choice set C_n into vectors $\mathbf{U_n}$, $\mathbf{V_n}$ and $\boldsymbol{\varepsilon_n}$, so that

$$\mathbf{U_n} = \mathbf{V_n} + \boldsymbol{\varepsilon_n}. \tag{22}$$

Now assume that the density function for the $J\mathrm{x}1$ $\boldsymbol{\varepsilon}$ vector is multivariate normal (MVN) with mean $\mathbf{0}$ and $J\mathrm{x}J$ covariance matrix $\boldsymbol{\Sigma}$. To be concrete, the MNP density function is given as follows:

$$\varphi_J(\boldsymbol{\varepsilon} \mid \mathbf{0}, \boldsymbol{\Sigma}) = \left(2\pi \mid \boldsymbol{\Sigma} \mid\right)^{-J/2} \exp\left[- \boldsymbol{\varepsilon}' \boldsymbol{\Sigma}^{-1} \boldsymbol{\varepsilon} / 2\right]. \tag{23}$$

Notationally, the corresponding cumulative density function is denoted as $\boldsymbol{\Phi}_J(\boldsymbol{\varepsilon} \mid \mathbf{0}, \boldsymbol{\Sigma})$, and the covariance matrix $\boldsymbol{\Sigma}$ as:

$$\boldsymbol{\Sigma} = \begin{bmatrix} \sigma_1^2 & & & & \\ \sigma_{21} & \sigma_2^2 & & & \\ . & & . & & \\ . & & & . & \\ . & & & & . \\ \sigma_{J1} & \sigma_{J2} & . & . & \sigma_J^2 \end{bmatrix}, \tag{24}$$

where the diagonal elements σ_j^2, $j=1,\ldots,J$, are the variances of the stochastic utilities, and σ_{ij} are covariances between stochastic utilities ε_i and ε_j.

Examination of the covariance matrix above makes clear that the MNP model is something of an "umbrella" model covering the choice models I've presented in preceding sections. For example, if $\boldsymbol{\Sigma}$ is diagonal with the same variance σ^2 for all alternatives, the MNP model mimics a MNL model; if it is diagonal but the variances are alternative-specific, the MNP will behave like the Heteroscedastic MNL and HEV models; and finally, if the diagonal is homoscedastic but off-diagonal elements are structured appropriately in a cluster fashion, the MNP will behave like one of the tree-based GEV models. It is easy to see that such a flexible model form would be an attractive formulation.

Choice probabilities can be defined relatively straightforwardly by working from first principles (see Daganzo, 1979, and particularly Bunch, 1991):

$$\begin{aligned} P_i &= \Pr\left(U_i > U_j, \forall j \neq i,\ i, j \in C\right) \\ &= \Pr\left(U_j - U_i < 0, \forall j \neq i,\ i, j \in C\right) \\ &= \boldsymbol{\Phi}_{J-1}\left(\mathbf{0} \mid \mathbf{V}_D, \boldsymbol{\Sigma}_D\right), \end{aligned} \tag{25}$$

where $V_D = \Delta_i V$ and $\Sigma_D = \Delta_i \Sigma \Delta_i'$. The $(J\text{-}1)\text{x}J$ differencing matrix Δ_i has elements

$$\Delta_i = [\delta_{kj}]_i = \begin{cases} 1 & \text{if } j \neq i,\, k = j-1 \\ -1 & \text{if } j = i,\, \forall k \\ 0 & \text{otherwise} \end{cases} \tag{26}$$

Note that the calculation of this probability involving J utilities requires the evaluation of the J-1 dimensional MVN cdf (this reduction in dimensionality comes about because utility differences determine MNP choice probabilities, just as in the other models examined heretofore). The final form of the choice probability for alternative $i \in C_n$ is given by the J-1 dimensional integral

$$P_i = \int\limits_{-\infty}^{V_i-V_1} \cdots \int\limits_{-\infty}^{V_i-V_J} \varphi_{J-1}\!\left(\varepsilon_{Di} \mid 0, \Sigma_{Di}\right) d\eta_{i1} d\eta_{i2} \ldots d\eta_{i,i-1} d\eta_{i,i+1} \ldots d\eta_{iJ}, \tag{27}$$

where $\eta_{ik} = \varepsilon_k - \varepsilon_i$. For the binary case ($J$=2), we can be somewhat more specific about this expression:

$$P_i = \int\limits_{\varepsilon_i=-\infty}^{\infty} \int\limits_{\varepsilon_j=-\infty}^{V_i-V_j+\varepsilon_i} \varphi_2(\varepsilon \mid V, \Sigma) d\varepsilon$$

$$= \Phi\!\left(\frac{V_i - V_j}{\sigma_D}\right) \tag{28}$$

where

$$\sigma_D^2 = \sigma_i^2 + \sigma_j^2 - 2\sigma_{ij}. \tag{29}$$

This binary probit expression illustrates several important points about the identification of elements in the covariance matrix Σ. First, note that the full structure of Σ is the following:

$$\Sigma = \begin{bmatrix} \sigma_1^2 & \sigma_{12} \\ \sigma_{12} & \sigma_2^2 \end{bmatrix}. \tag{30}$$

Seemingly, there are three elements of Σ to identify. In fact, this is not possible to do: expressions (28) and (29) clearly show that the elements of Σ only show up in a linear combination, and always in a ratio form with utility differences. As Bunch (1991) pointed out, in the binary case, *no* elements of the covariance matrix can be identified.

In general, because we can only really identify Σ_D, the covariance matrix of stochastic utility differences, we are at most capable of identifying $[J(J-1)/2 -1]$ elements of the original covariance matrix Σ. (The -1 in the expression will be explained below.) At the time of Bunch's (1991) writing, several unidentified MNP models had already been published in the literature, so it is clear that the identification restrictions on the MNP covariance matrix were not clearly understood. I believe this may still be the case, despite Bunch's (1991) important warnings. So let me summarize these restrictions very clearly below:

1. One of the variance elements must be normalized, say $\sigma_1^2 \equiv 1$. This is exactly analogous to setting the root node scale factor to unity in a Nested MNL or TEV model.
2. At most another $[J(J-1)/2 -2]$ elements of Σ can be identified.

Since Σ has $J(J+1)/2$ unique elements, and only $[J(J-1)/2 -1]$ are identifiable, that leaves $(J+1)$ that must be restricted, either by setting them to some constant or equating them to other covariance elements. (Note that these different restrictive actions lead to significantly different outcomes.)

Empirically, this leads to some ambiguity concerning the specification of the covariance matrix, analogous to one's uncertainty concerning the "right" tree structure in a Nested MNL or TEV model. Consider the case $J=3$, for which the full covariance matrix Σ has 6 elements:

$$\Sigma = \begin{bmatrix} \sigma_1^2 & & \\ \sigma_{21} & \sigma_2^2 & \\ \sigma_{31} & \sigma_{32} & \sigma_3^2 \end{bmatrix}. \tag{31}$$

The following four covariance matrices are identifiable since each has one or two unknown parameters (these are far from the full set of possible matrices one could define):

$$\Sigma_1 = \begin{bmatrix} 1 & & \\ 0 & \sigma^2 & \\ 0 & 0 & \sigma^2 \end{bmatrix} \tag{32a}$$

$$\Sigma_2 = \begin{bmatrix} 1 & & \\ \overline{\sigma} & \sigma^2 & \\ \overline{\sigma} & \overline{\sigma} & \sigma^2 \end{bmatrix} \qquad\qquad\qquad (32b)$$

$$\Sigma_3 = \begin{bmatrix} 1 & & \\ \rho_{21} & 1 & \\ 0 & \rho_{32} & 1 \end{bmatrix} \qquad\qquad\qquad (32c)$$

$$\Sigma_4 = \begin{bmatrix} 1 & & \\ 0 & 1 & \\ \rho_{31} & \rho_{32} & 1 \end{bmatrix} \qquad\qquad\qquad (32d)$$

The first matrix allows heteroscedasticity of alternatives 2 and 3 compared to 1, but forces independence across alternatives; the second matrix augments that specific heteroscedasticity assumption with covariation between alternatives, but forces the covariation to be identical across all alternative pairs; the third matrix assumes homoscedasticity and estimates two covariances (or, equivalently, correlations) between alternatives (1,2) and (2,3), while forcing the covariance between (1,3) to be structurally zero; and finally, the fourth matrix is conceptually identical to the third except that the pair of nonzero covariances are different. So, which is the "right" covariance matrix? At one level this is an empirical question, and should be answered case by case.

At another level, I believe this choice is also a conceptual issue. I would like to return to the overall choice model specification hierarchy laid out at the end of Section 1, which suggested that the specification of choice models should proceed as follows:

1. Specify the systematic component of utility.
2. Then specify a covariance matrix that first gives preference to identifying the variances.
3. Finally, if there are still identifiable parameters, look to the covariances. Be guided by "tree-like" thinking to promote parsimony.

Returning to the trinomial covariance specification example above (32a-d), my personal recommendation for a covariance matrix would be this one:

$$\Sigma_5 = \begin{bmatrix} 1 & & \\ 0 & \sigma_2^2 & \\ 0 & 0 & \sigma_3^2 \end{bmatrix}. \qquad\qquad\qquad (33)$$

This corresponds to a fully heteroscedastic MNP model, and was not included in prior examples.

3. ASSUMPTIONS ABOUT TASTE HETEROGENEITY

My main emphasis to this point has been on the assumptions concerning stochastic utility distributions in expression (1): dependence versus independence, homo- versus heteroscedasticity, and error term correlations. As we have clearly demonstrated in the preceding sections, a wide range of choice model specifications exists based upon varying these assumptions, even while maintaining the assumption that tastes are homogeneous across individual decision makers.

By "tastes" we refer to person-specific differences in the systematic component of utility (V_{in}, for alternative $i \in C_n$, person n). Nothing keeps us from introducing individual difference variables (e.g., income, age, variety-seeking propensity) into this function and applying it in any of the previously presented models. We have also seen that differences among individuals can be incorporated via the scale/variance specifications (and even via parametrizations of covariances). However, in this section we wish to more clearly define taste heterogeneity in the following manner:

1.   Each individual's marginal attribute utilities in the systematic utility function can be unique to that decision maker, and will be fully described by the $K \times 1$ vector β_n;

2.   For the sake of presentation, the systematic utility function will be assumed linear-in-the-parameters, thus:

$$V_{in} = \beta'_n X_{in} \tag{34}$$

The literature has presented two broad ways of modeling such taste heterogeneity: latent classes and continuous distributions of taste. We examine these in turn in the next two sections, closely tying the new material to the previous developments.

3.1. Latent Class Choice Models

In many applications, the assumption that tastes vary at the individual level may be overly detailed and the operationalization of such meticulous modeling insights impracticable. Marketing theory has introduced the intermediate concept of market segments/clusters/classes, which are finite in number and have within-segment homogeneity of tastes. In this section we will present a variant of the MNL model that incorporates latent classes, and was originally introduced by Swait (1994); though there are earlier versions of latent class choice models (e.g., Formann, 1992), Swait's presentation is closely related to our previous developments and carries through our hard-gained insights with respect to scale. The model presented below was originally developed for Revealed Preference (RP) single observation choice data, but is extended below to the SC case with repeated measures.

We observe N individuals at random from a population that is composed of S (unknown) classes. A class is characterized by its unique and homogeneous-within-class tastes β_s, $s=1,\ldots,S$. We observe $R \geq 1$ choices from each individual (let's assume the same number of choices for everyone), as well as socio-demographic and attitudinal variables Z_n. Each individual's choice set on the rth occasion is C_{rn}, $r=1,\ldots,R$; each alternative $i \in C_{rn}$ has attributes X_{irn}. However, we do *not* observe the individual's class membership, i.e., it is latent. That being the case, we are forced to develop a two-stage model: a choice model conditional on class membership, plus a class membership model. The probability of observing a choice $i \in C_{rn}$ is therefore given by

$$P_{irn} = \sum_{s=1}^{S} P_{irn|s} W_{ns} , \qquad (35)$$

for a given S, where $P_{irn|s}$ is the probability of choice conditional on membership in segment or class s, and W_{ns} is the probability individual n belongs to class s. These two models will be fleshed out in subsequent paragraphs.

First, assume that conditional utility functions like (1) exist for each class s. Then assume that the stochastic utilities within class are independent Gumbel variates with scale $\mu_s > 0$, $s=1,\ldots,S$. This assumption leads, of course, to the familiar expression for the conditional choice probability:

$$P_{irn|s} = \frac{\exp(\mu_s V_{irn|s})}{\sum_{j \in C_{rn}} \exp(\mu_s V_{jrn|s})} . \qquad (36)$$

Thus, within segment choice is characterized by the IIA property inherent to the MNL model.

Second, we must develop a probabilistic classification model W_{ns}. Postulate the existence of a membership likelihood scoring function Y_{ns}^*, defined through this expression:

$$Y_{ns}^* = \Gamma_s' Z_n + v_{ns} , \qquad (37)$$

where Z_n is the aforementioned vector of individual decision maker variables (socio-demographics, attitudes, perceptions, etc.) that affect classification probabilities; Γ_s is a segment-specific parameter vector; and v_{ns} is a stochastic error term. One may conceptualize Y_{ns}^* as a latent factor score that determines the likelihood of n being in segment s. The rule for class membership assignment is to place n in class s iff Y_{ns}^* is larger than the factor scores for all other classes:

$$n \rightarrow s, \ s = 1,..., S : Y_{ns}^* \geq Y_{ns'}^*, s' = 1,..., S, s' \neq s . \qquad (38)$$

Since the membership likelihood scoring functions are stochastic, class membership assignment can at best be probabilistic. Now assume that the error terms v_{ns} are IID Gumbel with scale factor $\lambda > 0$. (It is also necessary to assume that the v's are independent of the stochastic conditional utilities.) In that case, the class assignment probabilities will be given by this MNL model:

$$W_{ns} = \frac{\exp(\lambda \Gamma_s' Z_n)}{\displaystyle\sum_{s'=1}^{S} \exp(\lambda \Gamma_{s'}' Z_n)} . \qquad (39)$$

This model is a polytomous MNL model, since the alternatives are described by the same set of independent variables, but each alternative has its own set of weights for the independent variables. This model also corresponds to assuming the membership likelihood functions are orthogonal factors (due to the independence of the v's). Oblique factor solutions would be obtained if the v's were assumed correlated in some fashion (e.g., multivariate normal).

The joint use of (36) and (39) in (35) constitutes the full model describing a single choice. There are quite a few parameters to be estimated: S taste vectors β_s, and corresponding scale factors μ_s; S classification function parameter vectors Γ_s, as well as the scale λ; and finally, there is S itself. This latter parameter will be dealt with in a later section, but for now we enumerate identification restrictions to the remaining parameters for a given S.

1.   The conditional choice models are governed by the same identification conditions common to the plain-vanilla MNL model: only the product $(\mu_s \beta_s)$ can be identified without further restrictions (see below), so we commonly assume $\mu_s \equiv 1$, $\forall s$; as many alternative-specific constants as total alternatives being modeled, less one base, can be identified within each class.

2.   The scale factors μ_s can only be identified subject to the condition that some or all taste components be homogenous across some or all segments. One class must have a constant scale factor, and the other scales are identified relative to this normalization and that of the tastes. Such restrictions lead to interesting hypotheses concerning class membership: classes are assumed to differ due to differing levels of reliance on idiosyncratic utility sources (i.e., we're back to the strong influence of the stochastic utilities on choice), not taste differences.

3.   One of the classification factor scoring function parameter vectors
            cannot be identified, so one normalizes one such vector to zero, say
            (e.g., $\Gamma_1 \equiv 0$). The remaining Γ's are identified relative to this
            normalization. In addition, the scale λ must be normalized, say, to
            unity.

It was noted before that the conditional choice model (36) has the IIA property.
Does the property carry through to the unconditional choice probability? No, it does
not, as seen below:

$$\frac{P_{irn}}{P_{jrn}} = \frac{\sum_s P_{irn|s} W_{ns}}{\sum_l P_{jrn|l} W_{nl}} = \sum_s \frac{\left(\frac{\exp(V_{irn|s})}{\sum_{k \in C_{rn}} \exp(V_{krn|s})}\right) W_{ns}}{\sum_l \left(\frac{\exp(V_{jrn|l})}{\sum_{m \in C_{rn}} \exp(V_{mrn|l})}\right) W_{nl}} \qquad (40)$$

This expression cannot be simplified to rid it of the denominators of the MNL
models. Hence, the odds of choosing i over j depends upon, among other things, the
systematic utility of all alternatives in the choice set. Therefore, IIA does not hold at
the individual choice level, despite the fact that the class-specific stochastic utilities
are assumed independent. From (40) it can be seen that elimination of the terms

$$\sum_{k \in C_{rn}} \exp(V_{krn|s}), \qquad (41)$$

crucial to establishing IIA, is made impossible due to (1) heterogeneity in tastes
and/or (2) heteroscedasticity (i.e., different scales).
      The particular expressions we arrived at for this latent class model are specific to
the error term distributions we postulated. At any one of many stages in the model
development we could have made different assumptions and arrived at quite
different expressions for the choice models. For example, one might assume error
term distributions such that the conditional choice model (36) would be another
member of the GEV family, or even a MNP model, while maintaining the
classification model (39); alternatively, both the conditional choice and classification
models might be assumed MNP. To my best knowledge, there really does not exist
any theory to support the formulation of these complex models. Research work on
this topic would be helpful.
      Model (35) describes a single choice. In SC data it is common to observe R
replications, in each of which the choice set and attribute values might change. If the
replications can be treated as independent within a subject, then the joint probability
of observing the R choices $\{i_r^*, r=1,...,R\}$ is given by:

$$P_n = \prod_{r=1}^{R} P_{i_r n} = \prod_{r=1}^{R} \left(\sum_{s=1}^{S} P_{i_r n|s} W_{ns} \right). \tag{42}$$

We shall use this expression subsequently when we deal with the estimation of parameters via maximum likelihood. If the choices in the SC panel are assumed to not be independent, grave complications are introduced into the analysis: essentially, one must adopt some mathematical description of the dependence between observations. This opens a vast array of possibilities, which are beyond the scope of this chapter. Research need and potential in this area are great.

3.2. The Mixed MNL Model

One of the more important choice modeling technical developments in recent times was McFadden and Train's (2000) introduction and testing of the Mixed MNL model. This model not only addresses concerns about taste heterogeneity in a population, but also is found to have a high degree of flexibility that addresses the IIA property of the core MNL model.

Contrary to the latent class model described in the previous section, in the Mixed MNL model the individual tastes β_n are assumed to be multivariate normally (MVN) distributed in the population, like so:

$$\beta_n = \overline{\beta} + \tau_n, \quad \tau_n \sim MVN(\mathbf{0}, \Omega), \tag{43}$$

where $\overline{\beta}$ is the mean taste vector for the population, and Ω is the covariance matrix of the taste distribution. Rather than belonging to classes, as in latent class models, individuals are assumed to be draws from this taste distribution. The corresponding utility function for the rth replication now becomes

$$U_{irn} = \beta_n' X_{irn} + \varepsilon_{irn} = \overline{\beta}' X_{irn} + \tau_n' X_{irn} + \varepsilon_{irn}, \tag{44}$$

all quantities as previously defined. Note that the systematic portion of the utility now has two components, one common across individuals and another specific to decision maker n. Based upon various distributional assumptions concerning the τ's and the ε's, and the interrelationship between these random variables, one can arrive at different model forms incorporating heterogeneity of tastes.

To arrive at the model commonly termed the Mixed MNL, assume that the τ's are distributed per (43), that the ε's are conditionally independent of the τ's, and are iid Gumbel variates with identical scale μ. These assumptions imply that, conditional on a particular realization from the taste distribution, the choice probability for alternative $i \in C_{rn}$ is the simple MNL model:

$$P_{irn|\beta_n} = \frac{\exp\left(\mu V_{irn|\beta_n}\right)}{\displaystyle\sum_{j\in C_{rn}} \exp\left(\mu V_{jrn|\beta_n}\right)} , \qquad (45)$$

where

$$V_{irn|\beta_n} = \overline{\beta}'X_{irn} + \tau'_n X_{irn} . \qquad (46)$$

Now, to obtain the unconditional choice probability for alternative i, it is necessary to average expression (45) over the K-dimensional parameter space for tastes. Express the Kth-dimensional multivariate normal pdf with zero mean and covariance matrix Ω as $\varphi_K(\tau \mid 0, \Omega)$. Thus,

$$P_{irn} = \int_{\tau} \left(\frac{\exp\left(\mu V_{irn|\beta_n}\right)}{\displaystyle\sum_{j\in C_{rn}} \exp\left(\mu V_{jrn|\beta_n}\right)}\right) \varphi_K(\tau \mid 0, \Omega)d\tau \qquad (47)$$

is the desired unconditional choice probability. The model I term the Canonical Mixed MNL is simply to set the scale μ to unity in the above expression:

$$P_{irn} = \int_{\tau} \left(\frac{\exp\left(V_{irn|\beta_n}\right)}{\displaystyle\sum_{j\in C_{rn}} \exp\left(V_{jrn|\beta_n}\right)}\right) \varphi_K(\tau \mid 0, \Omega)d\tau . \qquad (48)$$

Evaluation of probability (48) can be accomplished by a number of simulation methods, all of which reflect the same basic mechanics of drawing L taste vectors from the underlying multivariate normal distribution (thus including the impact of the shape of the distribution of tastes), then estimating the choice probability by averaging over the L conditional choice probabilities (45), like this:

$$\hat{P}_{irn} = \frac{1}{L}\left(\sum_{l=1}^{L} P_{irn|\beta_l}\right) . \qquad (49)$$

Such methods of integral evaluation are broadly classified under the "Monte Carlo" simulation rubric. The most popular method for controlling the sampling process is due to Bhat (2001, 2003) and depends on quasi-random Halton sequences rather than on pseudo-random number (or Monte Carlo) sequences. Very significant convergence and computational advantages accrue to the use of the quasi-random methods over straight Monte Carlo methods. Bhat (2001) shows that reliable taste distribution parameter estimates can be obtained via Halton-based methods with as little as 100 draws, compared to an order of magnitude more draws for the pseudo-Monte Carlo methods. This advantage grows as integral dimensionality increases.

For the reader interested in the technicalities of simulation estimation, I recommend Train (2003). For our purposes here, suffice it to say that the estimation of these models is today quite practical and feasible.

Though we have shown the development of the Mixed MNL model, it is possible to straightforwardly derive equivalent versions for different kernel models: for example, the MNP, or one of the many other GEV models we've analyzed or mentioned earlier on. However, it is my belief that the Mixed MNL model is sufficiently flexible for most practical applications. In addition, note that the MVN distributional assumption made to arrive at (47) is relatively arbitrary. The literature has gone on to employ a number of other distributions (e.g., log normal, uniform, triangular, gamma) that seem more plausible in certain applications or for certain variables (e.g., price). Such extensions usually require that the distributions be assumed independent across attributes; however, it should be noted that most applications using the MVN have made the equivalent assumption of a diagonal Ω matrix anyway.

McFadden and Train (2000) established an important result for the Canonical Mixed MNL model (see Theorem 1, McFadden and Train, 2000): by the inclusion of appropriately defined variables in the utility functions, and association of stochastic mixing distributions with these variables, the Mixed MNL model can closely approximate a broad class of random utility models. The intuition for this is best explained by example: suppose that in a four-alternative problem it is desired to "nest" alternatives (1,2) and (3,4) (i.e., a two-level tree with two nests). One could do this by an appropriately defined nested MNL or TEV model, or one could use the Mixed MNL in the following manner:

1. Define dummy variables $Z_{irn}^1 = 1$ if $i=1,2$, $=0$ otherwise, and $Z_{irn}^2 = 1$ if $i=3,4$, $=0$ otherwise;

2. Include Z_{irn}^1 and Z_{irn}^2 in all utility functions, with associated parameter ψ_n^1 and ψ_n^2.

3. Associate with parameters ψ_n^1 and ψ_n^2 some suitable distributional assumptions (e.g., independent normals with means $\overline{\psi}^1$ and $\overline{\psi}^2$, and variance $\sigma_{\psi 1}^2$ and $\sigma_{\psi 2}^2$, respectively).

Then it should be clear that alternatives 1 and 2 will share a stochastic component ($\psi_n^1 Z_{irn}^1$) that is unavailable to the other two alternatives (since $Z_{irn}^1 = 0$

for them); conversely, the component ($\psi_n^2 Z_{irn}^2$) will be shared by alternatives 3 and 4, but not by the other two alternatives. These two variables will essentially induce a correlation within the pair (1,2) and another within the pair (3,4), respectively, leading to behavior very similar to a nested MNL or TEV model. It should also be noted that correlations between alternatives in a Mixed MNL model will also occur whenever a parameter is used in multiple alternatives. For example, a generic price parameter that's assumed to be stochastic will induce a correlation between all alternatives that share the same parameter.

We can clearly say that the Canonical Mixed MNL represents a tremendous advance in choice modeling capabilities. Its flexibility for describing complex behavior patterns, as seen above, as well as its relative ease of computation compared to MNP models, have made this model highly popular. The estimation technology required is perhaps a bit more esoteric than needed in simpler models, but rest assured that at this point the application of these models is quite straightforward to perform. The reader is also directed to the presentation of this model in Train (1999).

It is unfortunate, however, that the literature has not been very clear about the increased potential for confounding that exists in the Mixed MNL model between tastes (stochastic term τ_n) and stochastic utility (ε_{irn}). Specifically, let's return to expression (44), multiply through by the scale μ (making all the stochastic utility variates Gumbel distributed with unit scale) and calculate the variance of total utility (τ_n and ε_{irn} are assumed independent, as before):

$$
\begin{aligned}
Var(\mu U_{irn}) &= Var\left[\mu(\bar{\beta}'X_{irn} + \tau_n'X_{irn} + \varepsilon_{irn})\right] = Var(\mu\tau_n'X_{irn}) + Var(\mu\varepsilon_{irn}) \\
&= \mu^2 Var(\tau_n'X_{irn}) + \mu^2 Var(\varepsilon_{irn}) = \mu^2[X_{irn}'\Omega X_{irn}] + \mu^2(\pi^2/6\mu^2) \\
&= X_{irn}'\left[\mu^2\Omega\right]X_{irn} + \pi^2/6
\end{aligned}
$$

$$(50)$$

Two observations about the Mixed MNL can be made from this expression: (1) the model is inherently heteroscedastic, as seen by the alternative-specific variation introduced in the first term on the RHS of (50); and (2) it has the interesting property that the estimates of the covariance matrix of taste distributions are multiplied by the square of the Gumbel scale factor. Since the scale will be unknown in any given data set, the estimates of the taste covariance matrix elements that will be printed by any program are actually $\mu^2\omega_{lk}$, where ω_{lk} is the element in the lth row and k^{th} column of Ω. In turn, this means that we are recuperating the parameter distributions only up to scale μ, and we can only estimate the taste variances and covariances under the assumption of unit scale (i.e., the Canonical Mixed MNL). While prediction is unaffected by this property of the model, this result is, at another level, quite disturbing: it points at the impossibility of ever knowing taste distribution parameters!

This confound between taste distribution parameters and Gumbel scale in the

Mixed MNL model has been the subject of several comments by Louviere (2004) to a wide audience of health economists. Unfortunately, the literature seems still oblivious to this insight; I believe we continue to ignore it at our peril.

A straightforward extension of the previous derivation can lead to a Mixed MNL that has as its kernel the Heteroscedastic MNL model (expression 10). Term this the Heteroscedastic Mixed MNL model:

$$P_{irn} = \int_{\tau} \left(\frac{\exp(\mu_{irn} V_{irn|\beta_n})}{\sum_{j \in C_{rn}} \exp(\mu_{jrn} V_{jrn|\beta_n})} \right) \varphi_K(\tau \mid 0, \Omega) d\tau \quad . \tag{51}$$

Why generalize the Mixed MNL even further, given the potential for confound that we have just been discussing? Actually, this is one of those few cases where I think complicating things somewhat may actually be helpful. One way of circumventing the confound between tastes and scales is to add exogenous information about one or the other to the problem information to enable us to tease the two constructs apart. Suppose, for example, that we can formulate a scale factor model such as (7) that incorporates exogenous information vector Z_{irn}. That would enable one to identify scale factors, thus enabling identification of the taste distribution parameters.

I strongly recommend that this more general form of the Mixed MNL model be employed in situations where knowledge of parameter distributions are *per se* of substantive interest. Removal or reduction of the confound between tastes and scale can be achieved through the use of exogenous information, allowing improved estimation of taste heterogeneity distributions. Walker (2002) is an important reference for those working with the Mixed MNL model. She deals in some detail with the identification of parameters in the case of the Canonical Mixed MNL. While the reader is directed to that reference for further details, I wish to highlight one important message from Walker's work, specifically concerning the possibility of estimating a large number of random parameters from any given dataset. Very large data sets (as in many thousands of respondents in the case of RP data, plus significant replications of within-subject choice observations in the case of SP data) and strict adherence to identification restrictions are required to reliably estimate many random parameters. Thus, I strongly recommend that analysts should err on the side of parsimony when specifying random parameter models. This may seem like simple good sense, but it has been common to see Mixed MNL models with many (if not all attributes) with random parameters, estimated on some few hundreds of choices. In hindsight, this may be something of a stretch.

The Mixed MNL and its variants presented in this section can be estimated based on one or more choice observations per subject. If the replications are independent within a subject, then the joint probability of observing the R choices $\{ i_r^*, r=1,...,R \}$ is given by:

$$P_n = \prod_{r=1}^{R} P_{i_r^* n} , \qquad (52)$$

where $P_{i_r^* n}$ is given by either (48) or (51), or other Mixed models that were mentioned in the course of the discussion.

3.3. Continuous or Discrete Support?

In Sections 3.1 and 3.2, I have presented choice models that capture taste heterogeneity using discrete versus continuous support representations. In applying and comparing the two types of models discussed above, the question of which is the "better" representation always seems to arise. Andrews, Ainslie and Currim (2002) tackled this question head-on using an extensive simulation study mimicking household panel data (basically, panel revealed preference choices). They concluded that when choice data are dense (i.e., there's plenty of data), both latent class and Mixed MNL models perform equally well in terms of parameter recovery, fit and forecasting accuracy; however, the less data there are, the poorer the relative performance of the continuous support (Mixed MNL) versus discrete support (latent class) models. This is a very plausible result since the sparser data makes it more difficult to support complex parametric forms imposed by continuous support models.

Prior knowledge about the decision domain may lead one to opt for one or the other representation. For example, prior research might have identified that the population is actually made up of two price reaction groups, a low- and a high-price sensitivity segment (or equivalently, that it is at that level that marketing activity is to occur). It might be far more appropriate to represent this problem through a two-class latent class model rather than through some ill-fitting single-mode density function. Multi-modality of tastes is, then, one good reason to use latent classes. In rare instances, it may be that theory actually points to the existence of segments, and even the number of them. Wood and Swait (2002), for example, predict the existence of four segments in a population making decisions about bundles of telecommunications services. The segments are based on the existence of innovation-adoption groups, defined by two psychological constructs called Need for Cognition and Need for Change. The latent class MNL model presented in Section 3.1 was used to confirm the existence of these segments, as well as to "size" them in the particular application. However, it will not be often that researchers have access to such clear-cut theory to support the choice between discrete versus continuous heterogeneity representations.

Most applications of the Mixed MNL model apply the strong restriction that the covariance matrix of the parameters is diagonal (i.e., taste parameters are uncorrelated), a questionable assumption at best (though highly convenient from a computational perspective, explaining its pervasiveness in the literature). Provencher and Moore (2005) argue that the analyst's assessment of the degree of correlation between taste parameters should guide the selection of continuous versus discrete support models: the more plausible the assumption that the diagonal covariance matrix applies, the more recommendable it is to use the Mixed MNL with diagonal covariance matrix; the less plausible that assumption, the more recommendable the use of a discrete support model, which essentially allows for highly collinear tastes within the classes.

In my opinion, an interesting extension to the models in this section would be to combine them. That is, each of S distinct classes will have its own tastes, which will differ not only in mean but also in distribution. A classification model, such as (39), completes the specification. This will permit capturing multi-modal taste distributions, while still allowing for within-segment variation. This direction implies greater complexity; of course, it behooves one to counterweight this suggestion with the observation that greater model complexity does not necessarily imply better predictive capability or behavioral realism. For example, Provencher and Bishop (2004) found in their application that by some measures, the simple MNL model outperformed several latent class and Mixed MNL models in out-of-sample predictive ability. Nonetheless, I believe the effort may be sufficiently interesting to warrant further investigation.

4. SPECIAL TOPICS

Before we discuss estimation-related issues in Section 5, I would like to close the presentation of advanced choice models by briefly discussing two topics that have not yet received full attention in the choice modeling literature, but certainly are deserving of it: choice set formation and heuristics in decision-making.

4.1. Choice Set Formation

Every single model we have thus far considered has assumed that the choice set C_n containing the alternatives actually available for choice by person n is known with certainty. In fact, empirical choice modeling work commonly assumes that $C_n=M$, where M is the universal set of alternatives in the market (e.g., all parks in a region, all beaches in South Florida).[8] From a cognitive perspective, however, it is highly unlikely that this assumption holds in most empirical settings: it simply seems to require too much memory and processing effort on the part of decision makers to hold true. Occasional effort has been made to recognize these limitations and impose some *a priori* structure on choice sets. For example, in a beach destination choice study, one might limit the choice set to beaches within a two-hour drive from a subject's residence. Swait (1984) called this kind of *a priori* rule-based process *deterministic choice set formation*. To the extent that these rules capture true choice set formation, estimates of utility function parameters are sharpened due to the exclusion of irrelevant alternatives.

Many researchers in the field believe that the presence of "excess" alternatives in the choice set C_n is relatively harmless, and that any ill-effects are concentrated in alternative-specific constants. They also believe that bias will essentially be limited to these constants. These beliefs are fundamentally wrong: Swait and Ben-Akiva

(1986) show that mis-specifying choice set formation can introduce serious bias in utility parameters, and the bias is not limited to alternative-specific constants. Specifically, Swait and Ben-Akiva demonstrate mathematically for a particular binary choice scenario that, in the presence of captivity (i.e., the inability to choose any other alternative) to one of two alternatives, the following occurs: (1) the alternative-specific constant of the alternative with captivity is biased upwards, as expected; (2) but, in addition, the sensitivity to exogenous variables in the utility function is *decreased* due to ignoring captivity. Thus, generalizing their result, erroneous choice set formation will bias the entire utility function!

One way around this problem, of course, is to make choice set formation itself part of the model definition. Manski (1977) proposed this two-stage model of choice and choice set formation:

$$P_{irn} = \sum_{C \subseteq \Delta(M)} P_{irn|C} Q_C ,$$
(53)

where $P_{irn|C}$ is the conditional probability of choice given set $C \subseteq M$, $\Delta(M)$ is the set of all subsets of M (excluding the empty set), and Q_C is the probability that C is the true choice set (i.e., this is the latent choice set formation model). This model, while completely general, suffers from a "curse of dimensionality": the number of choice sets in $\Delta(M)$ is $2^{|M|}-1$. Thus, for 5 alternatives, there are 31 choice sets; for 10 alternatives, 1,023 choice sets; for 20 alternatives, 1,048,575 choice sets. Clearly, even with today's advanced number-crunching capabilities, such formulations are impractical for applications in which the number of alternatives is large, even with the use of deterministic choice set formation rules.

What is apparent today was even more so two decades ago, so Swait (1984) (see also Swait and Ben-Akiva, 1987a) considered a number of models imposing *a priori* limitations on the structure of $\Delta(M)$. For example, one might impose the limitation that only choice sets of size L or smaller are included in $\Delta(M)$. Another plausible restriction in some contexts might limit $\Delta(M)$ to captivity or full choice set, as in the Parameterized Captivity MNL model of Swait and Ben-Akiva (1987b).

Another approach to simplifying application of (53) is to assume that the choice set formation process is characterized by the independent availability of alternatives (Swait, 1984, Swait and Ben-Akiva, 1987a, Ben-Akiva and Boccara, 1995). While this does not decrease the number of sets in $\Delta(M)$, it does reduce significantly the number of parameters needed to describe the choice set formation process.

In an interesting development that links choice set formation to the GEV class of choice models, Swait (2001a) presents a variant of the MNL model he termed the GenL (choice set Generation Logit) model. Most GEV models, and certainly the ones we've presented in this chapter, view the choice set as fixed and concentrate on elaborating upon other constructs. For example, the Nested MNL and TEV models both introduce the distinction between elemental (or real) alternatives and construct (or nested) alternatives. These construct alternatives then become the basis for specifying correlations between alternatives. In the GenL model, Swait (2001a) defines the choice set as the latent construct of interest, and uses it as the basis for formulating the GEV density function. The GenL model suffers from the same "curse of dimensionality" we've been discussing here, but Swait (2001a) suggests several simplifications to $\Delta(M)$ that can make the model's application feasible in certain choice contexts. In addition, since the model belongs to the GEV family, it is possible to test whether behavior is consistent with utility maximization.

A very different approach to choice set formation is taken by von Haefen (2003), who proposes a theoretically consistent continuous demand system that incorporates probabilistic latent choice sets. Using Kuhn-Tucker demand model systems, von Haefen proposes an approach that has the great advantage of handling large numbers of alternatives. The "curse of dimensionality" that plagues current approaches is quite neatly circumvented by the proposed model system.

Choice set formation is clearly a difficult and challenging aspect of choice modeling, and it has yet to be satisfactorily addressed at either the research or application level. The point I wish to make and emphasize here is the need for the analyst to actively and seriously consider how choice set formation should be addressed in a given application. This is not a trivial matter, and therefore should not be left ignored in some dark corner of the choice analyst's mind. It has serious implications for modeling and policy analysis. For example, if a sub-population is captive to a given mode (say, auto drive) in its decision on how to commute from home to work, no amount of attribute change will induce a change in behavior. However, a model ignoring this aspect of choice set formation would overstate switching from auto drive to transit due to improvements in the transit system or additional costs imposed on the auto drive mode. Predicting switching when there will be none would be deleterious to the policy analysis and implementation process.

4.2. Heuristics in Decision Making

The topic we've just finished, choice set formation, is actually a special case of the application of "heuristics" in decision making. That is, individuals may simplify a complex decision problem by dividing it into two stages: (1) a quick, "cheap" triage of the larger set of alternatives to form a subset of alternatives (i.e., the choice set), (2) which are then studied in greater detail to arrive at the final choice.

The fully rational, fully informed, utility-maximizing decision maker of microeconomic fame has been profitably employed in economic analysis for a very long time. However, for just about as long other disciplines dealing with human decision making (principally psychology), and more recently, even economics, have pointed out that the type of behavior assumed in that framework is only one of many decision rules actually used by people (see, e.g., Bettman et al., 1991, Payne et al., 1993, Hensher, this volume). Psychological and consumer behavior research supports the view that decision makers are information processors with limited capabilities and resources, trying to make the best possible decisions within operational constraints (e.g., Ford et al., 1989).

As implemented in this chapter, the choice models that have been presented reflect the traditional economic paradigm of full rationality, full information and fully optimizing decision makers. In certain decision contexts these assumptions may be more or less plausible than in others, so it behooves analysts to give this matter some thought. What to do, however, if one concludes that this view of decision makers is unlikely to hold in some empirical context?

Despite the inherent difficulty of attempting to formulate models that are sufficiently flexible to capture a wide range of decision rules, I believe it is possible to take constructive steps in the right direction.

As discussed in the previous section, the analyst's attention can first be usefully directed at the issue of choice set formation. The application of deterministic choice set formation rules are a must, in my opinion, and this process can be driven by decision-maker characteristics. For example, Swait (2001b) considers the use of "cutoffs" elicited from respondents to model constraints directly in the utility function of alternatives, mimicking, if you will, the effect of choice set formation. If an alternative has a price p_i and the respondent has a maximum price constraint of τ (say, smaller than p_i), then the utility of alternative i will be penalized by the degree to which the constraint is violated. Where possible, and dimensionality considerations permit, the analyst can also formulate structural models of choice set formation based on expression (53).

Another window for the incorporation of "heuristics" into choice modeling is through the scale factor and the Heteroscedastic MNL model. Swait and Adamowicz (2001) propose that decision makers have a cognitive budget allocated to a decision problem. Complexity is assumed to demand greater effort on the part of consumers, so it is expected that variance (scale) will be increasing (decreasing) as complexity increases (decreases). For choice sets with dominant or nearly dominant alternatives, variance should be low. If tradeoffs must be made, or if the number of attributes or alternatives increases (i.e., complexity is greater), variance should again increase. As alternatives become more similar, however, there comes a point where the true utilities lie on nearly the same isoquant; the decision maker's perceptions of them will also converge to their being nearly identical. In these seemingly very complex cases, the increased variance arising from increased complexity will be offset by the fact that the utilities are all actually similar, thereby lowering the utility error variance. Thus, Swait and Adamowicz (2001) argue that at some point further increases in complexity will actually result in lower error variances. Based on this reasoning, they postulated the following quadratic function for scale:

$$\mu_n = \exp(\theta_1 H_n + \theta_2 H_n^2), \tag{54}$$

where H_n is a measure of the complexity of the decision of choosing an alternative from set C_n (specifically, the entropy of the choice set). Their empirical work, applying (54) in the Heteroscedastic MNL model, confirmed their hypothesis that $\theta_1 \leq 0$ and $\theta_2 \geq 0$.

Another useful concept from heuristic decision making that can be incorporated in choice models are the (combined) ideas of reference dependence and loss aversion (Tversky and Kahneman, 1991). These researchers postulated that reaction to an attribute level depends upon its relationship to some reference level, rather than to its absolute level. For example, the impact of distance in a fishing site choice situation is not that of absolute distance, but the distance savings or extra distance to the site compared to some reference site (e.g., most visited site, favorite site, an "ideal" site). In addition, Tversky and Kahneman (1991) suggest that losses loom larger than gains to decision makers; that is to say, the extra distance to fishing site *i* over that to the reference site will be more onerous (in absolute value) than the benefit accrued from the distance savings to fishing site *j*. Figure 4 illustrates both the reference dependence and the loss aversion ideas from Tversky and Kahneman (1991), for an attribute with positive utility (e.g., a quality attribute). It also shows a final aspect of their proposal: diminishing marginal impacts of both gains and losses.

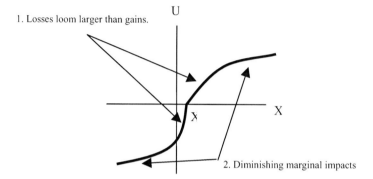

FIGURE 4. *Reference Dependence and Loss Aversion*

A final means of incorporating decision heuristics in choice models can be through latent class models. This is particularly useful when we consider heuristics that are attribute-based, because we can define classes that use only subsets of information. For example, suppose that we know there exists a group of fishermen who consider only distance and catch rate when making site decisions, whereas the remainder of the population of interest uses distance, yield and other quality attributes. We can then estimate a latent class model with two groups: Group 1's utility function will permit only distance and yield to have nonzero parameters, basically deleting other quality attributes from the estimation; Group 2's utility function will permit all three attributes (distance, catch rate, quality) to influence utility. While at first this approach seems infeasible simply because of the impracticality of enumerating all possible classes (a problem with dimensionality comparable to that of choice set formation), qualitative research may be quite helpful in indicating which decision protocols are most likely to exist in a given decision problem.

This section has tried to illustrate that it is possible to introduce into choice models many of the insights from psychology and consumer research, helping us relax some of the stronger assumptions built into the models concerning human decision-making. I have shown that basically all components of the choice model can be involved in this effort: the choice set, decision rule, utility function – both systematic and stochastic --and taste heterogeneity. This is a most fruitful area for future research.

5. PARAMETER ESTIMATION

In this section we will succinctly specify the (log) likelihood functions needed to implement estimation of the models in this chapter. Certainly other estimation methods exist (e.g., method of moments), but we leave that topic to other authors and the interested reader. The knowledgeable econometrician may want to skip directly to the material on the latent class models, but others may wish to read this section as a short review of maximum likelihood estimation theory.

5.1. A Review of Maximum Likelihood Estimation Theory

To lay the groundwork, we are considering the estimation of a parameter set Θ_n (the contents of which depend upon the model in question and at least some of whose elements are specific to person n) from the following data: $R \geq 1$ replications or choice scenarios were shown to each of N subjects, chosen randomly from the population of interest; each subject is described through a (socio-demographic) vector Z_n; in each scenario r, a choice set C_{rn} of goods with characteristics X_{irn}, $i \in C_{rn}$, is shown to the decision maker, who proceeds to choose a single good among them, presumably according to the principle of utility maximization. The choice is indicated via the indicator variables

$$\delta_{irn} = \begin{cases} 1 & if\ i \in C_{rn}\ is\ chosen \\ 0 & otherwise \end{cases}, \tag{55}$$

for which we further require that $\Sigma_i \delta_{irn} = 1$.

In any given replication/choice scenario, the choice probability for alternative $i \in C_{rn}$ is P_{irn}, the specifics of which will depend upon the model we are estimating. The likelihood of observing i being chosen from among the goods in C_{rn} is P_{irn}; hence, the likelihood of observing the specific R replications from subject n is simply

$$l_n(X_{rn}, Z_n \mid \Theta_n)) = \prod_{r=1}^{R} \left(\prod_{i \in C_{rn}} [P_{irn}(X_{rn}, Z_n \mid \Theta_n)]^{\delta_{irn}} \right), \tag{56}$$

assuming the R replications to be independent. (I have noted before the great difficulties associated with removing this particular assumption of independence. We continue under this restriction in this section.) Assuming a random sample, the likelihood of observing the choices of all N respondents is simply the product $L_N = (l_1 \cdot l_2 \cdot l_3 \ldots \cdot l_N)$. We estimate Θ_n by maximizing this product, or more commonly, by maximizing its log, with respect to the parameter set:

$$[\max]_{\Theta_n} \log L_N = \sum_{n=1}^{N} \log l_n(X_{rn}, Z_n \mid \Theta_n). \tag{57}$$

Under the assumption that we have selected the right choice model for P_{irn} and that the parameters are in the interior of the parameter space, the maximum likelihood estimator of Θ_n is known to have desirable properties: it is asymptotically consistent, unbiased and efficient. Empirically, the precision of estimates is evaluated and inferences are made through the empirical covariance matrix of the estimates, computed this way:

$$\hat{\Omega}_{ML} = -E\left[\frac{\partial^2 \log L_N}{\partial \Theta \partial \Theta'}\right]^{-1}. \tag{58}$$

Because this estimate of the covariance matrix depends critically on the assumption that there is no model mis-specification, one often sees researchers using White's (1982) robust alternative (also sometimes called the quasi-maximum likelihood – QML – covariance estimate):

$$\hat{\Omega}_W = \hat{\Omega}_{ML}\left(E\left[\frac{\partial \log L_N}{\partial \Theta'}\right]E\left[\frac{\partial \log L_N}{\partial \Theta}\right]\right)\hat{\Omega}_{ML}. \tag{59}$$

It is good practice to make this extra effort, something made easier by certain estimation software than others (e.g., Gauss MAXLIK routines default to outputting $\hat{\Omega}_{ML}$, but can compute $\hat{\Omega}_W$ as an option).

Individual parameter tests for a null hypothesis H_0: $\theta_k = v$, for some constant v, can be accomplished using asymptotic t-statistics t_k^*, formed as the usual ratios

$$t_k^* = \frac{\hat{\theta}_k - v}{\Omega_{kk}^{1/2}}. \tag{60}$$

These are asymptotically normally distributed. This test is most often used to explore whether $v=0$.

The most common omnibus test employed with ML estimators is the likelihood ratio test. When imposing M restrictions on a model form, the quantity

$$-2(\log L_M^* - \log L^*) \tag{61}$$

is chi-squared distributed with M degrees of freedom, where $\log L^*$ is the log likelihood at convergence for the unrestricted model and $\log L_M^*$ is the corresponding value for the restricted model. This omnibus test is most often used to test whether a group of parameters should simultaneously be deleted from the specification.

If the parameter set does *not* vary by individual, i.e., parameters are aggregate across the population, then the log likelihood function simplifies to this expression:

$$\log L_N = \sum_{n=1}^{N}\sum_{r=1}^{R}\sum_{i \in C_{rn}} \delta_{irn} \log P_{irn}(X_{rn}, Z_n \mid \Theta) = \sum_{n=1}^{N}\sum_{r=1}^{R} \delta_{i_{rn}^* rn} \log P_{i_{rn}^* rn}(X_{rn}, Z_n \mid \Theta),$$

(62)

where i_{rn}^* is the index of the chosen alternative in the rth replication of the nth subject. This is the usual expression used to estimate MNL, Nested MNL and other aggregate choice models. All the choice models in Sections 2 and 3 are generally estimated using this expression.[10,11]

An important (and often unstated) assumption of maximum likelihood estimation theory is that the validity of the entire framework depends upon achieving the *global* optimum of function (62). Numerical optimization algorithms applied to the ML estimation problem guarantee only that a stationary point will be achieved; it is up to the analyst to confirm that the point is indeed the global optimum. It was mentioned earlier that the log likelihood function for a simple MNL model is globally concave (Ben-Akiva and Lerman, 1985, pp. 118-119); this guarantees that the stationary point achieved by an optimization algorithm is indeed the ML estimator. With any other model in this chapter, we do not have this assurance. This means that it is up to the analyst to convince him/herself that he/she has achieved global optimality with a given solution. This is commonly done by using a large number of random starting points (e.g., tens of them) and observing final convergence. While this process is not fail-safe, it certainly increases the face validity of global optimality claims. In my opinion, while this is generally good practice, the need for this kind of checking increases with model complexity and sophistication.

When we're dealing with latent class and/or Mixed MNL models, where the parameter set is defined at the individual decision maker level, the log likelihood function does not simplify quite so much as (62). Note that in (62) the summations over subjects and replications are completely interchangeable; this is simply the result of the assumption of independence across replications and the fact that the parameter set is aggregate. With individual-specific parameters, however, the respondent-unit in the log likelihood function must preserve the knowledge that each set of R replications has its own unique parameter values. In the case of the Canonical Mixed MNL model, we utilize expressions (52) and (48) within log likelihood (57) to obtain parameter estimates (expression 48 is actually approximated by 49 when a simulator estimator is used). With latent class models, for a given number of classes S, we utilize (42), (39) and (36) in (57) to estimate parameters.

5.2. Estimation of the Number of Classes in Latent Class Models

Maximum likelihood estimation theory requires that the parameter space be continuous and estimates be in the interior of the space (away from any constraints, which make difficult the evaluation of parameter accuracy). Latent class models present a problem in this situation because parameter S (number of classes) is discrete. What to do? Basically, for a given S, there's no problem using maximum likelihood estimation and inference theory. So, the issue at hand centers around how to estimate S itself.

TABLE 1. *Measures for Selecting Number of Classes in Latent Class Models*

Measure	Definition
AIC: Akaike Information Criterion	$= -2(\log L_s^* - K_s)$
$\overline{\rho}_s^2$: Akaike's ρ^2	$= 1 - \dfrac{AIC_s}{2 \cdot \log L_0}$, where $\log L_0$ is the log likelihood of the sample with equal choice probabilities
AIC3: Bozdogan Akaike Information Criterion	$= -2\log L_s^* + 3K_s$
BIC: Bayesian Information Criterion	$= -\log L_s^* + (K_s \cdot \log N)/2$
Negentropy	$= 1 - \dfrac{\sum\limits_{n=1}^{N}\sum\limits_{l=1}^{S}\left[-W_{nl}\ln W_{nl}\right]}{N\ln(S)}$ where W_{nl} is the classification probability of person n for class l.

The literature has recommended the use of multiple information criteria for selection of S, much in the spirit of comparing nonnested models. These measures employ the log likelihood at convergence ($\log L_s^*$) with s classes, sample size (N) and number of parameters in Θ_s (K_s) to inform selection of S. The most commonly used measures and their definitions are given in Table 1 (see also Andrews and Currim, 2003, Ramaswamy et al., 1993). The first four measures address goodness-of-fit of a model with S classes, and are defined so that bigger is better. Each of the measures penalizes models with more parameters, thus promoting parsimony; in the case of BIC (Bayesian Information Criterion), this parameter penalty increases with sample size. The last measure, Negentropy (Ramaswamy et al., 1993), which varies between 0 and 1, has a different objective: it expresses how well-differentiated is the class membership component compared to random assignment of individuals to the classes. If the model's assignment mechanism is indistinguishable from random assignment, the W's will be equal to S^{-1} and Negentropy will therefore be zero; if the classes are well-distinguished (so that the W's are quite different one from the other), then Negentropy will be nearer to one. If the model achieves perfect classification (i.e., one W is unity, and all other W's are zero), then Negentropy will be exactly one.

The customary procedure for selecting S is to estimate models with 2, 3, 4, ... classes, with some top limit that seems reasonable for the number of individuals in the sample. In my experience, model quality begins to deteriorate abruptly when this reasonable number is passed, with models evidencing many extreme values (parameters tending towards $\pm\infty$) and very large standard errors (indicating identification difficulties); thus, this process of estimating S has a built-in safeguard of sorts. The researcher constructs a table of the measures above, and uses their convergent validity plus common sense to select the final S. After these more quantitative criteria have been employed, it is recommended that the researcher study the specific parameter solutions around the selected S. This closer examination may lead the researcher to increase or decrease the number of classes (usually the latter) used once the evaluation of neighboring solutions shows that a class seems somehow "unstable", or even that it is useful to break out a class into two subgroups. Common sense will play a significant role in this process: the researcher may wish to place more weight on non-statistical criteria than on the statistical ones. The interested reader may see an example application of this estimation procedure in Hu et al. (2004), and is directed to Andrews and Currim (2003) for a more detailed discussion of the technical issues surrounding estimation of S.

5.3. "Sharpening" Class Membership Probability Estimates

Once a latent class model has been estimated, the interesting question of class membership for individual subjects arises. Researchers often desire to "profile", or describe, the members of each (supposedly) homogenous-with-respect-to-taste segment. Latent class models, however, classify individuals probabilistically via the W's; this is conceptually confusing for non-technical types, so some effort should be expended in creating a bridge between the probabilistic classification of the statistical model and the deterministic classification desired for downstream applications.

One such bridge is simply to classify each individual uniquely into the class with highest estimated membership probability. If the estimated classification probabilities are sharp, or well discriminated, this is quite an acceptable procedure. However, practice shows that in most applications we are usually far from being so fortunate ...

An alternative to this "highest class" rule is to apply Bayes' Theorem in a creative way. Note that once the latent class model parameters are estimated, we can calculate estimates of the probability of each person's observed sequence of R (assumed independent) choices, given their membership in class s, $s=1,...,S$:

$$\hat{q}_{n|s} = \prod_{r=1}^{R} \hat{P}_{i_{rn}^{*}n|s} ,$$ (63)

where all quantities have been previously defined. The RHS of (63) basically conditions the likelihood of the observed sequence on the estimated coefficients. Via Bayes' Theorem, then, we can calculate posterior class membership probabilities like this:

$$\hat{Q}_{ns} = \frac{\hat{W}_{ns}\hat{q}_{n|s}}{\sum_{l=1}^{S}\hat{W}_{nl}\hat{q}_{n|l}} , s = 1,...,S.$$ (64)

This last expression essentially reweights the prior class membership probabilities (W's) in such a way that the posterior class membership probabilities increase for those classes that better predict the observed sequence of choices, and decrease for those that predict the sequence poorly. (A little algebra will reassure curious souls that $\sum_{s}\hat{Q}_{ns} = 1$.)

In practical experience, these posterior membership probabilities tend to be much better differentiated than the corresponding prior membership distribution. One can then use these posterior probabilities to assign individuals to classes, using, for example, the "highest class" rule. A shortcoming of this particular expression is that it does not recognize that the W's and q's are estimates subject to sampling error. One can elaborate upon (64) and make it subject to this source of uncertainty (e.g., by simulating draws from the parameter distributions estimated by maximum likelihood, and thereby building up a distribution for the Q's), but my guess is that the improvement may be marginal compared to the impact of estimating (64) in the first place.

5.4. Individual Parameter Values

Following estimation of either a latent class or a Mixed MNL model, it is possible to use the estimated class-specific parameter estimates or continuous multivariate representation of tastes to calculate point estimates of tastes for each individual in the sample. Because of marketing's partial roots in psychology, the attraction of having these individual-level parameter estimates runs strong in the veins of that discipline: the belief that individuals are essentially unique and idiosyncratic underlies this attraction. There is a long history of traditional conjoint applications in marketing, where the emphasis is on directly estimating individual parameter sets from ratings and simple tradeoff tasks. Obtaining individual-level parameters from a latent class or continuous support model is, therefore, a desirable end state for many marketers. Economics has tended to take a more aggregate approach, consistent with its orientation toward aggregate demand predictions; nonetheless, the ability to consistently estimate individual-level parameters from an aggregate taste heterogeneity distribution has become attractive to some economists (e.g., Revelt and Train, 1999).

Using exactly the same reasoning as employed in the last section concerning class membership probabilities, it is possible to use Bayes' Theorem to obtain individual parameter estimates from the taste heterogeneity distribution resulting from a latent class or Mixed MNL model. Let us address these two model forms in turn.

Suppose we have a latent class model with S segments and estimated taste vectors $\hat{\beta}_1$, ..., $\hat{\beta}_S$. Conditioning the likelihood of the observed choice sequence for individual n, we obtain the $\hat{q}_{n|s}$'s using expression (63). The conditional posterior taste parameter estimate $\tilde{\beta}_n$ for individual n is then given by (Revelt and Train, 1999, Kamakura and Wedel, 2004)

$$\tilde{\beta}_n = \frac{\sum_{s=1}^{S} \hat{\beta}_s \hat{q}_{n|s}}{\sum_{s=1}^{S} \hat{q}_{n|s}}. \tag{65}$$

Intuitively, this individual taste parameter estimate will favor those classes which yield higher sequence probabilities for the specific decision maker. Each individual's tastes are essentially a convex combination of the "archetypal" tastes associated with the latent classes.

In the case of the Mixed MNL model, with its continuous representation of taste heterogeneity, one can envision an infinite number of classes being applied to equation (65), which is to say, each person becomes a class onto him(her)self. Equivalently, one has a known distribution of tastes with estimated mean $\hat{\bar{\beta}}$ and covariance matrix $\hat{\Sigma}_\beta$. Simulate a large number of draws $\hat{\beta}_1$, ..., $\hat{\beta}_T$, from this taste distribution; for each draw t, calculate the choice sequence probabilities $\hat{q}_{n|t}$; then use Bayes' Theorem to calculate a conditional posterior taste parameter estimate (Revelt and Train, 1999):

$$\tilde{\beta}_n = \frac{\sum_{t=1}^{T} \hat{\beta}_t \hat{q}_{n|t}}{\sum_{t=1}^{T} \hat{q}_{n|t}} . \qquad (66)$$

If estimation of the Mixed MNL is being done via simulation methods anyway, (66) can be easily implemented as part of the estimation code.

Both (65) and (66) ignore sampling error, but as I mentioned before in the case of class membership probabilities, extending these expressions is relatively straightforward. This is left to the reader.

6. WELFARE ANALYSIS WITH MODELS FROM THIS CHAPTER

Up to now we have said little about an important topic for economists: welfare analysis. Alberini et al. (this volume) discuss this topic in some detail for the MNL model, for which standard results exist and are well known. We shall not delve into this topic in great detail, only enough to make some specific points and direct the reader to other sources that deal with the issue in more depth.

The Heteroscedastic MNL model is perhaps the most straightforward to address. With the parametrization of scale μ_{in} using an exogenous vector Z_n of person and context characteristics, one must simply use the full expression for the inclusive value, logsum, or expected maximum utility (Ben-Akiva and Lerman, 1985, p. 301):

$$E\left[\max_{i \in C} U_{in}\right] = \frac{1}{\mu_{in}} \ln\left(\sum_{i \in C} \exp(\mu_{in} V_{in})\right) . \qquad (67)$$

For models in the Nested MNL and TEV forms, Choi and Moon (1997) provide general formulae for computing expected maximum utilities from the underlying Generalized Extreme Value random utilities. Their methods are also extensible to other members of the GEV family of choice models.

Latent class models, particularly those that have the MNL model as the conditional choice component, are straightforward to use for welfare evaluations. Simply do the before versus after calculations at the class level for each individual as if one were working with a MNL model, then weight these conditional results by class membership probabilities (you will have to decide whether to use prior or posterior membership probabilities) to arrive at an estimate of an individual's welfare impact; these can then be weighted and summed over individuals to achieve a population level welfare impact estimate.

MNP models, as well as all versions of the Mixed MNL model, present something of an additional computational burden because the expected maximum utility cannot be calculated analytically; it must instead be simulated. For the MNP model, the reader is referred to Daganzo (1979). With respect to the Mixed MNL model, estimation of the inclusive value requires simulation of the taste distribution (with or without sampling error, per the analyst's choice).

In evaluating the impact of changes in the state of the world, analysts are often also interested in the marginal rates of substitution (MRS) between money and some quality attribute, or between quality attributes. In the models considered here, the utility functions have generally been thought of as linear-in-parameters, for which these MRS's will generally be ratios of estimated parameters; however, even with these specifications, introducing nonlinear transforms of the attributes (e.g., polynomials, logarithms) may cause conceptual and practical difficulties (e.g., MRS that are a function of policy variables, or extreme values for ratios). This is particularly the case when one is dealing with Mixed MNL models. Besides the difficulties that can arise from the nonlinearities just mentioned, it has become common to see multivariate random taste specifications that include components with normal, log normal, uniform and triangular distributions, to name the most frequently used. The use of these somewhat arbitrary distributions may introduce another layer of conceptual difficulty. To exemplify, consider these two questions that might arise under such conditions: What does one do if zero (or some other very small value) has a nonzero density for the denominator of a MRS? What is the distribution of a MRS formed by the ratio of a uniform and a triangular random variable? To illustrate the difficulties that arise from the introduction of random parameters for MRS evaluation, even in the "simplest" case of independent normal variates, their ratio is known to have a Cauchy distribution (Johnson et al., 1994, p. 319); well enough, but the problem is that this distribution has neither finite mean nor variance. Thus, the reader is alerted to the need to carefully consider the specification of random taste components, not just from the behavioral perspective, but from that of forming MRS's for impact evaluation. The interested reader is directed to Meijer and Rouwendal (2005), who treat the specification of these random taste distributions in some detail from the welfare analysis perspective.

7. A CAMPSITE SELECTION APPLICATION

The previous sections have introduced an extensive toolkit of models available for analysis of discrete choice data. In this section, I will undertake a specific modeling application using a subset of the models introduced above; this exercise will help to make certain concepts more concrete to the reader, and help raise certain issues thus far left untreated because of their empirical nature. The reader should be aware, however, that this exercise is developed and presented without any pretense of making an exhaustive comparison of all the models presented beforehand. Instead, the specific models presented here have been selected because, in my opinion, they have much potential for practitioners and researchers alike, and therefore warrant more in-depth exposure.

7.1. Brief Overview of the Data Collection

The data we employ in this section originate from the Foothills Model Forest Camping Survey – Phase II, a study conducted by the Canadian Forest Service in

1997. A total of 853 respondents (or 63% of those originally recruited) returned completed Phase II surveys. These mail surveys had several components: (a) attitudes about camping; (b) a SC questions about camping site selection; (c) attitudes and opinions about forest management options; and (d) socio-demographics. The reader is directed to McFarlane et al. (2000) for a detailed description of the survey and its administration.

Our focus will be upon the campsite selection SC tasks. This experiment presented decision makers with the choice of selecting among the following options: 1) one or two Provincial Recreation Area (PRA) campgrounds; 2) two campgrounds of types known as random and user-maintained formats (format was controlled by design); 3) the Jasper National park campground; 4) the Switzer Provincial park campground; and 5) the possibility of staying home. Thus, a choice set had either six or seven alternatives, depending upon the number of PRAs in the scenario. Each respondent was randomly assigned to a block of eight such scenarios. A sample choice set, with instructions to the respondent, is shown in Figure 5. The reader will note that the elicitation involved both first and second choices; we shall use only first choice data in this section.

As evident from Figure 5, campsites were characterized by eight attributes: Facilities available, Camping Fee, Firewood availability and price, Regulations concerning off-road vehicles and horses, Fishing options available, Wildlife present, Road quality and Location. Each of the attributes had two to four levels. Facilities available was fixed for a given type of site, and so does not require a design variable. In addition, one of the PRA campgrounds was either present or absent (see above). Note that the Jasper campground attributes were simply characterized in aggregate as being at "Current levels of service." A nearly-orthogonal experimental design was developed using 96 runs; the use of pure fractional factorials would have required significantly more runs, which caused concerns about sample size adequacy. Thus, it was felt that the design adopted was a good compromise between statistical quality and sample size requirements. Further details of the design can be found in McFarlane et al. (2000).

From the battery of attitudes about camping, a Confirmatory Factor Analysis (CFA) was used to create two construct estimates we shall employ in our model estimation. The two constructs, Satisfying Camping Experience (SCE) and Camping Self-Identity (CSI), are calculated as follows:

$$SCE = 0.046*X_1 + 0.065*X_2 + 0.591*X_3 + 0.826*X_4 \qquad (68)$$

$$CSI = 0.453*X_1 + 0.637*X_2 + 0.124*X_3 + 0.174*X_4 \qquad (69)$$

Here X_k, $k=1,\ldots,4$, is a value in the range 1 ("strongly disagree") to 5 ("strongly agree"), obtained in reaction to the following statements:

X_1	When I am camping I can really be myself.
X_2	Camping says a lot about who I am.
X_3	Camping is one of the most enjoyable things I do.
X_4	Camping is one of the most satisfying things I do.

These constructs are used simply for illustrative purposes. It is not my intention to recommend them over others for this kind of campsite choice problem.

The following tables describe hypothetical situations for camping areas in this study. Imagine that you are planning a camping trip. Consider carefully the importance that you place on the various features described for each camping area and decide which option you would pick as your first choice. Indicate your choice by checking the appropriate box. Now, imagine that your first choice was not available. Indicate which option would be your second choice by checking the appropriate box. Do this for all eight tables. *Refer to the glossary sheet for feature definitions and a map of the camping areas.*

Example:

Compare the features offered for each type of camping area.

FEATURES	User Maintained	Random	Forest or Provincial Recreation Area	Forest or Provincial Recreation Area	William A. Switzer Provincial Park	Jasper National Park	Stay home
Facilities	Pit toilets, fire pits, picnic tables, not serviced	No facilites, not serviced	Pit toilets, fire pits, picnic tables, gravel tent pads, water pumps, garbage cans, serviced	Pit toilets, fire pits, picnic tables, gravel tent pads, water pumps, garbage cans, serviced	Same as Forest/Provincial areas plus flush toilets, showers, electrical hookups, dump station, educational programs, serviced		
Camping fee (per night)	None	None	$9.00	$20.00	$15.00	Current	
Fire wood	None	None	$7.00	None	None	levels	
Regulations	No OHVs, no horses	No OHVs, no horses	OHVs, no horses	OHVs, no horses	No OHVs, no horses	of service	
Fishing	Streams or rivers	Stocked lakes or ponds	No fishing	No fishing	No fishing		
Wildlife	See moose, deer, or elk	See moose, deer, or elk	No moose, deer, or elk	No moose, deer, or elk	No moose, deer, or elk		
Road quality	Improved gravel, no logging trucks	Improved gravel, no logging trucks	Paved, no logging trucks	Paved, no logging trucks	Paved, no logging trucks		
Location	Near Edson (Site A)	Near Cadomin (Site D)	Near Hinton (Site C)	Near Hinton (Site C)	Near Hinton (Site B)		
a) Which of the above camping options would you choose? *(check only one)*	☐ 1	☑ 2	☐ 3	☐ 4	☐ 5	☐ 6	☐ 7
b) If you first choice was unavailable, what would your second choice be? *(check only one)*	☐ 1	☐ 2	☐ 3	☑ 4	☐ 5	☐ 6	☐ 7

Check one box for your first choice of camping area.

Check one box for your second choice of camping area.

Please continue with the eight hypothetical scenarios shown on the following pages.

FIGURE 5*. Instructions and Choice Set Layout, Foothills Model Forest Camping Survey – Phase II*

Source: Foothills Model Forest Camping Survey – Phase II, Canadian Forest Service – Used with Permission

TABLE 2. MNL, TEV and Heteroscedastic MNL Estimation Results

Variables	MNL	TEV	Heteroscedastic MNL
		(Asymptotic t-stats)	
Alternative-Specific Constants			
Random	1.373 (19.1)	2.667 (14.5)	1.029 (3.6)
User-Maintained	1.729 (24.7)	2.752 (18.0)	1.254 (3.7)
Provincial Recreation Area	1.412 (20.3)	2.662 (14.3)	1.364 (3.7)
Switzer	1.554 (21.9)	2.705 (15.9)	1.096 (3.6)
Jasper	0.088 (1.0)	2.405 (8.4)	0.069 (0.9)
Stay Home	-0-	-0-	-0-
Distance From Home (km)	-0.25 (-11.3)	-0.087 (-2.5)	-0.187 (-3.5)
Site Attributes			
Camping Fee	-0.403 (-22.5)	-0.102 (-2.5)	-0.376 (-3.7)
Firewood			
Available	0.139 (5.5)	0.034 (2.3)	0.115 (3.1)
Price, if available	-0.226 (-13.8)	-0.056 (-2.4)	-0.185 (-3.6)
Regulations			
No ORVs, no horses	-0-	-0-	-0-
ORVs, no horses	0.014 (0.5)	0.005 (0.6)	0.023 (0.9)
Horses, no ORVs	-0.010 (-0.3)	-0.002 (-0.3)	-0.022 (-0.8)
ORVs, horses	0.206 (6.8)	0.05 (2.3)	0.172 (3.3)
Fishing			
No fishing	-0-	-0-	-0-
Streams or rivers	0.219 (8.1)	0.051 (2.4)	0.168 (3.4)
Lakes or ponds (not stocked)	-0.008 (-0.3)	0.000 (0.0)	0.000 (0.0)
Stocked lakes or ponds	0.256 (9.8)	0.060 (2.4)	0.202 (3.5)
Wildlife			
See moose, deer, or elk	0.169 (10.6)	0.042 (2.4)	0.134 (3.5)
No moose, deer, or elk	-0-	-0-	-0-
Road Quality			
Paved, no logging trucks	0.108 (3.5)	0.025 (2.0)	0.085 (2.5)
Improved gravel, no logging trucks	0.013 (0.4)	0.004 (0.5)	0.014 (0.5)
Improved gravel, logging trucks	-0.078 (-2.4)	-0.021 (-1.8)	-0.064 (-2.0)
Unimproved gravel, no logging trucks	-0-	-0-	-0-

TABLE 2. *(cont.)*

Location			
Near Edson (Site A)	-0.179 (-5.4)	-0.047 (-2.3)	-0.139 (-3.0)
Near Hinton (Site C)	0.166 (5.4)	0.041 (2.3)	0.127 (3.0)
Near Cadomin (Site D)	0.175 (5.9)	0.046 (2.3)	0.144 (3.2)
Near Grande Cache (Site E)	-0-	-0-	-0-
*Inclusive Value Coefs**			
Theta (Random)	---	0.185 (-10.6)	---
Theta (User)	---	0.206 (-9.3)	---
Theta (PRA)	---	0.245 (-7.6)	---
Theta (Switzer/Jasper)	---	0.202 (-9.5)	---
Theta (Go Camping)	---	0.256 (-7.2)	---
Ln(Scale Function)			
Random	---	---	0.130 (0.6)
User-Maintained	---	---	0.163 (0.7)
Provincial Recreation Area	---	---	-0.100 (-0.5)
Switzer	---	---	0.170 (0.8)
Jasper	---	---	-0-
Stay Home	---	---	-0-
SCE	---	---	0.032 (1.1)
CSI	---	---	-0.011 (-0.3)
LL(Convergence)	-9476.71	-9449.76	-9464.78
Akaide Rho-Squared	0.1406	0.1426	0.1411
# Parameters	22	27	28
# Choice sets	5866		
# Cases	38712		

* t-stats for inclusive value coefficients are with respect to the null hypothesis H_0: $\theta=1$. All other t-stats are with respect to the hypothesis that the parameter is equal to zero.

7.2. Model Development

7.2.1. Initial Explorations

I first present some exploratory specifications that I estimated with this data, beginning with the MNL model. It's always a good idea to start with such a simple specification because it allows us to check previous estimation data preparation steps without the complexity of convoluted model forms that might mask simple data problems. Table 2 presents this model in the first column. Note that all price variables are negative, as expected; for qualitative attributes, aggregate rankings of the attributes seem reasonable with respect to *a priori* expectations.[72,73]

The second model reported in Table 2 is a Tree Extreme Value specification, estimated to test for the possibility that IIA violations occur with this data. Figure 6 depicts the proposed nesting structure that I hypothesized might account for potential IIA violations. Specifically, it assumes that within campsite types, alternatives share correlated unobserved utility/attributes that might induce IIA violations; then, at a higher level, all campgrounds share unobserved utility that induce another layer of IIA violations with respect to the Stay Home alternative. As can be seen from Table 2, this TEV model has five inclusive value coefficients (the inverse of the scale values used in Section 2.2.2 to define these models). To be consistent with the utility maximization framework, it is necessary that these inclusive value (or θ) coefficients be decreasing as one descends the tree (remembering that the root has an implicit coefficient of unity). In this model, this condition is satisfied.

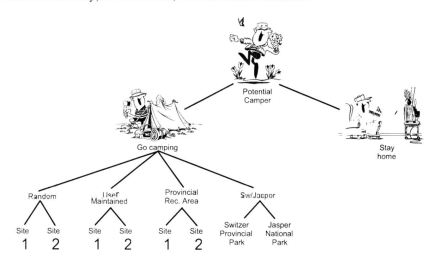

FIGURE 6. *Proposed Tree for Campsite Choice Model*

The MNL model first estimated is nested within the TEV model, so it is possible to use the chi-squared test to determine if the TEV model is warranted. Section 5.1 briefly reviewed this test. The empirical chi-squared value is $-2(-9476.71+9449.76) \approx 53.9$, with 5 degrees of freedom. The corresponding critical chi-squared value at the 95% confidence level is 11.07, so we strongly reject the IIA hypothesis imposed by the MNL model.

It is interesting to compare the utility function coefficients of these models: note that the parameters in the TEV model corresponding to the attributes (i.e., all except alternative-specific constants, or ASCs) are invariably smaller than their MNL counterparts. This is simply due to the scaling introduced by the inclusive value coefficients; if you divide the coefficients of the TEV model by about 0.25, you will obtain values of comparable magnitude to the MNL coefficients. It is also *very* instructive to plot these two sets of coefficients against each other, as in Figure 7, which contains all coefficients save the ASCs. What we see is a strong linear relationship between the two coefficient vectors, evidence of the fact that the two vectors differ by an almost constant scale factor of about 0.25. Swait and Louviere (1993) and Louviere et al. (2000, Chapter 13) should be reviewed for an interpretation of this phenomenon. For our purposes here, we note that the linear relationship implies that the marginal utilities of the attributes are essentially the same (up to scale) in both models, with one exception: in the southwest quadrant of the graph, one of the coefficients is somewhat out of pattern. This is the distance coefficient, and it seems that after accounting for IIA/scale differences, the TEV model estimates that the marginal effect of distance is greater than in the MNL model. Recognizing the impact of IIA violations, in this case, has led to a greater disutility for distance. We will be seeing more graphs such as this one, and I would urge the reader to make use of them as a practical means of comparing choice models; one shouldn't make statistical judgments on the basis of these graphs, but they will be useful in generating hypotheses and explanations about model differences.

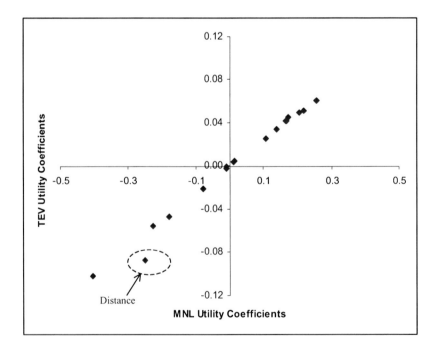

FIGURE 7. Comparison of MNL and TEV Coefficients

From the inclusive value coefficients, it is possible to estimate the degree of correlation within nests using expression (21). For example, among Random-type campsites, the estimated within-cluster correlation is $1-(.185/.256)^2 \approx 0.48$; among User-type campsites, 0.35; and so forth. These somewhat elevated correlation estimates intuitively explain why the MNL hypothesis is strongly rejected.

We will now take a somewhat different tack. The TEV model, thus far our preferred specification, assumes a homoscedastic error term, but permits correlations to exist between the pairs of alternatives within nests. As I motivated earlier in this chapter, another possible structure for the stochastic utility component is that it be heteroscedastic but allow for no correlations.

I explored this possibility via the Heteroscedastic MNL model presented in the final column of Table 2. In this specification, we elaborated on the simple heteroscedasticity hypothesis and asked whether this phenomenon might be a function of type of campsite, as well as vary by type of decision maker as measured through the constructs SCE and CSI (see expressions 68 and 69). Comparing the Heteroscedastic MNL (HMNL) to the MNL, the empirical chi-squared value is 23.86 with 6 degrees of freedom, which is larger than the 95% confidence level critical value of 12.6. Hence, we reject the hypothesis of homoscedasticity. However, note that none of the coefficients in the scale function are individually statistically significant, and the model improvement is much smaller than that generated by the TEV model. Therefore, we will drop this avenue of exploration and turn our attention elsewhere.

It is somewhat disappointing that the introduction of the two attitudinal constructs in the HMNL scale function did not generate any systematic improvements. After all, besides the individually varying distance variable, SCE and CSI were the first two decision maker characteristics used in modeling these data.

7.2.2. Exploring Taste Heterogeneity

In the first round of modeling, I purposefully kept the utility specification relatively straightforward to emphasize the basic issues of ascertaining data quality, correctness of coding, and tackling the important decisions concerning hetero- versus homoscedascity, as well as possible IIA violations. However, I did not do much in the way of introducing decision maker characteristics into the model, with the exception of the constructs included in the HMNL scale function. Note that in the HMNL model, the socio-demographics are essentially interacted multiplicatively with all the attribute parameters, potentially leading to a very flexible and responsive model; in this particular case, no significant goodness-of-fit improvement occurred.

In this section, I want to tackle the issue of taste heterogeneity, and I will do this using the latent class model presented in Section 3.1. While Mixed MNL models have become a relatively common means for capturing taste heterogeneity, I believe latent class models have great potential for practical application, particularly when class membership can be explained through socio-demographics. The model outlined in Section 3.1 permits establishing such a link, if it exists.

We continue to assume that the utility function is of the same form used in the models in Table 2. The class membership functions are based on factors given in expression (37), where we use as independent variables (i.e., the Z's in that linear model) a class-specific constant (or average) plus the two constructs SCE and CSI (expressions 68 and 69).

The first task is to determine the number of classes present in this dataset. To make this determination, I estimated models with one to five classes.[12] Table 3 presents the relevant statistics for supporting this decision, as explained in Section 5.2 and Table 1. As would be expected, the greater the number of classes S, the better the log likelihood. The other measures, however, argue for a more parsimonious specification. At first glance, it would seem that the choice is really between three and four classes, since the five-class solution presents only a small improvement with respect to the four-class solution. And between the three and four class solutions, the former seems preferable to me because it is more parsimonious while losing nothing to the latter on most measures. In many cases, in my experience, there will be a more clear-cut scenario for making the decision about number of classes: generally, after a certain number of classes, measures like AIC3 and BIC will begin to increase, creating a distinct minimum in the functions. Even then, however, the minima may differ by measure, so one may still have to make a difficult decision.

TABLE 3. *Estimation Results for Different Numbers of Latent Classes*

S	#Par	Log Lik	AIC	$\overline{\rho}^2$	AIC3	BIC	Negentropy
1	22	-9476.71	18997.42	0.1406	19019.42	9508.554	
2	47	-8581.60	17257.21	0.2193	17304.21	8738.248	0.84228
3	72	-8346.33	16836.65	0.2383	16908.65	8586.291	0.84233
4	92	-8196.86	16577.72	0.2500	16669.72	8503.479	0.82130
5	116	-8085.00	16402.00	0.2580	16518.00	8471.609	0.86457
3.1	60	-8359.23	16838.45	0.2382	16898.45	8559.196	0.84167
3.2	63	-8354.33	16834.66	0.2384	16897.66	8564.298	0.84333

Before proceeding with the development of the three-class solution, it behooves us to consider a possibility raised by Swait (1994) in the context of latent class models. The systematic utility function of any choice model generally has two major components: 1) a set of alternative-specific constants to capture the relative average attractiveness of each good, and 2) the attribute-specific contributions to the overall utility level. In a latent class model, the former component of systematic utility is essentially capturing a choice set formation effect that may differ by class. These are highly unlikely to be scalable across classes. The utility generated by the attributes, as pointed out by Swait (1994), *may* be scalable. This is an interesting possibility to pursue to simplify the model because the classes may potentially differ by choice set structure (e.g., one class may have a high average preference for staying home, compared to other classes), but may have marginal utilities that differ up to scale. In addition, Swait and Bernardino (2000) indicate that it is possible for only some of these marginal utilities to scale between segments.

How can we explore these possibilities with the present dataset? The first step is to take the attribute-specific coefficient vectors from the three-class solution and plot them one against the other, as done previously in Figure 7 for the MNL and TEV utility parameter vectors. Figure 8 shows three graphs, plotting the coefficients of each class against the other classes. In my opinion (and you're invited to disagree, since there is quite a bit of room for interpretation here), it seems that classes 2 and 3 share a large number of marginal utilities that are equal up to scale (see the straight line superimposed on the graph for this pair of vectors), whereas class 1 seems to differ substantially from the other two classes in terms of its marginal utilities.

Upon examination of these latest graphs, I tested the restriction that all Class 2 and 3 marginal utilities are equal up to scale, with the exception of Firewood Availability (but Firewood Price is restricted) and the three regulation parameters. With these restrictions, and with the necessary addition of the scale factor for the third class, we end up with a three-class solution with 60 parameters. The statistics for this model are shown in Table 3, in the row labeled "3.1" (i.e., variant 1 of the three-class model). This restricted model has measures quite comparable to those of the full three-class model. Since model 3.1 is nested within the full three-class model, we can use the chi-squared test for the restriction: the empirical value of the statistic is 25.8 with 12 degrees of freedom, so at the 95% confidence level the restriction is *just* rejected (the critical value is 21.0). A re-examination of the graphs in Figure 8 in light of this result suggests that perhaps the restriction of the three location parameters across Classes 2 and 3 may not be warranted (i.e., the utility estimates for these locations may not scale). Freeing these three parameters leads to a third three-class model denoted "3.2" in Table 3; a chi-squared test with respect to the full three-class model shows an empirical statistic of 16.0 with 9 degrees of freedom, compared to a 95% confidence level critical value of 16.9. Thus, we cannot reject the restrictions of the second restricted model at this confidence level.

This final latent class model is shown in Table 4. First we note that its goodness-of-fit is superior to that of any of the models in Table 2 by quite a bit: the Akaike rho-squared value is 0.2384, compared to 0.1426 for the TEV model, which had thus far been the preferred specification. The Akaike rho-squared measure penalizes a model for additional parameters, so we can rest assured that the improvement arising from recognizing the existence of taste heterogeneity is substantial and substantive. Three classes are represented, and membership in the classes seems unrelated to the two constructs SCE and CSI (again, a disappointment!), as evidenced by their non-significant parameters in the membership classification functions. It is estimated that the class sizes are 13.6%, 40.3% and 46.1% of the sample, respectively. (These sizes are computed by the estimation program, and cannot be inferred directly from the estimated parameter values.)

Figure 9 shows the aggregate predicted choice distribution for the different types of campsites, by latent class, and it is abundantly clear that the three classes are quite different from this perspective. For example, Class 1 has a much stronger predilection than either of the two other classes for staying at home; it also exhibits a much smaller preference for the "branded" campsites at Switzer and Jasper, particularly compared to Class 3. But that is not to say that Class 1 does not go camping: more than 75% of their choices are predicted to be for the Random, User-maintained and Provincial campgrounds.

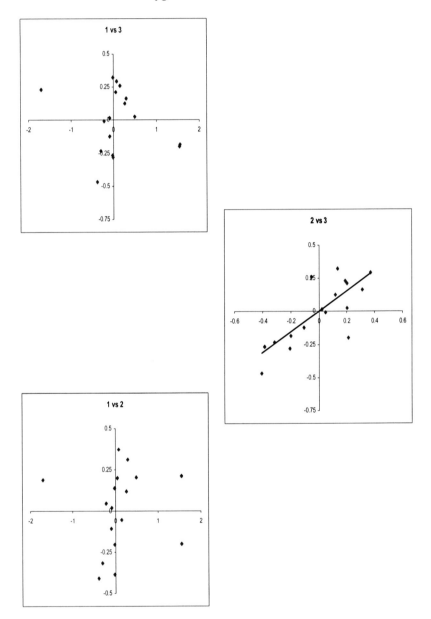

FIGURE 8. *Utility Coefficient Plots, 3-Class Solution*

TABLE 4. Latent Class Estimation Results, (3-Class)

Variables	Class 1	Class 2	Class 3
		(Asymptotic t-stats)	
Alternative-Specific Constants			
Random	-0.146, (-1.0)	2.898, (17.4)	0.667, (3.4)
User-Maintained	-0.051, (-0.3)	3.211, (18.8)	1.856, (9.5)
Provincial Recreation Area	-1.381, (-7.5)	2.281, (13.3)	2.839, (13.2)
Switzer	-2.565, (-5.8)	1.272, (6.8)	3.556, (14.7)
Jasper	-2.767, (-7.9)	-0.219, (-0.9)	1.811, (10.7)
Stay Home	-0-	-0-	-0-
Distance From Home, (km)	-0.025, (-0.6)	-0.346, (-14.0)	
Site Attributes			
Camping Fee	-0.369, (-4.9)	-0.485, (-19.9)	
Firewood			
Available	0.140, (0.9)	-0.059, (-1.1)	0.296, (6.9)
Price, if available	-0.300, (-3.4)	-0.291, (-13.0)	
Regulations			
No ORVs, no horses	-0-	-0-	-0-
ORVs, no horses	1.552, (13.9)	-0.191, (-3.6)	-0.203, (-2.9)
Horses, no ORVs	-1.680, (-7.2)	0.183, (4.2)	0.255, (3.9)
ORVs, horses	1.545, (13.6)	0.210, (4.2)	-0.211, (-2.9)
Fishing			
No fishing	-0-	-0-	-0-
Streams or rivers	0.303, (2.8)	0.264, (7.7)	
Lakes or ponds, not stocked)	-0.213, (-2.0)	0.025, (0.8)	
Stocked lakes or ponds	0.071, (0.6)	0.359, 11.6)	
Wildlife			
See moose, deer, or elk	0.043, (0.7)	0.223, (11.6)	
No moose, deer, or elk	-0-	-0-	-0-
Road Quality			
Paved, no logging trucks	0.255, (2.1)	0.126, (3.3)	
Improved gravel, no logging trucks	-0.080, (-0.7)	0.021, (0.5)	
Improved gravel, logging trucks	-0.087, (-0.7)	-0.121, (-3.1)	
Unimproved gravel, no logging trucks	-0-	-0-	

TABLE 4 (cont.)

Location			
Near Edson (Site A)	-0.024, (-0.2)	-0.179, (-3.9)	-0.338, (-4.4)
Near Hinton (Site C)	-0.011, (-0.1)	0.131, (2.8)	0.380, (5.7)
Near Cadomin (Site D)	0.497, (4.6)	0.205, (4.9)	0.040, (0.6)
Near Grande Cache (Site E)	-0-	-0-	-0-
Scales	1.0	1.0	0.857, (17.5)
Membership Classification Functions			
Constant	-2.017, (-2.2)	-1.709, (-2.6)	-0-
SCE	-0.092, (-0.5)	0.188, (1.4)	-0-
CSI	0.254, (1.2)	0.061, (0.4)	-0-
LL(Convergence)	-8354.33		
Akaide Rho-Squared	0.2384		
# Parameters	63		

However, let us remind ourselves that this class constitutes only 13.6% of the population. Class 2 is somewhat similar to Class 1 in that 90% of their choices are predicted to be for the Random, User and Provincial campgrounds, but its members are more prone to choose Switzer than to stay home. From a size perspective, however, Class 2 makes up 40.3% of the population, and is thus some 3x larger than Class 1. Finally, Class 3 (at 46.1% of the population, this class is about the same size as Class 2) tends to choose Provincial and National campgrounds, Switzer and Jasper, over the other alternatives, and chooses to stay home very infrequently.

Figure 9 and the discussion above highlight the "big picture" differences between the classes, and suggest there may be pronounced choice set formation heterogeneity between the classes. (But note again the differences in class sizes.) A detailed study of the parameters in Table 4 will also reveal marked differences in attribute valuations. For example, the impact of travel distance is the same (up to scale) in Classes 2 and 3, whereas Class 1 seems insensitive to distance variations within the range tested. Comparing price coefficients for camping fees and firewood, the classes seem to have remarkably similar price sensitivity, though Classes 2 and 3 have a somewhat marginally higher sensitivity to camping fees. Class 1 has a marked preference for sites that permit off-road vehicles, Class 2 prefers sites which has horses, while Class 3 has a strong preference for *not* having off-road vehicles present. Consistent with these preferences, Class 1 is indifferent to the presence of wildlife, whereas Classes 2 and 3 have a well-defined preference for wildlife being present around the campsites. Without being exhaustive (we leave this exercise to the reader), it is clear that the three latent classes uncovered by the model arise from substantially different tastes.

The model in Table 4, our final specification for the purposes of this exercise, would need to be refined by deletion of a number of non-significant parameters. This would be done in a straightforward fashion using appropriate statistical testing techniques. One might then continue the exercise and explore other specifications, particularly the Mixed MNL class of models. However, it seems to me that this latent class specification is quite a good model, and it has the advantage of yielding eminently plausible and interpretable segments. Its implementation in a Decision Support System (DSS) would be a great aid to those responsible for campsite design and management.

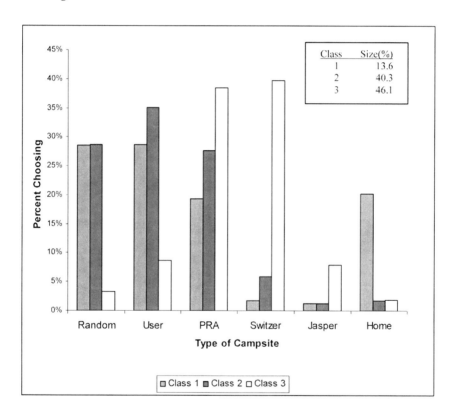

FIGURE 9. *Aggregate Predicted Choice Distribution from Choice Experiment, by Latent Class*

8. CONCLUSION

Since the 1970s, several disciplines (notably transportation, economics/econometrics, psychology and marketing) have contributed to a substantial growth in our capability to analyze and make inferences from discrete data, particularly choice data. By the beginning of the 1990s, this growth had been so substantive that in my opinion basic research in choice modeling slowed down significantly. However, with the development of faster computers and (particularly) simulation estimation methods, there has been a resurgence of interest in choice model extensions (e.g., generalizations of NMNL models), more complex model forms (e.g., new GEV models) and improved computational methods (e.g., for MNP and Mixed MNL). I believe the future of discrete choice modeling will be an exciting one, with many developments yet to come as theory is extended to allow better modeling of decision making.

9. ENDNOTES

I would like to extend my appreciation to Michael Williams, President of Advanis Inc., for his support in the development of this chapter. I would also like to thank Natural Resources Canada, Canadian Forest Service, Northern Forestry Centre, for the use of the data employed in the empirical section of the chapter; I particularly thank Bonnie McFarlane, who was invaluable in helping me obtain access to the data set. I also thank the Editor and Vic Adamowicz for their reading and rereading of the chapter, through which they contributed tremendously to its improvement. Notwithstanding this help, any errors, omissions, etc., are solely my responsibility.

[1] Scanner panel data records household-specific purchases over time at supermarkets. Household panels are tracked for long time periods, and panels are managed to obtain some degree of representativeness of the consumer population. In principle, though not necessarily in practice, all household purchases at participating stores are included in the databases.

[2] The cdf of the Gumbel (or Type I EV) distribution is $F(\varepsilon) = \exp[-\exp(-\mu\varepsilon)]$, $-\infty < \varepsilon < \infty$, where $\mu > 0$ is a scalar. Note that the variance of a random variable with a Gumbel distribution is $\sigma^2 = \pi^2 / 6\mu^2$.

[3] *Entropy* is a concept from information theory in electrical engineering (see Shannon 1948) that is used to express the information content in a signal. A set of outcomes $j \in C$ is associated with a probability distribution $\pi(j)$, and entropy $H = -\Sigma \pi(j) \ln \pi(j)$, where the sum is over all $j \in C$.

[4] Note that I have changed Bhat's (1995) notation to conform with my earlier exposition. His parameter θ_i is the inverse of my scale μ_i.

[5] McFadden (1978) originally proved the theorem for $G()$ homogenous of degree one (see also Ben-Akiva and Lerman 1985, pp. 304-310). Ben-Akiva and Francois (1983) showed that the GEV Generation Theorem was satisfied for any μ-homogenous function $G()$ (i.e. $G(\alpha y_1, ..., \alpha y_J) = \alpha^\mu G(y_1, ..., y_J)$, for α and μ non-negative).

[6] To make a quick digression, the top-level scale μ in GEV models (including the MNL, of course) plays the same role as the scale factor in the MNL model, a topic already extensively discussed in Sections 2.1.1 and 2.1.2.

[7] Note that for clarity of exposition we have omitted the possibility of independent variables in the composite utility of construct alternatives, but that is a straightforward generalization of expression (19) that in no way compromises the essence of this development.

[8] In empirical work using the MNL model with large choice sets, IIA comes to the rescue of the researcher faced with large choice sets. It is possible to obtain consistent utility function parameter estimates by sampling from M, rather than using the entire set. The reader is directed to the little-known results in Ben-

Akiva and Lerman (1985), Chapter 9, Section 9.3, who discuss various sampling rules and corresponding corrections factors. Their presentation is based on earlier work by D. McFadden on the Positive Conditioning Property of the MNL model (McFadden 1978).

[9] This expression for the log likelihood essentially treats each replication from a respondent as an independent observation. Since this overstates the sample size ($N \cdot R$ independent choice observations, rather than R "related" replications from N independent individuals), covariance matrix estimates will likely be underestimated; unfortunately, we don't know by how much they are underestimated, since that would require a description of how the R replications depend one upon another. (The reader can imagine the finitely countable number of hypotheses that might be generated about this dependence.) Louviere and Woodworth (1983) suggested multiplying the elements of Ω_{ML} by R (or equivalently, multiplying the standard errors output by estimation programs by $R^{1/2}$) as a very conservative correction. This is indeed *quite* conservative, since it discounts any additional information garnered from the replications; on the other hand, since it is conservative, inference-making will be that much more robust if this correction factor is used. A second option, which I believe preferable when available, is to use the QML Ω_{W} robust estimator for the covariance matrix (White 1982).

[10] All models presented in Table 2 assume that within-subject replications are independent. As noted earlier, this is likely to overstate t-statistics somewhat.

[11] It will be a maintained hypothesis in this section that the two price variables (Camping Fee and Firewood Price) have different marginal disutilities. Economists might prefer to see these coefficients constrained to be equal. I beg the understanding of economists for the atheoretical ways of an engineer.

[12] Estimation of the latent class models uses a log likelihood function that explicitly recognizes the repeated nature of the choice data. Specifically, the log likelihood function in expression (57) is employed.

10. REFERENCES

Allenby, Greg and James Ginter, 1995, "The Effects of In-Store Displays and Feature Advertising on Consideration Sets," *International Journal of Research in Marketing*, 12(1):67-80.

Andrews, Rick and Imram Currim, 2003, "A Comparison of Segment Retention Criteria for Finite Mixture Logit Models," *Journal of Marketing Research*, 40:235-243.

Andrews, Rick, Andrew Ainslie and Imran Currim, 2002, "An Empirical Comparison of Logit Choice Models With Discrete Versus Continuous Representations of Heterogeneity," *Journal of Marketing Research*, 39(4):479-487.

Ben-Akiva, Moshe and Bruno Boccara, 1995, "Discrete Choice Models with Latent Choice Sets," *International Journal of Research in Marketing*, 12(1):9-24.

Ben-Akiva, Moshe and Bernard Francois, 1983, "μ-Homogenous Generalized Extreme Value Model," Working Paper, Dept. of Civil Engineering, MIT, Cambridge, MA.

Ben-Akiva, Moshe and Steve Lerman, 1977, "Disaggregate Travel and Mobility Choice Models and Measures of Accessibility," Third International Conference on Behavioural Travel Modelling, Tanenda, Australia, 1977.

Ben-Akiva, Moshe and Steve Lerman, 1985, *Discrete Choice Analysis: Theory and Application to Predict Travel Demand*, Cambridge:MIT Press.

Bettman, James, Eric Johnson, and J. Payne, 1991, "Consumer Decision Making," in *Handbook of Consumer Behavior*, T. Robertson and H. Kassarjian, Eds., New York:Prentice-Hall, 50-84.

Bhat, Chandra, 1995, "A Heteroscedastic Extreme Value Model of Intercity Mode Choice," *Transportation Research B*, 29B(6):471-483.

Bhat, Chandra, 2001, "Quasi-Random Maximum Simulated Likelihood Estimation of the Mixed Multinomial Logit Model," *Transportation Research*, 35B:677-693.

Bhat, Chandra, 2003, "Simulation Estimation of Mixed Discrete Choice Models Using Randomized and Scrambled Halton Sequences," *Transportation Research*, 37B:837-855.

Bunch, David, 1991, "Estimability in the Multinomial Probit Model," *Transportation Research*, 25B(1):1-12.

Choi, Ki Hong and Choon Geol Moon, 1997, "Generalized Extreme Value Model and Additively Separable Generator Function," *Journal of Econometrics*, 76(1-2):129-40.

Chu, C., 1989, "A Paired Comparison Logit Model for Travel Demand Analysis," *Proceedings of the Fifth World Conference on Transportation Research*, Ventura, CA, 4:295-309.

Daganzo, Carlos, 1979, *Multinomial Probit: The Theory and Its Application to Demand Forecasting*, New York:Academic Press.

Dallaert, Benedict, Jeff Brazell and Jordan Louviere, 1999, "The Effect of Attribute Variation on Consumer Choice Consistency," *Marketing Letters*, 10(2):139-147.

Daly, Andrew, 1987, "Estimating Tree Logit Models," *Transportation Research B*, 21:251-267.

Daly, Andrew and S. Zachary, 1976, "Improved Multiple Choice Models," Mimeo.

Ford, J., N. Schmitt, S. Schechtman, B. Hults and M. Doherty, 1989, "Process Tracing Methods: Problems and Neglected Research Questions," *Organizational Behavior and Human Decision Processes*, 43:75-117.

Formann, Anton, 1992, "Linear Logistic Latent Class Analysis for Polytomous Data," *Journal of the American Statistical Association*, 87:476-486.

Gupta, S. and P.K. Chintagunta, 1994, "On Using Demographic Variables to Determine Segment Membership in Logit Mixture Models," *Journal of Marketing Research*, 31:128-136.

Hajivassiliou, V., 1993, "Simulation Estimation Methods for Limited Dependent Variable Models," in *Handbook of Statistics*, G.S. Maddala, C.R. Rao and H.D. Vinod, Eds., Amsterdam:Elsevier Science, 519-543.

Hensher David, 1997, "Value of Travel Time Savings in Personal and Commercial Automobile Travel," in *Measuring the Full Costs and Benefits of Transportation*, Greene D., Jones D., and Delucchi M., Eds., Springer-Verlag, Berlin.

Hensher David, 1998a, "Extending Valuation to Controlled Value Functions and Non-Uniform Scaling with Generalised Unobserved Variances," in *Theoretical Foundations of Travel Choice Modelling*, Garling T., Laitila T., and Westin K., eds.), Pergamon, Oxford.

Hensher David, 1998b, "Establishing a Fare Elasticity Regime for Urban Passenger Transport: Non-Concession Commuters," *Journal of Transport Economics and Policy*, 32(2):221-246.

Hu, Wuyang, Anne Hünnemeyer, Michele Veeman, Wiktor Adamowicz and Lorie Srivastava, 2004, "Trading off Health, Environmental and Genetic Modification Attributes in Food," *European Review of Agricultural Economics*, 31(3):389-408.

Johnson, Norman, Samuel Kotz and N. Balakrishnan, 1994, *Continuous Univariate Distributions – Volume 1*, Second Edition, New York:Wiley.

Johnson, Norman, Samuel Kotz and N. Balakrishnan, 1995, *Continuous Univariate Distributions – Volume 2*, Second Edition, New York:Wiley.

Kamakura, Wagner and Gary Russell, 1989, "A Probabilistic Choice Model for Market Segmentation and Elasticity Structure," *Journal of Marketing Research*, 26:379-390.

Kamakura, Wagner and Michel Wedel, 2004, "An Empirical Bayes Procedure for Improving Individual-Level Estimates and Predictions From Finite Mixtures of Multinomial Logit Models," *Journal of Business and Economic Statistics*, 22(1):121-125.

Kamakura, Wagner, Byuong-do Kim and Jonathan Lee, 1996, "Modeling Preference and Structural Heterogeneity in Consumer Choice," *Marketing Science*, 15(2):152-172.

Koppelman, Frank and C.H. Wen, 2000, "The Paired Combinatorial Logit Model: Properties, Estimation and Application," *Transportation Research*, 34B:75-89.

Louviere, Jordan, 2004, "Complex Statistical Choice Models: Are the Assumptions Ture, and If Not, What Are the Consequences?" CenSoC Working Paper No. 04-002, University of Technology, Sydney, Australia, 38pp.

Louviere, Jordan, David Hensher and Joffre Swait, 2000, *Stated Choice Methods: Analysis and Application*, Cambridge University Press:Cambridge, UK.

Louviere Jordan and George Woodworth, 1983, "Design and Analysis of Simulated Consumer Choice or Allocation Experiments: An Approach Based on Aggregate Data," *Journal of Marketing Research*, 20:350-367.

Manski, Charles, 1977, "The Structure of Random Utility Models," *Theory and Decision*, 8:229-254.

Manski, Charles and Steve Lerman, 1981, "On the Use of Simulated Frequencies to Approximate Choice Probabilities," in *Structural Analysis of Discrete Data*, C. Manski and D. McFadden, Eds., Cambridge:MIT Press, 305-319.

McFadden, Daniel, 1978, "Modeling the Choice of Residential Location," in *Spatial Interaction Theory and Residential Location*, A. Karlquist et al., Eds., Amsterdam:North Holland, 75-96.

McFadden, Daniel, 1981, "Econometric Models of Probabilistic Choice," in *Structural Analysis of Discrete Data*, C. Manski and D. McFadden, Eds., Cambridge:MIT Press, 198-272.

McFadden, Daniel and Kenneth Train, 2000, "Mixed MNL Models for Discrete Response," *Journal of Applied Econometrics*, 15:447-490.

McFarlane, Bonnie, Peter Boxall, Craig Hiltz and Michael Williams, 2000, "Decision Support System for Camping Site Choice," in The Foothills Model Forest, Draft Manual, Canadian Forest Service, October 2000.

Meijer, Erik and Jan Rouwendal, 2005, "Measuring Welfare Effects in Models with Random Coefficients," *Journal of Applied Econometrics*, forthcoming.

Morikawa, Takayuki, 1989, "Incorporating Stated Preference Data in Travel Demand Analysis," unpublished PhD Dissertation, Dept. of Civil Engineering, Massachusetts Institute of Technology, Cambridge, MA.

Payne, J., James Bettman, and Eric Johnson, 1993, *The Adaptive Decision Maker*, New York: Cambridge University Press.

Provencher, Bill and Richard C. Bishop, 2004, "Does Accounting for Preference Heterogeneity Improve the Forecasting of a Random Utility Model? A Case Study," *Journal of Environmental Economics and Management*, 48(1):793-810.

Provencher, Bill and Rebecca Moore, 2005, "A Discussion of "Using Angler Characteristics and Attitudinal Data to Identify Environmental Preference Classes: A Latent-Class Model," *Environment and Resource Economics*, forthcoming.

Ramaswamy, V., Wayne Desarbo, D. Reibstein and W. Robinson, 1993, "An Empirical Pooling Approach for Estimating Marketing Mix Elasticities with PIMS Data," *Marketing Sciences*, 12:103-124.

Revelt, David and Kenneth Train, 1999, "Customer-Specific Taste Parameters and Mixed Logit," Working Paper, Dept. of Economics, University of California at Berkeley, November 1999.

Schwabe, Kurt, Peter Schuhmann, Roy Boyd and Khosrow Doroodian, 2001, "The Value of Changes In Deer Season Length: An Application of the Nested Multinomial Logit Model," *Environmental and Resource Economics*, 19:131-147.

Swait, Joffre, 1984, "Probabilistic Choice Set Formation in Transportation Demand Models," unpublished PhD thesis, Dept. of Civil Engineering, MIT, Cambridge, MA.

Swait, Joffre, 1994, "A Structural Equation Model of Latent Segmentation and Product Choice for Cross-Sectional Revealed Preference Choice Data," *Journal of Retailing and Consumer Services*, 1(2):77-89.

Swait, Joffre, 2001a, "Choice Set Generation Within the Generalized Extreme Value Family of Discrete Choice Models," *Transportation Research*, 35B(7):643-666.

Swait, Joffre, 2001b, "A Non-Compensatory Choice Model Incorporating Attribute Cutoffs," *Transportation Research*, 35B(10):903-928.

Swait, Joffre, 2003, "Flexible Covariance Structures for Categorical Dependent Variables Through Finite Mixtures of GEV Models," *Journal of Business and Economic Statistics*, 21(1), January, 80-87.

Swait, Joffre and Wiktor Adamowicz, 2001, "Choice Environment, Market Complexity, and Consumer Behavior: A Theoretical and Empirical Approach for Incorporating Decision Complexity into Models of Consumer Choice," *Organizational Behavior and Human Decision Processes*, 86(2):141-167.

Swait, Joffre and Rick Andrews, 2003, "Enhancing Scanner Panel Models With Choice Experiments," *Marketing Science*, 22(4):442-460.

Swait, Joffre and Moshe Ben-Akiva, 1986, "An Analysis of the Effects of Captivity on Travel Time and Cost Elasticities," *Annals of the 1985 International Conference on Travel Behavior*, April 16-19, 1985, Noordwijk, Holland, 113-128.

Swait, Joffre and Moshe Ben-Akiva, 1987a, "Incorporating Random Constraints in Discrete Choice Models of Choice Set Generation," *Transportation Research*, 21B:91-102.

Swait, Joffre and Moshe Ben-Akiva, 1987b, "Empirical Test of a Constrained Choice Discrete Model: Mode Choice in São Paulo, Brazil," *Transportation Research*, 21B:103-115.

Swait, Joffre and Adriana Bernardino, 2000, "Distinguishing Taste Variation From Error Structure in Discrete Choice Data," *Transportation Research*, 34B(1):1-15.

Swait, Joffre and Jordan Louviere, 1993, "The Role of the Scale Parameter In The Estimation And Use of Multinomial Logit Models," *Journal of Marketing Research*, 30(August):305-314.

Train, Kenneth, 1999, "Mixed Logit Models for Recreation Demand," in *Valuing Recreation and The Environment: Revealed Preference Methods in Theory and Practice*, J.A. Herriges and C.L. Kling, Eds., Aldershot:Edward Elgar.

Train, Kenneth, 2003, *Discrete Choice Methods with Simulation*, Cambridge University Press, Cambridge.

Tversky, Amos, 1972, "Elimination-by-Aspects: A Theory of Choice," *Psychological Review*, 79:281-299.

Tversky, Amos and Daniel Kahneman, 1991, "Loss Aversion in Riskless Choice: A Reference-Dependent Model," *The Quarterly Journal of Economics*, 106(4):1039-1061.

Von Haefen, Roger, 2003, "Latent Consideration Sets and Continuous Demand System Models," Working Paper, Dept. of Agricultural and Resource Economics, University of Arizona, July 2003.

Walker, Joan, 2002, "The Mixed Logit, or Logit Kernel, Model: Dispelling Misconceptions of Identification," *Transportation Research Record* 1805, 86-98., also http://mit.edu/jwalker/www/home.htm.

Wen, C.H. and Frank Koppelman, 2001, "The Generalized Nested Logit Model," *Transportation Research Part B*, 35B(7):627-641.

White, Halbert, 1982, "Maximum Likelihood Estimation of Misspecified Models," *Econometrica*, 50:1-25.

Williams, H.C.L., 1977, "On the Formation of Travel Demand Models and Economic Evaluation Measures of User Benefit," *Environment and Planning*, A9:285-344.

Wood, Stacy and Joffre Swait, 2002, "Psychological Indicators of Innovation Adoption: The Interaction of Need for Cognition and Need for Change," *Journal of Consumer Psychology*, 12(1):1-13.

Yatchew, A. and Zvi Griliches, 1984, "Specification Error in Probit Models," *Review of Economics and Statistics*, 66:134-139.

CHAPTER 10

COMPUTER SOFTWARE TO ESTIMATE CHOICE MODELS

DANIEL HELLERSTEIN

United States Department of Agriculture, Washington, D.C., U.S.A.

GRBL2 [*] is a set of GAUSS programs for estimating a variety of econometric models used in environmental valuation. It is also a programming environment that provides a moderately rich set of i/o functions, and a fairly complete library of maximum likelihood estimation procedures.

Obtaining GRBL2

GRBL2 is an ongoing project. The latest (beta) version can be freely obtained from: http://grbl.danielh.org/grbl2/. You will download a .ZIP file that contains source code, documentation, and "compiled" versions of the programs.

GRBL2 is written in GAUSS for version 5.0. If you do not own GAUSS, a free run-time module can be used to run the compiled versions of these programs; this run-time module is also available at the above web address. Most users will find it most convenient to use these compiled versions, even if they own GAUSS 5.0 or above.

What does GRBL2 have?

As of this writing, GRBL2 contains the following estimators:

a)   Probit and Logit
b)   Single and double-bounded logit and probit
c)   2-stage double-bounded probit
d)   Multinomial logit (MNL)
e)   2-stage MNL

B.J. Kanninen (ed.), Valuing Environmental Amenities Using Stated Choice Studies, 295–296.

f)   Mixed Logit (several variants)
g)   gSpike and Poisson semi-non-parametric models
h)   A variety of WTP calculators (with support for Krinsky-Robb, Jackknife, etc.).

GRBL2 also contains several data-manipulation programs. Thus, even if you do not own GAUSS, these programs allow you to easily create, modify, edit, and display GAUSS datasets.

Why GRBL2?

To a large extent, this list represents models developed by me (and various associates) for our own purposes that we find useful enough to offer freely to the public. I plan to add other models over the next several months. These include:

- Models discussed in Alberini et al. (this volume) and Swait (this volume).
- Models written for an earlier (DOS) version of GRBL (such as a set of Poisson and Negative Binomial estimators).

It is relatively easy for competent GAUSS programmers to use GRBL2 to implement their own models. The technical documentation for both the MLE procedures and the input-output routines is thorough and I am willing to help you in a pinch!

ENDNOTES

*   Although this software has been used for United States Department of Agriculture (USDA) pro-jects, GRBL2 is in no way a product of the USDA. Use it at your own risk.

CHAPTER 11

JUDGING QUALITY

V. KERRY SMITH

Arizona State University, Tempe Arizona, U.S.A.. and Resources for the Future, Washington, D.C., U.S.A.

1. INTRODUCTION

Statistical methods for estimating parameters generally assume that there is a "true," but unknown, value for the concept being measured. Sometime after the estimation is complete and decisions are made, analysts learn "the truth." In these cases, quality can be judged by a comparison of estimates with what is learned *ex post*. In the case of economic trade-offs there is no process that allows analysts to learn these "true" values. Thus, in the absence of an ability to make these comparisons, how should a reader evaluate new efforts to measure the economic values for changes in the amount, quality, or access conditions to environmental resources? There are many different ways measures of economic trade-offs are used and many different "readers." As a result, any attempt to respond to this question will be incomplete. My strategy uses examples to convey the main ideas associated with judging the quality of these measures. It also relies on literature citations rather than detailed summaries.

Seven sections follow this introduction. Section 2 provides background, reviewing some of the material covered in more detail in the previous chapters of this volume. This brief summary helps to explain my proposed strategies for evaluating quality. Section 3 steps back from the task at hand and uses a simple, indifference curve-based framework to illustrate how the analyst's assumptions about individual preferences for nonmarket goods condition what can be learned from choice surveys.[1] Section 4 reviews a few aspects of how analysts usually evaluate the plausibility of results derived from stated choice (SC) studies. The examples are dominated by my own work with former students and colleagues. My reason for focusing on these examples is a simple one. In these cases, I know, as only an insider can, how the results in these studies were cross-checked and what

B.J. Kanninen (ed.), Valuing Environmental Amenities Using Stated Choice Studies, 297–333.
© 2006 *Springer.*

readers, review panelists (for litigation work), and referees requested to convince themselves that the findings in each case were plausible.

The fifth section discusses how information about complementary behaviors can be used to gauge survey responses. It also recognizes that as a set of applications in any particular area expands, the accumulated record can serve as a basis for judging new studies. The sixth section discusses a new context for thinking about the issues associated with quality assessment. Section 7 offers some practical suggestions to get started. The last section returns to where I started in this introduction. It discusses how judgments about the quality of estimates cannot be evaluated separately from the use of these measures. I use one of the most stark differences in these judgments by comparing how my question would be considered from a policy standpoint versus litigation.

2. BACKGROUND

Quality, like beauty, is in the eye of the beholder. One definition will never fit all needs. A quality study is one that measures the concept intended in an informative way. This formulation is deliberately vague. It avoids discussing formal definitions of statistical concepts of quality that inevitably involve bias/variance trade-offs. Instead, it focuses on evaluating economic plausibility within a setting that assures, as nearly as possible, that stated choices are authentic representations for the "real world trade-offs" made by the respondents who report them.

To appreciate why I propose a less tangible definition of quality, consider how quality might be defined with a statistical framework. The logical structure that underlies estimation and inference in classical statistics generally relies on the assumption that there is some unknown, true model to be estimated. Often the true model is assumed to have a parametric form. When a model is estimated, we argue that there are unknown, "true", values for its parameters. The properties of the methods used to estimate models are routinely judged in relationship to these unknown parameters. For example, an unbiased estimator for a parameter is one that, given the maintained assumptions underlying estimation, on average recovers the "true" value of that parameter. Unfortunately this logic leads us to frameworks to evaluate the quality of estimates for economic trade-offs that tend to treat them as if they were constants. As a result, the strategy leads to misleading conclusions regarding efforts to ask people about choices. For example, much of the nonmarket valuation literature has identified measures of economic trade-offs that vary with the context of the choice as evidence for serious failures in the neoclassical theory underlying benefit estimation.[2]

At a very general level, an estimate for an economic value is an answer to a specific question that involves comparing two alternative situations.[3] Suppose a change in something is to be made. Perhaps a natural area is to be clear-cut to provide land for a new high school and associated athletic fields. We might expect different individuals to evaluate this change differently depending on whether they live near the natural area to be transformed and/or whether they have teenagers who would attend the school.[4] A simple, static definition for an economic value measures the one-time dollar amount a person would pay or need to be paid (in compensation) to remain as well off with the school as without it. The amount that answers this hypothetical question can be positive or negative. This monetary quantity does not represent the "economic value of the school" for each person. Rather, the monetary measure defined by this question evaluates a specific trade-off each person is willing to make.

One way to distinguish a market from a nonmarket trade-off might be labeled the *trade-off resolution*. To my knowledge the concept I am describing has not been discussed in this way. When people have opportunities to make repeated choices for market goods and services, there are features about the exchanges each individual takes for granted. These features convey information to each participant. Faith and Tollison (1981) commented on some aspects of what I have in mind in their discussion of the timing of exchanges for different goods and services. We pay for a movie in advance and a restaurant meal afterward. Many services are paid for after the work is complete, but there are exceptions. For example, most medical professionals now require that the arrangement for payment be established in advance of service. Faith and Tollison suggest *ex post* payment is a rational response when there is the need to control the large transactions costs that can arise when there are substantial interpersonal differences in the information available to buyers and sellers. My point here is about the information that the analyst can expect people to know: the greater the consistency in the information about what is "gotten" from an exchange and what is "given up," the greater is the trade-off resolution associated with these transactions. The rules defining a market exchange specify exactly what is traded and the terms of the transaction. These rules isolate the object of choice (OC) as well as the elements that define the circumstances of choice.[5] OCs can be complex or simple. The decision to purchase a cup of coffee involves giving up money and receiving a cup of a specific amount and type of coffee (plus any sugar, cream, and other additives available to the customer at the defined price). The object of choice is the "thing" or set of "things" exchanged or altered by the trade. These can be amounts of commodities or services, states of nature, changes in risk, or changes in circumstances facing an individual (or others) which enhance that individual's well-being directly or indirectly.

My example of the transformation of the natural area to build the school has at least two "things" changing. First, there is the loss of some amount of natural area (in a particular way – e.g., clear-cutting). Further, we have the addition of a new high school. These two changes, along with the perceived process through which they "take place" (as well as any "end state" implications), may all be part of the object of choice. If this choice can be asked with a high level of *trade-off resolution* then we can be sure that the discrepancies individuals might have in understanding the object of choice, as well as in what they must give up to get it, are very limited. As a result, to estimate the economic trade-off, the analyst must identify all the elements in the exchange. With high levels of trade-off resolution, it is reasonable to assume that all participants are equally aware of these consequences and that a well-defined economic trade-off can be recovered from their decisions.

This discussion probably seems tortuous. However, it is important to try to be specific about the elements in each exchange. The translation of a choice – stated or actual – into a well-defined economic value relies on a complete specification of the circumstances of choice. These include the OC, the terms of the choice, and any other background factors that might influence the well-being an individual realizes from an exchange.

All of these considerations are implicit when an analyst writes down a model that is hypothesized to define an economic value. For example, we can specify that c in equation (1a) is an *exact* measure for the WTP (WTP) for Δq. Equations (1b) and (1c) offer bounds. Equation (1b) defines c as an upper bound for that WTP and (1c) specifies the case where it is a lower bound.

$$V\left(m - c, \bar{p}, \bar{t}, q + \Delta q\right) = V\left(m, \bar{p}, \bar{t}, q\right) \tag{1a}$$

$$V\left(m - c, \bar{p}, \bar{t}, q + \Delta q\right) < V\left(m, \bar{p}, \bar{t}, q\right) \tag{1b}$$

$$V\left(m - c, \bar{p}, \bar{t}, q + \Delta q\right) > V\left(m, \bar{p}, \bar{t}, q\right) \tag{1c}$$

The function $V(.)$ in these expressions is the indirect utility function. It characterizes the highest level of well-being an individual is able to realize in the presence of constraints. In this case, the components of these constraints are the level of income (m) (I have assumed this income is determined independent of an individual's choices in allocating his time between labor and leisure), the prices for market goods ($\bar{p}$), the total time available for all uses ($\bar{t}$), and the amounts of nonmarket goods (q).[6] Equation (1a) defines implicitly the WTP for Δq because it represents a situation of indifference. (1b) and (1c) isolate bounds because they correspond to situations where c exceeds the trade-off this person would be prepared to make, or is less than what she would give up. (1b) would correspond to a rejection of the OC if offered and (1c) an acceptance. Δq can be an increase or a decrease in the amount of one or more nonmarket goods (labeled as q). For an increase we would expect c to be a positive value, implying this person would pay to increase the amount of q available. When Δq is a loss in q then we would expect that c is also negative and it serves the role of monetary compensation for that loss.

These details are usually taken as given in writing down an economic model of the choice process. They come to the surface when the responses to well-defined SC questions must be "converted" so that they can be used to estimate economic values. My point is to remind you that the objective of a survey question is to provide enough information that we can be reasonably sure there is a high level of *trade-off resolution* for both the proposed change in nonmarket goods and the resources a person must give up to get that change. Survey researchers undertake focus groups, pretests and pilots to be sure that what is being asked is understood as the analyst intends. An important aspect of that process arises from the assurance that the trade-off presented or elicited from each person is understood in comparable terms. I believe economists involved in this process have adopted an implicit standard that this level of understanding is comparable to most market transactions. I am using *trade-off resolution* as a shorthand phrase to capture this idea.

Defining trade-offs with algebra is easier than defining them in "real life" with real people. All the elements in the transition from observed (or stated) choices to the modeled choices contribute to measures of economic trade-offs. As a result, the task of evaluating the quality of a choice analysis for changes in nonmarket services requires careful consideration of all of these elements.

The basic model given in equations (1a) through (1c) can also be used to describe responses to open ended, ranking, and rating questions. Cameron, et al. (2002) demonstrate that inverting the left-hand side of equation (1a) and solving for c yields a model for describing open-ended responses. Let $h(\ .\ )$ designate the inverse function for $V(\ .\ )$ with respect to the income variable. Responses to the choice process implied by equation (1a) are then modeled using equation (2).

$$c = m - h\left(m, \bar{p}, \bar{t}, q, q + \Delta q\right) \qquad (2)$$

The important lesson to be derived from tracing this logic is that comparisons across question formats must impose a preference structure to assure consistent comparisons in the estimates for economic trade-offs.[7]

Expanding this logic to other response formats is straightforward. For example, rankings simply increase the number of alternatives that are ordered in the (1b) and (1c)-type relations. Requests for individuals to provide ratings (as Layton and Lee, 2003, demonstrate) can be interpreted in these terms as well.[8] The primary differences, from the perspective of a quality judgment, arise from the form of the estimators used for each type of response elicited; assumptions about (and realities of) respondents' abilities to answer the questions posed; and the ability to use the information that can be recovered to measure economic trade-offs.

3. PREFERENCE RESTRICTIONS

Judgments about the quality of a valuation study are always conditional. If the analyst is prepared to add information to what is available from the choice survey, the opportunities to evaluate the survey's quality increase. This information usually amounts to some type of preference restriction. For example, the nonmarket good of interest might be assumed to be used with other goods and services. The pattern of use can imply restrictions on the marginal rates of substitution. This structure can make it possible to formulate thought experiments that serve as cross-checks on the estimated economic trade-offs.

To illustrate this point, consider a manipulation of indifference maps to represent how three goods contribute to an individual's well-being in a two-dimensional diagram. Samuelson (1974a) attributes the strategy to Hayek (1943) and Georgescu-Roegen (1952).[9] Using simple graphs that describe the trade-offs between two goods, we can introduce a third good by allowing it to alter the position of each curve, and then use the shapes of the indifference maps to illustrate either complementarity or substitution relationships. These alternative graphs replace conventional indifference curves where each curve is drawn to represent a separate level of well-being with separate curves constructed to hold utility constant and to vary the amount of a third good. This third good can be either a complement or a substitute for the two commodities plotted on the axes of the graph. The pattern and spacing of the curves in this case captures the substitution or complementarity.

For this illustration, the choices for all goods, the relative prices, and other aspects of the availability of the nonmarket good are assumed to be observed. Let z represent the numeraire (on the vertical axis), x an observable private good (on the horizontal axis), and q the nonmarket resource. The level of q distinguishes the indifference curves given in Figures 1a through 1c. Consider Figure 1a first. The curves labeled q_A, q_B and q_C hold the level of individual well-being constant at some specified baseline value and then vary the levels of q. q is assumed to be a desirable good so $q_A > q_B > q_C$ (with the subscripts corresponding to the levels used to identify the indifference curves). As q increases, the indifference curves corresponding to higher levels move *in* toward the origin. With each larger amount of q (a desirable nonmarket good or service), the amount of x and z required to realize the constant baseline level of well-being declines. This logic explains the movement inward of the curves. The specific features of the shape of the mapping of indifference curves is determined by what is assumed about the relationship between q and either x or z. These interrelationships focus attention on how the analyst specifies that increases in q will affect the amount of x and z consumed.[10] Different assumptions will imply different patterns for the marginal rates of substitution between x and z as q changes.

In Figure 1a, the indifference curves labeled q_B and q_C are constructed to appear to be parallel to q_A -- that is, the slopes of the curves are in a constant ratio when x and z are constant but q varies. For these curves, the vertical displacement measures the WTP (c in terms of the numeraire z) for an increase in q regardless of the level of x. Changes in q are comparable to income effects. In Figure 1a, we do not expect the demands for x or z to change differently with the level of q. At first this conclusion might seem to imply market demands for x and z are completely uninformative about the value of q. This setup actually parallels one definition for existence value. It corresponds to the definition implied when we assume preferences are additively separable in q.[11]

Changes in q improve well-being, but after controlling for income and relative prices, do not differentially alter the demand for x or for z. However, this conclusion overlooks one important aspect of how this information can be useful. When we are collecting SC information about the decisions that *would be made* for potential changes in q, we have estimates of what people would give up (measured in terms of a numeraire) to assure those changes. If we add questions about x, we can track changes in consumption of x in response to changes in q. With this structure – we have a clear expectation – there should be no incremental effect. That is, the change in q does not influence the marginal rate of substitution between x and z. As a result, if the relative prices of x and z do not change, we would expect no change in their demands. Thus, the added question about changes in x in response to q can confirm other aspects of a choice experiment. Even with a situation with no relationship between a market good and the nonmarket service, a supplementary question can offer useful information. Knowledge of preferences, in this case, can serve another role. We could use the price of x as the payment vehicle to estimate the WTP for an improvement in q from q_B to q_A. The pivot in the budget constraint z_1x_1 to z_2x_2 is the Hicksian equivalent price change for the quality change from q_B to q_A. Looking at Figure 1a, Smith and Banzhaf (2004a) have demonstrated that ½ (TN+SM) provides a first order approximation to the Hicksian consumer surplus -- in this case, the curves are exactly parallel (as implied by additive separability).

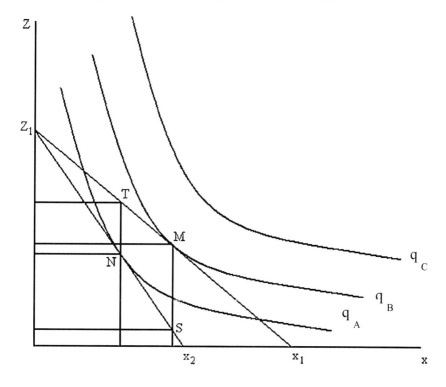

FIGURE 1a.

Figure 1b presents a situation where preferences display weak complementarity. x is the weak complement for q. The indifference curves labeled q_A and q_B correspond to the *same* level of utility or well-being along with the assumption that $q_A > q_B$. The curves intersect at R because weak complementarity implies that additions to q have no value when x is not consumed. As quality changes, the slopes of the indifference curves change at each level of consumption of the weak complement This format can also be used to define the Hicksian equivalent price (EP) change to the quality change. For a given income level, the EP is the price change associated with the pivot from one tangency to a constant utility indifference curve to a tangency of a new indifference curve at the same utility level, but a new quality level. In Figure 1b, this is illustrated as a move from mP_r to mP_s. q enhances well-being when the individual consumes a positive amount of x. More generally, provided we can also assume the Willig (1978) condition is satisfied, Marshallian consumer surplus per unit of use of x will provide a consistent price index adjustment for changes in q (see Smith and Banzhaf, 2004b).

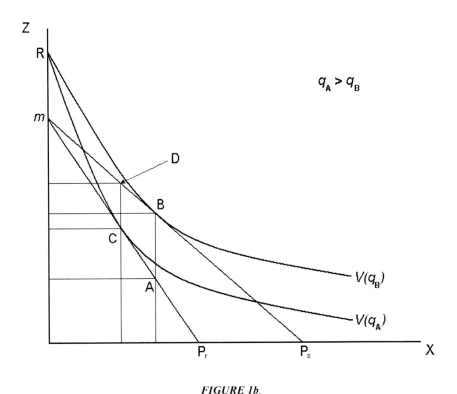

FIGURE 1b.

These results relate to SC tasks because changes in q should be reflected in the demand for x. In fact, if x and q are linked as weak complements and the Willig condition is satisfied, Palmquist (2005) has shown that we should expect the elasticity of price flexibility for q with income to be equal to the income elasticity of demand for the weak complement, x.[12] While we usually associate weak complementarity with revealed preference approaches, Palmquists's result implies that the two conditions can offer a behavioral prediction for SC surveys. With both conditions satisfied, separate estimates of the income elasticity of the marginal WTP for quality should be related to the income elasticity of demand for this weak complement. In addition, if the primary basis for being willing to pay to improve some aspect of the quality of an environmental resource stems from use-related activities, then we should expect nonusers to be disproportionately represented in the "no" responses to SC questions about these quality improvements. Conversely, those favoring improvements should all be users.

Of course, we may not always (or even frequently) be able to assume that there are observable complementary choices that can be used to derive measures of the value of q that stem exclusively from use. Perfect substitution between some private good and a nonmarket amenity is another example where we expect a change in an observable behavior to accompany a change in a nonmarket good.[13] In this case, we would expect it to be unnecessary to use a SC survey. With perfect substitution, changes in the expenditures for the perfect substitute would provide the desired measure. Of course, this conclusion relies on a mechanism that routinely keeps track of these expenditures. Often this does not happen, so a survey may be needed. Under these conditions, the restriction provides the means to develop a cross-check on SC responses.

Figure 1c illustrates a third case where q and x are weak substitutes. q has no value when the consumption of x is above $\bar{x}$. In this situation, the price of z provides the most direct basis for defining a change that is the Hicksian equivalent price change to the quality change, and the virtual price of z at this level of x offers the best index of a change in q.[14]

Weak substitution is interesting because it suggests a more general class of relationships. These links might be hypothesized to arise when there are discrete changes in the size of the contribution that q makes to well-being for different levels of consumption of one or more private goods. To the extent that we can confirm the presence of these types of transition points, we can use them to design additional questions that offer consistency checks. For example, if it is known that ambient concentrations of pollution only affect individuals who display "controllable" health conditions (e.g., over- or underweight) then we should expect respondents in these groups to react differently than those who would not fit these categories. These differential responses are not necessarily undermined by an assumption that people are also motivated by nonuse values. So long as there is no reason to expect these preferences would be linked to the health conditions, the differential response for those with the health condition compared to those without will continue to serve *its intended* role. That is, if the demand for improvement in environmental resources due to nonuse motives is randomly distributed among those with health conditions and those without, then these health states can still provide a differential signal of demand.

Two lessons emerge from this short overview of a few preference restrictions. First, when we make assumptions linking a nonmarket good to an observable market good, the conditions associated with these restrictions are usually consistent with being able to define an adjustment to the price for the linked private good (or for another, related private good). Basically, the preference restriction allows us to specify a price index that adjusts the price of the related private good for the amount of the nonmarket good.[15] In applications involving environmental amenities, this index specifies how a private good's price would change with changes in environmental quality. The logic underlying this process is analogous to what we would want to do if the quality of the private good had changed. While there are certainly a number of different assumptions that could be made, the point of making the connection to prices is that we can use it to construct tangible measures to compare to SC measures.

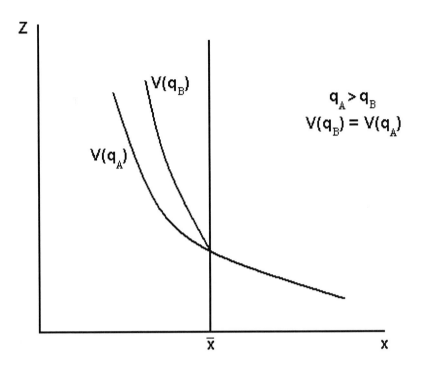

FIGURE 1c.

The process expresses a change in environmental quality as equivalent to a price change for the private good. For example, if we observe circumstances where environmental quality is constant, but a weak complement's price has changed ,then the observed adjustment in quantity demanded can be used to evaluate stated consumption adjustments in response to a proposed change in environmental quality. While the specific details and directions of change in the demand for private goods will be different, similar arguments could be constructed for the cases of perfect and weak substitution.

Overall then, these types of assumptions offer the prospect for confirming evidence based on stated increases or decreases in the consumption of the private good when the level of the nonmarket good changes. The greater the resolution in the prediction implied by theory, together with the ability to ask about such related behaviors, the more discriminating will be the assessment of the SC responses. Of course, the evaluation of the choice survey's results will be conditional on the validity of the assumed preference restrictions.

This first point implies the second lesson. It is difficult to offer general statements about a process that relies on using prior theory to judge the quality of a choice survey. A choice model must balance prior restrictions that limit its relevance, but increase the resolution in its predictions, with the generality of its description of behavior. This process implies that there are not simple, general guidelines on how theory can be used that relate to all situations. The context of each application matters.

Consider some recent examples from research in progress. Mansfield et al. (2004) propose using parents' behavior in preventing children with asthmatic conditions from being outside on days with severe ozone conditions. Their innovative strategy involves using a web-based survey that contacts parents (with children that have these health conditions) after days with severe ozone conditions to find out what they did. The revealed preference logic underlying averting models suggests that if parents know about poor air quality conditions, care about the effects they might have on their children, <u>and</u> have the ability to implement limitations on their children's behavior, we should expect to see some pattern of different responses to variations in air pollution.

A quality check would use questions about these related behaviors (structured so as to avoid signaling the desired response to those being interviewed). Krupnick et al. (2004), for example, propose using averting behavior to "check" the responses to a SC survey on the value of reducing contaminants in public drinking water supplies. In their case, the response was envisioned to be a change in the purchase of bottled water.[16]

The nature of the strategy, the information, and "controls" over other factors motivating people's behavior, differ with each example. The point is simply that if the process is to provide either a measure of economic value or a quality check for a SC question, judgments about its plausibility in either role begin with preference restrictions.

4. GUIDANCE ON FIRST STEPS

Assessment of the validity of measurement methods routinely begins with consideration of content, construct, and criterion validity. *Content validity* refers to whether the design and execution reveals the desired valuation concept. *Construct validity* concerns whether the SC responses are consistent with alternative measures of the trade-off and whether they are consistent with theory. *Criterion validity* requires a standard to judge the plausibility. This standard is especially difficult for nonmarket goods. These three criteria have been central to the evaluation of contingent valuation (CV) results since they were first outlined for this use by Mitchell and Carson (1989). Plausibility checks on the survey process do not replace this type of validity assessment. Rather, they provide the first steps in an analysis of quality after validity concepts have been considered.

Rules for quality control in SC surveys have emerged in a more systematic form in part as a result of the NOAA Panel's (Arrow, et al., 1993) recommendations. The Panel's guidelines were intended to be relevant for surveys that sought to measure nonuse values for litigation associated with natural resource damage assessment.

Subsequent research motivated by their proposed guidelines helped to reinforce these developments.[17]

The Panel's recommendations can be divided into two areas where they have had a direct influence on the first steps in judging quality: (a) good practices in questionnaire development and survey implementation; and (b) expectations from economic theory for the properties of the trade-offs elicited with CV surveys.

The NOAA Panel emphasized several aspects of the development of questionnaires, the survey design, and its implementation, including:

- accuracy in description of the object of choice (e.g., a program or policy intended to improve the amount or quality of a resource);
- pretesting of questionnaires to assure the potential respondents understood the key SC questions and background as intended;
- pretesting of information materials such as photographs or graphics to assure they served the role intended;
- checks for presence of interviewer effects if interviewers are involved in the survey;
- checks on understanding and acceptance of the context for the choice;
- inclusion of follow-up queries to the choice questions to assure respondents answered consistently with the intent of the trade-offs to be estimated.

Most of these elements are now part of the design process for SC questions.[18] Focus groups, pretests, and, in many cases, pilot surveys (i.e., initial surveys with a small number of respondents who fit the design criteria of the study) are a part of the design of large scale, SC surveys.[19] These design stages can provide indirect evidence that the questions were understandable and the proposed choices consistent with the trade-offs a research analyst intends to measure.[20]

Table 1 offers a few suggestions about how these types of comparisons might be implemented. The first proposes the use of tasks or even quiz questions to evaluate how well respondents understood the information presented. Two examples are cited in the table. The first, by Smith and Desvousges (1990), incorporated a judgment about how well respondents understood what they had received in the evaluation of a CV question. The task that was selected for this role required respondents to use information they received about the level of radon in their homes, along with a survey-provided risk chart, to estimate their approximate risk from the radon. Correct assessments implied understanding of the risk material. Incorrect assessments implied the opposite conclusion. The assessment (i.e., understand or not) was used as one determinant in a SC model seeking to estimate those respondents' demands for added information about radon as indoor air pollution. Correct use of the risk information reduced the effect of a respondent's radon level on the likelihood of demanding additional information.

The second example, by Krupnick et al. (2002), evaluated the effects of mistakes in understanding probabilities on the estimates of WTP for risk reductions. They used a grid with colored boxes to present mortality risk (as a relative frequency). After explaining the materials, a factual question about which chart represented greater risk was asked of each respondent. The authors kept track of who made mistakes.[21] Their analysis then used the results to evaluate the effects of dropping those respondents from the sample. Their implicit judgment was that those survey respondents who answered the initial question correctly had sufficient understanding and gave plausible responses to risk trade-off questions.

TABLE 1. *Informal Evaluations of Quality of Stated Choice Surveys*

NOAA Panel Suggestion	Practical Approach for Evaluation
Accuracy and understanding of the description of the object of choice	Quiz question about related implication implied by the character of the object of choice (e.g., Smith and Desvousges, 1990). Inclusion (in conjoint survey) of a choice which is obviously best[*] (e.g., Krupnick et al., 2002)
Pretesting of questions or supplementary materials	Comparison of performance between focus group, pretest, and alternative pilot surveys as information in survey question ns change (e.g., Carson et al., 1992)
Checks on understanding of choice implications	Evaluation of responses by features of respondents or for different subsets of sample that would be differentially affected by the choice questions (e.g., Smith, 1996, Mansfield and Smith, 2002).

[*]If this process includes a no choice question then the evaluation of a best decision is conditional on selecting one of the treatments aside from the status quo alternative.

The NOAA Panel and nearly all SC research has, by now, incorporated focus groups and/or some type of pretest into the design of questionnaires. When quantitative information is collected as part of these initial development activities (i.e., both focus groups and pilots) it can be used to evaluate the performance of the final survey results. One of the most detailed of these types of comparisons was undertaken in the Carson et al. (2002). Their survey sought to estimate WTP to avoid an oil spill comparable to the Exxon Valdez oil spill in 1989. Figure 2 reproduces estimates of the survival curves, based on Weibull hazard models. Each curve describes the probability of voting for a program to reduce the potential for damage from future oil spills.

The results are compared across three of the four pilot surveys and, together with a tracking survival, can be compared with the results of the final survey. Pilots II, IV, and the tracking survey were undertaken in the Dayton/Toledo, Ohio area. Each survey used a somewhat different distribution of one-time costs (per household) for the proposed plan. Nonetheless, estimated survival curves are nearly coincident.[22] While these types of comparisons are possible in a number of other large-scale SC analyses, to my knowledge they have not been incorporated in this way to judge the plausibility of estimates.[23] This means we are missing an important opportunity. To the extent that there are design variations in these initial pilots, such comparisons can offer informal evidence on the potential importance of these choices and, as a result, help readers to judge the quality of a SC survey and the potential sensitivity of the results to design decisions.

The last proposal for a plausibility check involves evaluating the implied consequences of choices. These are not identified to the respondents as being related to their stated choices. Thus, to the extent there is behavior consistent with the economic logic motivating each choice question, they help to confirm the implicit logic in trade-offs assumed to be present in each stated choice. Two examples illustrate this type of cross-check on survey responses.

The first stems from research undertaken to evaluate a suggestion by Kahneman and Ritov (1994) that for SC surveys to be believable they should "...demonstrate that contingent valuation properly discriminates significant causes from trivial ones" (p.28). The study (reported in Smith, 1996) compared two randomly assigned programs with the same payment mechanism and structure for the costs. Table 2 reproduces the text of the questions for each program. What is important for this example is that the payment vehicle for the program was an increase in the fees for vehicle registrations.

The most convincing evidence that the question was understood as intended (from the perspective of the journal referees) was the sign and statistical significance of a term controlling for the current number of registered vehicles each respondent owned. This question was asked along with other background information at the end of the interview. No specific connection was made in the survey between this number of registered vehicles and the proposed fee increase. That is, the survey did not present calculations of what the full costs of the program would be for each respondent. A negative and significant relationship confirms respondents understood that the costs they would experience from the increase in license fees would depend on the number of registered vehicles they had.

A second example of a cross-check on understanding involves using the type of respondent. Mansfield and Smith (2002) investigated two alternative plans for improving water quality in North Carolina rivers through stricter regulation of the hog industry. Two alternative plans were randomly assigned to different respondents. The structure of the payment vehicle and outcomes were described in identical terms. The plans were differentiated based on whether they emphasized stricter regulations or a cost-share program (i.e., the costs imposed on farmers would be subsidized as part of the proposed program). The cost share program was justified by describing the economic impacts associated with the employment multiplier effects of the hog industry. Background information in the survey, collected before information about the plans was available to respondents, asked whether each person was, or ever had been, a farmer. The logic for a respondent cross-check implies that it is reasonable to expect farmers and nonfarmers to have different responses to the two alternative policy descriptions. Mansfield and Smith found weak but confirming evidence that farmers or former farmers were opposed to both plans but slightly less opposed to the cost-share scheme. Nonfarmers did not display these differences. Thus, respondents do notice context. As a result, respondents' attributes, along with those of the survey questions, can offer plausibility checks on the understanding of the choice questions.

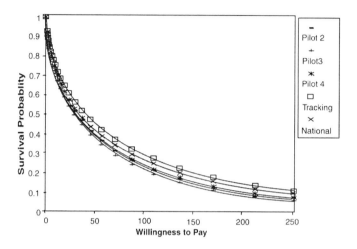

FIGURE 2. *Estimated Survival Curves Comparing CV Results across Pilots and Final Survey for Exxon Valdez Natural Resource Damage Assessment Source: Carson et al. (1992)*

The second area where the NOAA Panel focused attention was on properties of choices for measuring economic trade-offs that we expect to observe based on theory. In a least one instance, subsequent research has proposed more stringent standards than either the Panel or theory would suggest. The primary "test" in this category is the so-called scope test. The NOAA Panel's specific recommendation was:

Rationality in its weakest form requires certain kinds of consistency among choices made by individuals…Usually, though not always, it is reasonable to suppose that more of something regarded as good is better so long as an individual is not satiated. This is, in general, translated into a WTP somewhat more for more of a good, as judged by the individual. Also, if marginal or incremental WTP for additional amounts does decline with the amount already available, it is usually not reasonable to assume that it declines very abruptly (Arrow et al., 1993, p. 4604).

Subsequent research by Diamond (1996) and Hammitt and Graham (1999) has suggested that greater resolution can be expected with proportionality of the WTP measures to "size" of the object of choice. In Diamond's scheme, WTP measures for each of two different sized changes in the same nonmarket good, Δq_1 and Δq_2, would be related as in equation (3):

$$WTP(\Delta q_1) \geq \left(\frac{\Delta q_1}{\Delta q_2}\right) \cdot WTP(\Delta q_2) \qquad (3)$$

TABLE 2. *Example of Payment Vehicle Cross-Check*

Part I – Description of Object of Choice (randomly assigned)
A. Wildflowers The U.S. Department of Transportation is interested in improving the appearance and environmental conditions around interstate highways. North Carolina's program of planting wildflowers along its major highways is a small program that helps improve the appearance of highways. A recent national proposal would expand these types of programs. This plan would increase the planting of trees, evergreens, and ground cover, including wildflowers along fifty-yard corridors on either side of interstate highways throughout the United States. It would also pay for clean up and maintenance of areas after planting. *B. Tire Crumbling* The U.S. Department of Transportation is considering programs to recycle used car and truck tires. Of the 200 million tires discarded each year, about 168 million are sent to landfills or junkyards, where they are a fire threat and a breeding area for mosquitoes and rodents. The proposed system would make used tires into crumb rubber for asphalt to pave roads. Experience with this process indicates that it is more costly than current paving methods. Paving firms would need some public support to do it. This plan provides public support to private paving firms for facilities to convert used tires so they can be used for road paving.
Part II – Description of Choice Mechanism
To do so would require an annual federal surcharge in addition to current fees for state vehicle registrations. This would be ____ [randomly assigned $.50, $1, $2, $5, $10, $15 to each individual] per vehicle. It would be paid for each car or truck you have that requires a license plate each year. Please keep in mind your current household income and the number of cars and trucks you purchase licenses for. If you could vote on this plan, how would you vote? Yes, to support it. No, to oppose it. Don't know (do not offer this response).

Source: Smith (1996)

Graham and Hammitt (1999) have proposed a similar relationship for risk changes. Whether expressed in terms of a commodity or a lottery (i.e., a risk change), both studies add restrictions beyond the basic theory underlying choice to derive their proportionality results.[24] As a result, the scope test is probably not the "litmus test" originally envisioned by many economists. Theory implies that bigger amounts of the same object of choice should be worth more than smaller amounts. Judgments of how much larger the trade-offs for larger amounts should be require additional assumptions about preferences that are not easily substantiated.

Most discussions of validity follow Mitchell and Carson (1989) and consider the three C's – content validity, construct validity, and criterion validity. My discussion has suggested some simple additional gauges – direct and indirect – of whether the respondents: (a) understood the survey; (b) responded consistently with what would be implied given that understanding; and (c) provided information, which when interpreted in an economic choice context, adheres to general economic consistency conditions. Once these conditions are satisfied, the evaluation of quality can move to judgments about the robustness of estimates to alternative assumptions.

Robustness has many dimensions. I will discuss three aspects of the judgments associated with it: the influence of model specification; the treatment of unobserved heterogeneity (the error); and the composition of the sample used for the valuation analysis. This last element is essentially concerned with the importance of sample selection effects. Do respondents who agree to participate in surveys have special features that bias valuation measures?

All estimates require maintained assumptions about the structure of the data-generating process. In the case of SC studies, this process is a model of individual choice, as discussed in Section 2. In the case of a discrete response CV survey, estimates of economic parameters require a specification for the indirect utility function that is hypothesized to "explain" respondent choices.[25] This decision uses a specific algebraic form to represent the equation I presented in general terms in equations (1a) through (1c). For the two outcome cases, if we assume the survey allows for variation in both the cost (c) and the amount of the environmental resource (or nonmarket good) Δq, a linear form implies that equation (2) is replaced by equation (4).

$$c^* = \frac{\alpha_2 \Delta q}{\alpha_1} \tag{4}$$

In this case a linear indirect utility function would be given by $V = \alpha_0 + \alpha_1 m + \alpha_2 q$. Notice (4) leaves out the error. c^* describes the implied estimate for the maximum WTP, given a choice situation as implied in my earlier discussion. Alter the assumptions about the form of the preference structure and the estimated values for c^* would be completely different.[26] To my knowledge, the only study evaluating the potential error these changes can cause is one by Ju Chin Huang and me (1998, 2002). We designed a Monte Carlo framework to mimic discrete response CV questions. Three "true" specifications for preferences were used, varying, in addition to the algebraic form, the implied ratio of use to nonuse value embodied in a derived true WTP for each model. A simple discrete response CV model was estimated with data from each form. The experiments found that as the importance of the nonuse contribution increased, the error in measures of WTP became smaller. The intuition for our results is straightforward. Under these conditions, the omission of use-related variables (such as the prices of the related private goods) becomes less important.

Our analysis used a controlled, numerical experiment to evaluate modeling judgments. Specific analytical models were selected to describe preferences and a set of values for incomes, relative prices, and quality changes were specified. While we considered some variations in each of these decisions, the inevitable question one can raise about this strategy for evaluating modeling judgments is how relevant are these choices to actual applications? This issue is important. It implicitly asks whether the conclusions drawn from these types of controlled experiments can be useful for actual practice. To help answer this question, consider our finding that substitutes are less important when nonuse values become the primary motivation for choice. Can we expect to find that the treatment of substitutes explains differences in SC surveys in practice? I believe the answer is yes – our findings for this conclusion do appear to be reasonably robust.

An example illustrates why. The application involves a direct field comparison of CV and choice experiments by Boxall et al. (1996). They report using CV and SC for moose hunters to evaluate the trade-offs these recreationists would make to improve hunting success. The hunters were given the task of selecting a hunting trip in a particular area (a wildlife management unit) with an improved moose population versus not hunting in that area. The cost was described as increased distance required to hunt (and thus higher travel costs) with the improved moose population. In contrast to the CV design, the SC study involved presenting each respondent with 16 pairs of alternative descriptions of moose hunting sites varying the distance, the same measures of moose population, quality of roads and trails, encounters with other hunters, and logging activity. Each choice panel had a no-hunting option.

In comparing the separate subsets from the same overall sample, they derived three sets of results for the expected WTP for the same improvement in moose populations. These findings are summarized in Table 3. Comparing the first and second rows of Table 3, it is easy to see that the CV estimates are more than 20 times the size of the means from the SC study.[27]

The authors discuss potential reasons for these differences: eliminating experience, sample attributes, and the model. They conclude that the differences were due to respondents' perceptions of substitutes. To see their point we need to consider the expression for WTP within a linear random utility model (RUM). This relationship is given in equation (5).

$$\tilde{c} = \frac{1}{\alpha_1}\left[\ln\left(\sum_{i \in S}\exp(V_{i1})\right) - \ln\left(\sum_{i \in S}\exp(V_{i0})\right)\right] \tag{5}$$

$\tilde{c}$ is the WTP implied by the RUM (with Type I extreme value errors). V_{i0} and V_{i1} correspond to the values of the deterministic portion of the linear indirect utility function without and with the proposed improvement in *one* of the hunting areas included in choice set S.[28] This choice set is not carefully described in the paper, but presumably includes all the available moose hunting sites (15) along with the prospect of no hunting. When this set is reduced to the one site versus no hunting, we have the third row of Table 3. This situation provides a more comparable estimate than what is reported in the second row. The authors interpret this result as a situation where the survey respondents are "ignoring substitution options" in answering CV questions. I have a somewhat different view. The differences do arise from the treatment of substitutes in the two models. However, we cannot be sure that CV respondents ignored substitutes. Instead, what we know is that the authors' initial comparison failed to match both the object of choice and the apparent circumstances of choice between the CV and SC questions. We do not know that respondents failed to consider substitutes. They simply evaluated the alternative as presented.

In the CV question, all hunters could do was purchase (through travel) or not hunt. The SC task was treated as a decision that involved selecting one of the alternatives that allowed each respondent to use the improved site, to use one of the existing alternatives, or to not hunt. To mimic the CV question, the analytical translation of the choice process *must be* different. My point is direct: this dimension of robustness is a function of both the survey performance and the maintained assumptions of the model.[29]

In practice, the treatment of the error in CV and SC studies is realized in at least two ways. The first arises from the selection of summary statistics for measures of the estimates – mean, median, Turnbull lower bound mean, etc. It can also arise indirectly through the use of questioning formats such as "cheap talk" and degrees of certainty in stated choices (see Alberini et al., 1997, and Welsh and Poe, 1998) that imply the choice process is somewhat different from that envisioned in equation (1a) through (1c). The second approach to the treatment of error interacts with the choice for model specification. We can see it through the selection of mixed logit (or random parameter) choice models versus other formats (see Swait, this volume). I believe the most constructive way to consider these decisions parallels the suggestion of Herriges and Phaneuf (2002) in modeling revealed preference recreation site models. It is analogous to an assumption about the substitution among choice alternatives, i.e., the structure of a Slutsky matrix, in a model that might be used to describe a conventional demand model for sets of goods and services at positive levels of consumption for all commodities. These specification decisions for discrete choice models are equivalent to imposing restrictions on the correlations between the random utilities assumed to be derived from choice alternatives. Correlation in this context plays a role analogous to substitution in the continuous demand case. Thus, evaluations of the sensitivity of conclusions to these modeling choices must also address the economic assumptions that are implicitly *added* when we alter the summary statistics, make additions to choice questions, and determine the placement of errors in our model specifications.

*TABLE 3. Boxall et al. Comparison of Contingent Valuation and Stated Choice Studies**

Method	Expected Value
Contingent valuation	$85.59
Choice experiment with "full" choice set	$ 3.46
Choice experiment with "no" substitutes	$56.69

* Per trip WTP; these appear to be in Canadian dollars in 1992 but the paper does not describe specific dates.

The last dimension of robustness concerns the sensitivity to the sample composition. It underlies the NOAA Panel's rule of thumb for high response rate (e.g., above 70%) and proposals to use aggregate data to correct for selection effects in mailed surveys (see Cameron et al., 1999, and Smith and Mansfield, 1998). Evaluations of the importance of efforts to meet high response rates have been limited. Ideally, we would like to have some information about the relative effects of selection corrections versus high response rates on the properties of benefit measures. For the most part, the literature has overlooked this trade-off. Instead, surveys have turned to commercial vendors offering "captive" respondents. These are web-based surveys with panels of households who are paid in services or direct compensation to complete a specified number of internet surveys each month. Thus, for these groups realizing a high response rate is not the same as what is accomplished with a conventional response rate. The panel itself is subject to a selection effect. While it is possible to use observables to mimic Census-based descriptions by a representative sample, this strategy does not address the potential consequences of unobserved heterogeneity in the panel respondents signaled by their agreement to participate.

We should acknowledge that the past literature offers little guidance for most of the recent web-based surveys using internet panels through such commercial firms as Knowledge Networks or Harris International (see Alberini et al., 2004, and DeShazo and Cameron, 2004a, 2004b, as examples of these studies). The issue would seem to parallel the evaluation issues raised by Heckman and his collaborators (see Heckman (2001) for an overview of the research to that point). High response rates in this context would mean nothing. Similarly, comparisons between demographic features of respondents and characteristics based on census data or other criteria are largely uninformative for one simple reason: these respondents are *paid* to be part of these panels and participate in a set of surveys. They should be described as "professional" interviewees. It seems clear that declining participation in surveys (due to telemarketing and other factors) is transforming survey research. The literature on how to interpret these panels has not caught up to the practice. Are we training people to be professional subjects or simply improving the efficiency of the survey process? Is the pool of potential subjects so special due to internet use that re-weighting to match a desired demographic profile from the census does not accomplish its intended objective? These issues are part of current research and answers are not available.

What can be done in the meantime to judge robustness to this feature of the analysis (i.e., the specialized samples)? My response is incomplete but feasible: include several relevant (to the research objective of each study) questions that also appear on publicly available surveys that do not use web-based panels and compare their performance for seemingly comparable groups. This strategy would allow comparative evaluation. It offers a start in the analysis of the implications of web-based panels.

5. RELATED BEHAVIORS, JOINT ESTIMATION AND META-ANALYSIS

Many authors have described revealed-preference (RP) approaches to benefit measurement as "detective work." These methods require accumulating sufficient information about observed behaviors to permit estimation of the WTP for whatever amenity change is the focus of the research. Efforts to evaluate the quality of a SC study with related behaviors recognize that even when it is not possible to "connect the dots" for a full application of RP methods, there may be *signs* that specific stated choices are likely. Consistency in these terms between expected and realized signs for these changes in revealed behaviors does not guarantee a high-quality estimate. Nonetheless, it does raise confidence.

One way of considering this process is to review the strategies associated with joint estimation using RP and SC information and then to imagine a situation where the assumptions or data available are incomplete – what could one do? This thought process often yields quality checks. As I suggested in Section 3, the nature of these cross-checks depends on how much *we* are willing to assume about the role of the nonmarket good in preferences.

More specifically, the typical strategy for an RP/SC application begins with the indirect utility function $V(m, \bar{p}, \bar{t}, q, \varepsilon)$ and might match some expected property of the demand function for a use-related good, x, to a stated behavior as in (6a) and (6b).[30]

$$-\frac{V_p}{V_m} = x(m, \bar{p}, \bar{t}, q_o, \varepsilon)$$
(6a)

Prob(select stated choice) =
$$\text{Prob}\left(V(m - c, \bar{p}, \bar{t}, q_o + \Delta q, \varepsilon) - V(m, \bar{p}, \bar{t}, q_o, \varepsilon)\right)$$
(6b)

The first equation (6a) uses Roy's identity to define the demand for the use-related good. The second (6b) defines the probability that an individual would pay c

to assure an increase in quality from q_0 to $q_0+\Delta q$. Shared parameters between $x(.)$ and the function (in 6b) describing this probability provide the basis for the efficiency gains that are usually assumed to arise with this type of joint estimation.[31]

At a general level, the logic underlying joint estimation recognizes that estimates of c^* (the WTP) from SC responses are random variables. If we believe that there are past choices or other current, stated choices that are correlated with ε, then conditioning our estimate for $E(c^*)$ on these behaviors should provide a better estimate.[32] Using the framework to condition estimates from choice surveys does not necessarily impose as much structure as joint estimation does, but it implies that we can "check" our estimates based on these interrelationships. Let B describe a set of behaviors that lead to consistent predictions of the stated choice used to estimate c^*. Also, assume that $i \in B$ implies that individual i has or states he will undertake one or more of these behaviors. In this context, a cross-check amounts to examining

$$\Delta_i = E\left(c_i^* \middle| i \in B\right) - E\left(c_i^*\right) \tag{7}$$

In short, this *a priori* information is assumed to allow the analyst to sign Δ_i.

Avid fishers should have a greater likelihood of favoring policies to improve water quality in areas where they fish. Families with children with asthma should support policies to reduce air pollution that aggregates asthmatic conditions. Older respondents may well not support efforts to improve public rock climbing facilities.

Two features of these examples are important. First, all describe past (or concurrent) observable behaviors or characteristics. Second, the judgments are not always true. An example may help to explain this second point. Dale Whittington, who pioneered the application of SC methods in developing countries, recounted to me an early field experience in a rural agricultural area of Pakistan. He was investigating households' WTP for improved public water supplies via a policy that would provide village specific standpipes. These are public water sources at a central location in a rural village. An old man responding to the survey answered a discrete response question indicating he was willing to pay one of the largest stated annual fees for the system. While he lived reasonably close to the proposed site for the standpipe, it was also known (to Dale's interviewers) that he had his own indoor pump for a private well providing clean and more reliable water than what was expected for the proposed new public source.

The logic of equation (7) implies that his Δ_i should have been less than zero, but his response seemed to imply that his value exceeded the average value (provided the schedule of bids offered was selected correctly). Using this prior expectation as a gauge of quality would imply that the survey was inadequate. Actually, the verbal responses he offered (he was not, as I recall, specifically asked why he answered the way he did) acknowledged that he did not need to use the standpipe system. However, he felt the younger families in the village needed it and he was willing to pay to help them. The moral of this story is that the Δ_i we can observe is a random variable. We will label that measure as Δ_i^*. One way to apply this point is to acknowledge there is a probability that Δ_i will be incorrect, and we need to collect as much information as possible to be able to interpret our conditional expectations. As a result, we need to describe whether the behaviors are indeed consistent with the higher valuation.

To introduce the fact that hypothesized behaviors may not always signal correctly the intended size of nonmarket values, let π_i designate the probability that individual i will engage in one or more of the behaviors that are thought to be related to higher WTP.[33] In short, the information we bring for assessing what actual behaviors and characteristics imply for stated choices is inexact. Thus, the analyst should evaluate the weight of the evidence. Using an analog to what von Haefen derives (based on the law of iterated expectations) in the case of recreation site choice modeling we have:

$$\Delta_i^* = (1 - \pi_i)\left[E\left(c_i^* \middle| i \in B\right) - E\left(c_i^* \middle| i \notin B\right)\right] \qquad (8)$$

Equation (8) indicates that Δ_i^* is only as informative as our ability to model the outcomes, and our judgment about this skill is included here as an estimate of π_i. In most applications we would not be able to develop formal measures of Δ_i^* or π_i. This structure is an attempt to formalize why we look for complementary behaviors and what the sources of errors might be in using them.

There is another source for information to judge the quality of a new study – the accumulation of past research in an area. Meta-analysis is the process of developing systematic summaries of the results of past research. If a new SC study addresses a set of resources that have been studied before, then as with behaviors that may be correlated for the same individuals, one might hypothesize that the results from these studies should be correlated. Were the data available, one might consider a multiple sample with joint estimation of the choice models (see Imbens and Lancaster, 1994; Smith, 2004). As a rule, however, this strategy is not generally feasible. Meta-analyses may be the next best option.

One interpretation for how meta-analyses are used in this context would suggest that they allow construction of an estimate for the total (or marginal) WTP to compare with the new study's results. This is a different type of conditional expectation for c^*. If we understood the processes distinguishing the objectives of the earlier research comprising the meta–sample, and were able to develop a theoretically consistent summary, then it would be possible to describe the properties of any difference in the objectives of the past studies in comparison to a new study. A meta-summary would provide these controls. The conditional expectation from such a model would offer the described comparative estimate. Thus, the overall logic is broadly comparable to what leads to equation (8) with a different set of conditioning factors.

Clearly, the value of such comparisons depends on the comparability of what is being measured and the consistency of this earlier research. As Subhrendu

Pattanayak and I (Smith and Pattanayak, 2002) suggest, many meta-analyses have not considered the importance of economic consistency in their summaries.

In applied economic research, this type of comparison can be expected to be inexact for a simple reason. Replication is scarce. New SC studies usually involve both methodological advances and changes to *new* resources. The professional and external funding incentives assure that without these attributes the new studies would not have been undertaken. As a result, developing a comparable estimate from a meta summary (or any specific study) is likely to require considerable judgment. The comparisons envisioned reflect both the features of the new primary research and those underlying the construction of "comparable" research. As in the case of related behavior, these exercises do not provide a single, unambiguous basis for judging quality. Instead they become a part of the "weight of evidence" used to develop an argument supporting a study's results.

6. THE QUALITY OF RESEARCH STRATEGIES

Most of the discussion up to this point has described ways to think about the elements practitioners use to increase their confidence in survey results. For external consumers of SC studies, it suggests what to look for. For producers it provides my explanations of why people adopt specific cross-checks of their results. Other chapters in this volume have discussed how SC studies must address a full set of activities leading to the definition of: (a) the relevant attributes of the object of choice; (b) the design space for feasible variations in them, as well as the circumstances conditioning individual choices, and the trade-offs they are assumed to reflect; and (c) the details of the experimental design, sampling activities, information provided, format of the questionnaire, etc.

It goes without saying that the survey research process is a "roundabout" one. A sequence of steps usually described in a causal sequence (often with feedback loops in some of the intermediate stages) is required, including:

- background on problem definition,
- focus groups eliciting information about how people think about the problem and describe it,
- draft survey instruments,
- cognitive interviews for key elements of questions and explanatory materials,
- pretest interviews (e.g., telephone, mail, in-person, internet),
- experimental design,
- pilot samples,
- final survey,

Analyses of various types take place at each step in this process as other authors in this volume have described in detail. The external observer is expected to read descriptions of the process and somehow make a judgment. One might ask how this judgment is to be formed. That is, how do we know a good process from a bad one? Are there signals of problems or consistencies that the reader should look for in descriptions? This section proposes one way to think about evaluating the full process of survey design and implementation. It is easy to describe but difficult to implement. Simply stated – look at the process in reverse. Knowing the results of the final survey – would the analysis undertaken at the initial pilot stage have lead to results that are consistent with the final estimates? If the answer is no, then why did this happen?[34]

The rationale for my proposal stems from Arrow and Fisher's (1974) early suggestion about how to conceptualize learning and new information in the presence of irreversible decisions. There is an incremental value to new information, provided decisions have not been made that would preclude it being used. In the context of survey research, each new pilot or pretest may add information. Delaying final fieldwork to undertake these intermediate steps and checking the components intended for the final survey assumes that we are *using* the resulting new information to enhance the objectives of the overall research. As Fisher (2000) notes in formal terms, this is about being able to use the information before estimating the expected value of a choice versus being required to estimate expected values before choosing. Jensen's inequality, along with the convexity of the objective function, assures a nonnegative value of information, provided it is used. My proposal is to evaluate the survey research process based on these criteria. By looking back, we evaluate our judgments.[35]

How might this suggestion work? It is difficult to give a complete example because implementing the suggestion would change recordkeeping and might even alter the thought process in survey design. Nonetheless, I can use a natural resource damage application, the Montrose case, to provide a sketchy illustration. The case involved disposal of DDT and PCB off the coast of California over a long period of time and associated injuries to fish and birds.[36]

The survey design process involved developing two questionnaires that were randomly assigned to the survey respondents. The primary survey was a "base case" that described the injuries believed capable of being established based on scientific evidence. The second involved a smaller set of injuries designed to test scope effects. The base and scope surveys varied the injuries based on the number of affected species (base – 2 bird species and 2 fish, scope – 2 fish) and the time for natural recovery (base – 50 years, scope – 15 years). The plan to accelerate recovery was described as taking 5 years, so for the base survey this would reduce the time for natural recovery by 45 years (versus 10 for the scope survey).

Developing the surveys involved focus groups, pretests, and pilot surveys. Table 4 summarizes the key features distinguishing the pilot surveys. To illustrate my proposal in simple terms, I selected the overlapping cost amounts for the final survey with all pilots (i.e., $10, $80, and $215) and conducted some comparative analysis. Taking the final survey as if it provided the "true" values for the proportion supporting the plan, could distinctions in the pilot estimates for these proportions help to signal what was intended to be learned by the manipulation of information presented in each pilot?

As the last three columns of Table 4 suggest, this question is not directly answered, but there is some suggestive evidence. The reason these answers are very approximate is readily seen once the objectives of each pilot are stated. There was *not* one single or a well-defined set of changes in each pilot. As a result, there is not an unambiguous prediction for what to expect. Multiple dimensions were changed simultaneously, so expectations were impossible. Thus, one might ask, if an external observer cannot learn, how did the research team respond to the new information?[37]

This question captures the point of this proposal for evaluating survey design processes. If the analysts cannot specify a clear pathway for how they learned from the development process, then, all else equal, external observers should have less confidence in the final survey instrument. Of course, it is also important to acknowledge that questionnaire development is an inexact science. If the researchers knew in advance how people would conceptualize a resource, or how they could explain changes to it, as well as how to describe the implications of the terms of payment, the development process would be unnecessary. Survey development involves trial and error. The point is that the process should be judged by a set of expected outcomes from each step that is intended to be used in judging whether the changes to a survey instrument are accomplishing their intended objective.

The last three columns use a one-sample test of proportions (assuming normality). The proportion from the final survey is deliberately treated as the true value (measured without error) to evaluate the direction of effects anticipated from the pilot versus what was learned. In the second column of the table, I report the hypothesized direction for the proportion of yes responses in the relevant pilot compared to the base case of the final survey. For example, with pilot II, both the 50 year and the 150 year recovery subsets, I would expect that a plan to accelerate recovery for 6 species injured would be a larger object of choice than the same plan (in terms of time to completion) involving 4 species. This judgment is assumed to be the same for each potential one-time cost. The alternative hypothesis for each test is a greater proportion willing to support the plan. The p-values are based on one-sided alternatives. For pilot II, with the longest time for natural recovery, the results are somewhat supportive of my prior expectation at the middle design point. Surprisingly, the value for the highest cost is less supportive than the $80 design point.

My *ex post* judgments on Pilots III and IV are that they would be approximately equivalent to the base scenario. Only one additional species (California sea lions) distinguishes them. For pilot III at the $80 design point, there is a significant difference. One might argue that this design point should be most informative because of its proximity to the lower bound estimate of mean WTP.[38] Higher design points will be sensitive to respondent income; lower values may not force such careful consideration. Introducing the manipulation that reorders the plan and natural recovery appears to eliminate this perception of a difference in the two cases.

Clearly my proposal is just that – a suggestion for how to evaluate the survey process. Its value depends on whether it is possible to design and document how the steps in implementation lead to predictable outcomes and then to demonstrate retrospectively that the learning developed in the process of designing the survey instrument was embedded in the final questionnaire and design.

TABLE 4. Montrose Survey Pilot Samples Compared to Final Base Survey

Pilot	Hypothesis	Sample Size	Design Cost Amounts	Number of Species[*]	Special Features	Tests Pilot Compared to Base Proportions (p-values)		
						$10	$80	$215
II[**]	Pilot larger	460	10, 45, 80, 215	6	split sample: 50 versus 150 years for natural recovery	0.55 (0.73)	0.34 (0.07)	0.92 (0.26)
III	Approx. equal	324	10, 45, 80, 215	5	samples targeted at high and low response rate	0.17	0.03	0.20
IV	Approx. equal	473	10, 25, 40, 80, 215	5	reversed order of natural recovery and accelerated recovery; natural presented second	0.15	0.74	0.19

[*] The six species for pilot II included two fish species (white croaker and kelp boss), three bird species (peregrine falcon, bald eagle, and brown pelican), and California sea lions. In pilots III and IV, brown pelicans were dropped because it was believed continuing injuries could not be established. In the final base survey, California sea lions were dropped for similar reasons.

[**] The estimates in brackets are for p-values for the sub-sample with longer time for natural recovery.

7. PRACTICAL GUIDANCE

I promised that my discussion would offer some practical suggestions. These are divided into two parts: first suggestions for new survey researchers (the "doers"); second, suggestions for users. The first group is aspiring to evaluate quality as they do their research so they can use these activities to convince readers of the quality of their final product; the second is, presumably, seeking to gauge the quality of a completed study. All of my suggestions are confined to strategies for collecting or using information to evaluate the quality of a SC study. They are largely personal. I would be hard pressed to document a specific set of carefully structured studies that support each of them. Moreover, these do not represent a comprehensive list of all the elements one might expect to find in a high-quality SC study. The other chapters in this volume discuss many of these elements.

Doers

- Include questions in your surveys from established, publicly available surveys that are related to your objectives; this allows matching and cross-checks;
- include questions to assess the amount and quality of information respondents have about the issue being studied;
- gauge their understanding of what you present; keep track and analyze the factors influencing those who don't learn;
- look for parallels in attitudes, past behaviors, past choices, and stated behaviors that should be positively *and* negatively correlated with the goal of the choice questions;
- consider indirect implications of the payment vehicle – remember the vehicle registration story;
- collect verbatims; remember my story about the older respondents' demand for public water supplies;
- "most women don't engage in recreational hunting" (see Smith and Van Houtven, 2004, for examples from The National Survey of Fishing Hunting and Wildlife Associated Recreation); remember preferences in a household are different; a household choice is not necessarily the same as an individual choice; be clear on how the decision process is presented and who within the household might gain; it is important to take into account activities that require consideration;[39]
- cross tabulations should always be a part of the first stage analysis of all data collected (pretests, pilots, or final surveys); tabulate these responses against categorical variables as well as on the design features; they are essential in understanding how the survey was interpreted by different groups; often it helps to detect coding errors as well.

Users

- the "laugh test" sounds silly – nonetheless it is often the very first thing some investigators consider as a plausibility gauge; in my opinion, this process only detects the extremes – implausibly large or small values which almost never appear in the published literature;
- systematic plausibility gauges – some possibilities for evaluating estimates for WTP are:
    - as a percent of income (individual and family),
    - relative to expenditures for closely related goods or activities undertaken with the same frequency (e.g., once in a lifetime vacations versus annual vacations versus weekend trips);
- related and unrelated behaviors – look for consistencies and inconsistencies;
- use publicly available data to match the demographic profile of a study and compare related expenditures (if they are not reported in the SC study) for sub groups (e.g., age, gender, and income cohorts);

- consider "economic" parameters – Hanemann's (1991) simple approximation for the relationship between income flexibility for nonmarket goods and income elasticities, and Palmquist's result (2005) for cases involving weak complementarity can, in some applications, offer a basis for forming some intuition about what to expect in measures of behavioral parameters;
- consider historical analogies, Costa's (1999) use of recreation expenditures to evaluate living standards is the type of parallel to be considered; how such parallels might be developed depends on the specific application;
- look for results consistent with my list for "doers."

8. FINAL THOUGHTS ON THE END USES OF VALUATION INFORMATION

Over forty years ago, Krutilla (1961) admonished theorists to be more tolerant of the "perforated justifications" for the analysis that is available to evaluate policy because "...the alternative is not to retire to inactivity, but rather to reach decisions in the absence of analysis" (p. 234). His comment reminds us that measures of the economic value of a change in a nonmarket resource are often used along with other information to make decisions. Judgments about their quality should consider the nature of those decisions and the role the benefit information plays in how they are made.

Most environmental policies preclude the use of benefit information in the design of rules. A series of Presidential Executive Orders and legislative mandates, however, have given benefit-cost analysis a greater role in evaluating the regulatory alternatives once they have been defined through some separate process. Similarly, benefit measures are used in public investment projects and in activities related to the management of public resources.

For public policy applications, whether regulation, investment, or management, Krutilla's argument does not imply that any number is superior to none. This is a part of my initial definition of quality: the quality of an effort to estimate economic trade-offs should be judged based on whether the study is able to measure the desired concept, as intended, in an informative way. Measures of economic trade-offs used for policy actions do not prescribe decisions. They inform decisions along with many other considerations. Benefit-cost analysis helps to promote processes that identify all components of choice so that the "cards are on the table." As a result, participants in the process have incentives to identify outcomes that can *and cannot* be monetized.

The context for what can be measured is different when valuation information enters litigation. Depending on the statutes underlying the litigation, it has a much more specific role that is not necessarily intended to help structure a constructive dialogue. Often it establishes upper and lower bounds for a judicial (or a jury) decision. This role creates different incentives for how judgments are made by the analysts on each side of a case. For example, it may be desirable to avoid imposing prior restrictions on preferences that might provide an array of plausibility checks for choice surveys because mistaken restrictions can lead to *biased* estimates. These mistakes may well be small, so in other contexts analysts would be willing to argue that their overall effect is to, for example, improve mean squared error. Nonetheless, the term "bias" has a chilling effect on litigation proceedings. As a result, actions that might be construed as possibly biasing estimates are avoided at all costs.

Simple, direct methods that allow experts to form opinions about the lost benefits due to resource injury (as estimates of damages) are often favored over results that might be based on methods that could be "better" on statistical grounds. However, these "state of the art" approaches are usually described as too complex and lacking in "common sense." If laypersons can understand the logic and feel confident that the process measures what needs to be estimated, then the approach is more likely to be favored. What this means is that researchers face a very different mindset when they conduct analyses for litigation. Guidance for litigation purposes, such as that from the NOAA panel, should, therefore, not be expected to transfer completely to cases of policy evaluation.

We will never know the true value of any economic benefit measure. These measures represent summaries of past choices or assessments of the implications of potential choices. It is important to see benefit-cost analysis conducted for policy evaluation as a process that imposes a rational logic on the elements that influence a decision. The specific components of a benefit-cost analysis are organized in a particular way, describing the pros and cons of a choice using a common metric, to facilitate comparisons. Efforts to judge the quality of the benefit measures inevitably seek to develop survey and measurement strategies that are good substitutes for what I described as the *trade-off resolution* in market choices. They should enhance the confidence we have over some elements on the decision-making table. They will never be reduced to a checklist. Instead, they should be viewed as methods to describe the potential importance of choices that are part of policy analysis. Understanding them can help to improve the policy makers' appreciation of the uncertainties in the information available to them.

---

9. ENDNOTES

Thanks are due to Barbara Kanninen for very constructive comments on several earlier drafts and Kenny Pickle for patiently preparing several revisions in response to these suggestions and my own "endless edits." Partial support was provided by the U.S. Environmental Protection Agency through Star Grant # R82950801.

[1] The format was developed with H. Spencer Banzhaf to explain weak complementarity and the Willig condition (see Smith and Banzhaf, 2004a). I have used it subsequently to consider the variety of ways preference restrictions affect the definition of price indexes (Smith and Banzhaf, 2004b) and the characterization of interactions between economic and physiological factors in determining environmental vulnerability of heterogeneous groups (Smith et al., 2004).

[2] Another example of these failures is Tversky and Kahneman's (1991) hypothesis that people have reference dependent preferences. The basic idea is people perceive options available to them in a choice situation as gains or losses relative to a reference point. Hanemann (1999) has demonstrated that there is nothing in the theory of choice which is inconsistent with these behaviors, noting that,

> "…reference dependence *per se* is not required in order to generate the gain/loss disparity. …the essential requirement is convex indifference curves – i.e., less than perfect substitution in the indirect utility function…" (p. 78).

[3] This overview of the meaning of an economic value is based on the discussion in Bockstael et al. (2000).

[4] My example will abstract from issues concerning how the construction and operating costs of the new school are financed. These matters could also be considered as relevant to an individual's decision, but for my purpose here would make the example overly complex.

[5] For a more detailed discussion of the circumstances of choice, see Kopp and Smith (1997).

[6] This definition abstracts from the timing of choices. $\bar{T}$ in this case is treated as a resource, fixed in amount.

[7] This issue is a central motivation for Cameron et al. (2002). It is also the primary issue illustrated in Huang and Smith (1998).

[8] They require that the analyst consider these rating responses as incompletely observed (or censored rankings). This formulation allows ratings to be re-cast so that they are consistent with a choice model. It allows the responses to be modeled consistently with choices, rankings, and stated values.

[9] As noted in footnote 1, Smith and Banzhaf proposed that this structure be used to explain weak complementarity.

[10] There are interesting features of Figure 1a that have had different effects on the literature relating observed patterns of demand to preferences. For example, if we assume it implies additivity, $U(x,z,q) = \tilde{U}(x,z) + \overline{U}(q)$, then this is the condition Frisch used to isolate preference from demand without assuming cardinal preferences. His argument relied on observing market choices for all three goods (see Samuelson, 1974b). In the absence of choice information about q, this is the formulation Hanemann (1988) selected to characterize nonuse values. That is, there are no changes in the marginal rate of substitution between x and z with changes in q. It is this feature that is my emphasis here.

[11] I could also have produced parallel indifference maps with weak separability, but this stranger form limits the ability to use corner solution models to recover measures of nonuse values.

[12] This elasticity is defined as the percentage change in the Marshallian virtual price for q, e.g., $\left(V_q / V_m\right)$ with a percentage change in income.

[13] In this case, the change in the expenditures on the perfect substitute with changes in q measure the WTP for a change in q.

[14] See Smith et al. (2004) for further discussion of this case.

[15] We can treat these restrictions as implying scaling (or repackaging) restrictions on the amount of a private good or translation restrictions. In the case of the former restrictions, changes in the amenities can be used to define Hicksian equivalent price changes. For the latter, they can be used to define compensating income changes. See Smith et al. (2004) for further discussion.

[16] See Smith and Desvousges (1990) for an early example of this logic.

[17] The NOAA guidelines are not free of controversy. A leading critic, Harrison (2000) has noted that:
> The NOAA report was a great disappointment…Given the inability of CVM [CV method] practitioners and consumers to weed out sense from nonsense in the extant literature, it is unlikely that there will be much progress as the result of the NOAA report (p. 2).

Harrison documents differences between the Panel's recommended guidelines and experimental results completed at the time the report was prepared. While he is correct in suggesting that there was little "hard" evidence to support their detailed recommendation, I do not think the outcome has been as dire as he suggests. The report got researchers interested in testing its suggestions. Subsequent research on CV has offered a number of new methods and survey strategies. In fact, interest in SC surveys is partially a result of the high costs of meeting their standards with a CV survey.

[18] Laboratory experiments have made the process of evaluating alternative survey formats more systematic. Nonetheless, we remain at an early stage in understanding how to transfer findings from these controlled studies to field surveys for more complex goods.

[19] Unfortunately, the details of these activities are usually not reported systematically. The findings and responses are certainly relevant to the researchers' confidence that their approach addresses the question intended. Ideally, it would also be a larger part of the published research record.

[20] For example, Smith et al. (1997) used a rank logit analysis, estimated from questions posed in focus groups, to evaluate the relative amounts of beach quality associated with photos mailed to survey respondents a part of a larger survey measuring how households valued programs to clean up marine debris. The ranking of the photos was consistent with the independent ranks implied by the WTP estimates derived from the survey. This comparison suggests that the photos were effective in communicating similar relative amounts of debris across different groups of individuals.

[21] Over 10 percent of the respondents provided an incorrect answer.

[22] The median WTP measures are, as expected, quite comparable.

Survey	Sample Size	95% Confidence Interval for the Median
Pilot II	95	19.42 - 6.70
Pilot III	244	21.61 - 36.19
Pilot IV	175	24.53 - 44.04
Tracking	209	29.54 - 52.01
National	1,043	28.49 - 37.51

[23] For example, Welsh et al. (1995) report a detailed analysis of their pilot study for a final survey that sought to estimate the economic value of changing the water flow rate through the Glenn Canyon Dam to reduce effects of downstream resources but the estimates were never compared specifically with the final survey results. Nine survey versions were evaluated in the pilot surveys and six in the final. Changes were made in the description of the environmental consequences of alternative water flows based on improved understanding of the consequence of these programs. More detailed comparisons of the choices would offer another type of plausibility check.

[24] See Smith (1997) and Cameron and DeShazo (2004) for discussion.

[25] One could also begin as Cameron (1988) suggested by hypothesizing that choice is based on a variation function. This logic imposes a normalizing restriction that allows the sole parameter in discrete choice models to be identified.

[26] I am describing a side discussion of the fact that with discrete-response data estimates of α_1 and α_2 are not identified independently of a scale parameter. That is, what we can estimate is α_1/σ and α_2/σ, where σ is the scale parameter for the additive error, assumed to reflect unobserved heterogeneity in V.

[27] These estimates are random variables. Simple comparisons are certainly not tests. Nonetheless, the size difference is so large given the precision in estimating the individual parameters it seems reasonable to

conclude they would be significantly different. The authors do not report standard errors for their WTP estimates in each case.

[28] $\widetilde{c}$ is reported here as a positive quantity. The authors have it reversed in their original study.

[29] There is a growing literature in experimental economics suggesting that choice tasks involving public goods are sensitive to provision rate and modeling assumptions. See Boyle et al. (2004) as a recent example that compares real and hypothetical choices for CV and SC studies.

[30] Notice I added unobserved heterogeneity, ε, or a random error to the description given in equations (1a) and (1c).

[31] The rationale for joint estimation has been described in other terms, some less favorable to the quality of SC information. Cameron (1992), for example, describes it as a basis for imposing budget discipline. Adamowicz et al. (1994) emphasize the relative size of the scale factor associated with RP and SC unobserved heterogeneity.

[32] This logic parallels von Haefen's (2003) argument for using observed choice to provide more informative welfare estimates with random utility models for recreation site choice.

[33] This description can be made more precise if one is prepared to enumerate the behaviors. At this point, my objective is to lay out the implications of von Haefen's logic as it might be applied to interpreting cross-checks for SC models.

[34] Clearly, these are not independent. The final survey was derived from analyses and judgments made based on the pilot. There should therefore be strong interrelationships. If there is none, what does this outcome say about the learning that derived from the process?

[35] The decision to undertake the final survey in a research project is in many respects irreversible. Thus we are using the rhetorical question underlying the conditional expected value of information to evaluate the process used to learn in survey design.

[36] See Carson et al. (1994) for the report to NOAA on the CV survey and Smith (2004) for a brief, published summary of the study and its findings.

[37] I was a member of that team and I suggest that it was these incomplete predictions that caused considerable debate largely because well-defined hypotheses did not motivate the pilots.

[38] The estimated WTP for the base plan, $63.24, was the Turnbull lower bound mean for the final survey, which was conducted in 1994.

[39] Jenkins and Osberg (2005) consider the need for coordination in uses of leisure time. To play tennis, for example, one needs a partner. Discriminating tennis players also impose skill level requirements on their selected opponents. This requires coordination in the timing of leisure decisions. The need to coordinate is not limited to group sports; it can also arise in coordinating within-household childcare as well as an array of other types of activities. With SC, depending on the activities of interest, other forms of coordination should probably be investigated.

10. REFERENCES

Adamowicz, W., J. Louviere and M. Williams, 1994, "Combining Revealed and Stated Preference Models for Valuing Environmental Amenities," *Journal of Environmental Economics and Management*, 26: 271-292.

Alberini, A., K.J. Boyle and M.P. Welsh, 1997, "Using Multiple Bounded Questions to Incorporate Preference Uncertainty in Nonmarket Valuation," in W-133 Benefits and Cost Transfers in Natural Resource Planning 9th Interim Report, University of Nevada, Reno.

Alberini, A., M. Cropper, A. Krupnick and N.B. Simon, 2004, "Does the Value of a Statistical Life Vary With Age and Health Status? Evidence from the US and Canada," *Journal of Environmental Economics and Management,* 48: 769-792.

Arrow, K.J, R. Solow, R.R. Portney, E.E. Leamer, R. Radner and H. Schman, 1993, "Report of the NOAA Panel on Contingent Valuation," *Federal Register* 58: 4601-4614.

Arrow, K.J. and A.C. Fisher, 1974, "Environmental Preservation, Uncertainty, and Irreversibility," *Quarterly Journal of Economics*, 88: 312-319.

Bockstael, N.E., A.M. Freeman, R.J. Kopp, P.R. Portney and V.K. Smith, 2000, "On Measuring Economic Values for Nature," *Environmental Science and Technology,* 34(8): 1384-89.

Boxall, P. C., W.L. Adamowicz, J. Swait, M. Williams and J. Louviere, 1996, "A Comparison of Stated Preference Methods in Environmental Valuation," *Ecological Economics*, 18: 243-253.

Boyle, K., M. Morrison and L. Taylor, 2004, "Why Value Estimates Generated Using Choice Modeling Exceed Contingent Valuation: Further Experimental Evidence," Presented at the Australian Agricultural and Resource Economics Society Conference, Melbourne, 11-13.

Cameron, T.A., 1988, "A New Paradigm for Valuing Non-Market Goods Using Referendum Data: Maximum Likelihood Estimation by Censored Logistic Regression," *Journal of Environmental Economics and Management*, 15(3): 355-79.

Cameron, T.A., 1992, "Nonuser Resource Values," *American Journal of Agricultural Economics*, 74: 1133-1137.

Cameron, T.A. and J.R. DeShazo, 2004, "Valuing Health-risk Reductions: Six Years, Lost Life-Years, and Latency," mimeo.

Cameron, T.A., G.L. Poe, R.G. Ethier and W.D. Schulze, 2002, "Alternative Non-Market Value-Elicitation Methods: Are the Underlying Preferences the Same?" *Journal of Environmental Economics and Management*, 44: 391-425.

Cameron, T.A., W.D. Shaw and S.R. Ragland, 1999, "Nonresponse Bias in Mail Survey Data: Salience vs. Endogenous Survey Complexity," in *Valuing Recreation and the Environment,* Herriges, J.A. and C.L. Kling , (Eds.), 217-251.

Carson, R.T., W.M. Hanemann, R.J. Kopp, J.A. Krosnick, R.C. Mitchell, S. Presser, P.A. Ruud, and V.K. Smith, 1994, "Prospective Interim Lost Use Value Due to DDT and PCB Contamination in Southern California," Report to the Natural Oceanic and Atmospheric Administration, Natural Resource Damage Assessment Inc, La Jolla; California.

Carson, R.T., W.M. Hanemann, R.J. Kopp, J.A. Krosnick, R.C. Mitchell, S. Presser, P.A. Ruud, V.K. Smith, 1997, "Temporal Reliability of Estimates from Contingent Valuation," *Land Economics*, 73(2): 151-63.

Carson, R.T., R.C. Mitchell, W.M. Hanemann, R.J. Kopp, S. Presser, and P.A. Ruud, 1992, "A contingent valuation study of lost passive use values resulting from the Exxon Valdez oil spill," Report to the Attorney General of the State of Alaska.

Costa, D.L., 1999, "American Living Standards: Evidence from Recreational Expenditures," NBER Working Paper No. 7148.

DeShazo, J.R. and T.A. Cameron, 2004a, "The Effect of Current Health Status on Willingness to Pay for Morbidity and Mortality Risk Reductions," Unpublished Working Paper.

DeShazo, J. R. and T.A. Cameron, 2004b, "Mortality in a Morbidity Risk Reduction: An Empirical Life Cycle Model of Demand with Two Types of Age Effects," Unpublished Paper, UCLA Department of Policy Studies.

Diamond, P., 1996, "Testing the Internal Consistency of Contingent Valuation Surveys," *Journal of Environmental Economics and Management*, 30(3): 337-347.

Faith, R.L. and R.D. Tollison, 1981, "Contractual Exchange and the Timing of Payment," *Journal of Economic Behavior and Organization*, 1: 325-342.

Fisher, A.C., 2000, "Investment under Uncertainty and Option Value in Environmental Economics," *Resource and Energy Economics*, 22: 197-204.

Georgescu-Roegen, N., 1952, "A Diagrammatic Analysis of Complementarity," *Southern Economic Journal*, 19: 1-20.

Hammitt, J.K. and J.D. Graham, 1999, "Willingness to Pay for Health Protection: Inadequate Sensitivity to Probability," *Journal of Risk and Uncertainty*, 18(1): 33-62.

Hanemann, W.M., 1991, "Willingness to Pay Versus Willingness to Accept: How Much Can They Differ?" *American Economic Review*, 81(3): 635-647.

Hanemann, W.M., 1998, "Three Approaches to Defining "Existence" or Nonuse Values Under Certainty," Working paper, Department of Agricultural and Resource Economics, University of California, Berkeley.

Hanemann, W.M., 1999, "The Economic Theory of WTP and WTA," in *Valuing Environmental Preferences: Theory and Practice of the Contingent Valuation Method in the US, EU and Developing Countries,* Bateman, I.J. and K.G. Wells, (Eds.), Oxford: Oxford University Press.

Harrison, G.W., 2000, "Contingent Valuation Meets the Experts: A Critique of the NOAA Panel Report, Working Paper, Department of Economics, University of South Carolina, Columbia, SC.

Hayek, F.A., 1943, "The Geometrical Representation of Complementarity," *Review of Economic Studies*, 10(2): 122-25.

Heckman, J.J., 2001, "Micro Data, Heterogeneity, and the Evaluation of Public Policy: Nobel Lecture," *Journal of Political Economy*, 109: 673-748.

Herriges, J.A. and D.J. Phaneuf, 2002, "Inducing Patterns of Correlation and Substitution in Repeated Logit Models of Recreation Demand," *American Journal of Agricultural Economics*, 84(4): 1076-1090.

Huang, J.C. and V.K. Smith, 1998, "Monte Carlo Benchmarks for Discrete Response Valuation Methods," *Land Economics*, 74(2): 186-202.

Huang, J.C. and V.K. Smith, 2002, "Monte Carlo Benchmarks for Discrete Response Valuation Methods: Reply," *Land Economics*, 78(4): 617-623.

Imbens, G.W. and T. Lancaster, 1994, "Combining Micro and Macro Data in Microeconometric Models," *Review of Economic Studies*, 61: 655-680.

Johnson, F.R., K.E. Mathews and M.F. Bingham, 2000, "Evaluating Welfare-Theoretic Consistency in Multiple-Response Stated-Preference Surveys," TER Working Paper, Triangle Economic Research, Durham, NC.

Kahneman, D. and I. Ritov, 1994, "Determinants of Stated Willingness to Pay for Public Goods: A Study in the Headline Method," *Journal of Risk and Uncertainty*, 9: 5-38.

Kopp, R.J. and V.K. Smith, 1997, "Constructing Measures of Economic Value," in *Determining the Value of Non-Marketed Goods,* R.J. Kopp, W.W. Pommerehne and N. Schwartz, (Eds.), Boston: Kluwer Academic Publishers.

Krupnick, A.J., V. Adamowicz, D. Dupont, H.S. Banzhaf and M. Batz, 2004, "Preference Tradeoffs for Drinking Water Risks: Diarrhea of Death," Presented at the Allied Social Science Associations, San Diego, CA.

Krupnick, A.J., A. Alberini, M. Cropper, N. Simon, B. O'Brien, R. Goeree and M. Heintzelman, 2002, "Age, Health and the Willingness to Pay for Mortality Risk Reductions: A Contingent Valuation Survey of Ontario Residents," *Journal of Risk and Uncertainty*, 24(2): 161-86.

Krutilla, J.V., 1961, "Welfare Aspects of Benefit-Cost Analysis," *Journal of Political Economy,* 69: 226-235.

Layton, D.F. and S.T.Lee, 2003, "From Ratings to Rankings: The Econometric Analysis of Stated Preference Ratings Data," Unpublished Working Paper, University of Washington.

Mansfield, C. and V.K. Smith, 2002, "Trade-off at the Trough: TMDLs and the Evolving Status of US Water Quality Policy," *Recent Advances in Environmental Economics,* List, J.A. and A. de Zeeuw (Eds.), Cheltenham, UK: Edward Elgar.

Mansfield, C., G. Van Houtven, F.R. Johnson, D. Crawford-Brown and Z. Pekar, 2004, "Behavioral Reactions to Ozone Alerts: What Do They Tell Us About Willingness-to-pay for Children's Health?" Presented at the Allied Social Science Associations, San Diego, CA.

McConnell, K.E., 1990, "Models for Referendum Data: The Structure of Discrete Choice Models for Contingent Valuation," *Journal of Environmental Economics and Management,* 18: 19-34.

Mitchell, R. C. and R. T. Carson, 1989, *Using Surveys to Value Public Goods: The Contingent Valuation Method,* Washington D.C., Resources for the Future.

Palmquist, R.B., 2005, "Weak Complementarity, Path Independence, and the Intuition of the Willig Condition," *Journal of Environmental Economics and Management*, 49: 103-115.

Samuelson, P. A., 1974a, "Complementarity: an Essay on the 40th Anniversary of the Hicks-Allen Revolution in Demand Theory," *Journal of Economic Literature*, 12: 1255-89.

Samuelson, P. A., 1974b, "Remembrances of Frisch," *European Economic Review,* 5: 7-23.

Smith, V.K., 1992, "Arbitrary Values, Good Causes, and Premature Verdicts: Comment," *Journal of Environmental Economics and Management*, 22: 71-89.

Smith, V.K., 1996, "Can Contingent Valuation Distinguish Economic Values for Different Public Goods?" *Land Economics*, 72(2): 139-51.

Smith, V.K., 1997, "Pricing What is Priceless: A Status Report on Non-Market Valuation of Environmental Resources," in *The International Yearbook of Environmental and Resource Economics 1997/1998*, H. Folmer and T. Tietenberg, Eds., Cheltenham,UK: Edward Elgar, 156-204.

Smith, V.K., 2004, "Fifty Years of Contingent Valuation," in *The International Yearbook of Environmental and Resource Economics 2004/2005*, T. Tietenberg and H. Folmer, (Eds.), Cheltenham, UK: Edward Elgar.

Smith, V.K. and H.S. Banzhaf, 2004a, "Quality Adjusted Prices Indexes and the Willig Condition," Unpublished Working CEnRep Paper.

Smith, V.K. and H.S. Banzhaf, 2004b, "A Diagrammatic Exposition of Weak Complementarity and the Willig Condition, *American Journal of Agricultural Economics*, 86: 455-66.

Smith, V.K. and W.H. Desvousges, 1990, "Risk Communication and the Value of Information: Radon as a Case Study," *The Review of Economics and Statistics*, 72: 137-42.

Smith, V.K., W.H. Desvousges, A. Fisher and F.R. Johnson, 1988, "Learning About Radon's Risk," *Journal of Risk and Uncertainty*, 1: 233-58.

Smith, V.K., M.F. Evans, H.S. Banzhaf, and C. Poulos, 2004, "Rehabilitating Weak Substitution," Unpublished CEnREP Working Paper.

Smith, V.K. and C. Mansfield, 1998, "Buying Time: Real and Contingent Offers," *Journal of Environmental Economics and Management*, 36:209-224.

Smith, V.K. and L.L. Osborne, 1996, "Do Contingent Valuation Estimates Pass a 'Scope' Test? A Meta-analysis," *Journal of Environmental Economics and Management*, 31: 287-301.

Smith, V.K. and S.K. Pattanayak, 2002, "Is Meta-Analysis a Noah's Ark for Nonmarket Valuation?" *Environmental and Resource Economics*, 22: 271-296.

Smith, V.K. and G. Van Houtven, 2004, "Recovering Hicksian Consumer Surplus Within a Collective Model: Hausman's Method for the Household," *Environmental and Resource Economics*, 28: 153-167.

Smith, V.K., Z. Zhang and R.B. Palmquist, 1997, "Marine Debris, Beach Quality, and Non-market Values," *Environmental and Resource Economics*, 10: 223-47.

Tversky, A. and D. Kahneman, 1991, "Loss Aversion and Riskless Choice: A Reference Dependent Model," *Quarterly Journal of Economics*, 106: 1039-1061.

Von Haefen, R.H., 2003, "Incorporating Observed Choice in the Construction of Welfare Measures From Random Utility Models," *Journal of Environmental Economics and Management*, 45: 145-165.

Welsh, M.P., R.C. Bishop, M.L. Phillips and R.M. Baumgartner, 1995, *GCES Non-use Value Study*. Final Report, Prepared by Hagler Bailly Consulting.

Welsh, M.P. and G.L. Poe, 1998, "Elicitation Effects in Contingent Valuation Comparisons to a Multiple Bounded Discrete Choice Approach," *Journal of Environmental Economics and Management*, 36: 170-185.

Willig, R.D., 1978, "Incremental Consumer's Surplus and Hedonic Price Adjustment," *Journal of Economic Theory*, 17: 227-53.

INDEX

The Economics of Non-Market Goods and Resources